The New Stage of Capitalism: A Marxist Update on Its Evolution

Zhang Tongyu, Ding Weimin, Chen Ying
Translated by Zhou Kai, Zhang Pengyun

CANut

Originally published as Evolution and Fracture: How to Understand the Historical Process of the Development of Capitalism in 2004 by China Renmin University Press.

Original Chinese Edition Copyright © 2004 by Zhang Tongyu
ISBN: 978-7-300-05340-0

The New Stage of Capitalism: A Marxist Update on Its Evolution
ISBN: 978-3-942575-04-1

Published by
Canut International Publishers
Yorck Street. 66
10965 Kreuzberg
Berlin-Germany

Canut International Publishers
12a Guernsey Road E11
London 4BJ-England-U.K.

URL: http//www.canut.us
E-Mail: canut@aol.com

Publisher's Note

Capitalism research has been a constant research subject of critical thought in the world. Marxists and left activists are the irreplaceable actors for that criticism. And, generally Marx's Capital has been the basis of all debates and controversies. And we cannot ignore those several arguments holding the view that Marx's capital and capitalism and class analysis have proved invalid throughout the contemporary history. Another view holds that capitalism and capitalist society is faced by a disastrous regress to barbarism. As capital and capitalism develops forward, these debates will never end, but revival and creative progress of Marxist tenets on the issue based on the recent facts of the era has long called Marxists on this task. Due to several historical reasons and internal problems, several basic tenets of Marxist capitalism and capital analysis were damaged remarkably. We have chosen this book from Chinese scholars who have paid a valuable effort to revive those tenets together with a comprehensive analysis on contemporary developments.

Our title seems too radical, and we agree that capitalism has not entered into a brand new stage recently, though it has gained many new features with corporate capital and internationalization. We simply preferred to re-underline the state monopoly capitalism already long on the stage but shadowed by ideology or new facts.

As capitalism and capital was developed in the womb of the old society, socialism and social capital is dialectically developed in capitalism every hour and every day. This is the realistic basis of all the practice to deepen and accelerate this process. This is another way of saying socialism opposes private capitalist property and capitalism but is inherently combined and related with them in several patterns dialectically in the process of opposition. This is one of the the main aspects in this book inherited and revived creatively from Marx's work.

Originally, one of the aims of this scholarly book was to offer further research material for higher education in political or social economics in China. Their counterparts living in the same world can also find abundant material and different aspects in this book and especially on the globalism process.

Except for partial articles, it is yet a rare occasion that Chinese scholars' works are published or translated to other languages, but this fact is never related with qualities. It only means globalization in many areas lags behind, especially in publishing. Therefore we owe special thanks to the translators and China Renmin University Press who have paid valuable efforts in the realization of the English version of this book.

We hope the content of the book will give the readers in the world a sense of those important scholars' mind and aspects which in their creativity and endeavor reflect the qualities of China's Marxist researchers.

Canut Publishers
London, December 2010

Acknowledgements

This work is finally compiled by the Deng Xiaoping Theory and "Three Represents" Thought Research Center in China. The task of this research book is to find a proper method for "understanding the historical process of capitalist development". A research team mainly composed of instructors engaged in teaching and researchers studying on modern capitalist economy for many years and also some doctors has contributed to the main effort for this book. A draft is produced on the basis of earnest discussions held for more than several times, and we have solicited opinions of the leaders of the Deng Xiaoping Theory and "Three Represents" Thought Research Center as well as the China Renmin University Press throughout the process of writing. We have then made further revisions on the manuscripts collecting valuable opinions raised by the experts. The work presented to the readers now is accomplished by relevant scholars through joint efforts.

I would like to mention the names and thank my colleagues who have contributed to the chapters of this book. Chapter I, Zhang Tongyu; Chapter II, Ding Weimin; Chapter III, Chen Ying; Chapter IV, Li Chunlei, Ding Weimin; Chapter V, Liu Jie, Ding Weimin; Chapter VI, Bai Qunying, Zhang Tongyu; Chapter VII, Liu Zhiyang, Zhang Tongyu; Chapter VIII, Bi Rong, Zhang Tongyu; Chapter IX, Zhang Tongyu. Zhang Tongyu and I have assumed the work as chief editor, responsible for revising and finalizing the manuscript.

It was difficult for us to avoid some faults or errors due to the limitation of our theoretical preparation and pressing time. The opinions from readers will be greatly appreciated.

We owe special thanks to the leaders and scholars of the Deng Xiaoping Theory and "Three Represents" Thought Research Center and China Renmin University Press. I express our sincere gratitude to Guo Xiaoming for his valuable work in editing and publishing this book.

Chief Editor

Ding Weimin

Nankai Park, August 2003

Contents

Introduction: A New Approach to the Historical Process of Capitalism

With the advent of the new millennium theoretical circles in China attempted to sum up the Marxist theoretical achievements in the last decades and realistically face the new developments manifested by contemporary capitalism. The latest research has also offered a more comprehensive approach to the historical evolution of capitalism since its birth in West Europe. Naturally the new attempts have brought a deeper understanding of Marxist historical materialism and its classical main texts on capital and capitalism. The new exploration has three important starting points which can be summed as follows:

Firstly, in the historical process of the development of capitalism, the capital relation has gone through a series of self-regulation, reforms and improvements and these reforms have provided a space for the continuous development of social productive forces; secondly, basic laws, the nature of its system and the basic contradictions of capitalism have not been changed; thirdly, Marxism's historical judgment on the fate of capitalism is still relevant. In this book we will offer the readers a detailed, deeper analysis on capital, capitalism, and evolution of capitalism focusing on its internal contradictions.

I. Capitalist Development in a Steady Change Process

In the historical process of the development of capitalism, in order to meet the requirements of the socialization trend of productive forces, capitalist relations of production indeed have carried out a series of adjustments and reforms within the scope permitted by its fundamental nature. The adjustments and reforms of capitalist relations of production constitute the basic reason for the continuous development of the capitalist economic base. I think, driven by internal contradictions, the capitalist mode of production has experienced a historical process of continuous development and evolution.

Just from its rudimentary stage, the emergence and evolution of the capitalist mode of production have undergone a history of about 500 years and when calculated from the English Civil War, it has a history of more than 360 years. In this historical process, it has undergone four major historical development stages, and three major technological revolutions based on the changes of social production technologies. Correspondingly, the social productive forces of capitalism have undergone three major leaps. Capitalist relations of production have also experienced three major adjustments.

1. The Historical Stages of the Development of Capitalism

(1) The rudimentary and formation stage

The 14th and 15th centuries comprise the rudimentary period of the capitalist relations of production. The emerging workshop handicraft industry with capitalist production form in some treaty port cities along the Mediterranean was the earliest rudimentary form of capitalist economic relations. However, the handicraft workshops then were few, very immature and unstable.

The period from the 16th century to the first half of the 18th century is commonly held as the formation period of capitalist relations of production. The big geographical discovery in the end of the 15th century and the beginning of the 16th century had created the world market, which provided the capitalist workshop handicraft industry with important conditions and facilities. During this period, the workshop handicraft system had completed the transformation from simple co-operation to the workshop handicraft based on labor division, thus making the handicraft workshop system of labor division occupy the dominant position in the real workshop handicraft industry period. Simple co-operation was the initial form of workshop handicraft industry. It not only used manual labor as the base of production technology for its own survival and development and also we can say that it had no essential difference with the previous social production form as to its nature, therefore, it could not obtain the dominant position in the social production. In its production process, given that the workers had production technology that must be used in manual labor, the subordination of wage labor to the capital had still remained at the affiliation stage of formal subordination only, and hadn't developed into the actual subordination stage yet. This simple workshop handicraft industry of simple co-operation only had the nature of capitalist production in terms of production relations (i.e. social form of production). However, when the workshop handicraft industry of simple co-operation was developed into workshop handicraft industry based on labor division, the real workshop type handicraft industry had emerged. The factors such as the subjective labor division of workers and the objective division of labor tools had developed. Hence, a genuine manual workshop had already shown its superiority by improving labor productive forces; meanwhile, the emergence of labor division within the workshops had also provided a new means for capital controlling labor and made the affiliation of labor to capital begin to turn to actual affiliation. All of these had made the then existing production mode have more competitiveness and manifested that the workshop handicraft industry—as a transitory phase—contained the basic characteristics for the future factory system.

The main internal contradiction of capitalist economy then was the contradiction between capitalist production relations and the technological pattern based on manual production. Both developing social productive forces and creating a production technological basis suitable for capital that could realize the unlimited value-appreciation were inevitable requirements at that time. Without the fundamental transformation of social production technology, the capitalist economy could not eventually replace the feudal economy, and the struggle between the restoration and anti-restoration forces could inevitably congest that transition from the old to the new socio-economic formation.

(2) The first technological revolution and the laissez-faire capitalism period

The first technological revolution took place in the second half of the 18th century, which was the establishment period of the capitalist mode of production. The invention and utilization of the steam engine was the main sign of this scientific-technological revolution known as the "steam age". Machine production and the emergence of mechanization had made capitalist production relations achieve the production basis consistent with its nature and requirements, and socialized mass production began to take shape. The workshop handicraft industry was gradually changed to machine based industry, and the industrial revolution had established a specific capitalist mode of production with machine production as the basis and wage labor as the formation. In the second half of the 18th century, the industrial revolution hadn't reached full development, but it was an issue of further development. Family private factory system was quite common. In capitalist factories, the capital ownership relation appeared to be a simple private property right relation, the capital ownership and the rights of capital usage were completely unified, and capitalists were not only the owners but also managers. In the production process of capitalist enterprises, the relationship of wage labor to capital had eventually realized the transformation from the formal affiliation to the actual affiliation. The commercial capitalism had eventually changed from industrial capitalism into free competition capitalism. On the basis of the first technological revolution in the first half of the 19th century, the factory system was spread further with the further development of the industrial revolution, and joint stock companies already began to take shape in some sectors. However, the family private factory system still occupied the dominant position in the social production.

From the middle of the 18th century to the middle of the 19th century, during its nearly 100-year history of formation and development, the social wealth created by the capitalist mode of production amounted to more than the sum of the wealth created in all previous ages of humanity. This fact had fully proved the historical progress of the capitalist mode of production. The bourgeoisie then absolutely believed that the free market economic system had incomparable superiority and the free competition was the basic feature of this era. However, the inherent basic contradiction within the capitalist mode of production had also thoroughly emerged. Its main expressions were the economic crisis of overproduction that broke out periodically and the social instability caused by the intense industrial conflicts between capitalists and workers. Furthermore, the first technological revolution marked by the invention and use of the steam engine could not provide the technical basis for transforming all the industrial departments. Light industry was the leading industrial department at that time. Developing new social production technologies and adjusting the industrial relations were the prominent problems that the development of capitalist society had then faced.

(3) The second science and technological revolution and monopoly capitalism period

The second science and technological revolution took place in the second half of the 19th century, and was mainly marked by the invention and use of electric motors and power, called as the "electric age". As to the organizational form of capitalist enterprises, this stage was the period in which the joint stock company system in the industrialization began to develop and be gradually popularized. The second technological revolution had promoted the further development of the socialization of production, transforming the social industrial structure of the light industry domination to the heavy industry domination. The transformation of the industrial structure based on the new technological was not merely an opportunity but also a challenge to private individual capital. The emerging industrial sectors had undoubtedly offered opportunities for capital to make money. However, investing in the heavy chemical industry and other emerging industrial sectors required huge amounts of capital and was characterized as scale benefit, which was hard to achieve by relying on capital accumulation by individual private capital. Due to the highly socialized stage of productive forces, individual private capital could no more be able to embrace those greater productive forces unless they abandoned their original independent existence form. Thus capital's concentration had become the only choice to develop the capital ownership relation at that time. The share capital was the appropriate form of capital creation and accumulation, thus causing a general development trend for joint stock companies. During this period, as a more mature enterprise system, modern industrial joint stock companies occupied the dominant position in social production, and more than 80% of the enterprise income in the developed capitalist countries was created by joint stock companies accounting for less than 20% of the total enterprises. The dual separation which was manifested as the ownership rights and use rights of capital in the share capital form had recorded a significant progressive development. The generalization of share capital was the essential requirement in which capitalist economic relations could adapt to the development of productive forces, and it was the first adjustment of the production relations of capitalism in the scope permitted by its fundamental nature. Based on the innovation of the technological and enterprise system, from the end of the 19th century to the middle of the 20th century, the financial capital form of private monopoly had formed and developed, and gradually occupied a dominant position in social and economic life. The financial capital was a more advanced form of monopoly capital formed by sublating[1] the independent industrial monopoly capital and banking monopoly capital and allowing them to grow jointly. The essence of financial capital was all-round monopolization of social, economic and political life. The formation of financial capital was the inevitable result of the development of the internal contradictions of capitalist economic formation. On the one hand, due to the promotion and application of the results of the second science and technological revolution, the socialization level of the productive forces were further improved, resulting in the requirements for strengthening production and capital concentration and pushing the necessity of establishing larger-scale or huge industrial enterprises. However, the speed of the capital's socialization could not so quickly adapt to the rapid development speed of socialization of production. The accumulation and concentration capacity of the joint stock companies integrating individual dispersed private capital around themselves was not sufficient enough. Many production sectors could not realize the full occupation and control of those productive forces that had already achieved higher degrees of socialization. On the other hand, not only share capital system had provided a basis for the formation of monopoly, but the expansion of individual capital had resulted in production and capital concentration in the form of share capital, which had also greatly stimulated the inherent expansionistic impulse of capital. Therefore, a new round of higher degree of capital concentration had become a historical necessity: the capital's new ownership form under finance monopoly capital. The enterprises controlled by financial monopoly capital were companies being composed of several companies joining together, trusts merging by trusts, and manifesting multi-forms of joint stock companies. In order to strengthen their individual private monopoly powers, private monopoly capital had repulsed free competition, but they had intensified competition among themselves in several other forms which had

---

[1] Translation of the terminology in German (=Aufhebung).

led to the outbreak of the imperialist World War I. However, at the same time, formation of financial capital also reflected the socialization of ownership relations more profoundly than the share capital form, thus promoting the relations between possession, occupation, control and utilization of capital to a higher socialized degree. It enabled capital to make full use of the results of the second science and technological revolution and further promoted the development of social economy. Consequently, laissez-faire capitalism was changed into monopoly capitalism period.

In the monopoly capitalism period, the developed capitalist countries realized a thorough industrialization process. At the same time, it also exacerbated the basic contradiction of capitalism and social class contradictions. Large monopoly capitalist companies had recorded a huge expansion for monopoly, strengthening the non-rational elements in the development of the entire social economy and aggravating the anarchy of social production. Its results were the big crisis of the whole capitalist world from 1929 to 1933. The intensification of various contradictions resulting from the expansion of monopoly capital had finally led to the outbreak of World War II.

(4) The third science and technological revolution and monopoly capitalism period

The third science and technological revolution took place in the second half of the 20th century. It is mainly marked by the invention and use of a series of high technological products, which is represented by the computers, and it is known as the "electronic age". Modern science and technology, such as the development and utilization of nuclear energy by men, space technology marked by the launch of satellites, biological engineering technology marked by DNA recombination tests, mass production and wide use of microprocessors and development of network technology and IT industry, etc., rapidly developed in the last 50 years. Modern science and technology became the primary leading productive force due to its increasing prominent role in socio-economic development. Science and technological revolution and transformation optimized and enriched the elements of the productive forces, industrial structure was transformed from labor-intensive to capital-intensive and later to knowledge- and technological-intensive, and high-tech industrial departments rapidly developed and increasingly grew into the leading sectors in the economy. The industrial structures of developed capitalist countries transformed from an industrial economy to a knowledge-based economy, and social and economic life of the society recorded a comprehensive modernization and informatization. The unprecedented improvement of socialization degree in the productive forces, expansion of the business scale in enterprises and increase of risks in capital investments had forced the states to intervene in order to adjust the social and economic life. With increasing of investment risks and huge development of credit and financial markets, the investment ability of private capital owners needed to control the risks in the financial markets and check the investment risks had become increasingly insufficient. Thus with those new developments private property was compelled to entrust various financial institutions to invest, so the corporation form with financial institutions as shareholders rapidly increased. Capital organized in the corporation form in the developed capitalist countries had become to control more than 60% of total company shares. Thus the corporation capital form and state-owned capital form were two other major adjustments that the capital ownership relationship had encountered to suit to the requirements of the socialized development in the productive forces and had resulted in further socialization of the capital. Due to the development of productive forces and implementation of state intervention policies and "democratic capitalism" policies, all kinds of social contradictions had enjoyed an alleviating tendency for a period of time. However, in the 1970s, due to the inherent contradictions of capitalism along with the shortcomings of the state monopoly capitalism policy, the capitalist economies were faced with the general "stagflation" phenomenon. The new recession in the socio-economy had provided the opportunity for the rise of neo-liberalism which was against Keynesianism and state economic intervention. Since the late 1970s, neo-conservatism had increased its power and state capitalism had become weaker to some extent. As a result of the new development of social productive forces and the unprecedented active international capital, the development trend of globalization of the capitalist mode of production had gained a vigorous impetus. Generally speaking, this period was the development period of state monopoly capitalism.

2. New Features in Contemporary Capitalism

After analyzing the historical development stage of capitalist mode of production, I would particularly like to point out that capitalist economy has encountered major new changes and has some obvious new features in the last two to three decades of the 20th century.

From the perspective of the morphological characteristics of capitalist social economy, the economies of the developed capitalist countries have been developing towards informatization, post-industrialization, virtualization and globalization. Information technology is being fully applied to the social production and economic life, and accordingly social production and life styles have recorded profound changes. In the industry structure, the tertiary industry has replaced the leading position of other industrial sectors and become to occupy more than 70% of the total social economy and the virtual economy with financial assets has rapidly developed and become an element which has a significant influence on the real economy. We also observe that a variety of production factors and economic resources, in a larger scale, have been flowing internationally which is the part of economic globalization.

From the perspective of the essential characteristics of capitalist social-economic structure, we observe the following new features:

1) In terms of capitalist ownership relations capital ownership relation manifests a trend of accelerated development of socialization: on the one hand, because in the form, the development of corporation capital has completely cut off the links between the ultimate owners of capital and the actual dominator on capital, the power of private capital has consequently become limited and has been sublated in some aspects; but on the other hand, a high degree of socialization of capital strengthens the power of capital

in the hands of "positive" bourgeoisie that holds the direct ownership of capital, and consequently power of capital sees a transfer in different strata of bourgeoisie. In the capital structure, the capital of financial industry as compared to others has obtained an increasingly dominant position. With the rise of financial liberalization and the rapid expansion of virtual capital, and with the virtualized development of social economy, the capital of financial industry has attained a dominant role in the capital's accumulation and operations. The capital of the financial industry plays a decisive influence on the stability of the economy of a country and even the world.

2) In terms of the social class structure, the main classes in the society have seen that structural changes and evolution has speeded up. We observe rapid development in the number of corporation shareholders. The process of the financial institutions becoming shareholders in corporations has accelerated and thus separation between controllers of capital and ultimate owners of capital, the owners of entity capital and functional capitalists has been more distinct. Due to reforms in the social production technology foundation characterized by information technology taking the leading position—the working class ranks see an accelerated trend of expansion and multi-layered structure. In the recent two to three decades, the "middle class" has been in a trend of polarization. In the sphere of industrial relations, capital's attack and control on wage labor has manifested a strengthening trend. After the World War II, the capital's governance on wage labor has been improved, especially with the implementation of measures such as the "worker capitalization" and "management democratization" which have alleviated the labor-management conflicts to some extent. After the 1980s, although the capitalist economy has moved from stagflation to slow growth, bourgeoisie has made use of the benefits brought by the new science and technological revolution to further expand its own strength, but due to sharp segmentation in the labor market, the joint strength of the working class has been weakened. Under these circumstances, the control and attack of the bourgeoisie on the working class has strengthened, and industrial relations have turned to a direction unfavorable to the working class, which manifests

many similarities with the original model in the 19th century. Determined by the new science and technological conditions, the mode of labor may be further adjusted to enhance the capital control on working classes.

3) In terms of changes in distribution relations, we can observe an unstable adjustment process since the capitalist economy has got rid of stagflation and made into the low-speed growth, and the income of workers in most developed countries have relatively increased. However, the role of labor negotiation power in the income distribution determination is further reduced. Instead the role of the so-called "share system" has been increased, social welfare and social security systems are still in an adjustment period, and the change from welfare state to welfare society faces some difficulties. The income gap between the capital and labor is enlarged, the obvious polarization is strengthened, and the life pressure on working classes increases strongly. Besides, governmental intervention policies to income distribution by legislative bodies are neither clear nor stable. Due to the development of virtualization in the economic life and increase in the share of economic surplus through virtual economy has brought important changes in the redistribution of capital. Virtualization of the economy has caused new changes in the appropriation and distribution of surplus value and in the capital accumulation.

4) In terms of changes in the operation system of social economy, the struggle between Rhine model and the Anglo-Saxon model has become fiercer; the defects of Keynesianism and the policy of state monopoly capitalism have provided economic liberalism with an opportunity of regeneration, so the free enterprise ideology and policy of the neo-conservatives have increasingly got the upper hand, and the superiority of social market economy has been generally suspected. But on the other hand the results of neo-liberal policies mainly advocating Anglo-Saxon model seem disappointing, so the struggle between the two development models of contemporary capitalist economy has become fiercer, and the future of social economic development patterns has become a debate theme in western

countries. I think the outcome of the struggle between the two economic models is still uncertain. Generally serious economists have not forgotten the scars left by the "Great Depression" in the 1930s, which still aches from time to time, and scholars can not completely give up the necessity of state economic intervention, but we can observe that the state monopoly capitalism is passing through a period of adjustment.

5) In terms of changes in the international economic relations, an economic globalization process dominated by the developed capitalist countries has formed. The new developments in information technology, new changes in the world economic and political system, and especially the international environment after the Cold War have provided more favorable conditions for the globalization of capitalist mode of production. Due to globalization, over-accumulation and over-production, the realization of surplus value created by developed capitalist economies more and more relies on the potential markets in developing countries. For the developed capitalist economies, the importance of the world market compared to the domestic market is increasing. The economic globalization offers both opportunities and tough challenges for development of the majority of developing countries. In the process of economic globalization, both in the economic sphere and the political sphere the conflict between multi-polarization and unilateralism is further aggravated. This could lead to severer contradictions and conflicts with increasing demands for the establishment of a more just and new international economic order.

In short, the new features we have summarized above are ultimately inevitable results of the development of the inherent contradictions in the capitalist mode of production. This process includes the socialization of the form and operating mode of the capital and also new developments in the capital ownership relation and other basic economic relations determined by it.

II. Theoretical Trends Reflecting on the Capitalist Development

1. Recent Theories and Reflections in Academies

Since World War II, nearly all aspects of the global economy have encountered tremendous changes. And those abundant new phenomena and new features have aroused a wide attention in the academy. Mainstream scholars, left or right wing, do not deny that dramatic changes have occurred in the forms of capitalism. These changes observed and reflected by them are also keenly followed and debated by Marxist scholars though analytical methods applied and the conclusions are quite different. In the works of non-Marxist scholars on the contemporary capitalist economic development, there are prolific research results and several misleading ideas that could easily be noticed. But on the one hand, they have produced and recorded abundant objective descriptions on contemporary capitalism and its recent changes. They have also achieved quite sound analysis on some aspects of the capital operating mechanism, and the methods employed for empirical study and rich data analysis indeed deserve admiration. They have also reached several rational conclusions on the operational systems of capitalism and have proposed a set of new policy suggestions on improving market economy. Marxist scholars generally admit and appreciate these researches highly and their practical value. On the other hand, we generally observe that there is rarely a deep inquiry into the basic contradictions of capitalist mode of production.

They generally conceal and deny the opposing relation between classes and their arguments rarely surpass beyond capitalism and its historical limitations. In the recent decades we observe that mainstream academies in the West have produced various unique "qualitative change theories" which have dominated capitalism and societal studies. Below, we shall present a brief evaluation on those with most influential and systematic character. In the relevant sections of the book, readers will find more detailed reviews on them.

"Science and Technology Based Theories": This trend focuses on pure technological development to explore the contemporary development and changes in the society, and suggests that progress in science and technology has already influenced capitalism for a "qualitative change", and thus a new social system is formed. Though this trend had emerged in the post-war era, its influence in academies is deep and still affects recent generations. J. A. Schumpeter and Galbraith and several other important scholars advocate this view. Schumpeter has asserted that the technological innovation constitutes the fundamental driving force for capitalist development, but several components of the capitalist economic system hinder or weaken this driving engine. The solution is to promote public power and institutions controlling production process which could replace privately-run enterprises. Schumpeter has also suggested three possible forms through which capitalism could transform to a "new socialist" society. Galbraith has suggested to view science and technology as an independent factor of production, and claimed that this factor is increasingly becoming the key component for business success, so the future trend of social development is bound to give way to a new ruling social force and power will be controlled by "advanced experts" group possessing special knowledge on industrial technologies. He had also asserted that with the technological process and the new group assuming the social power, aims and objectives of the capitalist enterprises could alter accordingly, and the new enterprise will aim at societal stability, economic growth and technological improvement instead of profit maximization as a major objective. He also proposed a "new socialist" social model which will reform capitalism.[1] We have noticed similar approaches by other scholars who depend on the pure technological factor to explain the evolution of social economic formation and underestimate the function of capitalist economic relations, especially that of capitalist ownership of the means of production.

---

[1] J. A. Schumpeter: *Capitalism, Socialism and Democracy*, Edition 1, Beijing, The Commercial Press, 1979; J. K. Galbraith: *Economics and Public Goals*, Edition 1, Beijing, The Commercial Press, 1983.

This approach ignoring capitalist property leads to improper conclusions and shadows their assumptions on a socialized and a reformed capitalist society. Yet their ideas pinpoint to the critical role of science and technology in promoting socio-economic structures. To sum up we suggest that these views reflect—to a certain extent—the rapid socialization of capitalist production process and its contradiction between capitalist property and also describe the recent changes in the social power structure. By reflecting on certain realities in contemporary capitalist society these theories offer critical inspiration.

"Democratization of Capital": This theory reflects on the decentralization phenomenon in shareholder system of capitalist enterprises and suggests that decentralization of shareholder system promotes the democratization of capital, income distribution witnesses a revolutionary change, and thus "people capitalism" could become a reality. Bailey, an American economist, claims: "since private capitalist ownership is now transformed to a socialized group ownership form, private property has been divided into two parts as the 'passive' property and 'managed' property, the former reflects the status of stock owners (shareholders) and the latter indicates the nature of managers. The passive property is centered in banking financial institutions, the role of private ownership declines, and its position is replaced by the financial institutions. Capital still exists, but the capitalists are perishing." American economist Means asserts that "the recent trend, governance by big corporations leads to the termination of private capital ownership and elevates the 'collective capitalist' system to a dominant position." Drucker, a management expert from the US claims: "workers' pensions invested in corporate shares make them become the true masters of the means of production and this can be termed as 'socialism of pension funds'." American socialist Bailey affirms that "with the rapid development of industry, the income differences among citizens could be reduced, polarization phenomena in the capitalist society will disappear, ownership structure lose their significance, and the power and role of private ownership tend to disappear, so capitalists and workers can share similar status." In Germany, "democratization of capital" is praised as the basis of establishing "social partnership" in the society, and is evaluated as an important component of German model of "social market economy" theory. The "social market economy" theory of Freiburg school in the post-war era was expounded in detail by Ludwig Erhard in his work *Prosperity Through Competition*.[1]

"Capital democratization" and "people capitalism" ignore the dominant position of big shareholders in the companies and confounds the big shareholders with small ones, so its basic point of view seems shaky. However, there are some specific analysis that should arouse our attention, for example, the analysis on the relationship between "passive property" and "managed property", analysis on large companies' governance and the collective capitalist system, and analysis on the relationship after pension is transformed into share capital. Of course, implementing "capital democratization" policies has not changed the status of workers, but in essence, it has been supportive for capital accumulation. However, the change of income distribution relationship arising from the establishment of employee stock ownership in large scale is undoubtedly an important adjustment of the economic relation, which reflects the reality.

"Manager Revolution Theory": This theory is a summary on separation phenomenon of ownership and control rights in modern capitalist companies. Its main content is as follows: due to the separation of a company's capital ownership and management rights, shareholders have transferred management rights to the "manager class" which is specialized in the operation and management of enterprises, but due to the decentralization of stock rights, managers have grasped the real capital control right, and thus the control right over the social economy has already been shifted to this group. Many scholars believe that capitalism has accordingly developed

---

[1] A. A. Bailey: *The Power without Property Rights*, Beijing, the Commercial Press, 1962; *Capitalist Revolution in the 20th Century*, p. 7, New York, 1954. G. C. Means: *Company Revolution in U.S.A*, p. 51, New York, 1962. Bo Drucker: *Invisible Revolution*, New York, 1976. Daniel Bell: *The Coming of Post-industrial Society*, Beijing, the Commercial Press, 1984. G. Erhard: *Prosperity by Competition*, Beijing, the Commercial Press, 1983.

from family capitalism to managers' capitalism. This viewpoint occupies an important position in the western economics. Bailey and Means think that in the era in which they live, nearly half of large companies are "under the control of managers". The separation of ownership and control rights means that the modern companies no longer take realizing profit maximization as the objective, and large companies have attained the nature of democracy, reflecting a fundamental change in modern capitalism. Burnham believes that capitalism is giving way to "managerial society". During this transitional period, the majority of the capitalists in U.S.A. haven't participated in economic activities, and managers have been obtaining the ruling items in the society.

R. Maris had put forward that "'managed' capitalism was a terminology formed in Western Europe and North America in the middle of the 20th century. In such an economic system, production is concentrated in the hands of large joint stock companies. In many management departments, the classic entrepreneur has virtually disappeared". In the modern companies entrepreneurial functions have fallen into the hands of the managers, who have gained a different status from the traditional subordinate staff. These people can grasp power, but don't necessarily own stocks to share profits, and don't bear the property risk of loss. "Manager Revolution" theory has been more fully developed in the works of Galbraith. He argues the inevitability of "expert combination" controlling the social power and advocates that the reason lies in the fact that science and technology as the most important factor of production has started to play a decisive role in the operation of the modern enterprise, therefore, "expert combination" is bound to grasp social power. He has made a detailed analysis on the three advantages of the "expert combination group" grasping social power. He has also further analyzed the transfer process of this social power.[1]

---

[1] A. A. Bailey, G. C. Means: *Modern Corporation and Private Property*, pp. 87- 88, New York, 1944; J. Burnham: *Manager Revolution: The Things That Are Happening in the World*, pp. 101-102, New York, 1941; R. Maris *Economic Theory of "Manager" Capitalism*, p. 1, London-New York, 1968; J. K. Galbraith: *Economics and Public Objective*, Beijing, the Commercial Press, 1983.

"Manager Revolution Theory" obviously misinterprets the nature of the separation in the capitalist enterprise ownership and management, which I will specifically discuss later. However, this point of view indeed reflects the changes in the function of capital under modern social production conditions. It argues from a different aspect that with the development of production socialization, the socialized development of capital is an inevitable trend in modern companies. Many ideas of "Manager Revolution Theory" have reference values, such as analysis on the change of role of engineers and technicians and managers in the economic development, analysis on business objectives being re-adjusted, and analysis on the advantages of experts governing the modern state, etc.

"Theories on the Changes of Socio-economic Structure": This is a theory which claims that the capitalist system can continuously tend to rationalization through changes in the economic structure and through social reforms. Western scholars have many theories on the evolution of contemporary capitalist economic structure, for example, Hansen's "mixed economy", Galbraith's "new socialism", Bell's "post-industrial society", Brzezinski's "technical society", Toffler's "super-industrial society" and Drucker's "post-capitalism society", and all can be classified under this theory. Besides these well-known theoretical models, other theories with significant influence include "welfare state", "social partnership system", "post-civilization society", and "multi-dimensional society". Hansen believes that the "mixed economy" is the economy of "the private enterprises and government partnership and argues that the private capitalism and the "socialized" economy are mixed together. Samuelson believes that "pure capitalism has gradually evolved into a 'mixed economy' that maintains the initiative and control rights of both the public sector and private sector". Galbraith believes that the "new socialism" can be achieved in the scope of capitalism, if the power and merits of the two systems are equally adapted, by improving the status of the "market system (small business system)", suppressing the power of "plan system (large company system)" and eliminating its negative effects on the "market system". Furthermore, he comments that "the steps strode toward new socialism due to necessities have already exceeded the level expected by the majority". And he believes that the key to the success in societal reform is to eliminate the old misconceptions and form a new "public knowledge" and in this respect, it is most important to rely on the government's efforts. Bell analyses the contradiction between company's economization pattern and socialization pattern and advocates that the United States is breaking away from the society based on the private enterprise market system and moving toward a society which attains a development objective for the majority and social decision-making. The changes of corporation and societal characteristics have made the American economy qualitatively enter into the "post-industrial society". He has also described the basic characteristics and economic structure of the "post-industrial society" in detail.[1]

Those theories have a set of special explanations on the changes of socio-economic structure. However, almost all kinds of theoretical models have a common purport and belief, that is, the economic system of capitalist countries after the war is increasingly tend to rationalization. Their basic views have striking similarities: First of all, they all think that the macro-control policies of capitalist states have changed the capitalist economic structure and system characteristics; secondly, they think that the private ownership in modern capitalist economy has disintegrated, private capital owners have lost their social powers, and "managers" or "expert combination" have become the real rulers of the social economy; thirdly, they think that the nature of monopoly organizations has changed, and the control power and business goals of large companies have developed toward the direction of socialization. Finally, they generally oppose the basic conclusions of Marx's analyses on the capitalist economic formation. Although their ideas deny the obvious internal contradictions of the capitalist economy and undermine the nature of capitalist economic system, some

[1] A.H. Hansen: *The Economic Problems in the 1960s*, p. 76, Beijing, the Commercial Press, 1964; P. A. Samuelson: *Economics*, the 10th edition, p. 31, Beijing, the Commercial Press, 1991; J. K. Galbraith: *Economics and Public Objective*, pp. 217-218; D. Bell: *The Coming of Post-Industrial Society*.

economic phenomena and problems that they have noticed need our in-depth analysis. I think their theoretical viewpoints also provide us with necessary material to conduct deeper comparative studies.

"System Innovation Theories": This is a theoretical trend formed through systematic analysis on socio-economic history by the New Institutional Economics School. The representatives of this theory such as Coase, North, and others have conducted their own unique descriptions on the history of economic development of human society. Coase's transaction cost theory is an important work on this basis. Coase's representative work *System Innovation Theory* and North's *The Structure and Change in Economic History* offer comprehensive analyses on contemporary capitalism. In the opinion of North and others, system innovation plays the same decisive role as technological innovation in the process of socio-economic growth, and the success or failure of the system determines the social progress and regression. The periods with slower economic growth in the history lie in absence of a clear property right system, and the Netherlands and England had the attained leading roles as the earliest because they are the first to achieve reforms on property rights system. The rapid economic growth of the western capitalism is the result of the formation and development of private property rights. They think that the formation source of private property rights is rooted in the scarcity of resources. With the population growth, resources become scarce, thus forming the necessity of defining property rights.

The formation of private property rights reduces transaction costs, providing maximization of revenue. Countries, groups and individuals as subjects of system innovation are all economic persons, and the purpose and fundamental principle of innovation are to pursue the maximization of their respective benefits. Just this benefit motive promotes the system innovation and the minimization of transaction costs, and thus profit maximization is realized through innovation. North thinks that the private property right is the most efficient property right system, and he has made a detailed analysis on various attributes and functions of private property rights. He clearly points out that the aim of researching the property right system is to play all kinds of functions to reduce transaction costs and improve economic benefits through the definition, alteration, arrangement and implementation of property rights.

"System Innovation Theory" contains certain rationality. Its viewpoint that adheres to the system analysis and thinks system factor is an important factor in determining economic growth contains scientific components. By the innovation of the property right system, it emphasizes that a state that has important special functions is correct. Its understanding that property right system is based on market transactions and the analysis that the reasonable arrangement on internal property right structure of a company is an important factor that determines the operation efficiency of an enterprise are relatively objective propositions. However, its methodology of analyzing problems is based on individual utilitarianism and liberalism of neo-classical economics, its theoretical paradigm has some colors of orthodox economics. I think insisting that the private property right is the only effective system represents a one-sided approach, and furthermore, its analysis on the system innovation subjects and reasons has also nothing in common with Marxist economics, but all of those ideas need our special attention.

2. Relevant Theories of Contemporary Marxist Scholars

After the World War II, especially since the 1960s, Marxist economists have made a lot of studies on the historical process of capitalism. Here, I would like to give a brief introduction to the main points on several fundamental aspects.

Regarding the ownership relations:

Contemporary Marxists have generally paid much attention to new changes on the ownership relations, and have proposed that this is the core issue to understand the contemporary capitalist economic relations. Baran (1910-1964) and Sweezy (1910-2004) have analyzed the foundation and patterns of combination of private property and company. They think that the power relations in the socio-economy has changed, the functions of capitalism have changed, manager groups have achieved the control over companies, representing a permanent group, individual capitalists are replaced by the companies and the functions of the capitalists have been systematized.[1]

Braverman has analyzed the changes of the ownership structure of monopoly capital in modern companies, and argued that the modern company form has cut off the link between capital and individual owners, resulting in the socialization of capital forms and the specialization of management. He stresses that the separation of capital ownership and management is conducted within the bourgeoisie. The modern companies make capital enter into a kind of social cause form beyond the personal form.[2] Mandel has (1923-1995) analyzed the inevitable influence on capital ownership structure and the nature of management itself in the internal plan and organizational development of capitalist corporate system, pointing out that modern corporate management expands its powers but it determines the detailed issues and by increasing concentration of power it determines critical issues. Thus, he describes that the real dominator of company is still big capital. Since the interests of big shareholders lie in the value of their shares rather than dividends, it is the in-depth reason that a company attaches great importance to long-term plans.[3]

Regarding the industrial relation and the distribution relation:

Almost all of the main works of Marxists involve changes of the contemporary capitalist industrial relation and distribution relation, in which Braverman's *Labor and Monopoly Capital* offers the most profound research and discussion. This book pushes the study on the industrial relation under the monopoly capital a step forward. He thoroughly discusses the labor process and trends of changes under the capitalism conditions, particularly analyzing how to adjust mode of labor according to the principle of capital control practice. He has also studied the evolution of capital relations and

---

[1] Paul. A. Baran, Paul. M. Sweezy: *Monopoly Capital—On the Economy and Social Order in U.S.A*, Edition 1, Beijing, the Commercial Press, 1977.

[2] Harry Braverman: *Labor and Monopoly Capital*, Beijing, the Commercial Press, 1978.

[3] Ernest Mandel: *Late Capitalism*, Harbin, Heilongjiang People's Publishing House, 1983.

class structure in the new science and technological conditions. He has conducted an in-depth analysis on the structure of the management and criticized the ideas on "non-working class of the middle class".

British left-wing economist Harris and Fiennes claim that studying the transformation of the development stages of capitalist mode of production should analyze not only the function of accumulation and class struggle, but also the changes of possession and control patterns of surplus value and evolution process of socialization in the production, distribution and exchange relation as well as the changes of the whole social relations arising from them. The state in contemporary capitalism occupies a dominant position in the social reproduction. Due to "process control", "accounting control" and "financial control" over social reproduction by the state, it realizes comprehensive socialization in the social production, the state promotes changes in the surplus value possession, and the competition over the surplus value are gradually socialized.[1] *Monopoly Capital* written by Baran and Sweezy uses monopoly capitalism in the United States as the background and the production and absorption of "economic surplus" as the central clue to study the new features in contemporary capitalism, which has laid the foundation for the formation of "monopoly capital school" in the United States. They have analyzed the rule over American society by large monopoly companies and also changes in the nature of big companies, pointing out that the American monopoly capitalism is a system composed of large companies. Large company's rule over the economy and its connections with other economic subjects are mainly established through the market relations, and the nature of such a market relation is that big companies determine the market price to ensure absolute and relative growth over the possession of the economic surplus, which is an important feature of monopoly capitalism. They have analyzed the contradictions between production and distribution of economic surplus and demonstrated the profound class contradiction and

---

[1] Ben Fiennes & Lawrence Harris: *Re-reading "Capital"*, Jinan, Shandong People's Publishing House, 1993.

irrationalities in the distribution system of contemporary capitalism.[1]

Regarding the operation system of capitalist economy:

In this respect, O'Connor (1930-) has a profound point of view. He thinks contemporary capitalist states have two contradictory functions: Firstly, the accumulation function means that the state wants to maintain and create favorable conditions for capital accumulation benefiting the private capital. Secondly, the function of legitimating means that the state wants to maintain and create the conditions for societal harmony and maintain the existing dominance in the ideological spheres of the society. The dual economic function constitutes the dual movement of the state-owned capital to achieve the realization of those functions. Based on the above points of view, he has put forward the two theoretical propositions: a) The development of state-owned industries and the development of state expenditure have become the foundation of capital's monopolistic development and the leverage for the growth of the whole social production. The development of the monopolistic sectors requires the growth of state expenditures. b) The dual movement of state-owned capital is a development process with contradictions, and it is bound to exacerbate the inherent contradictions of capitalism. French Marxist scholars took the state monopoly capitalism in France as the background to analyze the respective characteristics of private monopoly and state monopoly and the consistent and conflicting relations between private monopoly and state monopoly and offered an in-depth analysis on the functions of state monopoly capital. They have suggested that governments use the method of "state capital depreciation" method to solve the difficulties in the operations of the private monopoly capital and alleviate the profound contradictions in the development of capitalism brought about by it. Mandel has studied the long-term basis of the operational objectives of modern large monopoly companies and their policies to strengthen planning and organization. He has also analyzed the strengthening of overall

---

[1] Paul Baran: *Increased Political Economics*, English version, 1968, New York; Paul Sweezy: *The Development of Capitalism*, Beijing, The Commercial Press, 1997.

economic planning and coordination activities relating the whole society, the difficulties in social planning caused by "rationalized" plans of companies, and the role of the internationally created "general production conditions" for private capital. He has asserted that capital's new characteristic manifests itself as a transformation from international accumulation to international concentration.[1]

Regarding international economic relations:

Baran's Theory of Developed and Less Developed Countries analyzes the economic relations between a small number of developed capitalist countries and the most less developed countries to reveal the nature of contradictions and unequal relationships in international economic relations. The "center-periphery theory" of Frank Gudrun (1929-2005) holds that in the contemporary capitalist world system, a small number of developed capitalist countries possess the central position, and the majority of least developed countries remain in the periphery or in the margins of the periphery. The interests of a small number of developed countries are realized by invading and occupying the interests of the least developed countries and sacrificing the future development of the least developed countries. His theory discloses the inequalities in the contemporary capitalist world system and upholds that developing countries should disconnect with advanced countries to get rid of economic exploitation and oppression. The modern world system theory of Wallerstein (1930-) contains obvious characteristics of Marxism, which conducts systematic analysis by deeming capitalism as a historical system. He discloses the nature of unequal exchange relations between the core regions and marginal regions in the world economic system and their future development trends, and puts forward the theory that world capitalist economy system will inevitably collapse.[2]

At present, the most debated issue is economic globalization, most

---

[1] James O'Connor: *The State's Financial Crisis*, New York, English version in 1973; Paul Pokhara, etc.: *State Monopoly Capitalism*, Beijing, The Commercial Press, 1982.

[2] Immanuel Wallerstein: *Historical Capitalism*, Beijing, Social Sciences Academic Press, 1999; *Modern World System*, Beijing, Higher Education Press, 2000.

Marxists and left-wing scholars hold critical attitudes toward economic globalization. They clearly point out that the developed capitalist countries play a leading role in the economic globalization, analyze the influence of globalization on world economic development in a more profound manner and assert that economic globalization is a double-edged sword for the majority of the developing countries.

Regarding system changes and its nature:

Basing himself on the long wave of the three science and technological revolutions, Mandel has divided capitalist development into three stages: "Laisser-faire Capitalism, Classical Imperialism and Late Capitalism", and has studied the different focuses in the activities of capital owners during different stages of capitalism. The focus in Laisser-faire capitalism was in the production field; the focus in classical imperialism was in the accumulation field; the focus in the late capitalism was in the reproduction field opening new investment objectives to expand the scale of enterprises. The basic characteristics of late capitalism are the co-existence of rapid development of productive forces together with increasing serious parasitism and waste phenomenon which causes a structural crisis in capitalism. P. Bokhara and some other scholars have also defined three stages of capitalism as: "primitive", "classical" and "monopoly capitalism" and divided monopoly capitalism into the two stages as the "general monopoly" and "state monopoly". They have analyzed the relationship between stages of capitalism and the evolution of the historical form of capital. Fiennes and Harris provided a scientific perspective for the study of contemporary capitalist mode of production. They have made a distinction between production modes and social formations, and made distinctions between the general capitalist mode of production and capitalist formations in specific countries. They have made a special analysis on the stages of mode of production and combined this analysis with the self-development process of capitalist mode of production. They have suggested that the study of capitalism should focus to reveal its hidden motives and trends behind the changes—from one stage to another—in capitalist mode of production.

Chinese Marxist studies:

Regarding the study of the historical evolution and forms of capital, economic theory circles in China generally advocate the three-stage theory in capitalist development: free competition, monopoly and the state monopoly and also suggest that the corresponding capital form that has occupied a dominant position can be defined as three forms. Their analysis is mainly based on Lenin's theory of imperialism. Chinese scholars have reached some outstanding results in the study of contemporary financial capital and state monopoly capitalism. Since the late 1980s, some scholars have put forward "social capitalism" theory. Lu Congming has postulated that contemporary capitalism is a social capitalism instead of the state monopoly capitalism. "The development of capitalism has experienced the three stages of competitive capitalism, monopoly capitalism and social capitalism. The basic meaning of social capitalism is that capitalist economy has realized a higher phase of the comprehensive socialization; in the developed capitalist countries socialism factors have gradually occurred and the transition to socialism has begun." He has briefly analyzed socialization of production, capital's socialization, state economic functions and roles, class structure, international relations and the evolution of domestic political relations and other topics in developed countries in the social capitalism stage and the basic characteristics of social capitalism. He has demonstrated the emerging socialist factors and their basic content in contemporary capitalist society, and deemed the transition of capitalism to socialism as a natural historical process. Yu Guangyuan and Gao Fang, two scholars, both have concluded that contemporary capitalism is social capitalism, but they have offered different analyses and unique models.[1]

---

[1] Yu Guangyuan: "Study Marx and Engels' Discussions on Social Capitalism", in *Study of Marxism*, 1988 (4). Lu Congming: "Is It State Monopoly Capitalism or Social Capitalism?", in *Economic Research Journal*, 1989 (4). Gong Weiping: "Capital Socialization and Capital of Socialization", in *Study and Exploration*, 1992 (1); *The Scope of Ownership*, Xi'an, Shaanxi People's Publishing House, 1994.

III. Marxism and the Latest Developments of Our Time

1. Analyzing the Characteristics of Capitalism

Fundamentally speaking, adhering to Marxism is to adhere to use the methodology of Marxism to understand and change the world. In Marx's *Capital*, the study on the capitalist mode of production offers an excellent model of applying historical materialism.

To illustrate the basic principle of historical materialism, Marx has given a classic formulation in the Preface of the book *A Contribution to Critique of Political Economy*: "In the social production of their existence, men inevitably enter into definite relations, which are independent of their will, namely relations of production appropriate to a given stage in the development of their material forces of production. The totality of these relations of production constitutes the economic structure of society, the real foundation, on which arises a legal and political superstructure and to which correspond definite forms of social consciousness. The mode of production of material life conditions the general process of social, political and intellectual life. It is not the consciousness of men that determines their existence, but their social existence that determines their consciousness. At a certain stage of development, the material productive forces of society come into conflict with the existing relations of production or – this merely expresses the same thing in legal terms—with the property relations within the framework of which they have operated hitherto. From forms of development of the productive forces these relations turn into their fetters. Then an era of social revolution begins. The changes in the economic foundation lead sooner or later to the transformation of the whole immense superstructure."[1]

The philosophical method of historical materialism and the theory on the law of the development of human society established by Marx provide

---

[1] *Selected Works of Marx and Engels*, Edition 2, Vol. 2, pp. 32-33, Beijing, People's Publishing House, 1995.

a scientific method and the guiding ideology for the study of the historical process of the development and evolution of capitalist mode of production. If we analyze this classical statement combined with his study on the capitalist mode of production and its development law, we can grasp the following theoretical points very clearly:

(1) Capitalism is a specific historical process of the development of human society.

Human society has experienced a development process from low levels to higher levels. "The development of socio-economic formation is a natural and historical process."[1] The fundamental motive force to promote this process is the development of social productive forces. The development level of social productive forces determines social mode of labor and ownership form of the means of production and the situation of the corresponding entire socio-economic structure. According to the law that the social relations of production should be suitable for the development of productive forces, social economic formation has experienced a development process from a low level to high level, thus showing the stages of historical development of human society. All social systems successively replace each other in the history are temporary stages of the development process of human society. Every stage has a natural and a historical foundation. Capitalist economic form is a necessary step of the development of human society. It has historical inevitability and progressive nature that replaces the feudal mode of production and has its special social and historical nature. The specific capitalist mode of production cannot be ascribed an eternal attribute. On the contrary, in the development process of human society, it only manifests a historical temporality and transition.

(2) Capitalism is a social organism that continuously develops and changes.

The development of a social economic formation is also a historical

---

[1] *Karl Marx and Frederick Engels*, Edition 1 of Chinese version, Vol. 23, p. 12, Beijing, People's Publishing House, 1972.

process in a continuous change. Capitalist mode of production is "an organism that can change and is always in the process of change"[1]. That this mode of production is a continuously changing social organism is rooted in its internal contradictions. Unlimited greed for profit in the capital is bound to push the continuous development of social productive forces as a means to achieve its objective, the contradiction between the trend of unlimited expansion of social production and private ownership relation of capitalism is bound to lead to constant adjustments and changes in the capitalist production relations and the constant socialization of productive forces also require corresponding socialization of capitalist ownership relations. As long as the adjustment of production relations within the scope allowed by the nature of capital has not yet reached their limits and that there will be still a room for change in capital relations, and economic formation of capitalism will not perish. "No social order is ever destroyed before all the productive forces for which it is sufficient have been developed, and new superior relations of production never replace older ones before the material conditions for their existence have matured within the framework of the old society."[2]

(3) The process of development and maturity of capitalism is a process of self-sublation.

On the one hand, "the productive forces developed in the afterbirth of bourgeoisie society create the material conditions solving this kind of confrontation at the same time"[3]; on the other hand, the development and deepening process of private ownership of capitalism is also a process of self-negation. This self-negation is conducted by the role of the inherent law of capitalist production itself. In the capital concentration process, it achieves the strengthening of big capital; meanwhile, it also realizes "sublation of capital within its own scope of capitalist mode of production as private

[1] *Karl Marx and Frederick Engels*, Chinese version, Edition 1, Vol. 23, p. 12, Beijing, People's Publishing House, 1972.

[2] *Karl Marx and Frederick Engels*, Chinese version, Edition 1, Vol. 13, p. 9, Beijing, People's publishing House, 1962.

[3] *Karl Marx and Frederick Engels*, Chinese version, Edition 1, Vol. 13, p. 9, Beijing, People's Publishing House, 1962.

property", and creates "a transition form to a new mode of production in the organization"[1]. The perishing of capitalist mode of production is an inevitable result of its inherent contradictions and the development of capitalist basic contradiction is the fundamental driving force which promotes this process.

In conclusion, the concept of evolution of different social formations, the concept of self-negation of self-development process of a specific social formation and the thought that the formation elements of a new society germinate in the old society elucidated by Marx are all basic theoretical principles and foundation of methodology that we should follow when studying the history form of capital and the evolution of its economic relationship.

2. Several Theoretical Issues of the Historical Status of Capitalism

What we are trying to prove is the basic law of the movement of production mode of human society, which proves that the social relations of production should be in conformity with the requirements of the development of productive forces. This law has shown an inevitable trend of socialization development in capital because it should also be in conformity with the socialization development of productive forces contained internally in the capitalist mode of production. The basic research task lies in revealing the objective necessity of socialization of capital and making clear profound changes of the development movements of the internal contradictions of capitalist mode of production embedded in an analysis of evolution series of various historical formation of capitalism. Developing the basic principles of Marxist theory should be in line with practice and logic of the system of Marxist theory itself. In the following, we will briefly present our approaches on the basic theoretical issues of those new phenomena in the contemporary capitalist mode of production.

---

[1] *Karl Marx and Frederick Engels*, Chinese version, Edition 1, Vol. 25, p. 493, p. 499, Beijing, People's Publishing House, 1974.

(1) How to stick to the productive forces criterion to judge the social changes in the capitalist mode of production

Using productive forces standard in understanding the historical evolution process of social formations is the essential character of historical materialism and the basis of its scientific character. Adhering to productive forces standard is to adhere to the primacy of the productive forces among other various basic factors that influence changes in the social formations. This is because in the various activities of human society, production activity which meets the needs of human survival and development is the most fundamental practice. Other activities of human society are based on it and developed in accordance with the development level of productive activities. And a certain mode of production must be a union of productive forces and production relation. In the dual attribute of mode of production, productive forces are the determinant aspect, and it contains the contradictions and relations between men and nature which is the material content of mode of production, and is reflected through mode of material movement in the social production process. The material mode of production mainly refers to the technological combination mode of subjective and objective elements.

Production relation is a social production mode which adapts to the requirements of the productive forces. As the social content of production mode, it includes the contradictions and relations between men and men in the production and reproduction process and is reflected by the means of social movement of production, while the social mode of production mainly refers to the ownership of means of production and the combination mode of the parties decided by it. The material means and social means of production are dual attributes of the same production mode and they reflect the contradictory movement relation between productive forces and production relations. However, the role between them is achieved through mode of labor, which determines that labor mode itself is bound to have a dual attribute in this element system, because technological combination of productive mode of people is not only determined by material mode of production, but also influenced, by social mode of production. In other words, the change of material mode of production determines the changes of labor mode, thus leading to the changes in the social mode of production; on the other hand, the social mode of production brands certain social marks in the mode of labor, thus affecting the material mode of production.

The basic characteristics of capitalist material mode of production are the revolutionary and social nature of its technical basis of production. "The technical basis of modern industry is revolutionary, but that of all the former production modes, it is conservative in nature." This revolutionary and social nature of material mode of production is interrelated, reciprocal, causational and mutually propulsive. The technical nature of the production determines the co-operative and social nature of production in the labor process, and the use of means of production, production process itself and the products are fully socialized. The socialization of production provides the necessary conditions and internal requirements for the changes in the technical foundation, and further changes in the technical foundation of production will develop the combination pattern of production mode and labor mode, causing an important socialization trend in the **material production of capital's form**. Adapting to that process, the **social production mode of capital** is also bound to have that trend of socialization in its nature; otherwise it cannot continue to develop itself. Therefore, we conclude that the characteristics of material production mode of capital determines the labor mode of capitalism, thus the social mode of production records regular changes, and capitalist mode of production is a social organism that changes continuously and is in the course of frequent changes. Since the development and change of the social organism of capitalism are rooted in the requirements of the development of social productive forces, and its development finally can only be explained by the contradictory movement between productive forces and production relations, the only scientific criterion for us to determine the social and historical nature of development and evolution of capitalism can only be productive forces. And when compared with all other factors, others are all minor and non-fundamental. Those criteria that use the pure technological point of view, cultural comparison approach, religious beliefs approach, ideological point of view, spiritual strength point of views, etc. to illustrate the historical process of development of capitalism cannot completely reveal its nature thoroughly, so their results may be one-sided, or even idealistic. The main criterion we should judge whether any adjustment or social change in any economic relation has a progressive nature or not should not be based on ideology, but instead whether it promotes the development of productive forces. Those changes and adjustments that protect and contribute to the development of productive forces will have progressive significance, and when not they will lead to retrogression. Only in this way, we can insist on the fundamental principle of historical materialism. Just because of this, I think that a series of self-regulation, improvement and improvement in the capitalist relations have provided social productive forces a space for further development. We can thus scientifically explain the fundamental reason why the capital relation itself can have changes. And we can understand those fundamental conditions throughout the historical process of capitalism in which the productive forces can constantly develop by analyzing its internal contradictions.

Some Marxists simply use a kind of ideology standard, and completely deny the social progressive significance of all the changes and adjustments occurring in capitalism. They think that any adjustment in capitalist economic relations will exacerbate or intensify contradictions with its productive forces. Then, the questions arise: Why does capitalism adjust its economic relations in every possible way? How did the three industry revolutions and two structural transformations in industry happen? In the minds of some Marxists, even those policies that are clearly favorable to the working class are assessed as reactionary, and they evaluate them as "anesthetic" and "soup of infatuation" for the working class. This approach will only draw conclusions inconsistent with the facts, and its theoretical foundation is shaky, too. I think we should face the fact that a series of self adjustments in capital relations have provided space for the development of productive forces, and explore the fundamental reason for the constant development of social productive forces of capitalism.

Of course, only by using productive forces criterion to judge the evolution of capitalism, we can find the social progressive significance of this evolution and can really find the historical limitations of the capital relation. We should also study the real social obstacles for the development of social productive forces, and discover and accurately judge retrogressive phenomena in the economic relations under some historical periods. In short we should explain the evolution of capitalism, including its objectivity, progress, tortuousness and limitation.

(2) Capitalism: the development and antagonism of its contradictions

Historical materialism considers that the successive replacement of different social formations and also development within each social formation can be understood by studying the basic contradictions within any social formation. It is clear that the internal contradictions of a social organism are the first reason in its development.

Of course, this applies for the capitalist social formation, too. So, how to understand the nature of the fundamental contradictions of capitalism and how these contradictions move has become a critical issue to correctly understand the historical process of development of capitalism. Using contradiction analysis is undoubtedly a scientific method of historical materialism. If the internal contradictions of capitalist mode of production are not correctly understood, then the internal contradictions in capital cannot be revealed. The internal contradiction in capital is the embodiment of the fundamental contradiction in the capitalist mode of production and it is just this contradiction which promotes the formation and evolution of capital's socialization process. Only by revealing the inherent contradictions of capital together with the historical process of capital's accumulation and evolution and by exploring the track of capital's internal contradictions in the development process of socialization of capital, can we explain the fundamental driving force of this process. I think we should correctly understand how this contradiction moves and thus clarify the reasons and transformation mechanisms in the evolution of capital forms and relations. We observe that there is a certain movement law in the socialization development process of capital and we will try to reveal that with the below explanations.

For a long time, the dominant point of view in Marxist political economy has asserted that the basic contradiction of capitalism and other contradictions arising from it were antagonistic and irreconcilable from the very beginning. But I think this point of view seriously violates the principles of historical materialism and cannot withstand the test of historical practice. How to understand the roles of the basic contradiction and other various contradictions inherent in the capitalist mode of production and how to judge the historical status of modern capitalism is a fundamental theoretical and policy (practical) issue.

The internal contradiction of any social formation contains the unity of oppositions between basic elements that form the inner relations. It contains the contradiction between socialization of production and the private ownership of capitalism. The unity of specific contradictions constitutes a specific capitalist mode of production, and a specific type of movement in its contradictions forms the reason for the changes in the capitalist mode of production. And the different particular forms—these contradictions attain—explain the characteristics of different stages in the capitalist mode of production.

I suggest that both compatibility and antagonism are the basic characteristics of these contradictions. Reaching to a complete antagonism even to an irreconcilable level of that contradiction is a situation which emerges when a production mode develops to its late stage. Here I should underline that capitalist mode of production cannot remain unchanged, on the contrary, its two basic elements, social productive forces and production relations, are in the process of constant change.

Private ownership of capitalism has shown many existence forms, and as a kind of private ownership it has manifested many realization forms, and the realization form of the ownership system of capitalism is steadily socialized together with the development of socialization of production, and thus opens up a space for further development of productive forces. In fact, capitalist mode of production in itself also has evolved through a number of development stages. Each new development stage is based on the preceding stage and is an inevitable result of development of its older stages. And every new form is a change of and denial of the previous forms. Without such changes, capitalist mode of production cannot survive, and the driving effect for changes arises from the internal contradictions of capital. Here I should point to a misunderstanding that some people equate contradictions and antagonisms and hold that antagonism will inevitably lead to the dissolution of a system. But this does not reflect the viewpoint of Marxism. The fundamental criterion to judge whether a social mode of production has become obsolete is social productive forces. It certainly depends on whether a mode of production itself has room for further changes and whether it can effectively promote the development of social productive forces. If capitalist mode of production still has a space and room for change and if it still allows a certain degree of or even rapid development of social productive forces, it will certainly not leave the historical stage. Therefore, I think, we should not only evaluate the capitalist mode of production as an inevitable historical stage in the development of human society, but also to evaluate it as a long-term process of development. Otherwise we cannot explain the nearly 500-year development history of capitalism and possible achievements that capitalism may attain in the future.

Thus we can conclude that long-term co-existence of capitalism and socialism in the future will be a high probability and the co-existence of the two social production modes with different characteristics constitutes an objective historical necessity. Without making a scientific judgment on this basic international reality we cannot ensure correct basic policies.

(3) Ownership forms and the nature of the contemporary capitalist system

Marx claims that the relationship to the means of production is the basis for the whole socio-economic relations system and emphasizes that the changes in the relationship to the means of production has decisive significance in the changes of a social formation. He had written: "Whatever the social form of production is, labor and the means of production are always the elements of production. However, under the situation of each other, both of them are only the possible elements of production. If a production is to be carried out, they must be combined. The specific ways and means for in which such a combination is realized determine that social structure is divided into different economic periods."[1] Marx had not only deemed the ownership of means of production as a symbol of dividing different social formations, but also argued that the internal social structure within the ownership of the means of production plays a decisive role to the other aspects of production relations. Therefore, ownership of the means of production is the fundamental sign reflecting the nature of a social system. Ownership of the means of production itself is a system consisting of a variety of different property rights. The more advanced the economic structure of a society is, the more complex is the internal structure of ownership of means of production. The possession, occupation, dominance (control) and use relations of the means of production constitute the fundamental aspects of the ownership system of capitalist means of production. Therefore, we should study the historical evolution of the capitalist ownership of the means of production and follow the emergence of other forms of ownerships which are different from single-private ownership of capitalism. Of course these changes in the forms reflect the changes in the inner system structure of the capitalist ownership of the means of production. Such as the emergence of the co-operative ownership of means of production which has occurred as a positive sublation in the capitalist ownership. More important, we can certainly observe a socialization trend in the internal structure of the private capital ownership. Although this trend or change is not so easy to deduce, it is the most fundamental aspect which has determined several stages of evolutions—in forms and inner

---

[1] *Karl Marx and Frederick Engels*, Edition 1 of Chinese version, Vol. 24, p. 44, Beijing, and People's Publishing House, 1972.

relations—within the capitalist ownership.

Another important aspect in the social form of capitalist production is the social combination pattern of the individual capital. The so-called social combination way of capital refers to the process in which individual capital based on capitalist private ownership is combined with the pattern of social capital. Social capital here does not refer to capital possessed or occupied by the society, but individual capital combined or associated in the form of social capital which appears as the opposite of single private capital. Such a change acquires the capital's function and realizes the aim of capital's augmentation. Whether individual capital exists in the form of independent private capital, or it practices external association (such as low-level partnerships), or it practices an internal combination by sublating its independent form under the condition of ensuring private property rights depends on the different social combination ways of capital. Certainly in all these practices or new forms private property rights are protected. Such combination ways also occur and reflect different property rights forms within the capital's inner system structure.

Capital's socialization process:

Observed from the surface, it seems that the inner social combination does not reflect the changes occurring related to the property rights of capital. But in fact, social combination form of capital has adapted to the socialization of production and thus undergone a series of historical changes. And as a result capital accumulation patterns, property rights relations, distribution relations and even the whole economic structure have encountered tremendous changes. Within the scope of capitalist mode of production, private capital adjusts and adapts to the development requirements in the socialization of production. These adjustments or adaptations are mainly realized by reforming the social combination pattern of private capital. In its development process, private capital constantly combine with each other, constituting a development process as capital's socialization, and in this process, social capital has constantly obtained its own various development forms, and the level of capital's socialization shows a trend of constant progress. The process of capital's socialization in terms of its nature is a process of self-sublation of capital relations within the scope of the capitalist mode of production. The formation and development of socialization not only is a product of the internal contradictions of capital but also determines the changes in its appearance and forms. Unless capital's socialization and the formation and development of social capital, capital cannot embrace the socialized productive forces, cannot control the material conditions of the production of surplus value, and thus faces a risk to lose its basis of existence as well. Therefore, in the analysis of the historical evolution of capitalist mode of production, it must be paid special attention to the study on the combination way of capital.

Of course, I should clearly point out that the above historical socialization process of capital ownership form certainly contains a sublation of private power of capital; meanwhile I should emphatically point out that all of these changes still take place on the basis of private ownership of capitalism within the scope allowed by the fundamental nature of capitalist ownership and within the principle of inviolability of private property. Owners of private capital still retain the above process insist on the premise of holding the ultimate ownership of the capital.

However, in the eyes of some scholars, as long as the fundamental nature of capitalist private ownership remains unchanged, it seems that capitalist appropriation of productive forces will not change. They have a rather vague understanding on the relationship between capital and wage labor, they emphasize the fundamental contradictory nature of the two but seem to ignore a deeper analysis on capital's inner relations. They correctly admit the antagonistic character of the fundamental contradiction in capitalism but fail to face up to the historical changes in capital's relations manifesting themselves in practice. They only concentrate on the continued fact that private ownership on capital remains, but neglect the study on the socialization of private capital. Such vagueness in theory prevents them to objectively reflect the historical process of the development of capital relation and impel a metaphysical understanding to the capital relation and its internal contradictions. The above mentioned approaches "firmly believe" that "capitalism is bound to perish"—the historical conclusions of Marxism—but in fact, if faith is not based on correct and objective theories, it cannot be solid. The purpose of the study on the development process of the combination means of capital society is to explain why, how and by which means capitalist mode of production progresses to its opposition, and more clearly illustrate the historical law of production, development and demise of capitalist mode of production.

(4) Historical judgment of Marxism on capitalism

In the Marxist classical works there are abundant explanations on the historical conclusion proving the inevitable demise of capitalism. However, the reality is that capitalism not only exists, but it also displays certain vitality. This fact leads to vague approaches and to some tendencies that publicly deny the scientific nature of Marxism; some people even have doubted their belief in socialism; there are also some people who firmly believe in the conclusions of Marxism, but deny the reality that capitalism still has certain vitality. Subsequently, various arguments that challenge Marxist views are active today.

The key question here is: Does the Marxist historical conclusion on capitalism conflict with the historical process of capitalism? I believe that they are consistent. The historical process of capitalism has not denied the historical conclusion of Marxism; on the contrary, it has proved that the development law of capitalism and its historical trend revealed by Marxism are scientific conclusions.

Classical Marxist scholars have applied historical materialism to study capitalist mode of production and revealed the movement laws of its emergence, development and demise, which is based on characteristics of internal contradictions of capitalist mode of production and the development of those contradictions. The contradiction between socialization process of production and capitalist private possession of means of production is inherent and remains the fundamental contradiction of capitalist mode of production. The fundamental nature of this contradiction determines the social characteristics and historical nature of capitalist mode of production, and the historical progress and limitations of capitalist mode of production are all rooted in that contradiction. The capitalist private possession relationship of means of production is different from private ownership system of small producers. It takes the gathering of production factors as its premise, and it is just this characteristic that has made it initiate socialized mass production. However, the development of socialized production in terms of its nature is opposite to the private possession of means of production. It determines that in the development process of production socialization, the capital relation is bound to constantly sublate its previous existence forms and realize the socialization of capital form and capital's possession means, thus promoting the productive forces' continuous development and socialized possession. The changes of characteristics in the self-development and self-sublation process of capitalism can be observed as different development stages, and the latter stage always contain the succession and a denial relation to the previous stages. However, the self-regulation, reform and the improvement of capital must be conducted within the limit that maintains its governance basis and adheres to the systemic nature. This limit not only defines characteristically the limit of all self-transformations in capital relation, but also points to the social and historical limits of this transformation process. That is to say, on the one hand, in the historical process of the development of capitalism, the capital relations have gone through a series of self-regulation, reform and improvement, providing space for the continuous development of social productive forces; on the other hand, the self-adjustment space of the capital relation does not have infiniteness or endlessness, and in the end, the revolution in its fundamental system is inevitable. However, no matter in what period and what way the changes in the basic system of capitalism will occur, the historical process of the development of capitalism has already demonstrated with eloquent facts that compared to classical capitalist mode of production, today's contemporary capitalist mode of production contains the formational elements for a new society and these elements are not reducing but instead increasing and capitalism is not distancing from the new society, but is progressing closer to it. These above reflect the consistency between the historical conclusion on capitalism by Marxism and the existing historical process of capitalism.

Different from the above thoughts, there are two other diametrically opposed viewpoints on the development and changes in capitalist mode of production. One viewpoint is that the capitalism that Marx had illustrated no longer exists. And they evaluate those practices as self-regulation, reform and improvement to prove that these have transformed the fundamental nature of capitalism and this approach is in accordance with the various "qualitative change theories" put forward by some scholars. We can prove that the fundamental basis as private possession relationship of capitalism remains the same, the fundamental nature of wage labor and capital relation remains unchanged, and the fundamental relations of distribution and possession of surplus labor result based on capital's dominance remains the same. In a word, under the condition that the essential characteristics of the capitalism system continues, it may be quite conservative to discuss a characteristically qualitative change in the system of capitalism. The above arguments need a sufficient empirical basis.

The second viewpoint is that no matter what adjustments and changes occur in capital relations, the ownership relation of capitalism does not have any change, and they deem the viewpoints that affirm the socialization process in the capitalist ownership relations as anti-Marxism. They also believe that due to the fundamental antagonistic and irreconcilable relation between socialist public ownership and capitalist private ownership, the formation elements of the new society cannot appear in capitalist mode of production. No matter what original intention this view contains, in fact, it will lead to the infinite vitality of capitalist ownership relation, otherwise how can a constant and unchanged capital ownership relation promote that continuous development in productive forces? If it is evaluated that capitalist ownership relation has a temporary historical nature, why does not this constant ownership relation perish with the development of socialization of production? This viewpoint is not only contrary to Marxism in theory, but also does not conform to the historical facts we observe in the evolution of capitalist mode of production. In any case, a constant and fixed capitalist ownership relation cannot co-exist with constantly socialized productive forces but pushes a variety of innovations in the modern enterprise as a long term trend. Part of the above viewpoints come from the textbooks of the former Soviet Union, and are still accepted as scientific thinking by some Marxists. That error of the approach was wide-spread for a long time and has caused a serious damage and its remains are partly still effective today. Adhering to and developing Marxism need us to dissociate with those misleading thoughts in theory and methodology. We should reveal the law of historical development in the capitalist mode of production and make a scientific illustration on the self-negating historical process in the capitalist mode of production. Our analysis and practical exploration should conform with the facts and should withstand the test of history.

(5) Clarifying the relations between capitalism and socialism

Historical materialism claims that the development of human society is a continuous historical process. Any social development stage is a prerequisite for its later stage. The result of its development is the condition and realistic foundation for its later stages and the relation between the later stage and the former stages always contains the inheritance and criticism of the former. Therefore, study on the theories of the development of capitalism needs to pay attention to the continuity of historical process. On the one hand, this continuity of history embodies the historical continuity of the development process of the capital relation itself in the capitalist social formation; and on the other hand, it embodies the historical continuity as the replacement of the old by the new social formation.

In regard with the continuity of the development in capital's self-relations, there is a lack of research material, and quite few people study the socialization process of capital as a continuous historical process. Some researchers have paid attention to some realistic issues that have occurred in a certain stage of this process, but not studied the whole process in total, so they have a limited value. Partialness and discontinuity hinder the cognition on the law of socialized development of the capital.

Social capital theory:

I think historical continuity and wholeness approach is very important for the systematization, integrity and profundity of theoretical research. This is also one of the important reasons why the research framework of "social capital theory" has not been established for a long time. Due to such incompleteness on social capital theory studies, we lack a historical analysis revealing the process in which the basic contradiction of capitalism indeed promotes the social development. Lack of researches on the historical continuity of capital relation adjustments which has occurred within the framework of capitalist mode of production determine that Marxists may have an unclear understanding on its future scope and underestimate the self-adjustment ability of capitalist mode of production. Thus, it may lead to mistaken judgments on the historical position and fate of different historical formations of capital in different development stages and lead to such conclusions that contradict with the facts in its history.

Accordingly, I would like to suggest the following six issues for deeper study: the relationship between socialization process of capital and the historical evolution of capitalist economic formation, the relationship between social capital and the historical formation of capital, the relationship between the stages of and the continuity in capital's socialization process, the differences and connections between different social capital formations and their status and roles in the respective historical stages (development process of capitalism), dynamic effects of the basic contradiction of capitalism in the evolution of the capitalist economic formation and lastly the relationships between the law of capital's socialization and the law of negation in the development of capitalism.

The historical continuity as the replacement of the old by the new social formations is also a very important theoretical issue. Regarding to the historical connections of the two modes of productions, capitalism and socialism, an opinion advocated in the political economics researches made in the former Soviet Union has been popular till today. It suggests that the capitalist private ownership and socialist public ownership are diametrically opposed; therefore, the formation elements of socialism are inevitably repelled by the former one, making it unable to form in the womb of the former one. This narrow viewpoint on the relationships of the two social modes of production not only violates Marxist theories, but is also not in line with objective reality. Marx has believed that the development of capitalist mode of production creates the material conditions for the formation of a new society and evaluated them as a transitional process for transcending the capitalist mode of production with a newer mode. For example, he has deemed formation of the joint stock companies and the banking system as the transitional forms preparing for the new form of society. In fact, socialized productive forces created by capitalist mode of production constitute material conditions for the socialist mode of production, in addition, capitalist mode of production also contains a series of factors such as social mode of labor process which corresponds to socialized mass production, the organizational forms of socialized production, the management mode of social labor formed in accordance with the technical nature of production process, social institutions (regulations) that control and intervene to the operation of social production process, the mechanism for macro-economic adjustments, the economic basis through which state-owned capital is formed and the social factors formed by socialization of private capital, etc.

Among them, some factors can be directly applied or inherited by socialist mode of production, but some factors can be applied after making several alterations, and there are also some factors which are only the starting points to form the socialist mode of production. These elements all embody the historical connections of the two production modes with different natures. Every major adjustment or change within the systemic structure of capital relation contains a negation to the private capital relation to a certain extent. It is just through this constant self-negation that capitalist mode of production progresses to disintegration. The self-negation of capitalist mode of production in its own development process is also a process that creates the necessary conditions for the formation of the new society.

History has shown that socialism is not only the opposite of capitalism but is also its successor. Ascertaining the social and historical nature and the characteristics of the current times has important significance to correctly understand the basic characteristics and the main tasks in the primary stage of socialism of China. In the current economic globalization process in the world, capitalist economic system occupies a dominant position. Knowing the new characteristics in the economic development of contemporary capitalism has practical significance for Marxists to formulate correct principles and policies in the international economic relations. Market economy is a legacy left by capitalism and I think it needs to be developed and critically inherited. Learning the successful experiences and bitter lessons of capitalism in the process of developing the market economy also has significance to build the socialist market economy.

The Inevitable Trend of Capitalist Mode of Production

One critical question for understanding the historical process of capitalism is how to understand the historicity of capitalism. It is the question that a lot of people find controversial. Marx and Engels have declared in the *Communist Manifesto* that based on the movement of the basic contradiction between the socialization of capitalist production and capitalistic private appropriation form, capitalism is bound to perish and communism is bound to succeed. But currently capitalism not only does not prepare conditions for its demise, but also records achievements in terms of productive forces, science and technological development and promotes several innovations and sustainable development. It is quite necessary to explain this process.

I. The Inherent Contradictions of Capitalist Mode of Production

As early as more than 100 years ago, according to the analysis on the characteristics of the inherent contradictions and development law of capitalist mode of production, Marx had revealed the historical inevitability that socialism will replace capitalism. On the inherent contradictions of capitalist mode of production, Engels had further formulated it as the contradiction between socialized production and capitalistic appropriation in his work *Anti-Duhring*. The concrete embodiment of this contradiction is the contradiction between the proletariat and bourgeoisie and the contradiction between the organization of production in individual plants and anarchy of production regarding the whole society. Such arguments of Marx and Engels have provided the most fundamental basis to understand the historicity of capitalism.

The basic contradiction in human society:

To understand the historicity of capitalism, one must first elucidate whether the basic contradiction of capitalism still exists or whether its nature is fundamentally changed. Marxism believes that the basic contradiction of capitalism is the expression of the basic contradiction inherent in the development of the human society in the current stage, i.e. the capitalist society. And the basic contradiction of human society is the basic reason that promotes the development of human society from the lower level to higher level as well as the basic reason that capitalist society is bound to be replaced by socialism. But during this long process, there are not only gradual quantitative changes but also qualitative changes in which one mode of production is replaced by another mode of production. Does the basic contradiction of capitalism manifest fundamental changes after a development of more than 100 years?

First, let us look into one side of this basic contradiction, i.e. socialized production. Under the current capitalism conditions, the means of production and productive forces are, in an unparalleled level, highly socialized compared to those 100 years before. In the aspect of the scientific research, in the past it was those individuals like Watt or Fulton who had engaged in invention activities, but now there are huge research centers with different scales or even covering an entire industry that are engaged in technological innovation. Moreover the modern scientific study and learning has been organized in a more social form. In the aspect of division of labor, no matter it is the social division of labor or technical division of labor or even the division of labor in a single enterprise, the progress is remarkable. The socialization degree of capitalist society is unprecedented compared to the former society. The enterprises in the past were engaged in small-scale production in a region in the form of family businesses and the products they produced were those products containing primary technologies. Whereas today, those that are engaged in production are manufacturers with wider social scale, their managers control business activities covering continental regions, and the required professional functions and the relationships between the specialized skills that they need to deal with are much more complicated. The products containing complicated technologies piled like mountains circulate through complicated networks before reaching their final consumers, which is also an important expression of the socialization of economic activities.

To sum up, as summarized by the contemporary Western left-wing scholar John McDermott: "What we have today is not only an 'organized capitalism', but also a capitalism with profound social characteristics, which is deeply dependent on society, and is extremely weak and vulnerable to the possible changes of society."[1]

Possession and appropriation:

Secondly, let's look into the other side of the basic contradiction of capitalism, i.e. the capitalistic appropriation. First of all, we need to note that the meaning of appropriation is different from that of possession. The former

[1] Quoted from Zhou Tong: "A Number of Situations in the Contemporary Socialization of Capital", in *Foreign Theoretical Trends*, 2002 (2).

one has the meaning of theft, misappropriation, etc. It is the abstraction of the nature of capitalist private ownership even the capitalist economic relation, while the latter is used to express the ownership category in its broad general meaning or to define the small private ownership—the terming was also respectively employed as such in the English version of *Capital* edited by Engels. Therefore, capitalistic appropriation is different from the possession in the small producers economic mode. The latter denotes the private ownership based on the own work of small producers, while the former is an abstraction of the capitalist private ownership based on appropriation of other's surplus labor. Thus contradiction between socialized production and capitalist private ownership aimed at and based on appropriation of surplus value without payment—unpaid part—is the correct understanding of the basic contradiction of capitalism.

As explained in the introduction of this book, during a period covering more than 100 years, the existence form of capitalist private ownership in its above explained specific meaning has had major changes, but its nature and status have not been changed. We can prove this point at least from two aspects: the internal driving force—reasons—and the law of economic crises which create successive crises in contemporary capitalism and bourgeoisie's dominating status in the economic, political and social life. One of the important tasks of the subsequent chapters of this book is to reveal the nature of economic relations of contemporary capitalism from those aspects such as changes in ownership relations, class relations, distribution relations, economic operation mechanism of capitalism and its internationalization.

We suggest that the nature and status of capitalist private ownership have not recorded a fundamental change, which does not mean that every capital has been preserved without a change. The reality is that due to the existence of external competition, each capital is under the pressure of competition and has the risk of bankruptcy at any time. Capitalism does not protect any particular capital or capitalist; during each major economic crisis, there are a large number of capital(s) that are destroyed and a group of capitalists that go bankrupt. However, just in this process, capital finds a new material and technological foundation required for surplus value production again, and in such a dynamic process, it maintains capitalist private ownership and the governance of entire capital and the fundamental interests of the bourgeoisie, thus retaining the basic contradiction of capitalism.

1. Two Forms in the Evolution of Capitalist Mode of Production

Although the basic contradiction of capitalism still exists, capitalist mode of production characterized by the unity of socialization of production and capitalist private ownership is still in further evolution. Obviously, this evolution is the result of its internal contradictions.

As early as 100 years ago, Marx had not only declared the historical inevitability of the demise of the capitalist system based on the analysis of its internal contradictions but further pointed out that, as a result of the role of its internal contradiction, capital gradually moves toward its own opposite through two ways.

The negative *"aufhebung"* and the active *"aufhebung"*:

Firstly, through negative sublation (=*Germ. Aufhebung*) of capital, there occurs a gradual transformation from classical capitalist mode of production to the joint (corporate) capitalist mode of production. Secondly, through active sublation of capital, a negation occurs and thus continues the struggle and opposition between capital and wage labor in the enterprises and even throughout the whole society.[1] The history of the development of capitalism for more than 100 years completely proves the correctness of the predictions made by Marx. First of all, capital's negative sublation enforces some aspects of economic relation of capitalism undergo major changes. The so-called capital's negative sublation refers to that under the effect of various contradictions, especially due to its internal contradiction, capital attains an increasing social character through self-regulation, reform and improvement. This is also pointed out by several Marxist political leaders after Marx and in our contemporary times. Since socialism, the opposite of

[1] *Karl Marx and Frederick Engels*, Chinese version, Edition 1, Vol. 25, pp. 497-498.

capitalism has emerged in 1917 and has shown a vigorous superiority for a quite long period of time, the capitalist countries, on the one hand, have done everything possible to fight socialism. Although the forms have constantly changed, the struggle has never stopped. But on the other hand, in order to maintain the survival and development of capitalist system, they have implemented a series of self-regulation, reform and improvement in several links and elements of capitalist relations of production and in its operation and management mechanisms, which also included applying several practices of socialism. Through these adjustments capitalist relations of production not only can further embrace the realistic productive forces, but also promotes the further development of those productive forces. In the same context of those self-adjustments the class contradiction and social contradiction under the rule of capitalism have a certain degree of ease as well.

The change of economic relations caused by capital's negative sublation as an important topic will be studied in the following chapters of this book.

Secondly, as explained by Marx, active or the positive sublation of capital plays an increasingly prominent role in the evolution process of capitalist mode of production. Different from capital's negative sublation, active sublation of capital does not result from the inherent contradictions of capital, instead it is mainly rooted in the contradiction between capital and wage labor. It is not a reflection of basic contradiction movement of capitalism in the aspects such as some links and operation mechanisms inherent within capitalist relations, but the changes in the quality of capital are caused by this contradiction. They are not marginal adjustments in the capitalist economic relations, but basically negate these relations.

Broadly speaking, after the capital was born and had begun to expose its internal contradictions, its active sublation had also begun. However, in the early stages of capitalism, this sublation was still in its childhood stage. The practices under the guidance of the theory of utopian socialism, especially all kinds of practices of employing non-capitalist economic forms to replace the capitalist enterprises organized by the utopian socialists, were the expression in the early stage of this active sublation.[1] However, with the development of basic contradiction of capitalism and the further intensification of wage labor-capital contradiction, after the middle 19th century, active sublation of capital began to gradually transcend its naive and utopian characteristics and has successively formed two types of positive sublations as the active sublation on individual capital and active sublation on the overall capitalism of some countries by relying on the consciousness and power of workers and the working masses. The occurrence of cooperatives discussed in Chapter III is the manifestation of the active sublation of the individual private capital. The success of socialist revolution in a number of countries during the World War I was an example of the overall sublation to capital. All these sublations illustrate the historicity of capitalism with real facts; it has also demonstrated that after the abolishment of the wage-labor system, formation of a new labor relation in the capitalist society (workers' and producers' co-operative factories) and the emancipation of working people are not only ideal, but manifested with initial-primary forms of the replacement in reality.

II. Capital's Negative Sublation as the Main Form of Capitalist Evolution

1. Capital's Negative Sublation

History and reality has shown that between the two forms in the evolution of capitalist mode of production predicted by Marx, capital's negative sublation (=*Germ. Aufhebung*) is its main form of development. The development of every system or a thing has its own laws. That capital's negative sublation being the main form in the evolution of capitalism is also by no means accidental. Specifically, I can suggest the following reasons:

---

[1] Marx pointed out: "Communism is an active expression of sublating private property (refers to capitalist private ownership—noted by the quoter); in the beginning, this emerges as common private property." (*Karl Marx and Frederick Engels*, Chinese version, Edition 1, Vol. 42, p. 117, Beijing, People's Publishing House, 1979.)

First of all, capital's negative sublation is an important condition for the survival of capital. Under the condition of today's contemporary capitalism, the direct manifestation of capital's negative sublation is that capital has gained further characteristics of social capital or (socialized character) through self-regulation as compared to former periods, through self-reform and improvement.

In fact, as the infant form and its universal form, capital's negative sublation, i.e. as a transformation process from individual private capital to social capital, was also displayed in the initial stage of capital when it first emerged. That is to say, once the capital was born, a constant transformation process began from private capital to the combined social capital form. During this initial period, although from the perspective of a single capital, the capital gives an independent appearance (as if it has an independent existence) since it independently completes its own circulation, turnover and proliferation, whereas when we look at it from the perspective of the society, "the capital(s)" eventually have inter-relations in the market or in the process of circulation, so capital operates as inter-related and inter-dependent social capital. Therefore, in order to gain the value of its proliferation, capital must always strive to realize the transformation from private capital to social capital and always needs to conduct further negative sublation movement. And this movement is an important condition for the proliferation of capital. As pointed out by Marx: "The market here has another meaning. It is just this interaction of each capital as individual capital that makes them establish themselves as a general capital; this interaction determines the independence in the surface and determines that independent existence of each single capital be sublated. In the form of credit this sublation is manifested by a greater extent. The highest form of this sublation is also expressed as the ultimate independence within the most appropriate form of capital, which is the share capital form."[1]

Secondly, capital's negative sublation offers a partial solution to its

---

[1] *Karl Marx and Frederick Engels*, Chinese version, Edition 1, Vol. 46, p. 167, Beijing, People's Publishing House, 1980.

inherent contradiction. According to Marx's arguments, the key reason for the constant transformation from private capital to social capital lies in capital's contradictory nature and that any capital is contradictory and it possesses a unity of two opposite and combined characteristics as private capital and social capital. In different stages of capitalism, due to differences in the degree and movement of that contradiction, the expression of this contradiction differs. For example, in the period of free capitalism (laissez faire), capital had generally existed in the form of individual private capital. In that period, when we observe the direct production process, general social capital characteristic cannot be directly grasped; only in the exchange process, when capital becomes a commodity in the market and such individual private capital is recognized by the society, that is, after its independent character and independent existence which is on the surface are sublated, its characteristics of social—general—capital, are exposed clearer. In the case of share capital form, capital "directly attains the form of social capital, i.e., those directly combined individual capital(s), and its nature of private capital is veiled. At the same time, in the external relations of share capital, "its enterprise is also exposed as social enterprise, different from and opposed to private enterprise"[1].

This shows: 1) In the period of free capitalism (laissez faire), the movement of the contradiction between private capital and social capital characteristictakes place only in individual private capital and capital's negative sublation is yet only in a potential state and it remains at the low-level. While in case of share capital, the movement of that contradiction has already attained an external expression, and the internal contradiction between private capital and social capital hidden within the capital has been revealed through an external opposition, i.e. the opposition between private enterprises and social enterprises, and capital's negative sublation has been externalized and thus has developed to a higher form.

2) It is just in the process of capital's negative sublation that the internal contradiction of capital, i.e. the contradiction between private capital and

---

[1] *Karl Marx and Frederick Engels*, Chinese version, Edition 1, Vol. 25, p. 493.

social capital characteristic is resolved to some extent. It manifests itself as capital's ongoing negative sublation, which sublates the independence on the surface that private capital has and also points to the socialist elements which its social capital character contains. Thus, inherent contradictions of capital at this low level phase or the opposition at external level is resolved. However, the inherent antagonism of this contradiction has not been fundamentally resolved. It is just this inherent antagonism that promotes the endlessness and formal transformations of its conflicts at the external level, thus providing a function-movement- space for capital's continuous negative sublation.

3) Capital's negative sublation can alleviate the basic contradiction of capitalism to a certain extent. Although in a direct sense, capital's negative sublation is the result of the movement of its inner contradiction, inherent dual nature of capital. Fundamentally, it is still the inevitable result of the basic contradiction of capitalism. The nature and characteristics of capitalist private appropriation determines that the capital is firstly private capital. But under the socialized production conditions, it is impossible for capital to limit itself in its own narrow sphere of self-sufficiency. Only through the exchange process, can capital deliver its commodity to the society and acquire the production factors (labor and material) it needs, thus continuously using the brand ("trade mark") of social capital; it can realize its aim to preserve and appreciate its value, and finally realize its own essential requirements. Conversely, if the capital cannot meet the above requirements of socialized production, it cannot play its role as social capital and finally can only lead to its own demise. Therefore, the fundamental reason for capital's negative sublation lies in the basic contradiction of capitalism.

Just for this above reason, the development degree of capital's negative sublation is determined by the conditions of the basic contradiction of capitalism. In the very early stages when the capitalist mode of production had emerged, at that time capitalist relations of production had contained an aspect which could not meet the requirements of productive forces, for this reason considered from the aspect of inevitability it could be possible that private capital could not be able to transform to social capital. But since both sides (ends) of the contradiction were adaptive in general at that time, there occurred a relatively smooth transformation of private capital to social capital. If I should give a further explanation, this transformation at that time could only be completed through external connections of each individual capital (i.e., through market connections and relations).

With the development and increase of productive forces and the sharpening of the basic contradiction of capitalism, the transformation from private capital to social capital becomes more difficult. It forces each individual capital to completely sublate its independent character and its independent existence on the surface and directly combine them from the internal, trying to finish the transformation of a part of private capital to social capital through the movement of its internal contradiction. This alleviates the basic contradiction of capitalism to some extent. However, share capital does not sublate the character of private capital fundamentally. Compared to original individual private capital, relatively share capital is social capital; if compared to the need of capital connection in a bigger scope, it is still private capital and needs further transformation from private capital to social capital. In this way, as driven by the basic contradiction of capitalism, capital's negative sublation re-occurs and re-occurs on a higher level based on a new foundation.

Briefly, capital's negative sublation plays an important role in the survival and development of capitalist mode of production in the form of easement of its inherent contradiction and effecting a partial solution in that contradiction. In fact, it is just this capital's negative sublation that makes economic relation of capitalism show greater flexibility and capacity for the development of productive forces and prevents the process of capital's active sublation to some extent. Meanwhile it makes itself become the main form of the evolution in capitalist mode of production.

2. Main Characteristics of Capital's Negative Sublation

As the main form of the evolution of capitalist mode of production, capital's negative sublation has the following regular characteristics:

Firstly, the process of capital's negative sublation is not only a capital transformation process from the private individual capital to the social capital form under the effect of the inherent contradictions of capital, but it is also a process in which social capital evolves from a lower to higher level. In the historical process of the evolution of capital's negative sublation and capitalism, social character of capital in the beginning is mostly apparent in the circulation field. Because the socialization only occurs in those frequent but temporary relations and linkages between individual capital owners and is not yet solidly established, thus in this phase, the social character of capital—which it already possesses—cannot be fully displayed. However, after the emergence of share capital form, the social character—being strengthened—appears more obviously, and the social character—with its initial independent existence—but not yet so solid—becomes apparent. In such a gradual evolution and with mixed external reflections the socialization degree of capital moves forward or capital evolves to higher and more complex levels. Initially **private monopoly capital** is formed on the basis of concentration and grouping of share capital(s) and then transform to state monopoly capital ownership based on the combination of private monopoly capital(s) with the state power, so its social character and its independent self-development progress and gain a more solid existence, i.e. the socialization level of capital is further elevated.

Secondly, in the process of capital's negative sublation, capital does not simply negate or totally eliminate previous low-level forms of social capital, but allow them "re-appear" in higher-level forms, thus improving the overall functions of capital. For example, after the formation of private monopoly capital and state monopoly capital, share capital form has not disappeared; on the contrary, it has continued to exist. Share capital is not only the initial basis for the formation of private monopoly capital and state monopoly capital, but also a higher form with a stronger social character which has surpassed or abandoned a lower-level form in which its social character has rather appeared in the market relations (at the initial stage of capitalism). Share capital negates the subject characteristics of its individual capital components and replaces them with a new form of subject with a new character (this new subject manifests a character of combined share capital). In this way, share capital, in order to achieve more power through capital appreciation, still needs to complete or push the transformation from private capital (in the form of share capital) to social capital (formed by the capital linkages in a wider range) through the market connection. Another example for that reality is that after the state monopoly capital form emerges the private monopoly capital form still continues to exist and further expands and so does the share capital form and it even enjoys a faster development. Share capital is not only the basis on which private monopoly capital and the state monopoly capital are formed, but it is also that form which also becomes the most basic or most important and common capital organization form. With such a multi-linear and an overlapping (side-by-side) co-existence and each form showing more or less staggered growth patterns, capital organization forms contain different levels of socialization and different features of socialization. All those processes and facts I have discussed above not only provide the basis for capital's sublation (both the active and the negative) but also facilitate and enhance adaption capacities of the capital (on the whole) to the requirements of further socialization of the production in the capitalist society.

Thirdly, in the various forms which emerge in the process of capital's negative sublation, the group subject-bourgeoisie act completely according to private capital characteristics. Whether it is share capital or private monopoly capital or state monopoly capital, they are all forms to guarantee capitalists to obtain more surplus value rather than to meet the needs of the society. When discussing the transformation from individual capital to share capital, Marx has made the following comment: "This transformation itself to share capital is still confined within capitalism; therefore, this transformation does not overcome the opposition between wealth as the nature of social wealth and that as the nature of private wealth, but only develops this opposition in a new form."[1] The opposite characteristics of both socialization and privatization inherent in the capitalist mode of production have become

[1] *Karl Marx and Frederick Engels*, Chinese version, Edition 1, Vol.25, p. 497.

increasingly evident in contemporary capitalist economies. All of these arguments also illustrate the limits of capital's negative sublation.

III. Capital and Evolution of Capitalist Mode of Production

1. Capital's Negative Sublation

Capital's negative sublation and the according evolution in the capitalist mode of production have important historical significance. When exploring the reason of capital's negative sublation, we have already pointed out that capital's negative sublation is an important condition for the survival of the capital. When analyzing the relatively higher forms of capital's sublation, i.e. state monopoly capital, we can have a better understanding on the significance of capital's negative sublation and its effects on the capitalist mode of production.[1]

Since the World War II, capitalism had developed into the stage of state monopoly capitalism, which constituted a new stage in capital's negative sublation and in the evolution of capitalist mode of production. At this stage, based on private monopoly capital, state's intervention to the economy was further strengthened, and states had not only entered into the process of capital movement on behalf of the creditors and investors of money capital and also as suppliers and buyers of advanced technologies, commodities and labor, but also started to regulate the reproduction of the whole society through economic plans and a variety of macro-economic policies. These interventions have injected further characteristics and factors of socialization within the private monopoly capital. The reality that state monopoly capital maintains the rule of private capital and ensures it to obtain more surplus

[1] Marx has pointed out, "Human anatomy is a key to monkey anatomy. On the contrary, signs of higher animals shown in lower animals can only be understood after the higher animals themselves have been known." (*Karl Marx and Frederick Engels*, Chinese version, Edition 1, Vol. 46, p. 43, Beijing, People's Publishing House, 1979.)

value is manifold. Below, I will only comment on state investments and intervention as an example to illustrate the amazing development in capital's socialization and the role of this socialization in preserving private capital character.

With state intervention in the economy (formed by capital's negative sublation), governments had attained the control of increasingly bigger shares in the gross national product (GNP). For example in U.S.A, the share of GNP controlled by the Federal Government of the United States had increased from 1.8% in 1913 and 6.6% in 1938 to 14.7% in 1950 and 18.6% in 1991.[1] The share of GNP controlled by governments at all levels (including federal, state and local governments) had increased from 7.4% in 1903 to 19.2% and 23.1% in 1939 and 1949, and then had increased to 28.8% in 1961 and 31.8% in 1989.[2]

Most of these resources were mainly used in the following aspects as public investment: 1) Direct subsidies to "private companies", for example, the enterprises in aircraft manufacturing and satellite communications companies.[3] 2) Bearing part of the investment burden made by big enterprises through tax reductions and tax exemptions. 3) Provide basic economic infrastructure, for example, to provide finance to be used in research and development, special roads and port facilities, etc. 4) Lease production facilities, materials, process equipment to private enterprises with prices lower than the cost price. This is a common practice in the investments

---

[1]   *Historical Statistics of the United States*, p. 225, 1104. *Statistical Abstract of the United States*, p. 312 and p. 386 in 1972; p. 315, 428, in 1992.

[2]   The data of 1903-1961 is quoted from *Monopoly Capital* by Baran & Sweezy, p. 140, Beijing, the Commercial Press, 1977. The data of 1989 is quoted from *Re-evaluating Contemporary Capitalist Economy* by Huang Suan & Zhen Bingxi, P152, Beijing, World Affaris Press, 1996.

[3]   Many high-tech companies in Silicon Valley heavily depend on research and development expenditures for the state's national defense, which is legitimized as technological innovation. Whether it is the computer industry or the electronics industry, military orders are still the main source of funds. For example, in opening up new fields of computer study, 60% of the funds comes from the national security budget. Quoted from the journal article by Gray, Mia and Elyse Golob and Ann Markusen and Sam Ock Park. Article was titled as: "New Industrial Cities? The Four Faces of Silicon Valley" from the journal of *Review of Radical Political Economics*, 4, pp. 1-28, 1998.

for national defense in the United States and other countries. The above four items are usually termed as "company welfare" provided by the government to private enterprises to distinguish them from "individual welfare". 5) Re-training and educating the workforce to adapt to the constantly changing needs of capital is also an important part. Regarding this, left-wing scholar John McDermot from the United States had made the following comment: in Marx's era, investments in these projects were completed by the capitalists themselves. However, "today, these public investments (education, research and development, infrastructure, domestic security environment, etc.) are at least equal to or nearly exceed the investment amount of the total industry of the United States". John McDermot used statistical figures to further illustrate his conclusions: In 1997, after deducting the amount of inventory adjustments, the total private investment in the United States was 818.3 billion USD including direct public support amount by the state. In this figure the so-called "company welfare", i.e. the investment directly financed by the U.S. government was 133 billion USD (calculated on the average statistical figures of the three research institutions). Additionally, the education funds allocated by the public sector amounted to 564.2 billion USD, the federal government allocated 32.2 billion USD for the development of natural resources, training and employment services and 55.6 billion USD was allocated by the federal state and local governments for infrastructure, preserving natural resources and waste treatment. The sum of those four publicly financed items was 785 billion USD. And when compared with the private investment of 688.3 billion USD (818.3 billion-133 billion) against 100 percent private investment, the government expenditure was 119 percent. Therefore, "without the investment by public sectors, private investment could not develop such large productive forces, scale, technological level and "income" in the contemporary economy. For example, if the government did not regularly commit for the training the labor force, it would be impossible to imagine today's U.S. economy and it would only reduce to "underdeveloped economy"[1]. These historical facts further demonstrate that capital's negative

---

[1] Quoted from "A Number of Situations of Contemporary Capital Socialization by Zhou Tong", in *Foreign Theoretical Trends*, 2002 (2).

sublation and evolution of capitalist mode of production are one of the most effective means.

2. Capital's Self-negation and Self-affirmation Process

This formulation, "Each part is directly its opposite"[1], creatively expresses an important aspect of contradictions, that is, the identity character in contradictions which can be observed in the development process of things. Capital's negative sublation and the resulting evolution process in the capitalist mode of production follow the same logic. That means the self-affirmation process of capital is also a process of self-negation of capital. In this regard, specifically, the following aspects are apparent:

Firstly, the appreciation nature of capital has its limits. Pursuit of maximum surplus value is the concentrated expression of the nature of capital. Previous data indicate that with the strengthening of state intervention, governments hold increasingly larger economic resources in their hands and moreover, a part or most of these resources come from enterprise profits collected as taxes from them by the state. Although most of this state investment will eventually return to general reproduction process of capitalism, the above mechanism of state control after all restricts the maximum pursuit of surplus value. For example if a part of that government expenditure is allocated to transfer payments to poverty-stricken residents and other social public objectives, we can evaluate this act as a restraint for the nature of capital and thus as its partial negation. American left-wing scholar Bowles and others have commented on this issue: the traditional viewpoint held that if there is an advantage, let the government invest! The state intervention will not affect private enterprises' logic of pursuing profit. But since the 1960s, the requirements relating to occupational labor safety, consumer safety, environmental protection and energy issues (such as the prohibition of nuclear energy) have shaken the primary status of profit in determining resource allocation and economic decisions, and thus government intervention and expenditure are conceived as "challenge to

---

[1] *Karl Marx and Frederick Engels*, Chinese version, Edition 1, Vol. 46 I, p. 28.

profit logic".[1]

Secondly, the capital's movement has a limited scope. Capital always needs to realize its economic goals in a certain (confined) space. The process in which it constantly strengthens its dominant position and scope of operation is also a process in which it strives to overcome geographic and national borders. Throughout its expansion process it should also face the challenges posed by former modes of production as well as a variety of non-capitalist ideologies, cultural and psychological obstacles. History has manifested that capital has a very strong penetration and expansion capacity, which proves its vitality. However, even in the rising stage of capitalism, Marx had already explained that its activities meet several restrictions, and such restrictions result neither from the natural conditions nor from social conditions besides the capital, but they are inherent in capital itself. The expansion or contraction of capitalist production is determined by the relation between capital and profit instead of relation between production and demand. "Therefore, when the other premise of the expansion degree of production is far less than enough, it means the restrictions on capitalist production have emerged."[2]

With the emergence of capital's negative sublation and state monopoly capital, the restrictions on capital's movement have new expressions, which are manifested such that private capital withdraws from some industries. For example, the improvement of social productive forces requires the construction of some infrastructure facilities or they should be strengthened and modernized, or the fruits of the new science and technology research require vigorous application to the newly emerging industrial departments and this is too high investment with low returns in the short term. Although they are absolutely necessary for the further development of social productive forces and could serve the social demand, due to high investment amounts, longer product development period, high risk, low or uncertain profit rate

---

[1] Bowles, S. and D.M.Gordon and Thomas E. Weisskopf. *After the Waste Land: A Democratic Economics for the Year 2000* [M], pp. 72-73, M. E. Sharpe. Inc, 1990.

[2] *Karl Marx and Frederick Engels*, Chinese version, Edition 1, Vol. 25, p. 288.

and other reasons, private capital abstains from investment or is unwilling to invest, so they can only be operated by state-owned capital. Although the state initiative observed in such situations does not mean the absolute reduction of the operation scope of private capital, but it shows obviously that requirements necessary for highly developed socialized production can restrain private capital's production and operation activities in some departments of the economy. It is obviously a kind of restriction on the activity scope of private capital.

Thirdly, the capital's activity mode meets restraints. Capital's supreme goal, as pursuit for maximum surplus value, is realized and expressed outward through free competition. Only through free competition, can capital impose this internal law of capital on the opposite party and itself. In the process of external competition the thing contained in the nature of capital "is realistically exposed as the external inevitability". Therefore, Marx had pointed out: "Free competition is the most appropriate form of the capitalist production process. The more free competition develops, the purer the form of capital movements is expressed"[1]. However, with the emergence of private monopoly capital, especially the strengthening of state's intervention in the economy, free competition is constrained to some extent, and it increasingly gives way to monopolistic competition under the conditions of state intervention.[2] This monopolistic competition is based on monopolistic position obtained by a small number of large monopolies in some sectors of the economy.

Within this monopolistic sector, although the policies of reducing costs are still applied, more often we can see monopolistic control mechanisms and cartel agreements such as control of production amounts, price arrangements, and inputs of key products, etc. Company mergers are the main policy used to solidify their monopoly position and competitive powers, so they increase

---

[1] *Karl Marx and Frederick Engels*, Chinese version, Edition 1, Vol. 46 II, p. 160, Beijing, People's Publishing House, 1980.

[2] Regarding the study on monopolistic competition in modern capitalist countries, see *The Monopolistic Competition in Developed Capitalist Economy* by Gao Feng, Chapter VII, Tianjin, Nankai University Press, 1996.

their control and fight against small and medium-sized enterprises and compete for bigger market shares and also fight against the influence of other large enterprises.

In recent years, due to global expansion of capitalist economic relations, the operation space of capital has expanded and the competition between capital groups has further intensified. Accordingly, some neo-liberal scholars believe that this process "will just bring about the end of capitalist monopoly era" and competitive market economy is revitalized again.[1]

It should be considered that new information means indeed have reduced entry obstacles to some industries and provided new survival possibilities for small and medium-sized enterprises. However, this does not mean that the trend of production concentration and monopoly has fundamentally been reversed. When we recall the worldwide enterprise merger and acquisition tide in the 1990s, only the typical new economy sector itself proves that the above optimistic view lacks appropriate basis.

In 1998, American scholar Mia Gray and others conducted an investigation on Silicon Valley titled as "model of the new economy" and demonstrated that Silicon Valley is far more complicated than the general public view. Silicon Valley is actually consisting of "four faces" including the flexible small enterprises. It is composed of defense industry, large enterprises, foreign companies and other large institutions which are often ignored. "The success and culture of Silicon Valley are the result of the existence and success of these large institutions to a large extent"; "among the enterprises in Silicon Valley, there is a quite serious imbalance of power"; "many large enterprises in Silicon Valley are market leaders, dominating their subordinated territory or the entire sector"[2]. So we say that "new economy" does not eliminate the monopoly, it merely makes monopoly being expressed in the form of network economy with large enterprises as the core. It can be anticipated that under the situation of increasing economic globalization, the

[1] Acs, Zoltan J. and Bo Carlsson and Roy Thurik. *Small Business in the Modern Economy*. Blackwell Publishers Inc., 1996.

[2] Gray, Mia and Elyse Golob and Ann Markusen and Sam Ock Park. "New Industrial Cities? The Four Faces of Silicon Valley" in *Review of Radical Political Economics*, 30 (4): pp. 1- 28, 1998.

network economy of this character will be extended to worldwide scale, and various international economic organizations will gradually replace national state's regulatory functions and they will undertake those functions.

In short, transformation from free competition to monopolistic competition has strengthened the dominance of monopoly capital, though at the expense of the freedom of small and medium-sized capital and limiting them a relatively smaller operation space. The growing strengthening of state intervention in the economy means that private capital(s) even now cannot have complete freedom to act according to their own will, and restricts their activities pursuing for surplus to an extent under the national legislation and economic intervention. Its economic significance is, as foreseen by Marx: "When capital begins to feel and realize itself becomes the restrictions of its development, it seeks refuge in some of these forms. Although these forms seem to make the dominance of capital absolute, since it meanwhile restrains free competition, this forecasts the dissolution of capital and disintegration of that production mode based on capital."[1]

3. Capital's Negative Sublation and New Social Factors

As a result of capital's negative sublation, we can observe generation of several factors possessing obvious characteristics with a new type of sociality. These factors are neither result of capital's active sublation (such as cooperatives), nor show complete characteristics of the new social economic system; they are several economic components, factors or immature forms— to an extent—with socialist characteristics. In direct sense, these factors are formed in the self-affirmation process of capital, some are even means used by capital to obtain more surplus value and maintain its own dominance, but these factors are the carriers of the socialist economic factors and can be regarded as symbols indicating that socialism can replace capitalism, and indicate that capitalism contains an irresistible trend for the evolution toward socialism.

Marx had commented on this issue: "New productive forces and

---

[1] *Karl Marx and Frederick Engels*, Chinese version, Edition 1, Vol. 46, p. 160.

production relations develop neither from nothing, nor emptiness, nor from the maternal-fetal of that concept which produces from itself, but are developed from within the existing production development process and internal traditional ownership handed down in the opposition to them."[1] Marx's arguments inspire a convenient methodology for us to study the generation of the factors of new society.

First of all, corporate shareholders (institutions) have become the main holders of corporate shares. Such joint stock companies have become the main controllers of the capitalist economy. Since the birth of joint stock companies, shareholders as the attributors of corporation were mainly individuals or families and the company's shares were mainly held in the hands of these individuals and families. Individuals or families had controlled share capital, and then they had later controlled monopoly capital formed by share capital. However, after World War II, the identity of big company shareholders began to change, various institutions and corporations (such as industrial and commercial enterprises, all kinds of banks, life insurance companies, pension funds, mutual funds, etc.) gradually replaced individuals or families to become company's principal shareholders, and individuals and families were put on the back burner. Corporation capital(s) have assumed dominant position in share capital, and its causes are manifold. Regarding this issue, Chapter III of this book will offer further aspects.

Here what we need to underline is the change in economic relations reflected by corporate stockholding system after 1960s.

Looking from the form aspect, we see the following: after the emergence of corporation capital, first there remains a control chain held by individuals controlling corporation capital (they control corporation capital through controlling the share capital), as the second part of the chain corporation capital controls share capital and then monopoly capital. Thus it can be concluded that the nature of economic relations in contemporary capitalism has not changed. But, if the first link of this chain is analyzed carefully, we can find some important differences. Individuals controlling corporation

---

[1] *Karl Marx and Frederick Engels*, Chinese version, Edition 1, Vol. 46, p. 235.

capital (or controlling corporation capital through controlling share capital) is the first link in the chain as the owners are all individuals, but their action purposes are very different: A part of them are investors, they invest in all types of industrial and commercial businesses and financial institutions to make profits, and they are the real controllers of share capital and corporation capital; the other part of the individuals are the are holders of various pension funds, and their purposes are to transfer a part of their immediate incomes to future incomes through savings and stably obtain pensions, thus forming a pension fund. This part as pension fund investments gradually breaks away from their holders and generates an interesting new phenomenon. Because on the surface, pension fund is a vertical movement among several generations, that is, workers when they have the ability to work and produce incomes they save and transfer their income to future income for those days they will lose laboring abilities; but in fact, their such act also produces a horizontal movement among workers, i.e. in the practical operation process, pension fund transfers only a part of the income of workers to the hands of workers who lose their labor ability. Regarding this reality, even U.S. *Business Week* had made a comment: "social insurance is basically a kind of contract between different generations. Through such a contract, in reality today's workers provide funds for the pension fund of yesterday's workers."[1] In this way, the difference between fund deposits gathered in the start-up phase of pension fund (at that moment, there were only deposits and workers were not paid annuities) and daily deposits and payment of annuities can be regarded as the genuine corporate funds which can be controlled by pension fund companies. Investing such funds into joint stock companies will certainly have a significant impact on corporate behavior.

Now, what we are concerned about is the nature of this kind of funds, they obviously do not have the characteristics of private capital. "In fact, today all the savings of modern society (refers to the developed capitalist society), including the 'public' savings and 'private' savings, have fallen into the control and disposal of the very few companies and individuals,

---

[1] Quoted from Mark Linde: *Anti-Samuelson I,* p. 150, Shanghai, Joint Publishing Company, 1992.

and considering the significance of the 19th century, these companies and individuals cannot be considered as the owners of these savings. If this is true, 'society' has the right to issue dominant voice for the decision and use of these investments, which is totally legitimate."[1]

Secondly, some workers have become the owners of the company's stocks. This is caused by capitalist governments' promoting employee stock ownership plans (ESOP). The purpose of implementing this plan by those capitalist enterprises is to ease the opposition between labor and capital, mobilize the initiative of the staff and maintain the rule of capital. However, objectively, it makes employees own holding shares as a part of property ownership of enterprises, thus making workers and the means of production reach a unity to a certain degree. In relevant parts of Chapter V of this book, the experiences and facts and related issues of stock ownership by employees in modern capitalist countries will be further introduced and analyzed. What we need to underline here is the significance of employee stock ownership. Compared with the public ownership, employee stock ownership is the stock holding by a "company insider". Besides the function to raise funds, these shares may guide and ensure employees to participate in management in order to improve enterprise performance and enhance the competitiveness of enterprises, which is beneficial to the capital. Therefore, employee stock ownership is a marginal adjustment of capitalist enterprise system or economic relations which have emerged under the effect of basic contradiction of capitalism, and it does not change the nature of enterprises which practice employee stock ownership system. But when we evaluate such an adjustment from another aspect, it is obvious that it has broken the capitalist production basis in which the basic condition is separation of wage labor and means of production. Thus it is a gradual system change with an important historical significance.

Thirdly, a part of the workers can participate in the enterprise management in different degrees. The different relations between men

---

[1] Quoted from Tong Zhou: "A Number of Situations of Contemporary Capital Socialization", in *Foreign Theoretical Trends*, 2002 (2).

and the means of production determine the different status of men in social labor organizations, which is an important basis for Marxism to divide classes. For a long time, bourgeoisie has monopolized the management of the enterprises by ownership of means of production that they have held. However, under the pressure of the requirements for production socialization and pressure from workers, capitalists have gradually transferred management and administrative rights to their agents, later they have allowed also workers to participate in management to a certain extent. For example, the legislation of the former Federal Republic of Germany in 1951 had regulated that in the iron and steel industry, worker's council should be elected by workers and it had the right to elect five members for the board of supervisors of the company. Board of supervisors consists of 11 members, and the other 5 members are elected by shareholders meeting, then the representatives of workers and representatives of shareholders jointly decide the eleventh member. Finally, board of supervisors elects board of directors. Board of directors should include one member elected by the representatives of workers. The legislation in 1952 had reduced the seats of workers' representatives in the board of supervisors to 1/3. In 1976, the seats of employees in board of supervisors in a big company with more than 2,000 employees were re-adjusted to 50%.[1] On the basis of company staff stock ownership, the management system in which the staff participates in management was further developed and has played a significant role in the improvement of enterprise performances. The National Center for Employee Ownership has conducted an investigation including 45 companies that implemented ESOP projects and 225 companies that did not implement that project. That investigation revealed that the profit growth rate of those companies that implemented staff stock ownership plans and allowed staff to participate in decision-making was 8 to 11% higher than those companies that did not implement such plans.[2] Although staff participation in the

---

[1] Ding Weimin: *Analysis of the Western Cooperative System*, p. 122, Beijing, Economy & Management Publishing House, 1998.

[2] Cheng Xue: "Advantages and Disadvantages of Western Employee Stock Ownership System", in *Foreign Economic and Management*, 1997 (1).

management of capitalist enterprises cannot fundamentally negate the control right of capital, especially that of big capital, and cannot realize genuine economic democracy[1], it finally has opened up a loophole for the traditional system of the monopolized management rights of capital, and meanwhile this can improve the management abilities of workers, last but not the least it demonstrates the importance of democratic management by workers' participation in socialized production conditions.

Fourthly, the big companies have become subjects of social plans to some extent. The complicated social division of labor formed by socialized production demands higher social cooperation. But under the condition of capitalist private ownership, such collaboration cannot be realized through direct social plans. In contemporary capitalism, in fact, part of the internal plan of a company has become a rough substitute for the necessitated social plan. Engels had commented on this issue: "The capitalist production operated by a joint stock company is no longer private production, but is production that makes profits for many people combined together. If we consider joint stock companies and then trusts which dominate and monopolize the entire industrial department, over there not only private production, is stopped but also non-planning disappears."[2] This observation can be proved with a great deal of experiences and facts. For example, in the United States, from the aspect of hiring people, besides the federal government, large companies are the largest units that hire people. The 500 top industrial companies employ nearly a staff of 15 million workers, accounting for 3/4 of the employment numbers of all industry companies. Strictly speaking, just as the internal division of labor in an enterprise

---

[1] American Sociologist Marsh made an investigation on enterprise management system of 48 large and medium-sized manufacturing enterprises in Japan in 1983 and proved that "contrary to belief of many western observers, Japan's participation in decision-making system has not led to the democratization of the factory. Although the companies allow workers to make suggestions and recommendations...but they refuse workers as a decision-making authority." See Marsh, R.M. "The Difference between Participation and Power in Japanese Factories," in *Industrial and Labor Relations*, 1992, January.

[2] *Karl Marx and Frederick Engels*，Chinese version, Edition 1, Vol. 22, p. 270, Beijing, People's Publishing House, 1965.

is different from the division of labor in society, the internal plan of an enterprise is different from general social plans. However, the internal plan of the large contemporary capitalist company also differs from the traditional enterprise plan. The main difference lies in that the sizes of modern large companies are immense, their output values usually exceed a number of medium-sized countries, and they are composed of numerous affiliated daughter companies. Being relatively independent production units, they practice their own daily business activities independently, therefore, the plans implemented by the headquarter of a corporation based on financial supervision and control have almost characteristics of social planning (i.e., economic activities of each economic unit are adjusted by a social center), and the headquarters not simply supervise and adjust or control each production or service unit. Therefore, in a certain sense, the pattern of macro-economic management in contemporary capitalism is primarily designed by large companies, while on the other hand "the government only supplements their management by making the ultimate decisions"[1].

To sum up the above ideas, we can conclude that capitalist negative sublation process generated by inherent contradictions of capital is both a self-affirmation process and a self-negation process of capital and generation process of new social factors as well. This process prominently expresses the historicity of capitalist mode of production. According to the realities in the capitalist mode of production, it can be expected that both capital's negative sublation and active sublation caused by this basic contradiction will continue their effects. But it can be attested that in capital's negative sublation process, the room for self-affirmation of capital will become smaller and smaller, while on the other side the characteristics as self-negation will become bigger and bigger, so the new social factors will be further generated in this process. At the same time, capital's active sublation, i.e., the opportunities for working class and all laborers to radically change the historical direction will not diminish. On the contrary, this trend will be much stronger enabling a qualitative leap to transcend capitalist mode of production.

[1] H. Braverman: *Labor and Monopoly Capital*, p. 238.

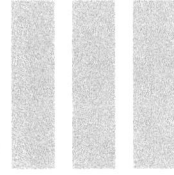

Chapter III

The Technical Progress Under the Capitalist System

Capitalism, so far, on the whole, still holds the leading position in technological development. The new technological revolution is changing the traditional capitalist mode of production and has become the main driving force of the growth in the contemporary economy. The facts show that this trend is primarily apparent in the developed capitalist nations and is promoted by the capitalist corporations. So, the question on how to understand capitalist economic relationship and the relation between technological progress and development of productive forces should be accurately answered. This is an important question to evaluate the historical position of capitalism. This chapter will mainly study the effects of the economic relations of capitalism on the technological progress and development of productive forces. I will analyze that question in the historical process of capitalist development.

I. Technology, Productive Forces and Capital

1. Technological Progress and Productive Forces

Currently, science and technology are rapidly developing, and today the idea put forward by Deng Xiaoping in the 1980s as "Science and technology have become the primary productive force" is widely accepted as true. Among economics scholars, technological progress is considered as an important element of the development of productive forces. In recent several decades, high-tech industry has been developing strongly. Especially since the 1990s, the fusion between information technology and capital has created the "new economy" in the United States. Due to its advantages especially developed capitalist countries pay more attention to technological innovation. It can be observed that a new round of technological progress tide is emerging, which is called as "the latest technological revolution", "knowledge economy", and "information economy", etc.

The tide of new technological progress has spread a profound effect and enterprises and governments are all stressing technical progress and have been increasing their investments in research and development (R & D) and technological innovation.

However, what is technological progress? How does it relate to productive forces? This is the issue that we should study first. In contemporary economics, "technical progress" is also called "technical change". It generally refers to technical factors that can improve production efficiency, and more specifically includes the two aspects as the use of science and technological knowledge and the changes in the production organization. Evaluated from a historical perspective, technological progress has upgraded the economic structures to higher levels or effected a big structural change from agricultural-oriented economy to industrial-oriented economy. For example, the New Palgrave Dictionary of Economics defines it as follows: technical change denotes the "transformation in the economic society from an agricultural basis to an industrial basis which began in about 1750s. Its own internal logic is that huge strength of technical change has initiated the process of economic change. This kind of logic expresses to utilize constant technical and organizational progress in order to pursue higher profits. Therefore it is constantly increasing the total output of unit labor force (which is the main source of improving the living standards), the progressive mechanization and automation of production methods and constant development of the economic structure."[1]

According to Marx, productive forces refer to the abilities that people apply the material goods to produce the products that can meet their needs in the production process. The definition in Chinese economics dictionary is that productive force is "the relation between people and those natural objects and natural forces that people use to produce material goods, i.e. those relations between men and nature in the production process. It shows men's ability—men the people in a society—to control and conquer nature.[2] In *Capital*, Marx pointed out, "Of course, productive force is always productive force of useful and specific labor. In fact, it only determines the efficiency of purposeful production activities within a certain period."[3] Therefore, the changes in productive forces can be used to measure production efficiency. And contemporary economics generally use the indicators such as "labor productive forces" and "total factor productive forces" to define that concept. Regarding indicators of the measurement, although there are different views and controversies in the theoretical circles, these two indicators have been commonly used in the international academy. As to the relation between the technological progress and productive forces, there is no doubt that the former effects and determines the latter one, and the latter reflects the extent of the former. In other words, technological progress is a means to increase productive forces, and changes in the productive forces are a sign reflecting technological progress. Specifically speaking, the technological progress

[1] John Eatwell, Murray Milgate and Peter Newman, *The New Palgrave: A Dictionary of Economics*, Vol. 4, p. 617.

[2] *Dictionary of Political Economy*, edited by Xu Dixin, Edition 1, p. 78, Beijing, People's publishing House, 1980.

[3] Marx: *Capital*, Edition 1, Vol. 1, p. 59, Beijing, People's Publishing House, 1975.

enhances the ability of men to control the realm of things, thus improving production efficiency, so measuring productivity level by production efficiency can express the degree of technological progress.

Technological progress can promote the improvement of productive forces, so can we conclude that all the science and technology applied in the production can improve production efficiency? Is the more advanced technology necessarily better for enterprises? In fact, this is not always the case, let alone some technology can bring about side effects. Besides, different new technologies have different influences on productive forces. Although science and technology can bring about high profits, they don't always (necessarily) promote productive forces. Under the economic condition of contemporary capitalism, the trend of technological innovation shows such controversial characteristics.

It is noteworthy that in capitalist economic conditions, whether to adopt new technology and what kind of new technology will be used do not depend on whether they can promote the development of productive forces, but only whether it can bring about more profits. From the perceptive of cost and revenue, it seems more profits mainly rise due to technological improvement, i.e. "production efficiency".

However, the ratio of costs and benefits does not always fully reflect the input - output ratio of specific products, i.e., the production ability of material goods only reflects a kind of "money-making ability". In other words, the "production efficiency" measured by such value indicators often cannot fully reflect the real productivity rate in the true sense. Because production efficiency is an indicator which shows changes in use values. The limitations of this measure often lead to a mistake and some people evaluate the effect of new technologies for improving the profit rate as a direct and a positive effect for the development of productive forces. I think this is scientifically not true. In fact, even when a higher profit is obtained by means of technological progress and by improving production efficiency, this kind of improvement in production efficiency is also restricted. Marx had once pointed out, "As for capital, the law of improvement of labor productivity is not applicable without conditions. As for capital, it is not applicable when living labor is generally saved, but only when the payment part saved by living labor exceeds the additional part of the past labor, this condition can improve productivity."[1]

In other words, under the condition of capitalism, the improvement of productive forces—productivity—can not only be expressed when saving from living labor occurs, so "savings on necessary labor and creating surplus labor are the characteristic of it."[2] Therefore, I can say that there exists a relationship of both difference and connection between improving productive forces—productivity—and improving profit rate. Confusing the improvement of productive forces and that of profit rate is just an expression of the narrow vision of the bourgeoisie. Section III of this chapter will discuss this in detail.

In the industrialization process, the application of new technologies has a primary influence on the production process. Therefore, the application of new technologies and improvement of production efficiency and profit rate have some internal relations. And production efficiency calculated on the basis of value can reflect changes, improvement and development, of productive forces only to some extent. However, in today's post-industrial economy, we generally observe that new technologies are hardly used for the improvement of production process, but instead for the product innovation. Thus high profits gained by product innovations are grasped mainly from new markets, and often have nothing to do with the improvement of productive forces.

2. Two Types of Technological Innovation and the Development of Productive Forces

In order to correctly illustrate the different effects by different technologies on the development of productive forces, we must distinguish between two different types of technological innovations, i.e. the production process innovation and product innovation.

---

[1] Marx: *Capital*, Edition 1, Vol. 3, p. 292, Beijing, People's Publishing House, 1975.

[2] *Karl Marx and Frederick Engels*, Chinese version, Edition 1, Vol. 46, p. 365.

No matter what new technologies are applied in production, they are all based on the premise of technological research and innovation. According to the definition of Schumpeter, technological innovation refers to the first use of new products, new processes, new methods or new systems in economic activities. Thus he makes differentiation between the scientific research in laboratories—scientific invention and discovery process—and the condition that technological innovation is incorporated into real economy and results of new invention conducted for the creation and improvement of products, production process and business systems. Certainly the second aspect is true.

Generally speaking, except the innovation of new products, **innovation of production process** includes new processes, new methods and even innovation of systems. **Innovation of production process** answers the question "how to better produce". And I think innovation or creation of new products only gives an answer to "what to be produced". Therefore, we should make a differentiation between two forms of the so-called technological innovation as innovation of production process and innovation of products.

(1) Innovation in the production process

Specifically, innovation of production process comprises of: the innovation of production tools, production methods, production materials and organization mode in the production process. It can be said that only innovation of production process can directly promote the improvement of productive forces, and thus it is the source of the development of productivity. Due to technological innovation, "production process receives the application of science, and science in turn becomes a factor in the production process, i.e. the so-called functions"[1]. On the one hand, this innovation greatly enhances the ability that men can control things in the production process, thereby improving production efficiency and enhancing production capacity. On the other hand, it is important to underline that science and technology become

---

[1] *Karl Marx and Frederick Engels*, Chinese version, Edition 1, Vol. 47, p. 570, Beijing, People's Publishing House, 1959.

the basic elements of productive forces after being incorporated into the production process, thus transforming the previous mode of production. As explained by Marx, "Capital does not create science, but it uses and possesses science for the need of production process."[1]

As the source of the development in productive forces, the innovation of production process manifests itself as the improvement of productivity through the changes in production process and in production organization. Changes in production process are the direct application of new technologies and new inventions in the production process. Improvement in production organization promotes the efficiency through changes in the pattern of production organization. Both changes in production process and improvement in production organization directly transform the results of scientific invention into productive forces.

Changes in the production process include changes in production tools, production materials and skills of producers or production methods. Among those three, changes in production tools are the most prominent. Marx had believed that the development of production tools reflected to what extent general scientific knowledge can be directly transformed to productive forces under certain social conditions, so it can be used to measure the development degree of productive forces. Therefore, Marx said: "The difference between various economic ages lies in how to produce and what means of labor is used to produce instead of what to be produced."[2]

The human production activity progressing from using primitive and simple tools to complicated machinery marks the different economic era in the development of productive forces. Especially the development of power (animals, wind-mill, steam, electricity, etc.) used in the production is the pilot and basis of changes in the production tools. The primitive production tools such as simple hoe, sickle, hammer, etc. were basically used relying on manpower; later, there were animal-driven tools such as plow, grind stone and vehicles used for transportation. The use of natural power makes human

[1] *Karl Marx and Frederick Engels*, Chinese version, Edition 1, Vol. 47, p. 570.
[2] Marx: *Capital*, Edition 1, Vol. 1, p. 204.

beings begin to create more complicated tools such as windmill, water mill, raft and boat, etc. Such tools have not only pushed productive forces far beyond the limitations of human physical force, but also expanded the space of human economic activities, thus contributing to the development of industrial and commercial activities. With the progress of scientific research, the power of production tools used by human beings has recorded constant revolutionary progress. The use of hydropower and steam power in the 18th century through the invention of steam engines, railways, trains and steam-ships had led to the first industrial revolution, i.e. large-scale industrial production.

As commented by Marx: "large-scale industries incorporate huge natural force and natural science into the production process, which is bound to greatly improve labor productive forces." The discovery of thermal power and electric power in the 19th century had pushed the machine industry to enter into the production pattern of internal combustion engine, electric motor and semi-automation and had further enhanced the rapid improvement of production efficiency. The information technology and the invention of integrated circuits in the 20th century have pushed the production into the digital and smart era. Complete automated production has enabled massive production quantities to be completed in a very short time.

Another prominent manifestation of innovation of production process is the changes in production organization forms such as changes from workshops of handicraft industry to factories of mechanized industry and then to production organization forms as work sites. Due to division of labor and the advancement of co-operative labor, changes in the form of production organization can often enable production factors gaining more efficiency, so it can improve overall production efficiency.

Adam Smith had also studied the relationship between the forms of production organization and production efficiency in his book *The Wealth of Nations*. He had given an extreme example of a pin factory which is still popular today: The factory changes the pin making method from independent manufacture work of every pin by each worker to labor division and cooperation that each worker only finishes one of manufacture processes, and this change had resulted in thousands of times improvement in production efficiency. From the historical evolution of production organization, we can see that the development of manufacturing industry from artisan-dominated workshops to factories that many laborers work together and then to large scale factories; from independent operation (whether by hand or machine) to the use of production lines and then to organization form of flexible multinational work-division and production. This evolution in every step had all meant huge improvements in production efficiency. The key reason for the huge effect of production efficiency brought by changes or evolution in production organization form lies in that production process not only involves the relationship between men and nature, but also includes the relationship between men and men. Whether people can effectively operate in production is bound to greatly affect the quantity and even quality of production.

As Marx said that "the development of human labor capacity is displayed in particular in the development of means of labor or the instrument of production and are called instruments of labor which are the most important things among means of labor—a standard of the degree of development to which human labor has attained."[1]

Changes in production organization are usually consistent with the changes in production process. The mode of production organization that applies simple hand tools as the means of production is impossible to imagine in the organization mode of large-scale factories, under the condition of using mechanized industry. Socialized production is adaptive to the production process of mechanized industry. "Skills of using labor tools are transformed to machines together with labor tools. Thus, the efficiency of tools is liberated from physical limitations of human labor. As a result, the technical basis of division of work-shop type handicraft manufacture had disappeared.[2] Therefore, the factory system that replaces handicraft work-shop is established on the basis of machined production. As pointed out by

---

[1] Marx (1954).

[2] Marx: *Capital*, Chinese version, Edition 1, Vol. 1, p. 460.

Marx: "The handicraft industry has produced machines, and large industry has excluded handicraft production and workshop handicraft production in the production field which was first occupied with simpler machines. Therefore, machine production has naturally emerged on the material basis that could not fit it. When machine production is developed to a certain extent, it will surely overthrow the basis that was readily encountered at first, and then has been further developed in its old form, and later set up a new basis corresponding to its own mode of production."[1]

In short, the change or evolution in production tools and in production organization forms is the basic form of innovations in production process. The changes in these two forms determine improvements in production efficiency. If an enterprise or a department, or even a country conducts such innovation earlier than others, it can master more advanced productive forces, and the unit production factors put into production process can be increased, so it will obtain an advantageous position in competition.

(2) Product innovation

Product innovation is to produce different products, including the development of new products and improvement or upgrading of the old products. Product innovation involves innovation in product quality, performance, designs and varieties, etc.

Viewing from the social consumption structure, we cannot say that "the difference between various economic eras has nothing to do with what should be produced", but also has great connections with what should be produced. In the historical process of economic development, each era has different new products which reflect the characteristics of the times. The original traditional products of each era also see improvements or upgrading.

From the aspect of supply, product innovations are always connected with certain productive capacities. For example, in the steam era, except the emergence of trains and ships, the most prominent product was a variety of textiles woven by machines replacing textile products woven by hand.

---

[1] Marx: *Capital*, Chinese version, Edition 1, Vol. 1, p. 419.

The new products in the electric power and thermal power eras include automobiles, radios, TV, etc. The wider use of those new products has not only greatly changed people's ways of life, but also made many traditional products become historical relics, such as coaches and primitive implements. Today, we live in the information age, there are more new products that are produced, and almost every product seeks change and innovation, therefore various new products are endless.

Different from innovation in production process, product innovation, especially the innovation of final products only solves the question of "what should be produced" and does not solve the issue of "how to produce"; therefore, it does not include a direct relation with the changes in productive forces. The production of new products does not necessarily need a change in their traditional production process. For example, when producing a kind of novel clothes, although there are a lot of design changes, there may be basically no change of production method and production tools. Of course, the production of new products often requires several corresponding/ appropriate changes in production processes. But if this change in the production process is made only to adapt to the production of new products instead of improving usage efficiency of production factors or production efficiency, then we can say the latter has nothing to do with productive forces. With the increase of product demand, if the production process is reformed in order to increase the output of production factors, then it will have an influence in the productive forces. For example, in the early stage of automobile production, there was no particular method of production, and the production efficiency was not high. Of course, later, automobiles changed from luxury goods of a small number of VIPs to a necessity of mass consumption. The standard production lines designed for mass production of automobiles and the corresponding forms in production organization (the Ford style, the Toyota style) have greatly improved production efficiency. Therefore, production of new products can only enhance the development of productive forces in the case that the new product is produced by the innovation in the production process.

On the other hand, when the innovative products are the intermediate products—as materials or production tools used to produce some other products—in the production process, the influence of those innovative products on productive forces occurs not indirectly, but directly. For example, as a commodity for individual or family consumption, a computer is the final product, and it has no direct influence on production process, so it has no direct influence on productive forces. But as a product consumed by an enterprise, the introduction of computers can improve production process, and thus has direct influence on productive forces. Because new products in the production process determine the changes in the way of production, production methods or production systems, which are all the basic elements in the development of productive forces.

And innovation in products can change personal consumption habit, quality of life and meet new needs, but doesn't have direct relation with the production process. Of course, if the consumption of new products can change the quality of workforce as consumers, that is to say it can support higher quality laboring, we can say that it has indirectly promoted the productive ability (force) of the laborer and thus promoted the productive forces. However, this is only a possibility, which can only play the role of promoting productive forces only after entering into the production process.

3. Technological Innovation and Capital

As to capital, the significance of technological innovation does not depend on promoting the development of productive forces, but on the increase of profit margins. In other words, the nature of capital is bound to pursue maximum profit, but not to care about the level of productive forces. Therefore, no matter what kind of technological innovation it is, as long as it can yield more profit, capital investment is correct and improves the economic efficiency.

Different kinds of innovation made by enterprises cause different methods of obtaining profit. In the case of appropriate market conditions, product innovation and product innovation in production process can make enterprises obtain higher profits. The former one increases profit by increasing sales; the latter one increases profit by reducing costs. Therefore, two kinds or modes of technological innovation bring two different economic effects: productivity effect and market effect.

Production efficiency effect can increase profits by increasing productive forces. And as to Marx, in the capitalist mode of production, "any improvements in labor productivity... are all the improvement in the productivity of capital", or "Only can this improvement be shown as the productivity of capital, it is the productivity of labor"[1]. As for capital, "machines are the means of producing surplus value"[2]. "If labor productivity isn't increased, the value of labor cannot be reduced, thus the surplus value cannot be increased."[3] Because within a certain work time range, "changes in the surplus value are based on the premise of the change in the value of labor caused by the changes in labor productivity."

A capitalist enterprise introduces advanced technology into production process through innovation of production process, and finally can achieve the effect which increases relative surplus value. It means that innovation in production process can yield more profits. According to Marx's theory of relative surplus value, we know that such an effect can arise only on the premise that innovation in the production process can reduce the value of labor. Moreover, in competition with other enterprises, individual enterprises improve production efficiency by innovations in production process, and that also means to obtain excess profits because other enterprises haven't grasped the same technology. In this case by improving production efficiency the products are sold with the old market price although the costs are reduced, that is to say that the products are sold at a higher price than their own value (or production prices), and the difference is the excess profits obtained by the enterprise.

[1] *Karl Marx and Frederick Engels*, Chinese version, Edition 1, Vol. 46, p. 306.

[2] Marx, *Capital*, Edition 1, Vol. 1, p. 408.

[3] Marx, *Capital*, Edition 1, Vol. 1, p. 569.

Market effect:

However, whether innovation of production process can yield more profits also depends on whether the products have appropriate market and whether it can reduce the value of labor. If the products have no market, no matter what advanced technologies or high production efficiency methods are employed, they cannot bring profits, so they cannot have any economic effect. In this case, the product innovation can solve the problem.

As to capital, the advantage of product innovation is that it can bring about the market effect. The market effect of product innovation is its role to open a new market offering new unique advantages provided by new products. Different from the innovation of production process, product innovation does not depend on reduction of prices in order to compete with other enterprises, but opening a new market by relying on new satisfaction provided by the product. The market effects of innovative products lie in that they can cause rapid increase for new demand. In the case that other enterprises cannot produce new products, the emergence of a new market will lead to the situation that demand exceeds supply. The market with demand exceeding supply means that a product can be sold at a price higher than its value, thus enterprises can obtain excess profits.

The reason why product innovation can play a role for opening a new market lies in that it can adapt to the new demand structure or changes in the old demand structure. The changes of market demand are not only influenced by the product prices, but also have connections with people's preferences or tastes. The significance of product innovation does not lie in reducing costs, but in meeting different demands. Therefore, product innovation does not mean a struggle between men and nature, but it means that human beings pursue for higher consumption needs. When the production capacity of social material wealth exceeds the level which meets the necessary needs of majority, and if production can meet the new demand choices of the people, it will be possible to have a market, and capital investment will be profitable.

The characteristics of the market effect lie in that new satisfaction provided by simple products themselves will be enough to open the market, and it even can achieve such effect even although the production efficiency is not high. Many people think that high profits of enterprises which make product innovation come from the improvement of production efficiency. But, in fact, their new technologies have nothing to do with production efficiency. Even some enterprises which make product innovations do not need to consider the question of how to produce, but see the production process of the new products as a secondary link and let the products to be produced by other manufacturers/producers simply through OEM contracts. However, even so, due to patent right of new products, investors of product innovation still can obtain higher profits. The reason is that the patent right of new products enables them to control what is to be produced and how many will be produced and even how to produce, but ignore the question whether production efficiency is improved in processing enterprises. In this way, innovation enterprises can control the standards and number of new products which will be put into the market, so they can control the situation that demand exceeds supply in the market. It can clearly be seen that the high profit resulting from the market effect is a monopoly profit. This monopoly is achieved by patent right for new products, and as the second step monopolizing and controlling the production numbers and control markets for those products.

Of course, innovation of production process can also cause the situation of demand exceeding supply in the market. Because lower costs will attract more customers with a price lower than other enterprises. However, this increase in demand is the result of struggle between competing enterprises. And it is not the result of creating new markets (or new demands). The economic significance of product innovation is that it can meet a demand different from the past, break the existing old market structure and open new markets.

The below scheme (Fig.3-1) illustrates the two different effects on enterprises that technological progress can have.

Technological progress can bring different economic effects to enterprises through the two different technological innovations. It can be shown by Fig. 3-1.

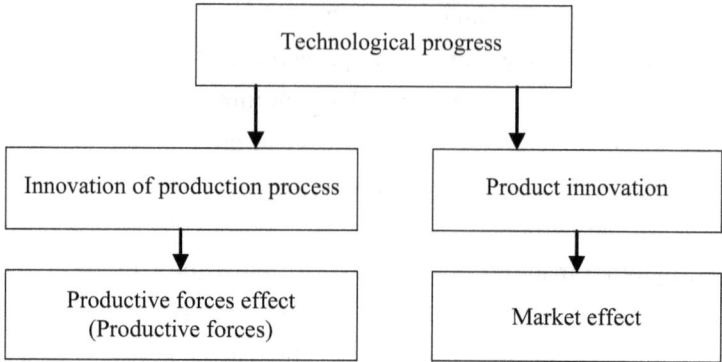

```
                    ┌─────────────────────────────────┐
                    │      Technological progress      │
                    └─────────────────────────────────┘
                         │                      │
                         ▼                      ▼
┌──────────────────────────────┐  ┌──────────────────────────────┐
│ Innovation of production      │  │      Product innovation       │
│ process                       │  │                               │
└──────────────────────────────┘  └──────────────────────────────┘
                │                                 │
                ▼                                 ▼
┌──────────────────────────────┐  ┌──────────────────────────────┐
│   Productive forces effect    │  │         Market effect         │
│   (Productive forces)         │  │                               │
└──────────────────────────────┘  └──────────────────────────────┘
```

Fig. 3-1 Two economic effects of technological progress

The connection between the two forms and different economic effects of technological progress are indicated with arrows. That is to say that technological progress has two forms of innovation: innovation in the production process and product innovation. The former one can bring production efficiency effect and the latter one can produce market effect.

II. Technological Innovation and Changes in the Industrial Structure

Historical change of industrial structure is another manifestation in the development of productive forces. There were two major changes in industrial structure throughout the capitalist economic history. The first was a change from the economy with agriculture as the largest industrial sector to the economy with industry as the largest industrial sector; the second was a change from the economy with industry as the largest industrial sector to the economy with service industry as the largest industrial sector. Those two changes of industrial structure had close connection with the work forms of technological innovation.

The first change in industrial structure was called "Industrial Revolution" that replaced the handicraft industry with the machine industry and its technological basis was the innovation in the production process. Marx had commented on this: "through its constant updated production revolution, large-scale industry made the production cost of products lower and lower, and mercilessly crowded out all previous modes of production. Thereby it finally conquered the domestic market for capital, by enforcing self-sufficient small production and natural economy of the farmer families take the road to ruin, and directly crowded out the direct exchanges between small producers, thus making the whole nation serve for capital.[1]

"Constant upgraded production revolution" described by Marx refers to the continuous innovation of production process. "Large-scale industry has incorporated huge natural forces and natural science into the production process, so it was bound to greatly improve the labor production efficiency. This point is very clear."[2]

Specifically speaking, the mechanization had changed the production mode relying on crafts of artisans under small production and natural economy conditions. "Large-scale industry had to grasp its special means of production, i.e. the machine itself, and it must use machines to produce machines. In this way, large-scale industry can establish the technological progress adapted to itself and be self-reliant."[3]

The establishment of mechanized industry not only means that the social productive forces have changed from manual labor based on labor to mechanized and automated production based on means of labor, but also decided the change of industrial structure. Industrial economy had replaced the agricultural economy. Since the establishment of the industrial economy, with the incarnation of capital, for the need of survival and proliferation, enterprises had to constantly improve technologies in mutual competition and constantly conduct innovation of production process, thus making the level of productive forces constantly improve. It can be said that "industrial revolution", realization of industrialization and the development of the

---

[1] Marx: *Capital*, Edition 1, Vol. 3, p. 1027.
[2] Marx: *Capital*, Edition 1, Vol. 1, p. 424.
[3] Marx: *Capital*, Edition 1, Vol. 1, pp. 421- 422.

industrial economy take constant innovation of production process as technological basis.

But the second change in the industrial structure was not "revolutionary" because it did not need to overthrow the existing mode of production. However, the change from an economy with the industry as the main body to an economy where "service industry" accounting for more than 70% of the national economy has displayed that productive forces have been developed to a certain higher degree. In other words, the constant innovation of production process of the industrial economy has made the development of productive forces develop to a high level so that less than 30% of the economic activities in the national economy are enough to provide all the material products needed by the society. When the level of productive forces is developed to such a height, the purchasing power level of society has been also improved to the historical stage of pursuing quality of life. In this time, reducing the product price begins to fail to change market demand. In order to get rid of the restriction of situation, capital, in order to pursue profit, has to rely on product innovation to open a new road for itself. So product innovation has become the main form of technological innovation in the "post-industrial economy" period.

There is an ultimate limitation in production efficiency effect caused by innovation in production process; the reason is the limiting line in demand growth in the commodity markets. The emergence of this limiting line in demand growth is the result of constant innovation in production process under capitalist competition. In other words, the development of technical basis in the industrial economy itself limits its own development space.

Because under the capitalist production condition, innovation in production process will cause a series of changes as follows: innovation of production process → improvement in production efficiency → reduction in product prices → increase in market demand → increase of market share of the enterprise → increase of output → increase of enterprise scale → increase of the total profit of the enterprise.

A series of changes indicate that the innovation of production process makes an enterprise gain a cost advantage in the competition with producers of similar products, so it can win more market share through expanding its production scale. On the other hand, the technological advantage by innovation of production process also creates conditions for enterprises to accelerate capital accumulation and expand the scale of production because the production efficiency effect also becomes a reason to expand the enterprise's production. I can summarize that as below: innovation in production process → improvement in production efficiency → unit production factor (especially labor) → improvement of output → increase in unit production factor → improvement of proliferation rate of capital → enhancement of the ability of expanding production scale.

However, the boundary for an increase in the market demand depends on demand elasticity of a product. When prices of products cannot be reduced no matter what measures are adopted, it means that the demand for such products has a lack of flexibility. Demand elasticity of a product is connected to demand preferences. With the improvement of the income level of people, demand preferences for many necessities no longer increase. It shows that the limit line of their demand growth has been near or reached.

And when the expansion of production scale exceeds this limit line of demand increase, it will no longer have economic effects.

Therefore, in the case that further increase in demand is very difficult, to apply innovative technology in the production process will rather result in greater losses. Because in this case, to further expand the scale of production will lead to overproduction and excess production capacity and the more it produces, the more losses it will have.

In the 1960s and 1970s, the industrial production in developed countries had recorded a significant contraction, known as the so-called "non-industrialization". This was because on the one hand, with the development of productive forces, domestic demand converged to the boundary, while on the other hand, the rapid economic growth in various countries in the world after the war had made traditional industrial sectors face international competition, particularly the pressure of low-cost competition from developing countries.

At the same time, the industry in developed capitalist countries was developing towards high-tech industries based on product innovation. Especially in the 1980s and 1990s, R & D investment in main developed countries increased rapidly, and its proportion in GDP increased. The technological innovation accelerated the change of sectoral proportions within the industry. And this in turn promoted the consumption demand for service industry in the social reproduction process, making the proportion of service industry in the economy rapidly expand to be the biggest industry department, and its role in the economy-industry has become more significant.

The shift from technological innovation to product innovation as the main form and the second industrial structure change can be seen from Fig. 3-2:

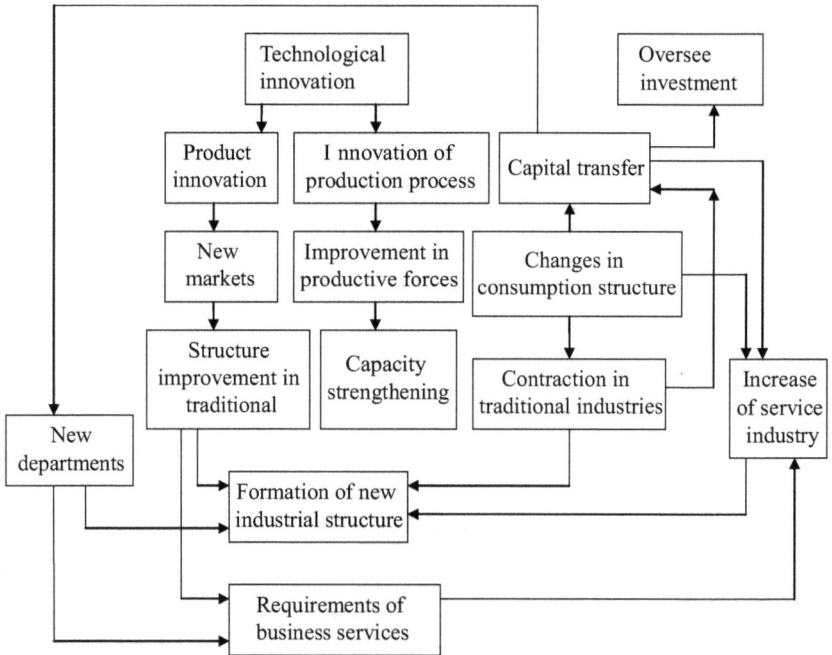

Fig. 3-2 The influence of technological innovation to the change in industrial structure

I can explain the technological basis for the second change as innovation in the production process creates space for product innovation. As shown in

Fig. 3-2:

1) There were two results by innovation in production process: the contraction in traditional industrial departments; changes in consumption demand structure. Because the innovation in production process in the long term had brought production efficiency and this increased the production capacity as long as the limit line of the product demand was not reached.

2) The product innovation had led to two results: increase of new sectors (especially the high-tech industry department); upgrading in the internal structure of traditional industry sectors.

3) Contraction of traditional industries had caused three changes: capital went to other sectors; consumption structure had changed and also provided conditions for new investments. The new investment areas include the new (high-tech) departments, foreign investment and the service industry.

4) The formation reason of the new structure was contraction of traditional industrial departments; increase in the service industry; increase of new (high-tech) sectors; structure upgrading in the traditional industry departments.

5) The reasons for the increase of service industry were the free capital caused by the contraction in the traditional industry departments; changes in the structure of consumer demand; increase in business service demand caused by the increase in the product innovation activity.

The formation of the new industrial structure:

1) The formation of new industrial structure is firstly started in the sectors of material production, especially when the internal structure has changed in the whole industry by the emergence of new sectors and vanishing of traditional sectors.

2) Technological innovation was the starting point of the structural change within the sectors of material production. The change of industrial structure is the result of more capital investment into the change process in the form of technological innovation. With reaching to the limit line of demand growth, the decline in the application of new type of technologies

into the production process caused capital to get out from traditional industrial sectors and enter to the more lucrative investment sectors, thus forming the new industrial structure of post-industrial economy.

In the 1970s, the traditional industries in developed countries fell into a serious predicament. First of all, the increase of raw materials costs and labor costs together with excess production capacity made traditional industries more and more unprofitable, and the entry barriers to high-tech industry sectors were high. The survival space for the traditional industrial capital in developed countries was shrinking. Secondly, after the war, the traditional industrial sectors of the developing countries had basically caught up with those of developed countries, and their labor costs and resource costs were lower than those of developed countries, therefore developed countries could not be competitive in the market for these products. Thirdly, after the war, the gap between developed countries was narrowed, and the competition in the production departments with certain technical content (such as cars, home appliances and other products) became fiercer. Some developing countries also had achieved very high competitive strength in these sectors, which showed that market of such products was reduced.

For example, "In the 1950s, the import of the United States was only a trickle, however, in the 1960s, it already became a turbulent river and finally in the 1970s and 1980s, the import already became a scourge. By the end of the 20th century, the trade deficit of U.S. had reached a degree that could not be imagined a few years ago."[1]

The industries in developed countries meet cost and technological competition at home and abroad, which means that the pressure of the profit rate decline is very big. To reduce the loss or risk of elimination, capital transfer is bound to occur. After experiencing an economic stagnation stage in the 1970s, an internal industrial adjustment was practiced.

I will explain that process more in detail.

Firstly, there were two new ways for traditional industries: capital

---

[1] Thomas K. McGraw: *Modern Capitalism*, Edition 1, p. 378, Nanjing, Jiangsu People's Publishing House, 1999.

transfer to low-cost developing countries through the multinational corporations; capital transfer to the service industry.

Secondly, R & D and human capital investments have been increased in the original high-tech industry sectors to improve competitiveness.

Thirdly, new high-tech sector (especially in the United States) represented by information technology and personal computers has been rapidly developed.

Fourthly, a huge amount of excess capital entered into the speculation field, which supported the financing of high-tech sector and other competitive sectors, but thereby caused the financial "bubble" and triggered "financial crisis" risks. However, overall, capital had moved out of the traditional industrial sectors and entered into the high-tech industry and service industry (tertiary industry), or was transferred to developing countries.

Since the 1970s, the capital's movement among different sectors in the developed countries had also displayed the changes in the condition of production technologies (or the forms of technical progress).

Before and after the two world wars, the developed countries already had the experience for product innovation, but this had not become the main form of technological innovation in industry. Only after the 1970s, product innovation—with the new and increasing intense competition—had become the most important competition means and survival condition for the developed countries.

Therefore, after the 1970s the change in the technological innovation mode had occurred as from production process innovation-oriented to product innovation-oriented has become the basic characteristic of industrial structure adjustment in developed countries.

The expansion of demand for the service industry (including expansion of private service product consumption demand and commercial service product demand of enterprises) had enabled investments become profitable. The capital investment in the service industry involves two aspects: on the one hand, increase of demand for service industry incurred to meet changes of the consumption structure, such as life service, tourism and entertainment, education, medical care and health care, etc.; on the other hand, increase of demand for commercial service caused by adjustment of the internal structure of the material production sector, such as law, finance, information, advertising and promotion, etc.

Especially, increase in demand for commercial service reflects the characteristics of the change of technological innovation form to some extent. Product innovation is more complicated than innovation of production process. It needs the following service: information acquiescence, technical identification, patent protection, financing and other service to apply the technical inventions into operation. It additionally needs advertising, marketing and other promotions to pass from a successful operation to successful sales because it can enlarge the market for this product only after it is recognized in the market. In addition, many new products may also need after-sales service, etc.

But the innovation of production process is much simpler. As long as machines with good performance are purchased, they can fulfill their purpose because the machine operation in the production process is not very complicated or remains under the guidance of engineers, and problems can be solved easily. However, product innovation is not so simple. It requires professionals and professional knowledge on the design, invention and innovation of new products to do technical guidance, training and adjustment, etc. in the production process. And those professionals and professional knowledge require the enhancement of education, culture and scientific research sectors which necessitates the mobilization of the whole society. Therefore, the post-industrial economy era is called as the "knowledge economy" era. In such a new era, the service industry also includes the development of those sectors. The service industry in post-industrial era is a very complex sector. Except the expansion of personal life scope, commercial service has been especially developed and accordingly it drives the development of education, scientific research and other sectors.

When we analyze from the aspect of technical basis, it seems that the first industrial structure change has involved the innovation of the production process and product innovation belongs to the second industrial change in the post-industrial economy. However, this can only show that the themes of technological innovation in the two eras are different, and it does not mean the absolute historical division of two technological innovations, because the industrial economy period cannot exclude the role of product innovation and the post-industrial economy period cannot exclude the innovation of the production process, either.

The first industrial structure change was revolutionary in comparison to the second one. The innovation of production process represents indeed a revolution of the process because it negated the previous mode of production on the technical basis. However, the second industrial revolution does not touch upon the mode of production, and does not totally negate innovation of the production process either, but complies with the adjustment of demand structure changes. Product innovation and innovation of the production process can be accomplished without getting into conflict, especially in the situation that market demand for new products is sufficient to meet large-scale production, and innovation in the production process can foster production efficiency effect to the capital. However, the second industrial revolution poses severe challenges to traditional capital accumulation way and laboring conditions. These challenges are: 1) changing the previous simple way of quantity expansion for capital accumulation, and instead using the method of quality innovation in products to obtain high added value to achieve capital accumulation in the market which should be enlarged. 2) The labor process begins to be incorporated into innovation activities, so labor is not entirely subordinated passively to the operation of machines, and the laboring process enters into a trend of creativity and initiative. Therefore, in the sphere of labor, the concept of "human capital" becomes important.

III. Capital and Its Restraints on Productive Forces

In the capitalist system, no matter what form of technological innovation is adopted or no matter what economic age we are in, the development of productive forces are subject to restrains by capitalist economic laws. In capitalist system, money-making is the supreme rule. Thus, although capitalist competition forces enterprises to continuously adopt new technologies, the development of productive forces has great limitations. Especially since the economies of developed capitalist countries advanced to the post-industrial times, restraints on the development of productive forces have intensified.

1. Restraints on Productive Forces in the Industrial Economy Period

In the capitalist industrial economy period, the character of technological innovation was the innovation in the production process. Through the previous analysis of this chapter, we have seen that comparatively, constant innovation in the production process had been favorable to promote the development of productive forces. However, in the capitalist system, productive forces formed in the innovation of the production process can only be shown as the productive forces of capital. That is to say, only when the innovation of the production process can relatively reduce the cost of production and increase profits, it has a sufficient economic significance for the capitalists. Therefore, in the capitalist industrial economy period, the limitations in promoting productive forces by technological innovation at least can be shown in the following aspects:

(1) Limitations in the usage of new technologies

The economic significance of innovation in the production process for capital lies in the effect that production efficiency generated by it can shorten the necessary labor time, accordingly relatively increases the time of surplus labor. Therefore, only on the premise of increasing surplus labor, the new technology can be applied. In *Capital*, Marx had profoundly revealed the limitations on capitalists to use machines. He had written: "If machines are only deemed as a means to make our products cheaper, the limit of using machines is that the labor expanded in producing machines is less than the labor replaced by using machines. However, as to capital, this limit is becoming narrower, because what appreciates capital is the value of living labor employed, not the previously materialized labor (machines); only in the case when there is a difference between the value of machines and the value of labor replaced by it, will the machines be used."[1]

That is to say, from the aspect of social production, if the use of new technology can save labor used for producing products, it means that the improvement of the productive forces effect is propelled in the production mode of the economy. However, for capital, the real significance of new technology is not to save labor but is to save cost (to buy machines or materials). Therefore, Marx had written that the limit that capital uses new technology is becoming "narrower". This is "because the profit of capital is obtained by reducing paid work instead of the previously materialized labor."[2] Capitalist production is the production that capital controls the production process, so the labor time saved by using new technology cannot liberate labor, but is used to produce more surplus value. If savings on the paid labor cannot exceed the increased cost owing to the usage of the new technology (or machine as said by Marx), the usage of new technology is meaningless for capital. Because if it is not profitable, the capitalist will not make new technological investment. It shows that in the system in which capitalists control the production process, not all advanced technologies that can increase production efficiency can be utilized. Innovation of production process can be used only under the premise that it can bring profit for capital.

(2) Side effects by the usage of new technology

Due to the innovation in the production process, capital rapidly expands, and in this process more and more social costs increase, thus forming an obstacle for further economic development. In the industrial economy period, a great deal of innovation in production process had been profitable for capital. Therefore, under the drive of technological progress, the industrial

[1] Marx: *Capital*, Edition 1, Vol. 1, pp. 430-431.
[2] Marx: *Capital*, Edition 1, Vol. 1, p. 431.

production in developed capitalist countries had continued to expand. "Due to the technical conditions, machinery, transport equipment, etc. in the production process itself, it is likely to most rapidly transform the remaining products to additional means of production in the biggest scale. A great deal of social wealth that is expanded with the increase of accumulation and may be transformed into additional capital frantically enter into the old production sectors with suddenly expanding markets, or emerging production sectors caused by the development of old production departments such as railway, etc."[1] This is the scene in the early stage of capitalist industrialization described by Marx. However, the social costs brought by expansion of the industrialization production scale were enormous. In the process of capital expansion, those social costs were not borne by individual capital, but instead by the whole society, so it severely limited the long-term development of human productive forces.

The social costs incurred from capitalist industry expansion were mainly apparent in two aspects: on the one hand, predatory consumption of resources occurred; on the other hand, serious environmental pollution was produced in this process. First of all, the mechanization and automation of industry needed to consume a large amount of mineral and fuel resources. In 1972, in Research Report the Limits to Growth provided to the Club of Rome by Professor Meadows from Massachusetts Institute of Technology, the necessary mineral and fuel resources needed in world industrial production was investigated and researched. The results had showed that "the world use rates of various natural resources had grown exponentially. The use rates of a lot of resources had increased faster than the population", and "according to the current rate of resource consumption and expected increase of those consumption rates, the majority of the resources which are important but cannot be re-generated will become extremely expensive after a hundred years." At that time, the problem had been that "those industrialized resource consuming countries completely relied on a set of international agreements signed with resource producing countries to obtain supply of raw materials

---

[1] Marx: *Capital*, Edition 1, Vol. 1, pp. 693-694.

needed by their industrial bases. One resource after another will become so expensive that people will not afford them"[1].

On the other hand, while production expansion with the application of innovative technology in the production process consumed a great amount of resources, it also produced increasing emissions, which polluted the environment and threatened human survival and development space. For example, carbon dioxide, heat and radioactive waste were polluting the living environment of human beings in a rate of exponential increase. Many toxic substances were discharged into the waters and the atmosphere from the industrial production process and agricultural pesticides. The report of Meadows had pointed out: "Now about 97% of industry energy production of human beings is from fossil fuels (coal, oil and natural gas). Those fuels that discharge carbon dioxide (along with other substances) into the atmosphere when burning. Currently, about 20 billion tons of carbon dioxides are emitted from burning fossil fuels every year." The thermal pollution to the atmosphere and rivers are making the global climate become warmer and the living organisms in oceans destructed.

Those consumption and destruction in the industrial economy make out the social cost for capital's pursuit of production efficiency effect, i.e. it is the cost of sacrificing the long-term development interests of human beings. Actually, the development level of modern science and technology can fully diminish the serious consequences of such damage, and most of them can be evaded by certain technologies, such as re-cycling harmful substances that might pollute the environment. However, the rule of capital dictates to reduce costs and increase profits. Without external pressure, a single capital will not automatically assume the responsibility of evading pollution which will increase its production costs.

(3) The conflict between development of productive forces and production relations

In production relations based on capitalist private ownership, constant

---

[1] D. Meadows, *The Limits to Growth*, p. 36, 45, Beijing, the Commercial Press, 1984.

innovation in production process results in a certain restriction, that is, the market continuously scales down. On the one hand, due to the innovation the proportion between means of production and labor, i.e. organic composition ratio of capital, constantly increases; on the other hand, the proliferation capacity of capital increases, so the capital increasingly concentrates in a small number of people who have capital and technological advantages. Therefore, the expansion of the market cannot keep up with the expansion of production. The ultimate result is that development of productive forces is restricted by insufficient demand.

Through continuous innovation in the production process, capital absorbs more and more unpaid labor force. It can be said that the development of productive forces provides a favorable condition for capital appreciation, thus changing them into the productive forces of capital. **"But social consumption capacity neither depends on absolute productive forces nor on absolute consumption capacity, but on the consumption capacity based on the antagonistic relations in distribution sphere; such a distribution relation makes the consumption of the majority of people in society be reduced to the minimum limit with only marginal changes and within very small boundaries. This consumption capacity is also limited by the desire that pursues for accumulation and desire for expanding capital and producing more and more surplus value. This is the law of capitalist production. It is determined by the constant revolution in the production method itself. Depreciation of existing capital that is constantly linked with this revolution, general competition struggle between capitalists and the necessity of improving production and expanding production scale to save itself and avoid extinction. Therefore, the market must continue to expand so that the connection of the market and the condition for regulating this connection increasingly adopt the form of natural law that does not transfer with producers and becomes harder and harder to control. For that reason, the method of expanding to the outer sphere is used as an attempt to solve this internal contradiction. However, the more the productive force is developed,**

the more probable it is to have conflicts due to the narrow foundation of consumption relationship.[1] This non-adjustable conflict described by Marx then is a true portrayal of the contradiction encountered by the development of productive forces in the capitalist industrial economy period. The Great Depression that swept global capitalist economy from 1929 to 1933 shows that capitalist production comprehensively had fallen into a severe situation difficult to extricate itself. If the Keynesian "demand management" had not reformed the capitalist economy with several adjustments in the framework of its system, it would be hard to imagine the current developed capitalist economy.

2. Restraints on Productive Forces in Post-Industrial Economy Period

Under the regulation of the Keynesian policies, the developed capitalist economy experienced a period of "Golden Age" of economic development after the World War II. Finally in the end of the 1960s and early 1970s, industrial economy reached its peak. The contradiction between production and consumption became sharp again. At that time, the reason for the inadequacy in aggregate demand was not simply the question of purchasing power, but in fact, the increases/changes in the factors of demand choices were the real principal contradiction. That is why later, the Keynesian effective demand management policy lost its effect. After the "stagflation" period in the 1970s, industrial capital gradually decided to focus on product innovation by employing technology.

As elaborated in the previous part of this chapter, the fundamental advantage of product innovation lies in its market effects, i.e., the effect of opening new markets. However, product innovation does not apparently have a considerable contribution to the development of productive forces in contrast to the innovation of production process. The reason is obvious that the technology used in product innovation solves the question of "what to be produced" instead of "how to produce", so it does not have a direct effect

[1] Marx: *Capital*, Edition 1, Vol. 3, pp. 272-273.

on productive forces. Besides, product innovation needs to consume a lot of social wealth because product innovation requires a series of activities such as acquiring market information, product design, scientific research, marketing and after-sales service and even financing and legal advice, etc. Those activities, together with production link can create wealth for the society, the other links all basically consume instead of producing material wealth.

According to historical data, we can see that the growth of production efficiency in developed capitalist countries has shown a downward trend since the 1970s. The downward trend in the growth rate of manufacturing industry which normally has the fastest production efficiency is the most obvious one.

Table 3-1 presents the data published in *Monthly Labor Review* in the United States in 1999. To ensure the convenience of the comparison, according to this group of index, we have calculated annual growth rates of production efficiency in the main developed countries. The results are shown in Table 3-2.

Table 3-1   Production index in the manufacturing industry in major developed countries
(Output per man-hour)   (The year of 1992=100)

	1970	1980	1990	1991	1992	1993	1994	1995	1996	1997	1998
U.K.	44.7	56.2	88.4	92.2	100	104.1	106.8	104.7	103.3	103.8	104.8
France	43.1	66.7	93.5	96.9	100	100.6	108.5	114.5	115.0	123.3	127.5
Germany	52.0	77.2	99.0	101.9	100	100.7	107.9	111.2	115.1	121.8	127.1
Italy	36.8	64.1	92.5	95.2	100	102.9	105.6	109.3	110.3	113.4	113.6
Japan	38.0	63.9	95.4	99.4	100	100.9	101.8	109.3	115.8	120.2	120.5
U.S.A	-	71.9	97.8	98.3	100	102.1	108.3	114.9	117.3	122.1	127.0
Canada	59.2	75.3	95.3	95.1	100	102.5	106.2	108.9	107.3	110.9	111.7

Source: *Monthly labor Review*, September 1999, p. 96.

Table 3-2   Average annual growth rate of the production efficiency of manufacturing industry in main developed countries   Unit: %

	1970-1980	1980-1990	1990-1998
UK	2.1	4.2	1.8
France	4.0	3.1	3.5
Germany	3.7	2.3	2.9
Italy	5.2	3.4	2.3
Japan	4.8	3.7	2.6
USA	2.8	2.9	
Canada	2.2	2.2	1.8
Average	3.5	3.1	2.5

From Table 3-2, we can infer that the average annual growth rate of output per man-hour of the manufacturing sector in the seven major developed capitalist countries from 1970 to 1998 has showed a downward trend. Especially from the average of the seven countries, the annual growth rate of manufacturing industry has an obvious decline trend: in the 1970s, it is 3.5%, in the 1980s, it is 3.1% and in the 1990s, it is 2.5%. Although from the perspective of countries, changes in production efficiency in all the major developed countries are very different. The production efficiency in France, Germany and the United States has rebounded in the 1990s, but the rises are small.

The decline of the growth rate in production efficiency reflects that the pace of technological innovation in the production process has slowed down. It is clear that the demand growth in the traditional products are close to the limiting line. The growth rate of production capacity tends to decline, therefore equipment replacement suffers resistance. However, these statistics only reflect the general trend in production efficiency in the manufacturing industry and wherein some different cases are also worth noting.

For example, the enterprises applying product innovation in manufacturing industry may have a rapid growth rate in production efficiency. As long as innovation made by these enterprises has a market effect and can open a large enough market, innovation in production process is profitable, thus production rate will still have a positive increase trend. Because in the case of large-scale production, the space of innovation in production process such as the usage of production lines and scale effect advantage of large-scale organizations, etc. is very large. However, the effect of product innovation on the increases in production efficiency by applying new technology has usually a false impression. Because the calculation of the production efficiency can only be output value of a unit of production factor, but a substantial part of that might be the result of the high added-value in the high-tech industry sectors and if so this number cannot reflect real improvements in the production efficiency. The added-value of the high-tech industrial sector is mainly produced by the market effect as the result of product innovation. Therefore, in an era of increased product innovation, statistical data of production efficiency usually cannot fully expose the real changes in the production efficiency. However, despite these factors, the production efficiency in the developed countries is still in a falling trend. It further indicates that with the form of technological innovation capitalism cannot give enough impulse to the promotion of productivity and productive forces and the impulse has weakened.

Of course, the decline in the growth rate of production efficiency during the post-industrial period is not necessarily an absolute decline in the level of productive forces. We cannot simply interpret that as product innovation hinders the development of productive forces but technology innovation merely does not have a direct effect on the changes of productive forces because its focus is not the production process, but the product. In other words, the product innovation does not exclude innovation in the production process, it merely does not involve the innovation of the production process, and thus it does not directly effect the productive forces or productivity.

IV. Change in the Form of Technological Innovation and Economic Growth

The previous industrial economy period based on the innovation in the production process was the period in which the growth rate of the economy had accelerated. On the one hand, the improvement in the production efficiency had greatly increased the ability to create social wealth; on the other hand, the economic effects brought by innovation in the production process had accelerated the speed of capital accumulation and had greatly stimulated the desire to expand the production scale. Therefore, the growth rate in the industrial economy period was unprecedented. However, later when product innovation had become the form of technological innovation the economic growth rate showed a falling trend. (See Table 3-3 and Table 3-4)

Table 3-3   Annual average growth rate of GDP in the major developed countries

Unit: %

	1970-1980	1980-1990	1990-1998	1999
U.S.A	3.2	3.2	3.0	4.2
Japan	4.4	4.0	1.4	0.3
Germany	2.7	2.2	1.4	1.5
France	3.3	2.4	1.4	2.9
Italy	3.6	2.2	1.3	1.4
UK	1.9	2.7	2.0	2.1
Canada	3.1	2.8	1.8	2.1
Average	3.7	3.3	2.1	2.4

Source: *OECD Economic Outlook* No.67, 2000, p. 190.

Table 3-4   Per capita real GDP growth rate in the major developed countries

Unit: %

	1970-1980	1980-1990	1990-1998	1999
U.S.A	2.1	2.3	2.0	3.2
Japan	3.3	3.4	1.1	0.1
Germany	2.6	2.0	1.0	1.4
France	2.7	1.8	0.9	2.5
Italy	3.1	2.2	1.2	1.3
UK	1.8	2.5	1.7	1.7
Canada	2.6	2.4	1.3	1.7
Average	3.0	2.8	1.5	2.0

Source: *OECD Economic Outlook* No.67, 2000, p. 190.

The statistical data in Table 3-3 and Table 3-4 show that except the United States, other major developed countries have prevalently had a falling rate of the economic growth rate since the 1970s. Both the growth rate of the real gross domestic product (GDP) and the growth rate of per capita GDP show a falling trend. This shows that although the technological innovation activities have received more and more attention (such as increase of R & D investment), because the product innovation activities cannot promote productive forces like in the innovation of the production process, this is bound to affect the growth rate negatively.

Since the 1970s, the slowing down of the economic growth rate in developed capitalist countries may have many reasons. But when we look at the issue from the perspective of change in the technological innovation mode, we can summarize it as follows:

Firstly, in the post-industrial period, change in the technological innovation mode has made a negative effect on the growth of production efficiency. The previous data have shown that since the 1970s, the growth in production efficiency in the major capitalist countries has shown a falling trend. And the change in technological innovation mode is an important reason for this trend. The economic effect of product innovation is opening markets, and it does not produce production efficiency effect like in the innovation of production process. With the changes in the social consumption structure in developed countries, the output of traditional products have approached to the limits. A large number of enterprises have to change from innovation in production process to product innovation because of the pressure of the smaller market. As a result, it inevitably decreases the growth of production.

Secondly, change in technological innovation mode is also the main reason for the change in the industrial structure. And change in the industrial structure affects the growth rate of overall economy. The competitiveness of technological investment in product innovation pushes a large amount of capital to enter into product innovation activities. Accordingly, a great deal of social wealth is consumed in the non-productive activities. Regarding this point, we have made explanations in the previous part of this chapter. At present, the industrial structures in developed capitalist countries have been developed to a level in which the proportion of the material production sector is less than 30% and the production of material products needs to be completed through the activities in other departments of industry linked with it. Therefore, I can say that "roundabout production" mode was replaced by "roundabout economy". The proportion of the consumption of material wealth in economic activities is larger than direct production of material wealth, so the economic growth rate is reduced.

Thirdly, the market effects of technological investment in product innovation co-exist and goes hand in hand with the monopoly in technology.

For enterprises, the patents of new products are the decisive condition for obtaining high added-value. Once a new product is produced by an enterprise, its profit difference will be great. The reason is: 1) The highly innovated products are unique and this factor determines the limit of its production scope, and the market needs an understanding and acceptance process/period for these new products. If the output/production is rapidly increased, it is bound to result in an over-supply and the enterprise profit will not be very high. 2) Development and design of new products require high investment on R & D. If the production of new products is not protected by patent rights, the profit of enterprises applying product innovation will be not as high as other enterprises, thus losing incentives for product innovation. However, patent rights protection constitutes in fact a protection to technological monopoly, which is a wall to free competition in the production and sales of the new products. The enterprises which apply product innovation rely on patent rights to restrict the production and sales in order to obtain monopoly profits. In such cases, the growth rate of production is restricted.

Fourthly, although the technological investment in product innovation can produce market effects, it cannot eliminate the inherent contradiction of the capitalist economy, i.e. the contradiction between production and consumption. On the contrary, with the change in technological innovation mode; large enterprises pay more attention to product development and design and transfer their production links to enterprises with relatively lower manufacturing costs. So a great deal of product processing is transferred to developing countries. Thus jobless situation in the labor markets in the developed countries is further aggravated, and increase in the workers' wages is highly restrained. Therefore, in recent decades, the income difference in the developed capitalist countries is increasing instead of narrowing. In addition, due to the increase of cross-national activities of monopoly enterprises, the gap between the rich developed countries and poor developing countries is widening. All this means that the issue of relatively diminishing market for capitalist production has not been fundamentally solved, but on the contrary, it has further deepened. Therefore, if this contradiction develops to an acute degree, recession and stagnation in the capitalist production will undoubtedly reappear. The periodicity of capitalist production inevitably inhibits the economic growth rate. I think the world-wide deflation and economic stagnation since the 1990s is the result of this contradiction.

Briefly, on the one hand, capitalist economic relation has promoted improvements in technology, development of productive forces and the upgrading in the industrial structure; meanwhile it limits the further development of productive forces. The development of productive forces has made more and more traditional products in capitalist countries reach the limit lines of their demand and production. Marx had commented on this issue: one important condition for the emergence of communism is that "all the sources of collective wealth fully flow" with the all-round development of individuals and growth of productive forces.[1] Some modern western left-wing scholars further define this condition as "affluence". The so-called "affluence" in theory is defined as the saturation of demand. When the marginal elasticity of demand for one product is approximately zero or below zero, then the product can be described as "affluent". Long-term statistical data, especially data from Western Europe, provide overwhelming evidence for that: "in rich countries a great deal of products can be classified into this category—which is the case not only for millionaires, but for most of the population"[2] It shows that the development of productive forces is providing an increasingly solid foundation for the establishment of a new society. At the same time, the conflict between productive forces and the capitalist production relations is sharpening, thus resulting as difficulties in the proliferation of capital. The change in technological innovation mode is the result and expression of this conflict. It eases the contradiction in a relatively small market to some extent, but cannot finally eliminate this contradiction, on the contrary, it makes this contradiction even further deepened. It shows a truth to the people: capitalism is by no means the end of human history.

[1] *Selected Works of Marx and Engels*, Edition 2, Vol. 3, p. 305, Beijing, People's Publishing House, 1995.

[2] Ernest Mandel: Power and Money: *A Marxist Theory of Bureaucracy*, Edition 1, p. 250, Beijing, Central Compilation & Translation Press, 2002.

Chapter IV

Historical Evolution of Capitalist Ownership

Ownership of means of production is the basis of capitalist economic relations. Since the establishment of capitalist mode of production, three major industrial revolutions have taken place, resulting in the rapid development of productive forces. The factors that promote the development of capitalist economy can be various, however, fundamentally speaking, its historical evolution is due to the capitalist economic relation based on the private ownership of means of production which suit to the requirements of development of productive forces and I think this is the most important reason which promotes the capitalist economic development. Therefore, to understand the historical process of the development of capitalist ownership relationship and its laws has become the key to analyze capitalist economic development.

I. The Development of the Capitalist Private Ownership

1. The Essential Characteristics of Capitalist Private Ownership

Generally most Marxist scholars and political leaders agree that capitalism has encountered a rapid development of production and productivity and the development of economy, science and technology has made many achievements. Chinese leader Jiang Zemin has also commented on this phenomenon: "the rapid development of production has not changed capitalist economic system—its basic inherent contradiction—especially the nature of capitalist private ownership." Same as the private ownerships in the slave society and feudal society, capitalist economic system is also based on private ownership, and the form of private ownership has not yet changed. However, compared with the previous private ownership of the means of production, its nature has changed significantly.[1] The special nature of this ownership is first manifested that capitalist private ownership is linked to commodity economy and market economy. In human history, capitalist economic relation is the result of the development of commodity economy. In the early stage of the development of commodity economy, economic exchanges between producers were on the premise of small private ownership based mainly on their own labor. Marx had defined it as: "previous forms in which laborers themselves are owners (means of production) or owners themselves are laborers." Thus it means capitalist ownership is formed by two extremes: one is capitalist as the owner of the means of production; the other is the free workers, who possess nothing but their own labor-power. The development of commodity economy determines that the means of production to be increasingly accumulated in the hands of the minority, while others become wage laborers that make a living by relying on their labor. Capitalist type of private ownership is gradually formed in this

---

[1] *Selected Works of Marx and Engels*, Edition 2, Vol. 3, p. 621, footnote.

process. Just because capitalist private ownership is associated with a certain degree of developed commodity economy, in the direct sense, capitalist private ownership has two characteristics:

1) The subject of capitalist private ownership adopts capital, as the form of the value, however, the subject of previous forms of private ownership used to adopt land, a particular form of thing. Although capital also needs to be manifested through a particular object, at the beginning, it could only adopt the existing thing in the form of means of production in the history. Marx had commented on this issue: "In the existing current technological condition in the history, make labor obey itself."[1] However, because the capital, in essence, is a value or economic relation taking proliferation of self-value as the purpose, it cannot be fixed in a particular department or a form of specific mean of production for a long time. On the premise of maintaining its value and proliferation, capital will continuously adopt or abandon a particular form of a thing to realize its essential requirements. This logic can clearly explain why the dominant industrial sector of capitalism has experienced changes from the cotton textile industry to heavy chemical industry, and later to machinery manufacturing and household appliances industry and finally to the information industry.

2) Capitalist private ownership is the large private ownership in which a minority group appropriates the monopoly of a great amount of means of production. It is not only because that capitalist private ownership is based on appropriation of labor of others, but also because it can, through the credit system, unite dispersed small and medium-sized individual capital(s) together to form larger capital(s) existing in the form of share capital thus creating the conditions of scale economies while retaining ownership of the original capital. All of these could not be achieved under the previous (pre-capitalist) ownership forms in history.

The special nature of capitalist private ownership is also manifested that it is based on the premise of the wage-labor system. However, the laborers themselves are not the objects owned by the bourgeoisie. In the form or

[1] Marx: *Capital*, Edition 1, Vol. 1, p. 344.

appearance, this wage-labor system recognizes that laborers are free people and they own their own labor-power, but the "hunger discipline" forces laborers must sell their labor as a commodity. As labor becomes a commodity, the currency can be converted into capital and capitalist private ownership based on appropriating-gets-surplus value of workers can be generated; on the contrary, capitalist private ownership becomes the basis of the above wage-labor system and the most important condition in which workers must sell their labor. As pointed out by Marx in analyzing the relationship between capitalist private system and wage-labor system: "Capital is based on the premise of wage labor, and wage labor is based on the premise of capital. Both of them are mutually restricted and mutually generated.[1] In the slave system and the feudal system, the laborers did not have (in whole or in part) personal freedom, and slaves and peasants themselves also (partially) were the objects owned by the ruling class (slave owners or feudal landlords). Marx had evaluated the slaves as: "there the worker is nothing but a living labor-machine, which therefore has a value for others, or rather is a value" (Marx, 1973, pp. 464-465). As one side of capitalist private ownership, the wage labor system not only ensures the subordination of labor to capital, but also provides a bigger space and motivation or pressure for regional mobility of workers and improvement of workers' skill and quality.

Below, I will analyze the constant development and deepening of the historical development of capitalist private ownership.

2. The Historical Evolution of Capitalist Private Ownership Forms

In the 17th and 18th centuries, bourgeoisie revolutions had occurred in Western countries, which had much speeded the transition from feudalism to capitalism. However, until the mid-and-late 19th century, with the development of the industrial revolution and the completion of the reform in agricultural capitalism, the industrial bourgeoisie had generally become

---

[1] *Karl Marx and Frederick Engels*, Chinese version, Edition 1, Vol. 6, p. 490, Beijing, People's Publishing House, 1961.

the leading force of the political life, and had finally seized the control of the state power, so capitalist system was truly consolidated. In the process from capitalist consolidation to expansion, gradual evolution of the existence and realization forms of capitalist ownership spontaneously occurred, which was closely connected with the Third Industrial Revolution. This process had developed under the effect of the contradictory movement and interaction between productive forces and production relation.

As early as in the middle 19th century, Marx had described the historical role of capitalism in promoting the development of productive forces: "The productive forces created by bourgeoisie in less than a hundred years are more and bigger than all the productive forces created by all generations in the past.. Subjection of nature's forces to man, the use of machinery, application of chemistry knowledge in industry and agriculture, running of steamships, railways, the use of electric telegraphs, reclamation of the whole continent and the canalization of the rivers, and the whole population conjured out of the ground—What earlier century had even presentiment that such productive forces were sleeping in the lap of social labor?"[1] Probably, in more than a century after him, the production created by capitalism could not be expected by the people who had lived in Marx's age.

In order to comply with the requirements of the development of socialization of production, capitalist relations have indeed experienced a series of adjustments and changes and the existence and realization forms of capitalist private ownership have changed continuously, too. Those are the fundamental reasons why capitalist economy could constantly develop. The historical process of the development of capitalism itself has undergone three major changes on the basis changes in social production technologies. Three major leaps of social production have taken place; the adaptation of capitalist production relation thus private ownership form has had three major adjustments.

The first scientific-technological revolution had occurred in the period

---

[1] *Selected Works of Marx and Engels*, Edition 2, Vol. 2, p. 277, Beijing, People's Publishing House, 1995.

from the second half of the 18th century to the early 19th century. It was the period in which capitalist mode of production was established, and the invention and use of the textile machines and the steam engines were the main symbol of this scientific-technological revolution, so it can be called as the "steam era". Machine production and the emergence of mechanization had enabled the capitalist relations of production to obtain the foundation of production technologies consistent with its characteristics, so the workshop manufacture type production was gradually changed into mechanized industry, and the industrial revolution had promoted the establishment of the specific capitalist mode of production which was based on machinery. Besides a smaller railway industry, this period was mainly characterized by dominance of the light industry, especially, the textile industry. In this period, the new entry of capital investments had seldom suffered technical scale obstacles, so the family private ownership type of investments could be possible and had been very common. The ownership and use rights of capital in these enterprises were completely unified, and capitalists were both owners and operators of the capital. In the first half of the 19th century, with the development of the industrial revolution, the factory system had further spread and joint stock type of companies had already emerged in some industrial sectors. However, the form of family type private ownership had still maintained its dominant position in social production. Under the then prevailing conditions of technical level and level of productive forces, such form of ownership in which complete unity of ownership with use rights had well met capitalists' needs of organization of production process and their pursuit of surplus value and accumulation of capital, and also had laid foundation for further technical development and improvement/promotion of productive forces. However, the continuous development of socialization of production made continuous changes and caused changes in the possession form of such capital property.

The second scientific-technological revolution had started in the second half of the 19th century, mainly marked by the invention and employment of electric motors and power. Meanwhile, with the development of the exploitation of petroleum and constant development of chemical, metallurgy, automobile and other industries, social production structure in the industrialization process changed from the light industry orientation to heavy industry orientation. The new revolution in production had brought both development opportunities and challenges. Investments in the heavy chemical industry required huge amounts of capital and was characterized by scale of economic profitability, which was hard to achieve by individual private capitalists through capital accumulation. Now, the original form of family type private capital ownership could not stand against the heavy chemical industry with large-scale production. If the individual private capital(s) would not transform their original form as independent existence, they could not be able to continue to maintain or reach a higher level of socialization in production. Thus capital concentration had become an effective way and a new choice for adhering to and developing capitalist private ownership. The process of heavy industrialization—capital concentration—was inevitably accompanied by the general and faster development of joint stock companies. According to the statistics of Bailey and Means, in 1930 of the 200 largest non-bank joint stock companies in the U.S.A., "most of them had asset size over 100 million USD; among them, 15 of them had assets over 1 billion USD. The total value of assets of these 200 companies were 81 billion USD, which was about half of the total property of all the joint stock companies in the United States"[1]. Development of joint stock companies and the development of capital concentration had resulted in a change: the ownership relation of capital had achieved a new socialization—different from its previous socialization characteristics. It had been the first adjustment made by private capital in those boundaries allowed by its fundamental nature. From the end of the 19th century to the middle of the 20th century, the private monopoly financial capital which had developed together with it, began to occupy the dominant position in economic life of the capitalist society. The formation of financial capital was an inevitable result of the

---

[1] Bailey & Means: *The Modern Joint Stock Company and Private Property*, Version 1, p. 22, Taipei, Bank of Taiwan, 1981.

development of the internal contradictions of capitalist economic system succeeding the joint stock capital form. On the one hand, it was the result of further promotion and application of the fruits of the second Scientific-Technological Revolution which had enabled a comprehensive socialization of production, thus the private monopoly financial capital could respond to the requirements of further strengthening in production concentration and capital concentration and had caused the inevitable trend: establishment of large-scale or huge industrial enterprises. On the other hand, joint stock company system had not only provided the systemic foundation for the formation of monopoly, but at the same time it had enabled the expansion of individual capital(s) —caused by concentration of production and capital—to the direction of the share capital form, and thus it had greatly stimulated the inherent motive of capital expansion. Therefore, we can say a new round of a higher level of capital concentration process had become an inevitable trend of capitalism. The enterprises controlled by private monopoly capital were corporations composed of corporations, trusts merged by other trusts, thus attaining multiple powers of a joint stock company. The further expansion of capital had promoted the integration between the bank monopolies and the industrial monopolies. Therefore, naturally the financial capital embodies a higher degree of socialization of ownership relation—more profound than the share capital form. It had promoted the possession and use relation of capital to a higher socialization level, which had enabled the capital fully utilize the fruits of the Second Scientific-Technological Revolution and had thus promoted the development of social economy.

The Third Scientific-Technological Revolution had started in the second half of the 20th century after World War II. Its main mark had been the information technology revolution represented by computers, the development and utilization of nuclear energy, space technology marked by the launch of man-made satellites, bio-engineering technology marked by the success of the test of recombinant DNA and invention and use of a series of high technology like synthetic materials. Modern science and technology had achieved a rapid development in the 50 years. New high-tech revolution had changed, optimized and enriched several elements of productivity. The industrial structure had transformed from labor-intensive to capital-intensive and further to knowledge and technology-intensive structure. High-tech sectors had rapidly developed and increasingly become the locomotive of the development of the economy. The social and economic life in the developed capitalist countries had been fully modernized, the increase in the socialization of production had reached to a unprecedented degree, and the enormous expansion and increase of capital investment risks had caused the necessity for state involvement in order to adjust the social and economic life. Under the new conditions of rapid development of production and the economic cycle factor, the states in the advanced capitalist countries were not only employed with limited functions as effecting government transfer payments and planning and implementing financial, monetary and macro-economic policy measures. Now the states were expected to directly undertake capital investments in research and development of science and technology and several industrial production sectors and thus attain a new form of capital which was owned by capitalist states; this was another adaptation to the continuous development of the socialized production. Therefore, during this period, state owned capital had enjoyed a fast development and had undertook new functions in combination and co-operation with private monopoly capital covering all aspects of social reproduction, so a new situation had occurred in which states were bound to adjust the social economy. At the same time, due to enormous increase of the investment risks and enormous development of credit and financial markets, the investment ability of the private capital owners had manifested obvious signs of inefficiency; to control the risks arising in the financial markets had become impossible; the ability to avoid investment risks by themselves alone had become extremely harder; therefore the private capital(s) had to entrust financial institutions for their further investments, so **a new form, corporations becoming shareholders of financial institutions, had encountered a rapid development**. "According to statistics, between 1987 and 1989, American institutional investor companies had possessed for more than 50% of the shares in the four segments of corporations including the biggest 50, the biggest 100, the biggest 250 and the biggest 500. In the remaining lower segments of corporation groups (the biggest 750 and the biggest 1000), the possession of shares holding were under 50% but above 40%"[1] So, we can say that corporation capital form, we have just defined, and state capital form had been another two major adjustments with which capital ownership relation had tried to respond to the development requirements of socialization of production and naturally had resulted in a further socialization of the capitalist ownership relation. The socialization of the ownership relation was a necessary adaptation to the requirements of socialization of production and had played an active role in the fast economic growth in the advanced capitalist countries in the post-war period. This period is the period during which private monopoly capitalism was transformed to state monopoly capitalism and at the same time to corporation type of monopoly capitalism.

The three scientific-technological revolutions have promoted the production to higher levels of socialization. The contradiction between production socialization and private appropriation pushes these constant self-adjustments in the capital ownership relation in the boundaries allowed by the fundamental characteristics of capitalism/capital with an aim to constantly appropriate the fruits of the advances in socialized production. Then, in the contemporary society, especially with the emergence of "new economy" in the developed capitalist countries led by the United States, have the fundamental nature of capitalist ownership relation and the core of capitalist production relation system changed? I offer the readers the following analysis as an answer to this question.

3. The Fundamental Nature of Contemporary Capitalist Ownership System

Lenin had once offered a sharp analysis: "When concentration is

---

[1] Gao Feng, etc.: *A Study on Ownership of the Developed Capitalist Countries*, Version 1, pp. 64-65, Beijing, Tsinghua University Press, 1998.

developed to a certain stage, it can be said that it is easier to progress naturally to a monopoly. Because it is easy for dozens of large enterprises to reach an agreement. On the other hand, it is just this large scale of the enterprise that causes the difficulties of competition and the new trend of monopoly."[1] Here, Lenin had analyzed monopoly as an inevitable trend of capital form change after capital concentration. When we observe the contemporary capitalist society, through its historical evolution, we can see that it has gradually formed several side-by-side ownership structures: with private monopoly capital ownership as dominant form, capitalist private ownership as the main body, capitalist state ownership as supportive and cooperative ownership and other ownership forms as complementary. Next, we will first review the developments in the contemporary capitalism.

Let's take USA as an example, in 1901, there was only one manufacturing company possessing assets of more than one billion USD; in 1970 the number was increased to 102, and in 1980 the number was increased to 291. By 1986, the big corporations possessing assets more than one billion USD dollars accounted for nearly 1: 200 of the total number of the companies in the total manufacturing sector, but their total asset amount and total profit amount respectively accounted for 69.9% and 69% of the total amount of assets and profit amount of the whole manufacturing sector. In the 1980s, the asset amount of the largest 100 industries in the U.S.A had increased from 760 billion USD to 1,540 billion USD. Their total assets compared (as a proportion) with the total assets of the largest 500 industrial companies had risen from 65. 0% to 74.1%. The total assets of the largest 10 industrial companies had increased from 280 billion USD in 1980 to 750 billion USD in 1988, and their total assets compared (as a proportion) with the largest 500 industrial companies had risen from 23.9% to 36.3%.[2] Also in the United States, in 1992, total assets of the largest 500 companies was 2,500 billion USD, and the average asset of each company was 5.1 billion

---

[1] *Selected Works of Lenin*, Edition 3, Vol. 2, p. 585, Beijing, People's Publishing House, 1995.

[2] Lin Huici, Zhang Tongyu, Li Yuanheng: *The Theory and Practice of Modern Capitalist Economy*, Edition 1, p. 34, Tianjin, Tianjin People's Publishing House, 1999.

USD; but in 1998, the total assets of the largest 500 companies had increased to 14,280 billion USD, and the average asset of each company had reached 28.5 billion USD, displaying a 5.6 times increase figure. The proportion of sales income of the largest 500 companies compared to GDP had increased from 39.3% in 1992 to 67.4% in 1998, an increase of 28.1%.[1] Such large-scale concentration of production provides important conditions for the monopoly.

Since the first large-scale company merger wave had occurred during period between the late 19th century to the early 20th century, three more merger waves had successively occurred during the 1920s, 1950s and 1980s. Driven by high-tech revolution based on information technology in the middle and late 1990s, the fifth wave of enterprise mergers had occurred again. This time, it was characterized by transnational mergers, and after these mergers and acquisitions, much bigger companies with assets of tens of billions USD or 100 billion USD had emerged. In 1990, global merger and acquisition cases had increased up to over 10,000 involving 400 billion USD transaction value; in 1995, the merger and acquisition cases were 20,000 involving 800 billion USD transaction value; within 5 years, both the number and the amount of transaction had doubled. In 1998, their volume had seen an increase by 50% compared to that in 1997, and had reached to more than 2,000 billion USD. In 1999, it was the year which reached a record high amount, with a transaction amount of merger and acquisition, officially announced, as 3,290 billion USD, with an increase of 32%. In 2000, global merger and acquisition transactions had amounted to 3,410 billion USD. Later the increase rate began to decline and it was only 3.6% on yearly basis. In 2001, the scale of merger and acquisition cases decreased sharply, and there were only 17 cases with a total amount of 40 billion USD. Then the fifth enterprise merger and acquisition wave had come to an end gradually after the economic boom.[2]

---

[1] Du Chuanzhong: "The Reason and Trend of the Rise of Concentration Degree in the Western Countries since the 1990s", in World Economy, 2002 (5).

[2] The year of the Mega merger, Fortune, January 11, 1999, pp. 62-67. Zhu Wei: "The Trend and Enlightenment of Global Enterprise Merger and Acquisitions in 2001", in World Economic Research, 2002 (3).

A series of data above show that the developed western capitalist countries still manifest a constant increasing development trend of monopoly in modern times. Then, concerning the property with such high monopolization, could the capitalist ownership relations record any change? Let's look at enterprise organizational forms in capitalist countries. The enterprises in modern capitalist countries can be divided into sole proprietorship, partnership and joint stock companies. The means of production of sole proprietorship enterprises and partnerships belong to individual capitalists. Sole proprietorship enterprise includes individual proprietorship enterprise, family enterprise, etc., most of which are natural person enterprises and don't have legal personality. In the United States, sole proprietorship enterprises are those with the largest number. According to the date from Statistical Abstract of the United States, in 1980, sole proprietorship enterprises have accounted for 78% of the total number of enterprises. Partnership is an enterprise that is jointly invested and operated and individuals jointly share the profits of the enterprises having generally two or more share owners. The number of such enterprises is small and it accounts for 7.5% of the total number of enterprises in the United States. It is mainly some advertising firms, law firms, retail stores and stock brokerage companies, etc. In 1980, the number of joint stock companies has accounted for 14.5% of the total number of enterprises in the United States.[1] The vast majority of the above large enterprises with monopolistic position are the monopoly enterprises of the joint stock company form. The so-called corporation stockholding is the newest form of private monopoly capital ownership in today's capitalist society. It can be explicitly seen that capitalist private monopoly capital ownership form is only changed from capitalist individual or collective appropriation form—wide-spread forms in the era when Marx had lived—to social forms of capital appropriation under the control of capitalists and the bourgeoisie. From the above-mentioned facts, we can easily draw the following conclusions:

---

[1] Zhang Tongyu: *Social Capital Theory: Study on the Socialized Development of Industrial Capital*, p. 198, Jinan, Shandong People's Publishing House, 1999.

First of all, private monopoly capital is still the core of the main foundation and production relations system of the contemporary capitalist economy. As the basic form of contemporary monopoly, mixed conglomerates have assumed an extremely important position in the capitalist economy. For example, in the mid 1980s, the sister enterprises of the six major monopolistic financial groups "Manager Association" accounted for less than 1:10,000 of the total number of private enterprises, but their sales and total assets were equivalent to 15.7% and 15.1% of the same indicators of all the industrial enterprises in Japan. If subsidiaries and affiliates under their control were included in the calculation, their total assets would account to 34% and their sales turnover to 27.6%.[1] Since the 1990s, the large-scale mergers had enabled capitalist monopoly to have further development. Let's take USA as an example, in 1992, the total assets of the 500 largest companies were 2,550 billion USD. In 1998, the amount increased to 14,281 billion USD, an increase of 5.6 times. The proportion of sales incomes of 500 large companies to GDP was 39.3% in 1992, and reached to 67.4% in 1998, an increase of 28.1%.[2] Progress of science and technology, expansion of international markets and intensification of worldwide competition are the results of the function of private monopoly capital to a great extent. In other words, they are the manifestation   of the strengthening of the function of private monopoly capital. We should not deny that middle and small capital(s) and small and medium-sized enterprises in developing countries account for the majority of enterprises, and they play an important role in the employment, and at the same time developing countries also possess broad market potentials to be developed and they also have a large investment space which could attract a substantial amount of excess capital from developed countries. But the real facts show that these economic factors haven't taken a leading role in the international economic development and growth. Private monopoly capital still remains as the core of capitalist relations of production.

[1] Sun Zhizhong: *Japanese Monopoly Capital*, pp. 1-2, Beijing, People's Publishing House, 1985.

[2] Du Chuanzhong: "The Reason and Trend of the Rising of Concentration Degree in the Western Countries since the 1990s", in *World Economy*, 2002 (5).

Since the times of Marx, what has changed is only the organization form and scale level of capitalist private appropriation, however, the nature of private appropriation has not been changed. As Marx had predicted: "With regard to the social form of stock system, it has to say that it has made some changes in the capitalist production relations.... However, the transformation itself to the share form is still limited to the boundaries of capitalism; therefore, this transformation has not overcome the opposition of wealth as the nature of social wealth and that as the nature of private wealth, but only developed such opposition in new forms."[1]

Secondly, the further capital concentration formed by group ownership form is the basic condition for capital to realize monopoly economy in contemporary capitalist economic life. In the case of excluding agreements, capital cannot have the strength to control the production and markets, so it becomes a decisive factor to attain a corresponding scale, and the (group ownership of) capital groups with private appropriation of means of production as a more solid foundation for its operations and socialized capital ownership forms create new conditions for further large scale concentration of capital. Just imagine if these newer forms of capital ownership were not implemented, or if recent modern shareholding system with strict norms was not implemented, could the capital concentration with such a huge scale be realized? If such various ownership forms with multi-level separation and distinctions were not implemented, and if the separation between ultimate ownership and direct ownership was not realized, and on the same basis, if the the separation of ownership and management could not be realized, then could it be possible to reach that maximum operational independence enjoyed by today's modern shareholder enterprises and could be possible to achieve such a high optimization in their operations? All those are entirely provided by the ownership form changes and realization pattern of the contemporary capitalism, i.e. the modern shareholder system. Therefore, I suggest that the development and changes manifested as increasing influence of private monopoly capital in the contemporary world is not only the result of the

---

[1] Marx: *Capital*, Edition 1, Vol. 3, p. 497.

function of those exogenous variables such as expansion of world markets and/or capitalist state apparatus intervening into the social-economy, but also the result of the ownership form changes brought by the three industrial revolutions, and moreover, the latter one provides the most important material conditions for the former one.

At the same time, modern monopoly capital ownership form determines the new features in the capitalist competition. Competition is the external performance of the nature of capital. The existence form of capital itself is closely connected with the competition forms of capital. As free capital is corresponding to competition and monopoly capital is associated with monopolistic competition, the existence form of today's modern capital has close connection with the capital competition form. It is just the changes in the modern monopoly capital ownership forms and the changes of monopoly form incurred, today's competition between capitals has the following new features:

Firstly, according to relevant data, "since 1955, the net profit rate of manufacturing, industry and transportation industry (including mining, manufacturing, construction, utilities, transportation, communication industry, businesses and miscellaneous service industry) in the United States has shown a balance of more than 8% on the average."[1] What factors have hindered the transfer of capital and formation of this average profit rate? Obviously, it could only be attributed to monopoly formed by the strength of capital itself. It is just the strong strength of capital and it could be the result of more and more specialized high technology and management pattern that has hindered capital's re-deployment, which is characterized by hindering incremental capital investments and avoiding competition between different departments to some extent. Due to difficulties in operation or technology, the cross-industry and cross-sector mergers of capital, which is characterized by acquiring stock capital, has rarely happened in the fifth merger wave since the 1990s.

---

[1] Lin Huici, Zhang Tongyu, Li Yuanheng: *The Theory and Practice of Modern Capitalist Economy*, p. 55.

Secondly, capital competition usually does not manifest itself by the negative and conservative competition forms of monopolizing advanced technology or markets, etc. But more often it manifests itself by active progressive competition such as adopting/acquiring advanced technologies, implementing optimized management, improving service quality, improving product efficiency and product quality. This form of competition pays more attention to the production laws and market laws, so this new form of competition has the characteristics of long term vision and strategy. This change is clearly manifested as constant expansion of joint stock companies under the condition of intensified competition. Rapid increases in corporation capital and gradually gaining the control of company management have led to the result of the **"manager revolution"**. The current competition for products or markets often doesn't include price competition; instead, it includes non-price competition such as "competition for newer products, newer technologies, newer supply sources and newer organizational forms". Such non-price competition provides a decisive favorable condition for cost and product quality. This type of positive competition impacts not only the profit margin and the output margin of existing enterprises but also their basis and existence.[1]

Thirdly, the development of economic globalization determines that the today's monopoly competition to be carried out in the international sphere. Intensified monopoly and more intense competition have even caused a global overproduction.[2] International competition has also acquired such changes, methods and ways, as mentioned above. In short, the expansion of markets, improvements in the socialization of production, constant development of corporation scale towards a conceptualized monopoly, constant changes in the ownership form of modern monopoly together with the Scientific-Technological Revolution and more intense competition; all these factors in turn further promote the changes in enterprise organization

---

[1] Baran & Sweezy: *Monopoly Capita—On the Economy and Social Order in USA*, p. 74.

[2] Gao Feng: *"New Economy" or New "Economic Long-Wave"*; Zhang Yu etc.: S*enior Political Economy—The Latest Development of Marxist Economics*, p. 315, Beijing, Economic Science Press, 2002.

forms and the further evolution of capital ownership form, thus determining such an evolution process to become an inevitable trend.

Finally, the change occurred in the ruling/management form of the private monopoly capital has consolidated group ownership form of capital. This fact not only ensures that the monopoly enterprises achieve increase of profit through monopoly prices. More importantly, after constant expansion of individual capital scale, they can achieve more optimal scale economies and technological progress and thus be able to reduce their production costs to below standard ration and ensure profit rates higher than average level. And the increase of profits and expansion of enterprise accumulation determine that cross-share-holding(s) between companies can become possible and practical, and therefore contemporary capitalism can have a more obvious appearance and characteristic of group ownership form. Thus, compound form of ownership based on capitalist private ownership becomes an inevitable phenomenon of strong increase of individual private monopoly capital and change of the monopoly form.

In regard to the above discussed development and changes in the capitalist ownership forms, their historical course and on today's realities, the academic circles at home and abroad have suggested abundant views and explanations. We would like to review some of them in the next chapters. But, next I would like to comment on "qualitative change theories of capitalist ownership" and employ Marx's method to offer a further analysis.

Qualitative change theories:

Considering the fact that the developed capitalist countries continuously adjust and change the capitalist ownership relation, some scholars have put forth a variety of "qualitative change theories" on capitalist economic relations. These theories include several arguments mainly as: "democratization of capital" or "people capitalism", "management capitalism", "the western countries have being bourgeoisified", "corporate capitalism", "welfare capitalism", etc. On the other side there is also another view that advocates that the existence form of capitalist ownership remains fundamentally unchanged and that the formation factors of new society cannot appear in capitalist mode of production. In the above two main viewpoints, advocating the theory of "unchanged" actually equals to recognize the eternal vitality of capitalist ownership relationship. How can constantly ongoing capitalist ownership relationship promote the continuous development of productive forces? This view not only contradicts to the method of Marxism that analyzes capitalism with the development foresight in theory, but also is not in line with historical realities in the evolution of capitalist mode of production.

I think, "the qualitative change theories" exaggerate the further socialization of capitalist mode of production and result in some important misinterpretations. Below, I would like to comment on those ideas:

"People's capitalism": This is a summary made by some scholars according to the phenomenon of decentralization in enterprise stocks in the contemporary capitalist countries advocating that stock decentralization has led to a revolution in ownership system and income distribution, thus leading to the "democratization of capital" and "people's capitalism". On the surface, it is true that the stock decentralization in western developed countries after World War II has made new progress. Stocks are becoming further smaller and the number of shareholders has obviously increased. The governments in several countries have also promoted employee stock ownership plans, which also played a role in the expansion of this phenomenon. In the late 1980s, concerning the proportion of shareholders in the total population, it was 18% in the United States, 12% in UK, 18% in Japan and 12% in Germany. However, viewing from the internal structure of the shareholders, there is still a situation of scattered small shares and highly concentrated large shares. In the United States, 2% shareholders own 82% of company shares and 83% of municipal bonds; in the United Kingdom, there are 0.5% adults own 70% of company capital; in Japan, 4% population has 1/3 of national total; in Germany, 1.7% of the population owns 74% of the total productive capital.[1]

---

[1] Zhang Tongyu: "The Nature of Contemporary Capitalist Ownership Has Not Changed", in *Higher Education in China*, 2000 (19).

Therefore, a large amount of social wealth is still concentrated in the hands of a small number of wealthy people and the capitalist nature of property appropriation has not been changed. The small number of shares owned by workers anyhow cannot be deemed to have realized "democratization of capital" and it is impossible to change their fates, either. Workers have not appropriated a great amount of social wealth because they are holding stocks, let alone becoming the masters of capitalist society; they can only make a living mainly by selling their labor.

Contrary to "democratization of capital" and "people's capitalism", the polarization of modern capitalist society has shown an increased trend. There still exists a large population that needs relief. The contradictions between the rich and the poor are still very prominent. From 1973 to 1995, deducting inflation factors, per capita gross domestic product in the United States had increased by 36%; however, the actual wage / hour of ordinary workers had decreased by 14%. The income gap between top 10% high-income earners and 10% workers in the bottom was expanded to 11:1 in 1992 to 75:1 in 1999. The proportion of poor population living below the poverty line was 16.5% in the United States, 15% in UK and 10% in Germany.[1] These figures are even near to figures of the above-mentioned shareholders. The real purpose of governments and enterprises in western developed countries who are keen for equity decentralization and expanding shareholders of workers lies in that through issuance of small stocks social idle funds are mobilized to accelerate accumulation of company capital and equity decentralization is a method favorable to strengthen the effective control of the small number of large shareholders. And secondly "employee stock ownership" creates an illusion among the workers that the enterprise and they form a "community of interests", so it is helpful to ease the class contradiction and maintain social stability. Therefore, the viewpoint of "people's capitalism" suggesting the opinion that workers stockholding have changed the nature of capitalist ownership is quite untenable. A small number of capitalists exploiting surplus

---

[1] Zhu Guohong: "Correctly Understanding the Self-regulation, Reform and Improvement in Developed Capitalist Countries," in *Fudan Journal (Social Science Edition)*, 2000 (6).

labor of the vast working population is still the fact in today's capitalist countries.

The viewpoint of "management capitalism": The viewpoint that the so-called "manager revolution" has led to "management capitalism" is an argument made by some scholars according to some phenomena brought by separation of ownership and management rights in the joint stock company. They have also admitted that because the development of joint stock company has created a "manager class", "manager class" can be regarded as "an agent of the people". However, as we deepen the analysis, we can see that as possessors of surplus value, the status of capitalists has not been changed at all, and under the joint stock company system, the nature of capital ownership has not been changed either. First of all, capital owners haven't let the power passing to another hand. Under the condition of separation of capital ownership and management rights, the operational functions actually implemented by capitalists in the past are transferred to pure managers, and owners of capital are transformed to pure money capitalists. Accordingly, in the micro-economic level in the enterprise there are three basic powers that are mutually connected: capital ownership, control rights and management rights. The separation of capital management rights and ownership means that the owners of capital have left the production process, and don't directly engage in business activities, but the shareholders have not lost the ownership of capital, and the big shareholders still enjoy the unique governance structure in the joint stock company and hold the corporate control rights. The development goals and major decisions of the company are made by major shareholders and the Board of Directors under their control, and managers only implement those decisions and organize and manage business activities. Secondly, senior managers are still part of the capitalist class. For example, in the 500 largest companies in the United States, 90% of the general managers own their company's stock, of which 75% of general managers at least own stocks above 100,000 USD, 45% own stocks of more than 500,000 USD and 30% own stocks of more than 1,000,000 USD. Another fact is that the average annual salary of general managers in 652 large companies in the United States is more than 500,000 USD, in which, the annual income of 133 general managers is more than one million USD.[1] Enterprise Manager is an occupation and managers do not purely form a separate new class; since high-level managers possess capital and obtain additional income from the profits, we can say that they belong to the class of capitalists and another part as the middle and lower level managers and general managers may belong to the wage-labor class. Today generally, the number of general managers and white-collar workers in the economy has surpassed the number of blue-collar workers. It can be related to the new internal division of labor under the condition of the development of science and technology. It is highly optimistic to argue that the "manager class" represents the interests of vast workers and has become "the agent of people". Thirdly, capital owners are the personification of the capital ownership and senior managers are the personification of capital functions. Both may have contradictions in the profit distribution and utilization, and even have conflicts for capital control rights, but still they have common attitudes, the pursuit of profit maximization of capital. In fact, after World War II, the exploitation rate of capital on wage labor has been significantly increased. In the manufacturing industry in the United States, the exploitation rate in 1950 was 111%; in 1960, it was 122%; in 1970, 141%; in 1980, 161%; in 1989, 209%.[2] These facts also explain the function of senior managers as the agents of capital appreciation and that they have not deviated from the nature of capital to become "agents of the people".

The viewpoint that "modern capitalist society has already been bourgeoisified": Western scholars that put forward that western countries have been bourgeoisified argue that the following: Firstly, the members of society with middle income in today's developed countries have become the majority. Secondly, mental workers in today's developed countries have become the majority and they possess higher intellectual properties and

[1] Zhang Tongyu: "The Nature of Contemporary Capitalist Ownership Has Not Changed", in *Higher Education in China*, 2000 (19).

[2] Zhang Tongyu: "The Nature of Contemporary Capitalist Ownership Has Not Changed", in *Higher Education in China*, 2000 (19).

are the "new ruling class". "The development of science and technology will lead to demise of the labor position in the traditional sense and result in subsequent disappearance of the working class in the traditional sense. In such case, scientists, engineers, managers and operators of automated production cannot assume the former position of the working class; instead, they will form a new 'possessor class', and to some extent, become part of the 'ruling classes'. At the same time, the middle class in the society will be increasingly expanded with constant reduction of the proletariat and the bourgeoisie. That is to say that the society will become 'middle class' society."[1] Thirdly, today's developed countries have entered the so-called "staff society". **Human Resources School,** one important school of American mainstream economics, even believes that the post-industrial trends have effectively overcome the traditional division between capitalists and workers; occupational difference caused by education has become the most convincing clue to explain the differentiation and inequality of different groups in the society; the emerging of "the new ruling elite" marks the end of traditional "ideological system". They naturally deny the decisive role of Marxist ownership of means of production in class analysis and conclude that capitalism has encountered a qualitative change. Here I would like to refer Ding Weimin's factual analysis "The Historical Process of the Development of Capitalism: Investigation Focusing on New Economy", published in *Contemporary Economic Research*, 2001 (9).

The viewpoint on bourgeoisification and the theory of three classes and opinion that the Proletariat and bourgeoisie transform to a middle class cannot explain the fact of the expansion of polarization in modern capitalism. The so-called new class formation that possesses the knowledge is misleading because the function of knowledge and information can only be realized with the combination of capital, and once it combines with capital, knowledge and information can only obey and serve the capital, or help the capital to create greater value or to assist the capital to extract more surplus value. In

[1] Brandt, and others: *The Future Socialism*, Edition 1, Preface, p. 8, Beijing, Central Compilation & Translation Press, 1994.

fact, in capitalist enterprises, the owners of means of production and their agents do not only perform power, but also employ some systems to ensure that they obtain necessary management information, and aim that employees can only obtain one-sided information, forming a condition as asymmetry of information. American sociologist Marsh has made an investigation on the management system of 48 large and medium-sized manufacturing enterprises in Japan in 1983. This investigation has also proved that the distribution of decision-making power and accordingly distribution of information are closely related to the internal hierarchy system in the Japanese enterprises.[1] In the capitalist economy, that using power to form a system for controlling information is an important mean for the bourgeoisie to maintain its ruling position. I think, to draw a rigid and an absolute division line between the owners of material capital and owners of human capital argued by "human capital" theory is also misleading. Without owners of human capital, owners of means of production can organize production by themselves; without means of production, owners of human capital cannot form a true labor force.

Therefore, it is un-scientific to neglect the appropriation means and quantity of means of production to offer a true class analysis in the capitalist society. Separated from means of production, labor cannot produce an economic value; as a reality in the history of socio-economic formations different relationship (form of union) between men and the means of production is still the main reason that forms the wage-labor system. Capitalist ownership is a form in which laborers themselves are not owners and the owners themselves are not laborers. In this form the union (relationship) of laborers and means of production appears as the union of the laborers and the owners of means of production. The laborer is the owner of his labor capacities. As Marx had commented: "the process therefore that clears the way for the capitalist system, can be none other than the process which takes away from the laborer the possession of his means of production; a process that transforms, on the one hand, the social

---

[1] Ding Weimin: "The Historical Process of the Development of Capitalism: Investigation Focusing on New Economy", in *Contemporary Economic Research*, 2001 (9).

means of subsistence and social means of production into capital, on the other hand, transforms immediate producers into wage-laborers" (See Marx, 1954, p.714) If capitalist ownership of means of production is not abolished, capitalism's basic economic relation will not change. And on the other side after the capitalist ownership of means of production is abolished, the future communist ownership will realize again the situation that unites the laborer and owner of the means of production into one, but this time on a higher base: "It is the negation of negation: This does not re-establish private property for the producer, but gives him individual property based on the acquisition of the capitalist era, i.e. based on co-operation and the common possession of the land and of the means of production." (Marx, 1954, pp. 763-764)

Although the middle class of contemporary capitalist society has certain material wealth, their social status indeed has not changed and is manifested as follows: Firstly, as to the relation of social means of production, the "white-collar workers" are all workers that are separated from the means of production. Secondly, from the status in the social production relations system, even though most of them engage in mental work, they are controlled by capital, have no independent status and all are workers that directly or indirectly provide capital with surplus value. Thirdly, when we consider their means or ways of obtaining share of wealth, in the modern capitalist production enterprises, with the exception of a small number of senior employees, the majority of scientific and technical personnel, managers and professionals still rely on hiring their labor in exchange for wages. Their labor is an indispensable part of the whole commodity production process, and their wages still belong to variable capital of capitalists. Therefore, considered from the characteristics of appropriation of means of production, as a class, the middle class does not exist, so of course, it may be important for them to become the ruling class of capitalist society.

Regarding the viewpoint of "corporation capitalism": Those who advocate "corporation capitalism" argue that due to the new corporate shareholder form of the corporate enterprises and financial institutions, corporate enterprises have become the real owners of capital and actual controller of the social economy and corporations have replaced the powers and roles of capitalists. Furthermore, some scholars further put forward that the fundamental nature of contemporary capitalist ownership is corporate capitalism, and not a capitalism with private monopoly capital ownership as the main orientation.

After World War II, the companies, enterprises, banks, cooperatives, insurance companies and various financial institutions in the western developed countries had successively bought shares and the stockholding rate of the corporation has constantly risen. In the United States, it rose from 8% in 1952 to 46 % in 1996, in Japan, it rose from 35% in 1950 to 67% in 1995 and in Germany, it rose from 52% in 1960 to 72% in 1995. Shares of corporate type of shareholders have rapidly increased.[1] Through various forms, private property is concentrated in social economic organizations, and is transformed to a corporation capital form. In such conditions, personal property ownership and enterprise equity are separated and individual shareholders are transformed into corporate shareholders. Moreover, due to multi-layered pattern of private capital ownership and economic activities in the reality, it results in the restriction on the power of private capital owners. However, it cannot be concluded that the fundamental nature of capitalist relationship has changed.

First of all, corporation capital is bound to be based on private capital. The property controlled by the economic organization as a legal person comes from the private property, and corporations are not the ultimate owner of capital. Therefore, the ownership nature of corporation capital in the last analysis belongs to the category of ownership of private capital.

Secondly, the nature of capital functions carried out by corporation capital as a collective body of private property has not changed, and corporate bodies and their representatives only act as agents of the owner of private capital to engage in business activities. The activity aim of corporation capital has no essential difference with private capital.

[1] Zhang Tongyu: "The Nature of Contemporary Capitalist Ownership Has Not Changed", in *Higher Education in China*, 2000 (19).

Thirdly, the ultimate beneficiary of corporation capital operation is still the owner of private capital. Private capital not only holds the ultimate ownership of corporation capital, but also owns the income ownership of capital profits.

In short, in order to meet the objective requirements of the development and progress of the socialization process of production, the various changes and further socialization of the capitalist property relation manifests just a self-adjustment realized in the scope and boundaries allowed by the nature of capitalist private ownership. It has not indeed changed the nature of capitalist ownership.

Regarding the viewpoint of "welfare capitalism": The scholars that hold the viewpoint of "welfare capitalism" believe that the social security systems like the annuity system (also known as the pension system, unemployment insurance and medical insurance) implemented in the developed countries dissolve the contradiction between labor and capital, thus providing conditions for the stability and development of capitalist relations of production. Therefore, they have termed today's capitalism as "welfare capitalism".

We should see that the welfare policies implemented in modern capitalist countries indeed have played a role in varying degrees in easing the class contradictions in the capitalist society. However, this policy does not fundamentally overcome the class contradiction of capitalism. Only from the limitations of the implementation of these policies, this viewpoint is hard to set up. Let's take the pension system of capitalism as an example. Even in those countries with high welfare, the coverage of pension system rarely reach 100%. Moreover, the pension programs usually only cover the citizens who work in the formal sectors. The so-called formal sectors refer to state organs, institutions, companies, enterprises and other departments, and don't include many small individual companies, individual farmers and agricultural workers and members of other non-constant employment.[1] Because the pension program is generally divided into mandatory participation and non-

---

[1] Zhang Junshan: *The Pension System in Capitalism*. Gao Feng: *The Economic Relations and Operating Characteristics of Modern Capitalism*, p. 79, Tianjin, Nankai University Press, 2000.

mandatory participation, different pension programs have different content coverage. Mandatory pension program has looser provisions for the granting of benefactions; at the same time, because of its mandatory provisions, members of these programs normally can enjoy the right of relatively small amount of retirement income for the old age years. As for the non-mandatory pension program, it is mainly a private pension plan held by an employer, and those who obtain income rights are usually only a part of members. For example, a study in 1972 showed that only half of the full-time workers in the private sector in the United States could join a private pension program, and among those participants, only 1/3 of them had the right to enjoy retirement income in the old age.[1] It can be seen that the so-called welfare capitalism is not the welfare paradise where everyone is assured.

In fact, let's still continue to take the pension system as an example. The pension arrangements under capitalism must be adapted to the requirement that capital appropriates surplus labor as well. Therefore, the expansion of pension coverage is conditional. Considering the reality that standard government pension coverage is much wider than private pension coverage, it reflects that the closer it gets to capitalist production process, the more its characteristics reflect the requirements of capital. And when observed from the perspective of the conditions required for benefits, it also reflects this reality. Government pension programs reflect the capital's requirement for a more stable social environment from the social perspective, therefore, participants of this pension program should meet the requirement of capital from many aspects such as years of service, premium payment years and the continuity of employment to obtain the conditions of receiving retirement income in the future.

From another perspective, some scholars think that pension fund companies are the main shareholder corporation of the joint stock companies, and the beneficiaries and owners of pension fund companies are workers and employees, therefore, they argue that the pension fund is a form of laborer's

---

[1] Zhang Junshan: *The Pension System in Capitalism*. Gao Feng: *The Economic Relations and Operating Characteristics of Modern Capitalism*, Edition 1, p. 82.

ownership. From perspective of the characteristics of the pension fund system itself, such view is weak, let alone the coverage of pension program. This is because:

Firstly, from perspective of the operators of the pension funds, as an investment institution, most of the assets of the pension funds are owned by individuals, but the corporation capital ownership is not a direct private capital ownership. Compared to individual direct investors, pension fund is a joint capital form. The stock owners of pension funds not only stay away from the production and operation process, but also don't directly hold shares of joint stock companies. In the direct private capital ownership, the personification form of corporation capital is individual capitalists; in the corporation shareholder ownership(joint capital), control management and personification form of corporation capital are senior managers of the joint stock companies. The joint capital of pension fund form is the concrete manifestation of socialization of capital appropriation, and here senior managers are an important part of joint capitalists. Therefore, at present, corporation capital ownership is the specific performance of collective ownership of private monopoly capital under the conditions of modern capitalism.

Secondly, studied from the perspective of employees that participate in the pension fund company, it is still a saving behavior for them. Through this behavior, employees exchange one part of their immediate income for a future income. However, pension fund operators are generally big financial enterprises controlled by monopoly capital. Those financial institutions clearly deem pension fund management as their part of their operation and an important way to improve the profit rate. In the real practice, in the initial stage of pension funds, the difference between funds absorbed from members and the daily costs and monthly pension payments can be seen as the capital to begin with, which is owned by and available for big financial institutions for a relatively free use in investment. And the participants of pension have no right to inquire all those at all. Therefore we say that the mechanism of pension fund has transformed a part of funds originally owned by the workers to appropriation of big financial institutions (although the nature of the pension fund itself is not private), and these financial institutions use these funds to acquire shares of some other big companies again. Therefore, the factual specific analysis also shows that the development of corporate stock ownership such as pension fund does not weaken and change the monopoly capital ownership; instead, it further strengthens such ownership. Meanwhile, it also effects some changes in the internal structure of monopoly capital ownership. The original two-tiered structure, that is, the big capitalists possessing the ultimate ownership and control rights of capital whereas business operators grasping the capital operation right, is gradually evolved into the three-tiered structure where the financial capitalists grasp the ultimate ownership of a part of capital, the big capitalists and big financial institutions jointly hold the control right of this part of capital plus the ultimate ownership and control right of another part of capital originally owned by them and as a third party the enterprise operators grasp the capital operation right. In such a new ownership structure, big capitalists are still in the core position. It is through this increasingly complex ownership structure that monopoly capitalists control the developed capitalism and the advanced productive forces in advanced capitalist countries and realize their rule over social and political life.

After the above explanations on the changes and evolution in capitalist ownership, we need to delve in two other aspects. The relation of ownership changes with the internal law in the evolution of capital forms. And we should conduct a deeper analysis on the ownership structures.

II. The Ownership Structures in Contemporary Capitalist Countries

In the production relations, the ownership of means of production plays a basic and decisive role. Any society is a complex system of production relations. There are various ownerships of the means of production with different natures. From the perspective of historical development, the current society usually contains the remains of the former social relations of production and the budding of relations of production of the future society, so the co-existence of several ownerships of the means of production with different natures is inevitable. However, in the society with co-existence of multiple ownerships of means of production, there is always one form of ownership which plays a basic or dominant role. The relations of production composed of it become the economic base of society and determine the basic nature and characteristics of that society. For example, the history of the industrial revolution for nearly one hundred years from the second half of the 18th century to the first half of the 19th century was the period that the capitalist mode of production was gradually established. During that period, the de-centralized individual capital form and the factory system took a dominant position in social industrial sectors. In the second half of the 19th century, modern industrial share capital replaced the individual capital and the joint stock companies replaced the factory system to occupy the dominant position in social production. The drive of the second technological revolution and the development of production concentration and capital concentration made the financial capital of private monopoly formed in the end of the 19th century and early 20th century which gradually assumed a dominant position, and after the World War II, the corporation capital of private monopoly rapidly rose and assumed a dominant a position. Meanwhile, it should be noted that state-owned capital, during a certain period, rapidly developed to become a capital form which took important position in social production. Although capitalist cooperative economy has not taken a dominant position since its birth and during later periods, it can still be evaluated as a new micro-economic pattern, and it is also an ownership relationship of means of production with certain characteristics.

Therefore, under capitalist conditions, the private ownership of capitalist means of production is the foundation, but there are also various specific forms such as individual capital, share capital, private monopoly financial capital, private monopoly corporation capital, state-owned capital and the cooperative economy, etc. Especially in the conditions of modern capitalism, the emergence of the ownership structure with capitalist private monopoly capital ownership as the dominant form, capitalist private ownership as the mainstay, bourgeoisie state ownership as the assistance and cooperative ownership as complementary is not accidental. It is the inevitable result of movement and role of the inherent contradiction of capitalism (especially the basic contradiction). These will form the content of our following analysis.

1. Individual Capital Ownership

The so-called individual capital ownership does not just refer to capital ownership operated by one person, but also includes the cases of a partnership. Neither sole proprietorship nor partnership separates the right of ownership and operation right. It refers to capital ownership that the owners directly operate and manage and directly enjoy the right of claim for surplus. Therefore, the basic structural characteristics of individual capital ownership are that ownership structure is single and the ownership and management are combined together. Here a capitalist is both the owner and manager. He owns all the property rights of the enterprise, including business the decision-making right, supervision and management right, surplus claim and property transfer right and the property right owned by him is complete. The identity of authority and owner of the enterprise is unified, therefore the nature of capitalist private ownership has got its most complete manifestation in this form of ownership.

In the history, the period when the producer enterprises with individual capital ownership structure dominated has gone through Western European capitalism workshop handicraft from the middle of the 16th century to the mid-18th century and the factory system in the form of machine production from the late 18th century to the early 19th century. Based on the same premise, there are also some differences between the ownership structures of the two. Handicraft workshop is a production organization based on manual labor technology, in general, it uses a smaller quantity of capital and the scale of enterprise is small; usually, it adopts a sole proprietorship, and the capital ownership right and management right are completely unified; the internal management structure of the enterprise is simple and does not have complicated hierarchy. Factory system is the enterprise system formed on the basis of the machine industry. From the very beginning, the amount of capital that it needs is much bigger than handicraft workshop and the production scale of the enterprise is bigger; in the case of basic single structure of capital ownership, as a result of the development of credit system, the capitalists have made greater use of loan capital, and thus the separation between ownership capital and function capital is not an individual phenomenon. Due to the need of expansion of production scale and improvement of technology level, the functions of management and supervision of production are further developed. The management departments of the enterprises have began to increase and the hierarchy also becomes increasingly complicated.

In the period of handcraft workshop period, capitalist relations of production has been formed, this is because: Firstly, the contradictory relation between capital and wage labor has been formed, and workshop handicraft industry has realized the separation of labor and capital. At the beginning, the free workers used their own tools to produce for businessmen at home, and later they became tenants that used working tools owned by other people and paid a use fee and lost their own means of labor, and finally they were concentrated in the manufacturer's workshops and became wage labor that relied on selling their labor to get a salary. Secondly, due to development of production socialization and development of capitalist private ownership, the attribute of private nature and social nature of capital was also established manifesting itself as the contradiction between private production and product sales. The capitalists could no long deem the product sales issue as the biggest issue like the previous masters of workshops. Thirdly, the property right relationship of the workshop handicraft industry reflects the essential characteristics of capitalist private ownership that capital ownership and capital function are unified. The capitalists are both workshop owners and the actual operators. The private right of capital is fully reflected here. But the workshop handcraft industry can neither grasp all of social production nor change social production fundamentally. Its relatively narrow technological base is not only contradicted to the social demand created by itself but also incompatible with the nature of unlimited proliferation of capital. Therefore, the capital relationship at that time could not establish a material and technology foundation suitable to itself, which shows that capitalist mode of production has not been solidly established yet.

The factory system based on machine production makes the capitalist mode of production to be fully socialized. The transformation of the capitalist mode of production from the stage of manufacture to the stage of machinery or modern industry is on its way. Social productivity possesses the capacity of rapid expansion, and it is consistent with the nature of unlimited proliferation of capital. Moreover, the factory system has established the absolute rule of capital. The abilities of workers are incorporated into machines which in turn, with a new division labor process, divides the production activities of workers. Thus machines have become a powerful weapon for capital to rule workers, giving the command function and discipline necessary for the socialized production which is under the absolute authority and dictatorship of capitalists, and thus the formal subordination of labor to capital is finally transformed into the actual subordination to capital. After the capitalist mode of production is thus fully formed, the contradictions and struggles between the working class and capitalist class have been gradually increased to the major class contradiction in the then society. It is manifested by the struggles of the working class in various forms and the violent and legal intervention to such struggles by the state. Individual capital ownership is also faced with challenges of the rapid development of production socialization, that is, the increasing complexity and the huge production and labor process, requiring more and more huge property ownership as the basis. Consequently individual capital increasingly loses the ability to control the productive forces, so it is bound to develop toward socialization direction in property possession and this socialization form of property possession based on private ownership could only be the joint stock company. Therefore, the inherent dialectics of the development of capitalist mode of production is that it pushes the productive forces to full socialization, while at same time the capital itself enters into an evolution attaining a more socialized nature. Thus private capital walks to its opposite in its own development. These two processes are two railways of the one and same process.

The vast number of small and medium-sized enterprises based on individual ownership still account for the absolute proportion in the contemporary developed capitalist countries, but the production and management activities are no longer dominant in the economy. For example, in 1980, among 14.6 million industrial and commercial enterprises in the United States, 78% sole proprietorship enterprise and 7.5% partnership only accounted for 9% and 4% of the total operation revenue and the joint stock companies which accounted for 14.5% of the total number accounted for 87% of total operation revenues.[1] Moreover, small and medium-sized enterprises have a very strong instability. For example, there are 600,000 small and medium-sized enterprises started in the United States each year, but 250,000 enterprises become bankrupt or merger with others; the annual establishment rate of Japanese small and medium-sized enterprises is 7% and the annual closure rate is 5%.[2] Only a few of them can grow into big enterprises, and the majority of big enterprises adopt the form of the joint stock company.

2. Share Capital System and Its Development Forms

As an enterprise organization form, a joint stock company has a long history. The organization principles of classical commercial joint stock companies have laid the foundation for modern joint stock companies from four aspects: 1) socialization of fund-raising and diversity of forms; 2) containing relatively independent capital (independent from personal wealth); 3) family factors and personal relation factors in partnerships and unlimited companies have later begun to transform to capital co-operation factor; 4) and the principle of limited liability has begun to take shape (LTD companies). On the other hand, such companies were also the main tool for

---

[1] Zhang Tongyu: *On Social Capital: Study on the Socialization Development of Industrial Capital*, Edition 1, p. 198.

[2] Quotated from Xiao Qinfu: "The Ownership Structure of the Market Economy in Contemporary Western Countries", in *Commercial Economy Studies*, 1994 (9).

the British, Dutch, French ruling classes to carry out overseas expansion and colonial plunder. In essence, they were special integrated institutions of economy, politics and military that those countries conducted foreign expansion, therefore, at the end of the 18th century, they declined together with the commercial capitalism.

The modern joint stock companies emerged with the further development of the Second Scientific-Technological Revolution and the industrialization process. One of the features of the Second Scientific-Technological Revolution was the demand for a more solid capital base. The changes of industrial structure caused by the new scientific-technological revolution, especially the development of heavy chemical industry and transport industry technically required that new enterprises should have a huge amount of capital. The independent/individual entries into these new emerging industries by individual private capital was restricted due to their limited capital amount. The further socialization of production required that the socialization of capital accumulation must find a new form to suit this requirement, thus inevitably, the concentration of industrial capital and demutualization had shown a rapid development. Higher precision in the production technologies and professionalization of the management in the production organization also required that the actual operators of enterprises should have professional science, technology and management knowledge. And the modern factory system (stage) in which individual capitalists had only relied on private capital ownership to directly control and organize enterprises were faced with difficulties, so the separation of capital with ownership rights had become an inevitable process. Therefore, the traditional enterprise system characterized by individual ownership of private capitalists could no longer meet the development of social productive forces, i.e., social production. The socialization of capital ownership had become an inevitability to break through the quantitative restriction of individual private capital. Therefore, inevitably gradual development in the ownership relation occurred in which the joint stock company mode of production replaced the factory system mode of production.

The main features of modern joint stock companies are the solid establishment of the principle of limited liability and corporations controlling property, as well as a standardized stock system and stock transfer principles. A joint stock company is a capital concentration form that gathers scattered and independent private capital together to conduct unified operation through the issuance of stocks. Compared with single private capital, it has encountered the most obvious change in the ownership structure, which is the separation of capital ownership and capital function, i.e. the capital management right. Marx had also commented on this issue: after the emergence of joint stock companies, "the capitalists who played the role in the actual implementation were changed into simple managers, i.e. the managers of other people's capital; and on the other hand, capital owners were transformed to simple owners, as pure currency capitalists."… "And thus this capital ownership is now completely separated with its functions in the reproduction process in reality. It is just like this function is completely separated with capital ownership from managers." Once the diversification of capital ownership is developed and equity is dispersed to a certain extent, larger shareholders can control the joint stock company by lesser stocks owned by them. In Patman Report published by the Banking and Currency Committee of the House of Representatives in USA, it was revealed that as long as 5% of the stocks were grasped, the control of an enterprise could be seized. The reason is that the main purpose of many smaller shareholders is to preserve their wealth and obtain stock dividends or stock appreciation incomes, they generally don't care for the control right of the company, and cannot participate in the general assembly of shareholders, either. When the shares possessed by large shareholders are in a small amount, sometimes smaller majority shareholders also entrust the managers to vote for themselves or give major decisions for the enterprise. And in a direct sense, the result of this behavior seems to be that the managers have seized control rights over the enterprise. The influence of capital owners on the company operation is no longer directly conducted by voting with hands. However, capital owners can also use "voting with their feet" to indirectly influence the operation activities of enterprises. The constraint mode of capital owners on the operators in the company is converted to the constraint mode of reselling their stocks in the capital market. By this usual applied method the direct restraint mechanism is converted to the indirect restraint mechanism, thus ensuring that the control rights of the enterprise is ultimately grasped in the hands of the owner of big capital.[1] Such a combined form of the capital ownership, control right and operation right actually reflects the characteristics of the internal structure of modern capital ownership.

In the past, the ownership of individual private capital was a complete property right, and share capital decomposes the original ownership of private capital into two relatively independent rights. As equity, capital ownership is only a simple and incomplete legal right, and is no longer a complete property right. Thus property developed and transformed into equity is a major revolution and the first qualitative leap experienced in the development of the capital ownership relation itself. Only in share capital form, the ownership and management right of capital inevitably achieve separation and capital ownership structure is changed from a closed structure to an open structure. The openness of this capital ownership structure constitutes the necessary precondition for the large-scale concentration of capital. With increase of the development trend of production socialization, equity has the trend of increasing decentralization and capital management right has an increasing concentration trend, which shows that capital ownership relation not only has changed but also is still in a continuous development and change.

3. Private Monopoly Capital Ownership

The continuous development of modern joint stock company with the background of industrial concentration and capital concentration has resulted in capital ownership of private monopoly form. According to the stages of historical development, private monopoly capital ownership can be divided

---

[1] The "corporation control right market" theory put forward by American Economists H. G. Mannesmann discloses this process from one aspect. Gao Feng, etc.: *The Theoretical and Empirical Analysis of Merger & Acquisition of Chinese Enterprises*, pp. 40-41, Beijing, China Financial & Economic Publishing House, 2001.

into financial capital ownership form and corporation capital ownership form of private monopoly.

The financial capital of capitalist private monopoly is an economic phenomenon which emerged in the end of the 19th century. But it took a dominant position in the social economy in the first half of the 20th century, i.e. before World War II. The enterprises dominated by financial capital were corporations consisting of corporations and trusts merged by other trusts. They were huge monopoly enterprises and multi-mode of a joint stock company. As a monopoly capital form caused by the integration of industrial monopoly capital and bank monopoly capital, before World War II, finance capital's main characteristic was the family control of private capital. Bank monopoly capital and industrial monopoly capital were formed at the same time, and both of them had mutually penetrated each other and mixed to grow together. Concentration of industrial capital promoted and drove the concentration of bank capital, and the mutual penetration of industrial monopoly capital and bank monopoly capital formed a small number of large financial consortia in its formation process. In the 1890s, the high centralization of American bank capital began to take place. In the early 20th century, a situation was formed in which a small number of banks headed by the Morgan and Rockefeller with Stillman, Harriman and Kuhn–Robbie, etc. seized control on the whole banking industry around them.

The formation of financial capital mainly came from the two motive forces. On the one hand, the changes of industrialization had led to rapid development of production socialization, thus requiring the concentration of capital and further socialization. On the other hand, share capital had realized a concentration in production and capital concentration which had resulted in rapid expansion of individual capital(s) and had profoundly stimulated the inherent expansion motive of capital. To further strengthen the concentration process of capital and even form monopolies had become an inevitable target of big capitalists. Under the drive of this double dynamic, the principles and operation forms of joint stock companies were further activated and applied to form large monopoly companies through merger or by enlargement of joint stock companies. The development of industrial concentration had caused industrial capital trusts had dramatically expanded demands for bank capital. Concentration of bank capital and formation of bank monopoly made banks use their large amount of capital funds as basis to monitor and control its parent (sister) industrial enterprises, making them the actual controller of industry. Capital combination and interest combination of industrial monopoly trusts with monopolized banking industry were financial capital. Financial capital is not only an inevitable product developed by virtue of the form of the joint stock company but also embodiment of rapid expansion of capital and the nature of pursuing surplus value. Financial capital had started a new type of social relations of production, marking that capitalism was transforming from the free competition stage to monopoly stage. In the condition of monopoly capitalism, it was financial consortium formed by integration of industrial monopoly capital and bank monopoly capital that had assumed a dominant position in social economy.

Financial capital's control over the company can take a variety of ways and forms, and the most typical control form is to realize the "pyramidal" control through the "participation system". Under the conditions of decentralization of shares, the control principle of share majority no longer becomes necessary, and financial oligarchy can completely establish its control through the means of a minority shareholding. Thus through the "participation system", monopoly capitalists can control a capital amount of dozen times or even a hundred times higher than their own capital. This corporate control form of financial capital no doubt pushes the separation of share ownership and company control to a higher level. In the "pyramidal" control system, the separation of share ownership and control rights are realized through multi-levels. Under the "parent company form" the control over companies through all levels can be achieved which means all companies are highly concentrated in the hands of a small number of financial oligarchies, and boards of directors of these subordinated parent companies are only a simple tool to enable or help the concentration of control rights. Here, what is left to the parent company leadership is a kind of supervision right and the management right is exercised by the managers which is quite far from the control right. In this control system, as long as their strength is less than the financial oligarchy, not only small and medium-sized capitalists but even big capitalists can be controlled by the financial oligarchies. It can be seen that the nature of financial capital is monopoly, but it constitutes a higher level of monopoly capital form based on the mutual combination of industrial monopoly capital and bank monopoly capital.

The big corporations controlled by financial oligarchies reflect profound changes in the capital ownership relation. In the form of financial capital, the changes in capital ownership show multi-level virtual characteristics.

At the beginning, it was that money capitalists who had invested in the banks in the form of share capital. Such act had created the first tier of the virtualization of capital ownership because thus the capital was decomposed into a virtual form—stock form—and real capital ownership form constituting bank assets. Then bank capitalists had invested those assets into the industrial sectors stock in the form of share capital to combine with industrial capital, utilizing the second virtualization of equity and real capital. The basic method that monopoly capital controls other enterprises is equity participation, there appears the phenomenon of holding the stocks of other companies and a similar pattern—second virtualization of capital ownership. Therefore, a large monopoly company not only shows itself as a multi-mode of joint stock company for many parties, but it also has the same meaning in the evolution of capital ownership. Ownership of private capital, time and time again, is sublated with such a virtualization of ownership, and increasingly alienates with the real movement of capital.

In the formation process of financial capital, the changes of capital ownership relation such as: **the multi-level virtualization of capital ownership, and separation between share ownership and the capital control right, and that between capital control right and capital operation right, and the non-individualization trend of property in the formation course of big monopoly company. These steps had certainly improved the socialization degree of capital with a big leap. The**

development of production socialization pushes the development of such high-concentrated and socialized capital form of financial capital; monopolistic organizations have united similar type of enterprises and have combined these enterprises under a central management organization, thus forming a higher-level social enterprise form than the individual joint stock company. It is the nature of financial capital as **socialized capital** and monopoly company as **social enterprise** which has enabled the promotion of the rapid development of productivity. I think that in the past Marxist studies, only the monopoly character of financial capital was emphasized and that its socialization contradicting the reality was not emphasized, so these works could not scientifically and completely evaluate its historical status and its future fate.

After World War II, the financial capital in the developed countries encountered a new development. The commercial banks could no longer have an independent control right over the non-financial industry. Instead, insurance companies, pension funds and mutual funds along with commercial banks altogether jointly become big shareholders of the non-financial industry to control the industrial and commercial activities in the developed countries. But more significantly, financial monopoly capital of private capital with an individual or family characteristic had taken a back seat, various corporate institutions and corporate legal persons had become the main shareholders of companies and the corporate stockholding capital had become dominant form of capital ownership.[1] Let's follow these changes of the three most developed capitalist countries in this regard, i.e. the United States, Japan and Germany from the 1950s to the 1990s as an example. In the U.S.A between 1952 to 1996 the shares of companies were reduced from 89.7% to 49.0% and the shares of financial institutions in the companies increased from 8.2% to 46.0%. In Japan, between 1952 and 1995; the shares of individuals were reduced from 61.3% to % 22.2 and the shares of corporates increased

---

[1] Chen Juzhi: *The Development of Financial Capital after the War*. He Zili: *The Formation of Corporation Capital after War*. Gao Feng: *The Economic Relations and Operating Characteristics of Modern Capitalism*, pp. 257-348.

from 35.5% to 67.0 %. In Germany, between 1960 and 1996; the shares of individuals were reduced from 30.3% to 14.6% and the shares of corporates increased from 52.1% to 72.4%.[1]

In the form of corporation capital, compared with the financial capital stage, the shares of the large joint stock company had become more dispersed, small number holding had become a general trend in equity controlling. In fact, it's easy for people to ignore that the monopoly nature of corporation capital was further strengthened than that in the stage of financial capital. For example, in the United States, the industrial weighted average concentration degree of eight enterprises had increased to over 50% in 30 years after 1960. And the overall scale of oligopoly was also constantly expanding.[2] The difference was that legal person replaced an individual or family to become monopoly power that grasped the economic lifeblood.

There were many conditions and reasons that led to corporation shareholder form in major capitalist countries after World War II. However, after all it is the development of the basic contradiction of capitalism, and it is an inevitable result of contradictory movement between development of production socialization and capitalist private appropriation. On the one hand, with the development of scientific-technological revolution, transformation of the industrial structure and intensifying of the competition in domestic and international markets, in order to enhance their own competitive power, the requirement of enterprises for capital union and scale expansion had shown an increasingly strong trend, so it was ineluctable to re-arrange enterprise relations and at the same time form a huge demand for capital. On the other hand, in the new structure of social productive forces and the complex environment of capital markets, it became increasingly difficult for private capital owners to manage this developed social forces, and their direct investment capacity became relative declined, and they had to rely more and more on the capacity of all kinds of institutional legal persons to convert their

---

[1] Quoted from Zhang Tongyu: *Social Capital Theory: Study on the Socialized Development of Industrial Capital*, Edition 1, pp. 322-324.

[2] Du Chuanzhong: "The Reasons and Trend of Concentration of Industry in Western Countries since the 1920s", in *World Economy*, 2002 (5).

private properties into capital. These contradictions accelerated the process of corporation shareholders becoming legal persons, promoting the formation of corporation capital ownership form.

In the capital form of the institutional legal person, there can be two types of combination forms of the ownership—control right and management right of capital. Firstly, institutional shareholders adjust their shareholding structure and pursue an indirect control method against the managers of companies in accordance with changes of the capital market, so they try to reach their aims primarily by "voting with their feet". In this case, the direct control right and management right of company capital are directly held by the managers, and the ultimate ownership of company capital is separate with the direct control right and management rights. Secondly, institutional shareholders pay attention to the rights of shareholders and take the direct control method in the operation of company, and they express their wills mainly through the "voting with hands". In this case, the ultimate ownership and control right of company capital are unified, but they are separated with the management right. However, no matter what kind of separations take place; these separations manifest the fission of capital ownership relations, that is, complete property ownership relation is divided into relatively independent rights. Thus in essence, it also manifests a kind of weakening and defect of capital private property rights, and ownership of private capital is more and more weakened or degraded to a new "creditor's right". This phenomenon is more apparent in the corporation capital form. The appropriation relation is changed into a collective appropriation system of monopoly capital, and a considerable portion of private property owners as private capitalists have become merely an entire rentier class. This is the difference between corporation capital and former private capital or financial capital in terms of the ownership relation.

Corporation property ownership emerges with the joint stock company together. Corporations becoming shareholders is only an inevitable result of the development of the joint stock company. The viewpoint that thinks corporation capital violates the principle of joint stock company argues that corporation becoming shareholders makes natural person shareholders a mere figurehead and corporation capital makes the corporation existence distancing from natural persons. But this argument cannot explain that the existence of corporation capital is unreasonable. On the contrary, this phenomenon just explains that capitalist private property right system is unreasonable, and demonstrates increasingly that private appropriation of property cannot adapt to the development of socialization of production.

Corporation capital provides enterprises with expansion of the production and management scale as an advantage, and also scale economic advantage when conducting diversified operations, all of which bring those enterprises higher incomes. They own a number of stand-alone products or different operating items which enable the speed of commercial circulation to accelerate through the coordination in the enterprise. All these advantages of corporation capital promote the development of production socialization thus reflecting its superiority to the former ownership relations in the history of capitalism. However, the ownership relation of corporation capital still has obvious system defects and historical limitations. On the one hand, after all, corporation capital still has not broken away from the foundation of private ownership, its fundamental nature has not changed, the direct source of individual corporation property is still private capital and private property, and the behavior of the corporation is still constrained by the owner of private capital and reflects the interest of the owner of private capital. Such relation itself demonstrates that corporation capital is still capital and in essence, it still preserves the basic attributes of the capital relation. Though the contradiction between socialized production and capitalist private property has got a certain degree of ease in the form of corporation capital, this contradiction has not been resolved, and it is still the basic contradiction of the socio-economic structure in which corporation capital takes a dominant position. On the other hand, corporation capital ownership has not overcome the opposition between capital and labor, and the contradiction between wage labor and capital in capitalist relations is still the core relation. Such capitalist relation is manifested in all aspects of social life, and the inequality of the capitalist exploitation system and the result as the periodic contradictions due to the shortage of effective demand of society are still manifested in the corporation capital form. Such contradictions are still the main factors that impede the development of socio-economic formation of the society.

4. State Ownership

Private capitalist ownership of means of production is the basis of the capitalist production relation. Capitalism of free competition is developed into monopoly capitalism, and private monopoly capital ownership becomes the ownership form which has assumed a leading position in the 20th century. After monopoly capitalism is developed into state monopoly capitalism, the private monopoly capital ownership still remains the general basis of state monopoly capitalism, but the state ownership of means of production has become an important feature of state monopoly capitalism. State ownership also refers to the ownership relation of state-owned capital and we should clearly explain the distinction between its broad and narrow meanings. In its broad meaning, the ownership relation of the state-owned capital refers to an economic relation in which a state owns and controls or directs its assets of production and circulation and exchange relations between the sectors of the whole economic life, i.e. nearly all the operating assets. This is generally termed as state capitalism in Marxist political literature. In its narrow meaning, the ownership relation of the state-owned capital refers to the economic relation that a country owns and controls its productive assets, that is to say, the economic relation in which the state appropriates means of production, mainly by state-owned enterprises. The distinction between the broad meaning and narrow meaning is of important significance because it is only in the narrow state-owned capital form the state forms ownership relation to social means of production (not general means of labor), and only by this ownership relation has a decisive significance to the development and evolution to capitalist mode of production. Below, I will only discuss the state-owned capital ownership in its narrow meaning.

The capitalist state ownership was formed together with the bourgeoisie state, therefore, state-owned capital also obtained three corresponding forms of classical state-owned capital, modern state-owned capital and later contemporary state-owned capital in the three historical development periods of free competition capitalism, private monopoly capitalism and contemporary capitalism.

In the free competition period of capitalism, the western countries still widely believed that the market, an "invisible hand", can spontaneously realize the optimal configuration and allocation of resources. A small amount of state-owned capital did not constitute an important part of general social capital, and it mainly existed in the departments such as national defense and military industry, postal service and state-owned railways. This is the classical form of state-owned capital. On the eve of the First World War, in order to prepare for the war, Germany, Russia, Japan and other countries increased state military procurement, and established and expanded a number of steel and munitions factories through state investment or through the mode of "nationalization". Although state-owned capital made a rapid development, it obviously had a military nature and a temporary nature. The economic crisis in the capitalist world from 1929 to 1933 led to a heavy blow to capitalist economy, and meanwhile it also manifested the bankruptcy of the free market economic theory and policy. In order to get out of economic difficulties, the major capitalist countries successively adopted the state monopoly capitalist policy, strengthening the economic functions and implemented all-round social and economic interventions. In the 1930s and 1940s, state-owned capital began to develop rapidly. Also nearly in this period the transformation from the classical form of state capital to the modern form of the state capital began. During World War II, capitalist state ownership obtained a rapid development, and gradually constituted an important part of the general social capital forming the modern form of state-owned capital.

After World War II, the state monopoly capitalism was further developed in theory, policy and practice. Accordingly, the contemporary state-owned capital form had also been formed and developed. After World War II to the end of the 1970s, Austria, France, UK and Australia were the countries with a higher degree of nationalization. The nationalization of the United States was lower, and the level of the Federal Republic of Germany was between them, but was closer to the former. By the 1970s, "The fixed capital of state-owned enterprises in UK accounted for more than 40% of the total investment in the whole country and the number of employees accounted for 15.4%; the investment of the state-owned enterprises in the Federal Republic of Germany accounted for 31% of the total investment in the whole country and their employees were over 2.5 million; the state-owned enterprises in France accounted for 38% of the total investment in the whole country and the number of employees accounted for 30% of the total employees; the state-owned capital amount in the United States was 208.6 billion USD (in 1976), and employment number accounted for 16% of the total employment; the fixed capital of the state-owned enterprises in Japan accounted for 19.6%, and the number of employees accounted for 8% of the total employment in the whole country."[1] The coverage of state-owned capital is not only limited to the state-owned enterprises in the industrial field that people often recognized, but also in the tertiary industry (service industry), such as education, scientific research and public service facilities, etc., state-owned capital had also accounted for a very large proportion.

After World War II, the formation and development of the state-owned capital in the main capitalist countries have many reasons, but the most fundamental reason is still the deepening of the basic contradiction of capitalism. The further development of socialization in production objectively requires the coordination of the country's entire economic plan. Economic crisis, the role of the economic cycle and stagflation of the developed capitalist countries during the 1970s brought forward higher requirements in the degree, means and mode of the state intervention. The development of science and technology and the rise of new emerging industrial sectors started to need the support of huge amounts of capital, and ecological and environmental problems also required a well-developed social public service

---

[1] Quoted from Gao Feng, etc.: *Study on the Ownership of the Developed Capitalist Countries*, Edition 1, p. 92.

system. All these required further changes in the capitalist economic system in the permitted limits of capitalism. To establish capitalist state ownership of the means of production through the means such as nationalization is one important aspect of the changes in the capitalist economic system.

The nature of the ownership of contemporary capitalist countries is also reflected in the dual attributes of the ownership relation of state-owned capital, i.e. its direct social nature and private nature. Direct sociality means that the capital is owned by the state and is controlled and used in the whole society in accordance with the needs of the development of social production. This capital ownership form has achieved a direct social nature. Compared to various capital historical forms such as private capital, share capital, private monopoly financial capital and private monopoly corporation capital, the ownership relation included in state-owned capital has an essential difference. It is a social public ownership of the capitalists and it undermines the private ownership, negates the sacred foundation of the capitalist society and sublates the attribute of private ownership of capital. It is the advanced form of self-adjustment of capital ownership relation in the scope of capitalist mode of production. However, at the same time, the ownership relation of state-owned capital also includes profound class nature and hidden private nature. The ownership subject of state-owned capital is the state, and capitalist states are the state of bourgeoisie in essence, "having the nature of class ruling machine."[1] The state-owned capital ownership relation as determined by the nature of state has profound class attribute. On behalf of the whole capitalist class, the state appropriates and controls the means of production, so the capitalist state-owned capital ownership is a kind of ownership of "general capitalist". It maintains inherent connections with capitalist private ownership and has both class nature and private nature, which is a new ownership relation in the history of capitalism with its unique characteristics. Just for this reason, it is different from the public ownership in socialist countries, reflecting the limitations of capitalist state-owned capital.

---

[1] *Karl Marx and Frederick Engels*, Chinese version, Edition 1, Vol. 17, p. 356, noted by the editor, Beijing, People's Publishing House, 1963.

Same as nationalization of the private economy, privatization of state-owned economy had also appeared a long time ago. After the First World War, a wave of privatization of state-owned enterprises appeared in a number of capitalist countries. In the end of 1970s, especially after 1986, a wave of privatization rose in the developed capitalist countries again. For example, from 1979 to the end of 1985, British Government sold the shares of state-owned enterprises to individuals with a revenue of 10 billion pounds, accounting for more than 1/3 of the total capital of state-owned enterprises. In 1987, more than 1,080 enterprises from 14 economic sectors in France were privatized. After this wave, it was spread to other countries in Western Europe and the United States, Canada, Japan and other countries. After the temporary suspension due to the stock market crash worldwide in October 1987, it continued in the 1990s.[1] Its direct reason was the "stagflation" phenomenon—production stagnation and inflation co-existent—which the capitalist economies generally faced in the 1970s and the rise of neo-conservative economic liberalism ideology. Sale of partial state-owned enterprises to the private sectors aimed not only to alleviate the financial burden of the country, but also to receive an amount of income to overcome financial difficulties. The fundamental reason of the wave of privatization was the development of science and technology and the adjustment of the industrial structure. The leading and dominant position occupied by traditional industrial sectors in social production was increasingly replaced by new emerging industrial sectors. The traditional state-owned enterprises gradually lost the necessary social economic and technological basis of their existence and development, and also partially lost the foundation and status and role of leading the industry. However, the structure pattern of state-owned capital was formed by the behavior of government instead of market behavior. Therefore, the re-structuring of state-owned capital cannot be spontaneously adjusted through the market mechanism, and it can only be realized through the policy behavior of government.

---

[1] Zhang Tongyu: *Social Capital Theory: Study on Socialized Development of Industrial Capital*, pp. 371-372.

It should be noted that existence and development of capitalist state-owned economy is a result of objective necessity. When the new contradiction arising from privatization and economic liberalization sharpens and when factors of state-owned economy are accumulated to a certain extent, in the future it may probably lead to a new round of nationalization fever.

5. Cooperative Ownership

The cooperatives in capitalist countries are different from the enterprise form of a joint stock company which occupies a dominant position. The cooperative system contributing to the formation of cooperatives is different from the enterprise system of corporate system, and the ownership of cooperatives is different from the ownership form of private capital ownership. To analyze this form of ownership presents a particular significance for understanding the development of capitalist ownership relation.

The cooperation as the germination of cooperatives refers to cooperation in economic relations and it is an economic activity for the direct purpose of mutual benefits on the basis of individually owned resources. As the cooperative behavior for the purpose of mutual assistance becomes regular, especially the role of some mutual aid activities in the social economic activities becomes increasingly important, and people cannot use other economic forms to achieve these purposes, these acts are generally fixed in some system or contract form in a long or short term, and thus a number of economic organizations emerge with the nature of cooperatives. For example, before 2,000 BC, there was an embryonic form of common farming system in Babylon. In ancient Chinese, there were cooperative associations for the purpose of mutual assistance. However, these did not form a relatively stable system with definite connotation in ancient history. More often, they were like a kind of cooperative behavior.

In the 1760s and 1770s, cooperatives in the modern sense appeared in UK, France, Germany and other countries. A variety of the embryonic forms of cooperatives appeared successively. During the same period, the

United States, Japan, Italy and other countries also had different cooperative organizations. However, they were not typical modern cooperatives or the representative forms and there was no universally recognized management, organization and operating principle to be followed by future generations. By 1844, the British Society of Equitable Pioneers Roach Dell was established and it became the most representative cooperative in the modern sense that was universally recognized. Since then, cooperative model was gradually expanded to other countries in Europe from the middle and late 19th century. From the late 19th century to the early 20th century, it was quite spread in North America, Latin America, Australia, Asia and Africa. By 1937, the member of such cooperatives around the world had reached 100 million; during World War II, although their development was disturbed, by 1951, the members of cooperatives throughout the world had been restored to 120 million; in 1982, it had increased to 326 million; in 1984, the member of the international cooperative alliance had increased to 500 million; by 1995, the members of international cooperative alliance had reached 750 million or more. For example, in the United States, cooperatives were established in various industries. There were 3 million people living in the apartments of housing cooperatives. Supply and marketing cooperatives could provide food and daily necessities of 123 million USD per day. Cooperative medical service organizations and other non-profit organizations provided 220,000 patients with medical service every day, and credit cooperatives dealt with 13.3 million checks, amounting to 1.3 billion USD. In 1994, the total output value of cooperative enterprises in the United States reached 100 billion USD.[1]

According to the principles of cooperatives form which was reviewed and amended in the 23rd Congress of the International Cooperative Alliance in 1966, cooperatives should comply with the following rules:

Firstly, the voluntary participation principle. The members of cooperatives should have freedom to voluntarily join, organize and withdraw. Of course, when joining the cooperative, a member has to pay share capital,

---

[1] Gao Feng, etc.: *Study on the Ownership of the Developed Capitalist Countries*, pp. 167-169.

which determines that cooperatives have the nature of private property. Viewing from the share capital system of cooperatives, we can draw a conclusion that the western cooperative is a property system that is different from the typical socialist enterprise and is mainly based on the mode of individual production, but it also has big difference with capitalist enterprises. It is a property mode of individual ownership of the resources of almost the same amount in the same scope, and the individual and the resources are directly combined in a certain scope.

Secondly, the principle of democratic management. Major issues in the cooperative should be determined by the general assembly of members, and all members should have equal voting rights. Furthermore, if we analyze the working system under a cooperative, we can draw a conclusion that its property right system is the individual ownership of joint workers' for joint work on the basis of share capital system.

Thirdly, the principle of limiting equities and dividends. In cooperatives the investment in shares by the member will be mainly used for the service of cooperatives instead of making profit. Therefore, generally many cooperatives stipulate not to pay dividends on share capital; if to be paid, it is generally limited. For example, the U.S Cooperative Law stipulates that the annual dividend distribution for a cooperative share will not exceed the stock dividend rate of 8%.

Fourthly, the principle of sharing surplus return. A certain part of the annual surplus of cooperatives is used to develop the businesses of cooperatives, a second part is used for the public service aims and the rest could be distributed among the members in accordance with the proportion of business exchange amount between members and cooperatives in that year. When the cooperative is in a loss, members shall bear the financial responsibility in accordance with the proportion of business exchange amount between members and cooperatives.

The organization and management features of a cooperative can be typically summarized as **one person one vote** (not according to share amount like in the stock companies), the members of a cooperative often share surplus claim rights equally and the management of cooperatives should reflect the common interests of members. Here, it is clear that cooperatives do not have majority stock holders like in the form of the joint stock system, and the rights of members are equally shared which neglect share amounts.

Let's take "Mondragon", a Spanish production cooperative, as an example of the internal relation of cooperatives. Since founded in the 1950s, "Mondragon Group has made considerable development in the fields of education, industry and the banking industry. By the end of the 1970s, the group has had a worker team of more than 15,000 cooperative members, 70 cooperative factories and credit cooperative banks with 93 branches."[1] In the governance structure of Mondragon, the general assembly of members practices a collective authority which replaces the authority of capitalists. The assembly of shareholders enjoys the supreme rights to govern the cooperative, and decides the other rights of the cooperative such as daily production amounts and management rights, and supervision or auditing rights under its authority, thus negating the essential content of the hierarchy in the capitalist enterprises. A permanent supervisory board of management group is elected by the general assembly of members, in which the manager is elected by this supervisory board and this manager is responsible for leading the specific activities of production and operations. There is a management affair committee and a social affair committee which are responsible for coordinating and standardizing the decision-making activities of managers and they seek the harmony between the supervisory board and managers. The general assembly of members also elects an audit committee to audit the implementation of finances, policies and procedures.

Regarding the ownership structure of cooperatives, I would like to offer a further analysis. Since the initial share capital of the cooperative company is owned only by investor members (not by the whole social group) and some cooperatives may allow to pay dividends, the character of initial share capital of cooperatives is different from the typical fund in socialist public ownership of the means of production described by Marx. And it is also different from

---

[1] Gao Feng, etc.: *Study on the Ownership of the Developed Capitalist Countries*, Edition 1, p. 190.

the collective ownership in China. Furthermore, since the cooperatives integrate all the funds owned by individuals into a capital fund which is collectively dominated and used by the cooperative, and since a cooperative highly values individual participation to the collective management right, the capital ownership of a cooperative reflects an ownership relation which has major differences with capital ownership of small-scale producers. The main aim of the share capital of a cooperative is not to make profit. Based on cooperative's unique ownership of means of production, labor controls capital fund, which means the associated labor controls and uses the capital fund and these two unique elements reflect a negation to the nature of capital, so it is different from capitalist enterprises. Therefore, the nature of the ownership reflected by the initial capital funds of cooperatives in capitalist countries is a combination of individual ownership of property with the management right of the workers collective.

Furthermore, since they can enjoy the right to collect benefits as dividends and a surplus return, the cooperative members are able to "deprive" the "privilege" formerly enjoyed by industrial and commercial capital. The cooperatives enable that profit returns to the hands of their creators (workers), so the ownership character of a cooperative also contains the individual member's right to collect a surplus earning.

In addition, due to provident fund accumulation system formed since early days of its emergence, this phenomenon causes the several rights in the cooperative ownership form gradually develop to the direction in which collective operation rights are highly valued which guarantees the long-term development interest of the cooperative. This fact determines that cooperative ownership contains the co-operative ownership of the property as one if its natures. Therefore, cooperative is an ownership structure which integrates four elements: individual ownership of a collective property, co-operative ownership of property, collective ownership of workers and individual rights to collect the surplus benefit.

When we analyze the reason for the emergence and development of cooperatives, we can easily see the inherent contradiction of capitalist mode of production, i.e. the contradiction between socialized production and capitalist private ownership of the means of production is the fundamental reason for the emergence and development of cooperatives. The embodiment of this contradiction is the contradiction between capital and wage labor, and is intensively reflected in both the direct production process and circulation process of capitalism. In the direct production process, these contradictions are mainly manifested as capitalists making use of means of production to extract surplus value of workers. In the circulation process, commercial capitalists make use of several tools such as prices to strengthen the exploitation of the consumers. In this background, the unemployment, poverty and low social economic status of the workers caused by the unique economic law of capitalist mode of production is the fundamental reason that they attempt to break away from the wage labor system with different explorations and re-master their own fate out of this system. And some elements and results of capitalist mode of production provide the conditions for such efforts of the workers. The emergence and development of cooperatives demonstrate with facts that capital wage labor system is not the only feasible form of microeconomic system in modern society. Also through this mirror of cooperatives, the internal contradictions, historical drawbacks and historical limitedness of wage labor system can be clearly reflected.

The cooperative ownership denies the contradiction between socialized production and capitalist private ownership within enterprises. However, this form of resolving this contradiction is not the public ownership of the means of production envisaged by Marx; instead it is only the cooperative's compound pluralistic ownership of means of production which also includes private ownership of a limited group. Although this form of ownership overcomes some drawbacks of capitalist private ownership and can play a positive role for the development of productive forces, when compared to public-social ownership of the means of production, it shows a certain degree of private nature such as the exclusive ownership right of a natural person to share capital, having negative role or a restraint which is unfavorable to the development of productive forces and the achievement of cooperative aims. Therefore, considering the cooperative's unique characteristics and limitations, it may be reasonable to predict that cooperatives may never become the main enterprise system in the capitalist economic system. If I view them from the aspect of realizing the social leap, socialism replacing capitalism, we also have reasons to believe that the productive forces that could be created by the cooperatives in the contemporary capitalist countries can hardly become the main material foundation for building a new society.

However, viewing from the aspect of the realization of social system changes or social progress, I would like to say that though we cannot say that cooperatives prepare the material condition for the emergence of a new society, the cooperative itself indeed contains a number of elements of a new socio-economic formation. This is mainly shown as follows: Firstly, cooperative labor system of a cooperative displays the new labor relation between men and men to some extent after the abolition of wage-labor system. It shows to the people that the liberation of workers is not just an ideal, but can become a reality. Secondly, the provident fund system of the cooperative makes the cooperative gradually accumulate a part of common property belonging to the collective of members. In such a collective property, that kind of social property nature belonging to everyone but not exclusively possessed by an individual envisaged by Marx is reflected as an initial manifestation. Thirdly, the collective management system of the cooperative not only becomes a means of implementing production and management activities better but also provides a way to achieve equality between people in the production process. It is obviously beyond the equality category of bourgeoisie and is really a progressive step towards the real equality aimed under the conditions of the new society. Fourthly, the system of distribution which is mainly practiced as according to work contributed and implemented by cooperatives also has the nature of distribution according to work contributed under the new social conditions of socialist transition. It is a constraint and negation to distribution system according to capital. Therefore, due to the above characteristics, we can fully suggest that cooperatives in capitalist countries are economic elements with obvious characteristics of socialism.

6. International Capital and the Ownership Relation in Capital's Internationalization

The above analysis on the ownership structure of capitalism and its evolution provides us with an understanding venation on its development process from history to today. However, this is not a complete understanding on the historical process of capitalist ownership. Because the economy between the capitalist countries are inter-related and mutually constrained, capital is also international by its nature. Marx had also commented on this issue: "Because the bourgeoisie has opened up the global market, all the production and consumption in all the countries become international." "The raw materials processed by the capitalist industry are no longer local raw materials, but instead they are raw materials from very remote areas; their products are supplied not only for consumption in their own countries but also for consumption all over the world at the same time."[1] We should take insight into the historical fate of capitalist private ownership and forecast the future of capitalism. Moreover, we also need to conduct an analysis on the internationalization of capital, an important aspect of capitalist world economic process to understand the ownership relations in capital internationalization.

Since Chapter VIII of the book will specifically discuss the issues of economic globalization, here I will only study the very necessary aspects of the ownership relation in international capital and capital internationalization. The other important aspects of economic globalization will be discussed there.

Capital's pursuit for surplus value is not restricted by national boundaries. Naturally internationalization of capital means that the movements of capital are conducted throughout the world and beyond national boundaries. The so-called international capital does not refer to a

[1] *Selected Works of Marx and Engels*, Edition 2, Vol. 1, p. 276.

specific capital form independent or quite distinct from the individual capital, share capital, private monopoly capital and state-owned capital, and it is just a manifestation of capital in various ownership forms in a wider range and in the international market across national boundaries. From the angle of industrial classification, we can sum up the international movements of capital into three forms as industrial capital, commercial capital and financial capital. Such three forms of capital have their own specific forms. Among them, industrial capital mainly refers to the international capital that directly invests in the manufacturing industry; commercial capital is the capital engaged in international commodity trade and service trade; financial capital includes the international capital engaged in international loans, securities, foreign exchange deals, insurance and other financial investments. The internationalization of these three forms of capital has followed different development routes in different periods of capitalism. In the period of free competition of capitalism, we can more obviously observe the internationalization of tangible commercial capital; in the monopoly capitalism period, we can more obviously observe the internationalization of loan capital of industrial capital and financial capital. After World War II, the internationalization of the three forms of capital has made a considerable development. In the recent years, the more prominent is the internationalization of industrial capital and financial capital.

From the beginning of the 16th century to the 1770s was the rudimentary stage of the formation of the world market. The goods that flowed across the borders were still mainly luxuries, but the products of small producers and workshop handicraft industry also increased day by day. Before capitalism was fully established and became dominant, the commercial capital had occupied a dominant position in the world market. From the 1770s to the 1870s was the initial formation and development stage of the world market. At that time, gold and silver were already the world currency, thus contributing to the formation of world prices. The law of value had begun to play a role in the world market, and different countries had made use of the "absolute cost" and "comparative cost" of products to conduct the international exchange of commodities. The main pattern of the world division of labor was that "industrial products from Europe and America and raw materials from Asia, Africa and Latin America". The western countries had also used the aggressive and cruel war tools to conduct colonial plunder to other countries. The last three decades of the 19th century was the transition period of capitalism from free competition to monopoly, and a large amount of surplus capital created by monopolies was exported to other countries in pursuit of high profits. It included both capital loans and direct investments.

After World War II, with the rapid growth of economies in different countries, the development of internationalization of capital has been rapid. In the aspect of internationalization of commercial capital, "the value of world exports was 64.1 billion USD in 1950, it was 1,997.8 billion USD in 1980 and it was 3,530 billion USD in 1991.[1] In 1998, the world's merchandise exports amounted to 5,414.8 billion USD. In 1950, the service trade can be ignored; in 1985, it was 380.9 billion USD, and in 1998, it increased to 1,326.3 billion USD. In 1998, the commodity trade and service trade amount accounted for 23.4% of the 28,862.2 billion USD of the total GDP in the world.[2]

In terms of internationalization of industry capital, private foreign direct investments among the developed countries had only reached to 67 billion USD in 1960, increased to 275.4 billion USD in 1975 and reached 693.3 billion USD in 1985, accounting for 97.2% of the total amount of foreign direct investments in the world. In 1992, the total foreign direct investment in the world amounted to 2 trillion USD.[3] From 1995 to 1999, the world's total foreign direct investment had increased from 355.3 billion USD to 1,005.8

[1] *Modern Capitalism Economic Theory and Practice* edited by Lin Huici, Zhang Tongyu, Li Yuanheng etc., Edition 1, p. 315.

[2] He Zili: "Economic Globalization and Modern Capitalism", in *Nankai Journal (Philosophy and Social Science Edition)*, 2002 (2).

[3] *Modern Capitalism Economic Theory and Practice* edited by Lin Huici, Zhang Tongyu, etc., Edition 1, p. 332.

billion USD, and in 2000, it reached 1,149.9 billion USD.[1]

Let's look at the internationalization of financial capital, from 1976 to 1980, the annual internationally dealt and marketed securities issued was 36.2 billion USD on average, and the average annual internationally syndicated consortium loans in the same period were 59.4 billion USD. Between 1986 and 1990, the above data reached 234.7 billion USD and 103.1 billion USD on average, and in 1992, the numbers increased to 357.2 billion USD and 117.9 billion USD respectively. By 1996, the total international finance including bank loans, bill financing and bond issues had reached 1,513.9 billion USD. In the foreign exchange market, in 1989, the daily global transactions on the foreign exchange had amounted to 590 billion USD, and in 1998, this data had reached nearly 1.5 trillion USD. In the international fund market, the total financial assets of all types of institutional investors had increased from 13.9 trillion USD in 1990 to 23.6 trillion USD in 1995.[2]

From the above data, we can draw a conclusion that the speed of internationalization of global capital is much faster than the growth rate of the global economy. The law of surplus value, the basic economic law of capitalism, is still the theoretical basis to understand and explain the rapid development of the internationalization of capital. The internationalization of capital, no matter what form is adopted and what position it takes, still assumes a common mission, which is to establish and strengthen the rule and exploitation of capital in the international scope, maximize the value proliferation of capital value and serve the capitalists who export capital, especially monopoly capitalists, plundering the highest profits. The fact of increasingly intensifying polarization of the rich and the poor in the world explains the above-mentioned law. For example, the total assets of Bill Gates, Prince Abdel Aziz Al Sand and Philip Anschutz, the three richest people

---

[1] Liu Changli: "The Rapid Development of International Direct Investment and Cross Border Merger & Acquisitions", in *World Economics and Politics*, 2002 (1).

[2] The above-mentioned data is from the book *Modern Capitalist Economic Theory and Practices* edited by Lin Huici, etc., p. 326; He Zili: "Economic Globalization and Modern Capitalism", in *Nankai Journal (Philosophy and Social Science Edition)*, 2002 (2); Zhu Naixin: "2001/2002 World Economic Review and Outlook", in *Forum of World Economics and Politics*, 2002 (1).

in the world in 1999, were more than the total wealth of over 600 million population in the 26 poorest countries in the world. The rich accounting for 20% of the population consume 86% of goods and services, and the 20% poorest citizens of the population only consume 1.3% of the world wealth, almost half of their wealth 30 years before.[1]

The changes in capital ownership relations are still applicable to the international movement of capital. The development law of capital's socialization is embodied in the evolution process of private monopoly ownership to international monopoly ownership and then to international corporation ownership in the internationalization movement of capital. In the internationalization movement of capital, same as the structure I have suggested in previous pages, the leading ownership form has also been an evolution from private family capital ownership to private monopoly financial capital and then to private monopoly corporation capital. The multinational corporations and multinational financial institutions that play a leading role in today's contemporary global market also operate in the form of corporation capital ownership. In the internal structure, their property rights, management rights and management or operation patterns have no difference with the contemporary corporate joint stock company form. In fact, most of the large-scale leading companies in the world also implement the world-wide operation strategies and the ownership structure of capital also develops towards the direction of internationalization. Capital's pursuit for surplus value is not limited by national boundaries. As long as it can produce surplus values for capitalists, regardless of the nationality of enterprises and what organization form is adopted, the profit of an enterprise belongs to the capitalist class power organized beyond the national boundaries.

More and more mergers of multinational corporations and their transnational investments make the original nationality of enterprises become blurred, but shareholders of enterprises, i.e. investors and owners, always have definite nationalities. They always need the support of the state machine

---

[1] Tang Renwu: "The Polarization Brought by Globalization and Its Countermeasures", in *World Economics and Politics*, 2002 (1).

to protect their private property and interests, and they still need to depend on the capitalist system which protects private ownership of means of production to help them obtain surplus value worldwide and expand their markets. As analyzed above, UK, the Netherlands and France had supported share capital form for their overseas expansion and colonial plunder at the end of the 18th century; large multinational corporations, corporation capital as the main ownership form, seek excess/surplus profits in every corner of the world today. In every epoch of capitalism, capital always needs that support by the state machine. Here I would like to suggest an analogy that similar to the phenomenon that the state represents the whole capitalist class to appropriate and control means of production, and thus the capital ownership of the capital state is characterized as a kind of ownership of "general capitalist", I can suggest that the international capital ownership embodies the plundering of excess profits by the "collective" of and for interest of the monopoly capitalist class and also embodies various specific relations with the states of the developed capitalist countries and various specific relations with other capital ownership forms which naturally seek surplus value as their aims.

Similarly, the basic contradiction of capitalism, the contradiction between socialization of production and private appropriation of the means of production, also exists in the internationalization movement of capital. The manifestation of this basic contradiction is reflected as follows: firstly, contradiction between adjustment challenges suffered by the economies in different countries and the practices of international capital to plan or design the global economy; secondly, the contradiction between careful organization and scientific management of multinational corporations and blind expansion and disorderly development of the world market; and thirdly, the contradiction of unlimited expansion trend of the global production capacity and limited capacity of the world market, etc. The imbalance of those contradictions directly results in imbalances of the global economy aggregate and structure and various sectors and spheres of the world economy, and then further leads to fluctuations, instability and crises in the global economy.

III. The Historical Fate of Capitalist Private Ownership

Capital is the subject of capitalist mode of production. As to Marx, the mode of production and production relations connect with each other and are interdependent upon each other. They are not only connected and interdependent upon each other but also react upon each other. From Marx's relevant expositions we can conclude several ideas. The historical process of development and evolution of capitalist mode of production driven by its internal contradictions is inevitably manifested as the development and evolution process of capital's historical form which takes the dominant position in the socio-economic formation in a certain epoch. In turn, the development and evolution of historical form of capital in a certain epoch contain major changes in the capitalist ownership relations. Disclosing the nature of socialized changes of capital ownership relation contained in the development of capitalist mode of production is an important theoretical contribution of Marxist social capital ideas. Here based on the above analysis of the evolution of ownership forms, we will take Marxist social capital ideas as the foundation to reveal the inherent evolution law of capitalist private ownership in order to further reveal the inevitable historical trend of capitalist private ownership.

1. The Reasons of the Evolution of Capitalist Ownership

In Marx's studies, the term "social capital" had first appeared when he analyzed "the role of credit in capitalist production" in his work *Capital*. He had written "that capital that is based on social production mode and takes social concentration of means of production and labor forces as the premise has directly obtained the form of social capital here (i.e., those directly combined individual capital) to be opposed to private capital, and its enterprises are also manifested as social enterprises to be opposed to private enterprises. This is sublation of the capital as private property in the scope of capitalist mode of production.[1] The social capital mentioned by Marx

---

[1] Marx: *Capital*, Edition 1, Vol. 3, p. 493.

here is the share capital ownership. Because share capital directly combines individual capital together to obtain a form of social (union) collection and differs from individual private capital that exists independently, it attains the form of social capital. As a form of social capital, share capital is opposed to private capital, and as a social enterprise, a joint stock company is opposed to a private enterprise. The formation of share capital in the form of social capital should be based on "social production mode" and on the premise of social concentration of means of production and labor.

To understand the transformation process from private capital to sociality, we should firstly understand the private and social nature of capital. The private character of capital stipulated by capitalist private ownership is reflected as the private power of capital in the economic relations, that is, the actual economic power that individual capitalists as owners of capital and the personal possession, control and use of capital. The sociality of capital can be composed of two levels: on the one hand, as the alienation form of labor, capital reflects exploitation relation that it freely occupies the surplus value created by wage-earners, which is the relatively stable content in the social mode of capital production and determines the exploitative nature of capital relationship. This is the first level of sociality of capital. On the other hand, with the strength of social combination and social power in its embodiment, capital reflects the combination way of capital itself to realize the exploitative relationship, which is the very content that constantly changes in the social mode of capital production and reflects the relationship that the combination way of capital constantly changes with the development of social productive forces occupied by it. This is the second level of sociality of capital. Thus private capital also includes a social nature that is different from and opposed to its private nature, that is, the sociality that private capital reflects as the transformation form of social work, strength of social combination and social power. Therefore, capital has private nature and sociality simultaneously.

The contradiction between private nature and social nature of capital is prominently manifested as the contradiction between the infinity of expansion of capital as a social force and limitedness of private appropriation capital amount. Only combined with certain social forces, can capital achieve proliferation of its value, and as the combination of social forces, the possibility of expansion of capital is without borders, however, the number of private capital is always limited. Infinite capital proliferation and the capitalists' desire for wealth endow capital an impulse of an unlimited expansion, and it pursues to combine social strength in a wider range to achieve the proliferation of value. However, this process will be encountered with more and more restrictions on the quantitative reach of individual private capital. Accordingly, a trend that wants to sublate the individual private appropriation form is formed in the development of capital itself. This contradiction not only inspires the continuous accumulation in the forces of capital, but also is the reason that leads to constant changes in the private appropriation relation and even the structure of capital ownership. With capital's continuous appropriation of increasingly socialized productive forces, the appropriation means and existence forms of capital are increasingly socialized. This is the connotation of the socialization process of capital.

From the initial individual capital in the workshop handicraft industry and the machine industry period later to modern share capital is the evolution and formation process of social capital. Social capital is the direct product of the private nature of capital and the development of social contradiction and the movement form of the internal contradiction in capital. Social capital forms have overcome the limitations of appropriation way of private capital to a certain degree so that individual private capital can suit the means of capital concentration, which is also an adaptation to the requirements of the development of social production. This is the very reason why socialized development of capital accumulation mode and operation mode have effectively promoted the development of social productive forces and increased the production of surplus value to a new level of history. Therefore, Marx had written that, as social capital, share capital is "the most appropriate form" of capital. However, it is proven that the process of capital socialization has not ended yet. As the externalization of the internal contradiction of private capital, social capital has only created new forms of contradictions. The result of this contradictory movement has been further evolution and development in the forms of social capital: financial capital of private monopoly and corporation capital of private monopoly. In these later social capital forms, the private capital ownership of a majority of private capitalists receives more and more restrictions, but they still retain the claim for surplus value. Let's look at the state capital generally evaluated as the completed form of social capital. Here, private capital ownership is no longer directly reflected, and the state directly appears with the identity of organizer of production in order to alleviate the contradiction between socialized development of production and capitalist private appropriation. However, the state capital ownership of capitalism is still an ownership form of the "general capitalists". State capital still keeps the internal connections with capitalist private ownership and also has class and private nature, reflecting the limitations of state capital of capitalism.

Cooperative ownership in capitalist countries is a positive sublation to individual capital. While it sublates the opposition between wage labor and capital among its cooperative members, it eliminates the phenomenon of labor alienation to certain different degrees; however, it usually restores the employment-labor-relationship with external men with an identity of the collective capitalist, and its manifestation is that some cooperatives carry out external employment, which also shows the limitation of this type of positive sublation occurring in cooperatives. Of course cooperative ownership denies the contradiction between socialized production and capitalist private ownership in the cooperative company, but the form of the solution to this contradiction is not public ownership of means of production envisaged by Marx, instead it is the composite ownership of means of production of the cooperative. Although this form of ownership has overcome some drawbacks of capitalist private ownership and plays a positive role to the development of productive forces, when compared to public ownership of the means of production, it shows some degree of private natures (such as the exclusive ownership of natural person to share capital), which plays a negative role unfavorable to the development of productive forces and progress of cooperatives. Therefore, sublation of individual capital cannot become the main and ultimate form of sublating capital, and cooperative ownership cannot become the ownership form that could assume a dominant position in capitalist ownership structure. I think, according to historical and realistic facts, it can be expected that under the effect of the basic contradiction of capitalism, the two forms of the evolution in the capitalist mode of production will still continue to progress for a long time in the future. On the one hand, I can argue that there is still a vast room for development of **capital's negative sublation** movement. This argument connotes that capital can use and mobilize more social resources to serve itself through the forms such as share capital, financial capital, corporation capital and state capital. As to the denotation, it means that capital can also obtain bigger and more stable markets through external expansion and international coordination so as to conduct negative sublation at a higher level and in a bigger scope. On the other hand, **capital's positive sublation** will also be adhered to and continued. It is not only because labor has the requirement of breaking away from the constraints of capital in essence, or from a more general sense, human beings have the will to eliminate alienation and return to human nature at a higher level, but also because that workers will obtain increasingly more conditions for sublating capital and realizing all-round development of human beings. Therefore, in the capitalist countries, the ownership structure that takes monopoly capital ownership as the leading, capitalist private ownership as the main body, state ownership as the assistance or supporter and cooperative ownership as the complement will survive during a quite long time in the future history. Besides capitalist countries, some socialist countries will also co-exist and survive for a quite long time in future history.

In the socialist countries, with the self-adjustment and improvement of socialist economic relations, the superiority of socialism will be further displayed. In this background, the working class and vast working people will take the initiative to complete the reforms and innovation in the new system based on highly developed social productive forces and more mature elements of the new society, which also means organizing and pushing the capital positive sublation, i.e. using new ownership forms and economic relations to replace capitalist economic relations based on private ownership. In this way, it will be possible to achieve a qualitative leap in capital sublation and complete negation of the capital.

2. Capitalist Ownership and the Evolution of Ownership Structure

With the increasing expansion of capital flow between developed countries and that between developed countries and developing countries, the scale of international flow of capital is constantly expanding and the structure of capital ownership is also developing towards a more international and globalized direction. In recent years, the multinational companies with assets of 100 billion USD after recent huge acquisitions constantly emerge, since large-scale companies are organized and managed in a quite planned way, which partially eases the contradiction between socialization of production and capitalist private ownership. At the same time, those above facts also show that the capitalist monopoly still continues more and higher concentration and develops towards the internationalized monopoly. However, the phenomenon of capital's continuous development towards the monopolistic concentration and the law of socialization of capital fully prove what predicted by Marxism, that is, socialism replacing capitalism is an inevitable result of the movement of the basic contradiction of capitalism and the historical trend of capital's sublation. This trend is both manifested through capital's sublation and socialist factors gradually formed in the evolution process of the form of capital ownership.

Observing from the capital standpoint, those factors or means that maintain capital domination in various forms and in different degrees are consciously applied. However, just because those factors or means directly reflect some features of socialism, from the perspective of wage labor, the emergence of those socialist factors under the condition of capitalism are spontaneous elements. These characteristics are the special expression of the law of capitalism instead of socialism in capitalist economy.

Because the state capital is the highest result of capital's sublation at this stage, the socialist factors are particularly manifested in capitalist state-owned enterprises and their economic activities. Fundamentally speaking, state ownership economy is to serve the general interests of the bourgeoisie. However, on the other hand, it has eventually broken through the restrictions of private capital. According to the general rules of social reproduction and the requirements of development of technology under the condition of socialized production, in order to achieve social stability, state ownership assumes certain social service functions such as strengthening infrastructure construction, supporting new emerging industries, researching for high technologies, providing a series of non-profit products and services necessary for general citizens and controlling environmental pollution. The starting point of such operations is no longer to make profit. Just for this reason, it has some similarities with the objectives of public ownership enterprises in the new society.

In addition, monopoly capital ownership is based on higher level of social productive forces, so the new social factors also appear in the existence form of ownership, i.e. in large companies such as workers owning company shares, the workers participating in production management, etc. as well as the development of cooperative economy analyzed before.

Capital's pursuit of surplus value is increasingly not restricted by national borders and the ownership structure of capital also develops toward the direction of internationalization. However, the imbalance of economic development widens the gap between the rich and the poor and between countries and regions, objectively increasing the possibility of occurrence of contradictions and conflicts. A sound and effective international economic regulation mechanism has not been formed yet. Therefore when some link of capitalist economy is broken, it is bound to have a domino effect, and thus we can say that capitalism is still facing severe potential challenges. No matter which objective trends or laws push the conditions for the new socialist economic system replacing the capitalist economic system, class struggle and revolution will be the necessary fundamental driving force in the transformation process from the old system to the new one.

Capitalist Social Class Relations and Its Historical Evolution

The class relation is the manifestation in the inter-personal relations of the economic relation in class society. The evolution of a social economic relation is prominently shown in the changes of class relation; or it can be said that change of class relation in a society is a concentrated reflection of the evolution in the socio-economic relations. When studying modern capitalism, we should adhere to this point of view and method more comprehensively. Thus, one important aspect of understanding the historical process of the development of capitalism is to investigate the nature and changes of the class relations of the capitalist society to envisage the future trend.

I. The Basic Class Relations in the Capitalist Society

In modern capitalism, each person defines his own identity from different angles such as the blue-collar worker, office staff, expert, consumer, young people, black, woman, environmental protection worker, poor people, member of a labor union, student or Catholic, etc. Therefore, this reflects that there are various complex relationships between men. It seems that people can very easily find similarities and a common language with others. However, although the relationships formed by the occupation, religious belief, education level and consumption experiences, etc. have different level of influences in social life, they are not the fundamental, long-term effective and decisive force for social development. The interest relation determined by the positions of people in the material production is the basic relationship of society and the nature and condition of this relation is the basic force that determines the social situation and social trends. My analysis on the class relation of the capitalist society will start from this basic relation.

1. The Basic Capitalist Economic Relation

The reason that we emphasize that the relation formed in the material production of people is the basic relation of the society is because that material production takes an extremely important position in the survival and development of human society and it is a basic human practice, so controlling the production not only can meet the need of survival and development, but more importantly, can fundamentally ensure to take a favorable and active position in socio-economic life, politics, ideology and other aspects, and then further determines the whole society.

Some scholars assume that in the capitalist society, all the subjects that participate in the production of the material goods have property rights (capitalists have the ownership of means of production existing in the form of capital and workers have the ownership of labor force), so in capitalist production process, even if there are two classes on different economic basis, their economic relation reflects equality and mutual benefit. For example, Samuelson has pointed out, "In the competitive model, there is no difference whether capital employs labor or labor employs capital."[1] In his view, the

---

[1] P. Samuelson, "Wage and Interest: A Modern Dissection of Marxian Economic Models", in *American Economic Review*, December 1957.

reason why capital hires labor is simply that capital is more scarce than labor. That is to say that the difference between the supply and demand in the capital market and labor market forms the pattern that capitalists employ, control and manage workers in capitalist production process.

In the condition of capitalism, workers indeed possess the ownership of their labor forces and accordingly they have personal freedom. It is an important feature of capitalist economic system and the important basis that capitalism could replace the feudal system. However, can we think that workers in capitalism have obtained equal status as the capitalists? In other words, will workers be able to restore equal status with the capitalists if the capitalist market conditions are improved?

In fact, if we delve deep into the historical source and the deepest level of social economic structure, we can clearly see the truth. Looking back at history, we can see that capitalists and wage-earners, the two basic main parts that compose capitalist enterprises and the capitalist society, are not inborn; instead they are the products of the development of history and the result of the development of commodity economy. When being produced, they were not equal. The foundation that capitalist economic relation could emerge was the rapid development of commodity economy and accompanied primitive accumulation conducted by the emerging new nobility to meet their greed as the feudal society was perishing. The rapid expansion of commodity economy and the competition between the owners of goods were bound to lead to the polarization of social classes, and the brutal primitive accumulation also accelerated the process. Losers in this process lost the means of production by which they could realize their labor forces, and apart from their labor force, they had nothing to be sold; and the winners naturally became capitalists and used the means of production accumulated in their hands to hire labor forces to carry out production. This polarization of the commodity had prepared the basic conditions of the capitalist production. The capital relation was established on the premise of the separation of labor with the ownership of its realization conditions."[1] Under such conditions,

---

[1] Marx: *Capital*, Edition 1, Vol. 1, p. 782.

if the workers did not sell out their labors to the capitalists, they could not get means of livelihood to survive. Marx had described this: "If labor ability cannot be sold, it is useless to the workers. Moreover, workers will feel a cruel natural inevitability that the production of his labor ability needs a certain amount of survival materials, and its reproduction constantly needs a certain amount of survival materials." So, he had proposed like Sismondi that "if the ability to labor... is not sold, it equals to zero."[1] Some modern scholars also have profound arguments on it. For example, when criticizing the proposition that "every transaction is strictly voluntary" under the market economy condition put forward by Friedman, a right-wing scholar, C. B. Macpherson has pointed out that to ensure the background condition of full voluntary exchange "is not to freely enter a particular exchange, but is not freely to enter all the exchanges", and "Under capitalist conditions, workers do not have means of production, and they cannot organize production, so they cannot freely enter the exchange.... This is compulsory."[2] This is the fundamental reason that workers sell their labor forces. Capitalists can organize production by themselves by the virtue of the means of production in their hands, and maintain the production and their lives by their material wealth. Therefore, it can be seen that in capitalist economy, even if workers have ownership of their labor capacities, even if the constraint on workers by the primitive accumulation of capital and pressure on workers by relative overpopulation are subtracted, the relation between the haves and haven'ts is unequal. This is a kind of asymmetry of the forces of competition caused by asymmetry of distribution of means of production. Only the "advantages" of capitalists and "disadvantages" of workers resulted from the private ownership of capitalist means of production have already determined the internal structure and social status of workers in capitalist enterprises and capitalist society. In such a structure, workers have to sell their own labor capacities and accept capital's rule on them.

The above arguments prove the basic opinion of Marxism once again

---

[1] Marx: *Capital*, Edition 1, Vol. 1, pp. 196-197.

[2] C.B Macpherson, *Democratic Theory*, Oxford, Clarendon Press, 1973, p. 146.

that the nature of the ownership of means of production plays a decisive role for the socio-economic relations and their social nature. Just according to this point of view, we can define the nature and basic class relation of different societies, especially the capitalist society. The basic class relation of capitalism is that the capitalists control wage-earners and exploit surplus value created by them. It runs through the whole process of the production and development of capitalist society and is manifested in all the aspects of the whole social economic activity.

Under capitalist conditions, each person is directly and indirectly connected with the above capitalist fundamental economic relationship, or further, more and more people become the bearers of this relation; their existence determines their consciousness, and people's behaviors and ideologies are bound to reflect certain provisions of this basic economic relation. From perspective of the working class employed by capitalists, although they have differences in vocation, education level, sex, age and religious belief, etc., "any person that needs work for survival and has conflicts with his boss will understand a fundamental incompetence and affiliation, which is the main point of the working class in capitalist society that classical Marxists emphasized.[1]

Viewing from the other party of this economic relation, i.e. the bourgeoisie, under the condition of modern capitalism, a number of interest groups have been formed in the bourgeoisie, and the relationship among those interest groups is a derivative relationship and they are gradually formed with the development of modern capitalist enterprises. At the initial stage of the development of capitalism, sole proprietorship enterprises take a dominate position in capitalist economic activity, the ownership and control right of enterprises are unified and there are not different interest groups among capitalists. However, with the expansion of the scale of capitalist enterprises, under the command of the same capital, a large number of workers that work together need managers and supervisors to carry out management in the name of capital in the labor process. It shows that as a result of the division

---

[1] David M. Gordon etc. *Segmented Work, Divided Workers*, Cambridge University Press, 1988. p. 5.

of capital functions, the classes that represent and realize the different functions of capital within the bourgeoisie have begun to take shape. In joint stock companies which take a dominant position in modern capitalist economic life, the function of capital is further divided and fixed, purchasers of shares, i.e. shareholders, become the owners of enterprises, and operation and management of enterprises are respectively executed by the directors and senior managers. Thus in the modern capitalist enterprises, various capitalist interest groups have taken shape.

In essence, the fundamental interests of each interest group within modern capitalist enterprises are coincident, their purposes of activities all serve to realize maximum capital proliferation and their economic income is also wholly or mainly from the surplus value. However, due to different position and role of each interest group in value proliferation activities, the obtaining ways and amount of surplus value differ, and contradictions arise among several interest groups. One important manifestation of this contradiction is that senior manager class as direct managers of enterprises sometimes makes use of the advantage that they hold the management information more than the owners to seek interests for themselves and even damage the interests of the owners. The "corporate governance structure" in modern capitalist enterprises is the system arrangement for dealing with the relationship of shareholders, directors and senior managers gradually formed in the enterprise management process. An important content of this system is to carry out the principle of shareholders (especially the big shareholders) first, meanwhile distribute the operation and management rights and interests of enterprises to the various interest groups. From Marx's point of view, in essence, the so-called corporate governance structure is to use enterprise system to define and standardize the responsibility, rights and benefits of capitalist groups such as shareholders, directors and senior managers in the realization of the value proliferation, so as to form the incentive and constraint of the owners to the managers and finally realize the economic relation formed by maximum surplus value. Thus it can be seen that in spite of some contradictions existing between the capitalist interest groups in modern capitalist enterprises, against the working class, their goals are consistent, that is, to produce and realize more surplus value through more effective control of wage labor. In short, under the condition of capitalism, although people have different specific identities and economic behaviors, it would be better to accept the concept of class and methods of class analysis rather than refuse this concept and method. Thus, we can have a more profound and more consistent explanation to their goals and behaviors.

2. The Form of Industrial Relations in the Direct Production and Operation Process

The industrial relation—employee and employer—is manifested in all the fields of the capitalist economic activity. I will first analyze the form of this relation in the direct production and operation process of capitalism.

In terms of its form, industrial relation in capitalist direct production process is different from the relationship between workers and capitalists in the circulation field. In capitalist economy, whether it is production process or circulation process, between capitalists and workers, there is the relationship of rule and being ruled. Marx had pointed out that capitalist production process is always the separation of reproduction of labor force and its working conditions. Workers must continuously sell their labor force to the labor markets, so "before selling themselves to capitalists, workers have already belonged to capital.[1] However, in capitalist labor market, the relation between capitalists and workers still appears in the form of commodity exchange of the owner of money and owner of labor force. In this sphere, the principle of equivalent exchange still applies. However, once the exchange ends, the situation will change.

The capitalist production process begins after capitalists purchase the means of production and labor force. When labor force plays its role as the existence and subsistence in this process, capital is "developed to a mandatory relation, forcing working class to do more work beyond the narrow scope of their own lives.[2] As a mark, labor's direct subordination to

[1] Marx: *Capital*, Edition 1, Vol. 1, p. 634.
[2] Marx: *Capital*, Edition 1, Vol. 1, p. 344.

capital begins.

In the capitalist production process, labor's subordination to capital has very distinctive features: Firstly, it is the product of the sale of labor instead of the result of political or social inherent rule or subordination relationship that observed in slaves' subordination to slave owners and peasants' subordination to landlords. Therefore, it is a purely economic relation. Secondly, the nature of labor's subordination to capital is capital's appropriation for surplus value instead of appropriation for surplus labor or surplus products. Marx had pointed out that "Capital has not invented surplus labor. In all the places where a part of people in the society enjoy the monopoly right of means of production, workers whether free or not free, must add excess work time to produce means of livelihood for the owners of means of production besides the living items necessary for maintaining their own lives."[1] In capitalist society, due to the generalization of the commodity economy, surplus labor is expressed in the form of surplus value, therefore, in capitalist production process, the workers' subordination to the owners of production conditions is manifested as labor's subordination to capital's self proliferation. Finally, labor's subordination to capital is manifested as capitalists and their agents' supervision and management on labor in the industrial process. "A worker works under the supervision of the capitalist, and his labor belongs to the capitalist. Capitalists conduct surveillance to make labor be normally conducted and the use of means of production in line with their purposes, that is, raw materials are not wasted, instruments of labor are cherished avoiding possible damages...."[2] The purpose of such supervision and management is completely for preserving and proliferating the value of capital, because "only when such preservation is achieved, proliferation can be carried out most appropriately and precisely, and thus the actual labor process can be realized."[3]

From the above we can see that labor's subordination to capital in the

---

[1] Marx: *Capital*, Edition 1, Vol. 1, p. 344.

[2] Marx: *Capital*, Edition 1, Vol. 1, p. 210.

[3] *Karl Marx and Frederick Engels*, Chinese version, Edition 1, Vol. 47, p. 101.

process of capitalist production is formed by buying and selling of labor force. On the one hand, this has some similarity with the subordination relation occured in the former production process based on private ownership; on the other hand, it has distinctions in form. Marx summed it up as "the labor process becomes a means of value proliferation and the self proliferation process of capital, i.e. the means of production process of surplus value. The labor process is subordinated to capital (it is the process of capital itself), and capitalists enter this process as managers and commanders; this process is also the process that capitalists directly exploit the labor of others. I call this as labor's formal subordination to capital."[1] The important expression of this subordination is that workers work under the supervision of capitalists and their agents, labor has become more tense, the duration of the labor process becomes longer, and labor has more continuity and becomes more orderly, so as to ensure capitalists to get more surplus value. This is the first and basic expression form of industrial relation in capitalist production process.

Labor's formal subordination to capital is only the relation formed because of buying and selling of labor force and it does not require a change in the mode of production. Therefore, it has become the main form of capital controlling labor in the initial stage of establishment of capitalism. During this period, on the one hand, due to capital primitive accumulation and capital accumulation, more and more people had become workers employed by capitalists, the groups of wage-earners continued to expand, and a labor market formed; on the other hand, because the workshop handicraft industry based on manual labor was still the main mode of production at that time and skilled workers still accounted for the larger proportion, they could be able to control the labor process to different levels by their skills and thus could bargain and struggle with the capitalists. Therefore, at this stage, capitalists could not fully realize the control over labor.

With the transformation of the mode of production owing to capitalists'

---

[1] *Karl Marx and Frederick Engels*, Chinese version, Edition 1, Vol. 49, pp. 78-79, Beijing, People's Publishing House, 1979.

pursuit for surplus value, capital obtained new means of controlling labor thus labor's actual subordination to capital had gradually formed. This was the second expression of industrial relations in capitalist production process. Labor's actual subordination to capital had occurred on the basis of labor's formal subordination to capital, but it was different from labor's formal subordination to capital. It was the labor's subordination to capital formed as a result of production and evolution of capitalist mode of production. This subordination had already appeared in the workshop handicraft industry based on the division of labor. At this stage, the internal division of labor in the workshop handicraft industry had made the activities of handicraft industry decompose, labor tools a bit specialized and workers become "local workers" (instead of journeymen) with the unilateral information and capacity. The work division and combination of workers formed a social form. "This social form with combination of labor as the existence of capital is opposed to workers. It is combined to become fatality to be opposed to workers. That a worker is dominated by this fatality is because that his work ability becomes a completely unilateral function. Leaving a general institution, this unilateral function is nothing. Therefore, it completely needs to rely on this general institution. Workers themselves become a simple part of this institution."[1] When capitalist mode of production was developed to the stage of machine industry, labor's actual subordination relation to capital had already become mature. Capitalism's use of machines not only continued to strengthen the old division of labor within enterprises, but also made the skills of using tools together with the labor tools shift from workers to machines. In workshop handicraft industry, it is workers that use machines, and the movement of means of labor starts from workers; in the machine industry, it is the workers who serve the machines, and the workers follow the movement of means of labor, thus forming drive system that machines control workers. Connection with the formation of capitalist mode of production and deepening of workers' actual subordination to capital is that capitalists obtain more relative surplus value (instead of absolute surplus value).

---

[1] *Karl Marx and Frederick Engels*, Chinese version, Edition 1, Vol. 47, pp. 319-320.

The nature of capitalist industrial relation is to extract surplus value through wage labor. In the situation that labor is only subordinated to capital in form, capitalists can only obtain absolute surplus value through the extension of working days and increase of labor intensity. However, in the production under the unique capitalist mode of production (after the intermediate phase is bygone) and capital's actual subordination to labor, capital not only achieves new opportunities of seizing absolute surplus value, but also obtains this unique and typical new means for the production of relative surplus value, thus making capital's desire for surplus value fully satisfied. "Once the more the better production of surplus value generally becomes the direct purpose of the production...'produce for production'—the production as the purpose itself—will indeed take place with labor's formal subordination to capital. However, only when the unique capitalist mode of production is developed and labor's actual subordination to capital is also developed with this production mode, can this inherent trend of the capital relationship be realized in an appropriate manner."[1] Therefore, only in the stage of labor's actual subordination to capital, the industrial relation which is most favorable to the realization of the capitalist nature becomes mature.

3. Performance of Industrial Relations in Capitalist Reproduction Process

To investigate the reproduction process is a dynamic investigation to the production process. In order to ensure the continuity of the production process, the circulation and consumption issue should be highlighted. Therefore, the investigation on the industrial relation in the capitalist reproduction process mainly investigates the expression form of this relation in the general capitalist economy, especially in the circulation and consumption process.

In this aspect, Marx had also provided us with an important research methods and results. Marx had pointed out, "The production has the form of capitalism, so the reproduction also has the same form. Under the capitalist

---

[1] *Karl Marx and Frederick Engels*, Chinese version, Edition 1, Vol. 49, pp. 97-98.

mode of production, the labor process is only manifested as a means of the value proliferation process, and similarly, the reproduction is only manifested as a means of reproduction that takes prepaid value as capital, i.e. the value of self proliferation."[1] As we have analyzed earlier, the formal subordination of labor to capital is formed on the premise of separation between laborers and the means of production, therefore, the separation of labor products and labor and the separation between objective working condition and subjective labor force are in fact the foundation and starting point of capitalist production process (its productive forces). Through continuous reproduction, this foundation or starting point becomes permanent. Among them, the continuous production and reproduction of the labor force are an important aspect. On the one hand, capitalists and workers must be allowed to consume, the only way to continue to maintain the production and supply of labor; on the other hand, capitalists must allow workers to consume. Only in this way, the reproduction and supply of the labor force can be maintained; on the other hand, the personal consumption of workers must be limited to the level that can only maintain reproduction of the labor force, so as to ensure they will not become the haves and break away from the operating orbit set up by capital. In this way, from the perspective of the whole society, "the working class, even outside of the direct labor process, is also subordinate of capital like dead work tools. Even personal consumption of the workers, to a certain extent, is an element of the reproduction process of capital. However, in this process what is concerned is not to let this production tool with self-consciousness run away when it continuously makes the labor products of workers from this end move to the other end. Workers' personal consumption, on the one hand, ensures them to maintain themselves and reproduce themselves; on the other hand, consumption of the means of livelihood ensures that they continuously re-appear in the labor market"[2]. It becomes the necessary condition in the reproduction process of capital.

Why can workers' personal consumption be limited to the level that can

[1] *Capital*, Edition 1, Vol. 1, p. 621.
[2] *Capital*, Edition 1, Vol. 1, p. 629.

only maintain reproduction of labor? Here it needs to study the role of the labor market. The labor market of capitalism is formed under the joint role of labor supply and demand. Their conditions have a significant influence on prices of labor force. In some stage in the development process of capitalism, because the acceleration of capital accumulation may result in tension in the labor market, making the price of labor increase, the industrial relation should be eased. However, because the increase of the price of labor can only be restricted within the limit that "not only makes the basis of capitalist system not be violated but also ensures reproduction of the scale expansion of capitalist system". "The nature of capitalist accumulation will never allow any reduction of the degree of labor exploitation or any increase of labor price which may seriously endanger the continuous reproduction of capital relations and reproduction of continuous expansion of its scale."[1] When the profit rate is seriously eroded by the increase of labor prices, the bourgeoisie can reduce the demand for labor to force the decline of labor prices by reducing the level of accumulation or through the contraction of government plans. However, the more frequent observed fact is that the improvement of the capital technology composition and organic composition brought by capital accumulation. While absorbing labor force, capital also reprobates labor force so that the working class can produce capital accumulation. Meanwhile they also produce the means that make themselves become relative surplus population by increasingly expanding the scale. Relative surplus population forms a huge reserve army of the capitalist industry, which makes a part of workers become part of the non-scarce resource and thus the labor market becomes a market of supply exceeding demand. It has an important significance for pressuring down wages, strengthening labor discipline and ensuring smooth proceeding of capitalist reproduction.

If we connect each link of capitalist reproduction for investigation, we can further find that capitalist ownership has not only caused labor's subordination to capital but also formed some specific mechanisms. It makes the workers subordinate to the need that capital obtains surplus value in the

---

[1] *Capital*, Edition 1, Vol. 3, Chapter XV, p. 681.

movements of various contradictions. When the accumulation is speeded up, capital's demand for labor increases. When it positively influences the production of surplus value, it may be favorable for the commodity sales and the realization of surplus value owing to the increase of workers' incomes and the improvement of their purchasing power. When the relative surplus labor causes a decline in the prices of labor, it is favorable for the production of surplus value, but however, because of the decline of the actual purchasing power of workers, it is unfavorable for the realization of surplus value. This is the important performance of the inherent contradiction of capitalist economy between surplus value production and realization of surplus value revealed by Marx.[1] The focus of the economic policy of bourgeoisie governments is conversed largely on easing the two aspects of this contradiction. It shows that the loosening of industrial relations in some link of capitalist reproduction cannot fundamentally change the status of workers. If capitalist private ownership is not abolished, the workers cannot obtain their own liberation at the root.

II. Recent Changes in the Industrial Relations

Since the 20th century, under the role of the basic contradiction of capitalism, capitalism has developed from the stage of free competition to the stage of state monopoly, and capitalist economy and society have had many changes. The scientific-technological revolution not only has further improved the labor productivity, more effectively changing all aspects of human life, but also profoundly changed capitalist mode of production, causing several new features in the relationship between labor and capital.

1. The New Changes in the Industrial Relations

The formal subordination of labor to capital is further developed. It is firstly manifested in the number of people employed by capital continuing to increase. This is mainly because capital still manifests a strong expansionary

---

[1] Marx: *Capital*, Edition 1, Vol. 3, Chapter 15, and pp. 269-296.

force since the 20th century. First of all, this expansion manifests continuous infiltration of capital, turning more and more social life into the activities that they can control. For this point, Braverman, an American left-wing scholar have pointed out that "only in the monopoly stage, capitalist mode of production takes over all the needs of individuals, families, and society, and when making such needs subordinate to market, it also offers them new forms to adapt to the needs of capital. If you do not understand this development, it is impossible to understand the new professional institutions—therefore you cannot understand the workers."[1] In the developed capitalist countries, the most significant consequence of this expansion is bankruptcy of more and more small farmers, joining in the team of the wage laborers. For example, the family farms in the U.S.A can only make about 20,000 USD even in a good harvest year, which cannot meet the need of expanding the herd and using modern equipments. Under the pressure of intense competition, since the 1980s, there are three farms in bankruptcy on average in the State of Minnesota per day, which disappeared from commercial activities.[2] Secondly, this expansion is also manifested as the expansion of capital in space. After World War II, the vast majority of the former colonial countries in the world had obtained national independence. According to the relevant information, among 193 independent sovereign states in the world, there are 128 states that obtained independence after World War II. Wherein, 28 states achieved independency in the late 1940s and 1950s; 40 states in the 1960s, 28 states in the 1970s, 9 states in the 1980s and 23 states got independent in the 1990s. The primary task of such countries after independence was to realize their economic industrialization. However, the shortage of their own internal capital and the capital export of developed capitalist countries and the development of domestic capital in those countries made the majority of these countries embark on the road of capitalism. The disintegration of socialism in the former Soviet Union and Eastern European countries and the pressure from the developed capitalist countries had further accelerated this process

---

[1] Hariri Braverman: *Labor and Monopoly Capital*, Edition 1, p. 239.
[2] William M Stern: *Low Return of Lake Land*, Forbes, 1994-08-15.

and choice."[1] Obviously, it could not be a road which allows independently developing national economy. However, viewing from the result, no matter it is in the developed capitalist countries, the middle developed countries or still developing countries, the number of people employed by the capitalists to make a living by selling their labor is a growing trend. Let's take the United States as an example, according to the information from Statistical Abstract of the United States, in 1900, the number of wage laborers in the United States accounted for 67.9% of total employment population; in 1950, it increased to 79.7%, and in 1980, it risen to 91.2%. This reflects the strength of the expansion of capitalist economic relations.

The further development of labor's subordination to capital in form is also expressed as that the degree of capital's direct control over labor is deepened, which is prominently manifested in the change of capital's labor management from the experience based management to scientific management. In *Capital*, Marx listed a large number of examples to describe the capitalists and their agents' direct management and supervision on workers.[2] However, at that time, the management and supervision was still in the stage of intuition and experience. However, in the end of the 19th century, marked by the emergence of Taylor system, a variety of "scientific management" theories and methods were successively generated. Since the 20th century, in the developed capitalist countries, some modern management schools with significant impacts in the management have gradually emerged, which are actually based on the cornerstone of Taylor system. The essence of these theories is to make labor better meet the needs of capital through the so-called "rationalization of labor". "They are all to ensure how the workers can better subordinate to capital in the form. As a result, in the same 9 to 10 hours

---

[1] From 1978 to 1992, more than 70 countries implemented 566 programs of stabilization and adjustment imposed by International Monetary Fund (IMF) and World Bank. Those programs have greatly changed the production mechanism of those countries and made them reincorporate the vast areas of the former Third World into the capitalist system in the world in accordance with the instructions of transnational countries" ["Globalization and the Formation of Transnational Countries", in *Journal of Foreign Theoretical Trends*, 2002 (5).]

[2] Marx: *Capital*, Edition 1, Vol. 1, Chapter 8, pp. 258-335.

of work, they can squeeze out double the amount of work as that compared to in the past from a worker and relentlessly strangulate all his strength and extract the ability of nerve and muscle of employment slaves bit by bit at a speed three times faster than the original one."

After World War II, in order to meet the requirements of the new scientific-technological revolution, the "scientific management" in capitalist countries has shown some new features: 1) Management means were further modernized. Capitalists made use of the results of the new scientific-technological Revolution to apply the latest scientific and technological means such as electronic technology, control theory and systems theory to the production process, further strengthening the control and supervision on workers. 2) The labor productivity system established by "Fordist system of labor organization" was finally restrained. As commented by Schumpeter, "accordingly people had begun to criticize 'destruction of creativity' to eliminate such restraint and finally entered the work society of Post-Fordism". The development of new scientific-technological revolution required to promote the creativity and initiative of workers. Therefore, the bourgeoisie had greatly promoted the so-called "civilized management". In the guise of the humanitarian labor process, capitalists and their agents had put forward the management theories such as "industrial psychology" and " human relations" and paid attention to strengthen the study on the management of psychological factors of workers, meet the workers' "psychological needs", give workers "spiritual encouragement" and create "cordial and harmonious" relations between employers and employees in the production, so as to achieve the purpose of creating more surplus value for the capitalists and workers subordinating to capital in the situation of "ease of mind". 3) Associated with the above-mentioned changes, capitalist enterprises used more and more "management experts" to conduct management in site so that the economic relationship in the enterprise was performed as labor relation. However, those management experts finally served for the proliferation of capital. Therefore, in fact it is the industrial relation that reflects the nature of labor relations in capitalist enterprises. 4) Realizing control over workers through the employee stock ownership plans. Since the 1970s, with the support from the governments of the developed capitalist countries, many enterprises began to implement the "employee stock ownership plans". According to the statistics of the ESOP Association in the United States, in 1974, there were only 200 ESOPs, but in 1984, ESOPs were increased to 2,500, 11.5 times more than that in 1974; in 1990, it climbed to 10,000, increased by 49 times than that in 1974; in 2000, this number was further increased to 11,500, which was 56.5 times than that in 1974.[1] Generally speaking, the employee stock ownership plan has not changed the worker's position in the enterprises.[2] However, it plays a role in different degrees in ensuring employees' participation in management and mobilizing workers' initiative. An investigation on 350 high-tech companies made by the United States Struggle for Employee Stock Ownership Commission found that the development of companies that made use of this program was 2 to 4 times faster than the companies that did not make use of this program. U.S. Senator Russell Long reported that the investigation shows that after changing the traditional form of management sales, employment and profits have increased considerably and we have to find a way to ensure that ordinary employees have the opportunity to participate in the management of stock.[3] It shows that the bourgeoisie has begun to attempt to make use of the property right system reform to adjust industrial relation and achieve the control over the enterprises by this opportunity and obtain more surplus value.

In the direct production and operation activities of modern capitalist

---

[1] http://www.the_esop_emplowner.org/pubs/stats.html.

[2] Information shows that in most cases, the result of employee stock ownership plan is that the vast employees only hold a small number of shares of the enterprises. For example, from 1973 to 1988, the proportion of the employee stock ownership in listed companies in Japan was only 0.66%-1.42%; in the middle of the 980s, 3/4 of the employee stock ownership plan in the United States only owned less than 25% of the stocks of corresponding companies, and the median of this proportion is 10% (quoted from doctoral dissertation of Liang Aiyun, Department of Economics, Nankai University: *Analysis of the Employee Stock Ownership System in Western Developed Countries*, p. 67).

[3] Li Zong, Jia Huaqiang & Xie Zhiqiang: *Study on the Important Issues of the Development of Contemporary Capitalism*, Vol. 1, Beijing, Central Party Literature Press, 2000 edition and relevant management information on the United States.

enterprises, labor's subordination to capital in form (formal subordination) is further developed. It is also further observed that in the labor's subordination to capital, an unproductive excess labor obviously increases. This is a structural change connected with the changes in production, realization, transfer and distribution of surplus value. In Marx's era, because industrial capital and surplus value production took a special dominant status in capitalist economy, the productive labor took a larger proportion in the labor force employed by capital. However, under the condition of modern capitalism, as the production process of value and surplus value has gradually become the norm, capitalists increasingly focus their attention on the realization of the value of production. At the same time, with more and more surplus value created in the production, the capital specializing in credit, speculation and other aspects significantly increases. The effect of these two aspects, namely, using capital to realize, appropriate and distribute surplus value also needs to hire a large number of labor force. Although such labor is the requisite of capitalist mode of production, it is still non-productive. As a result, it causes that non-productive labor takes a bigger and bigger proportion in the labor employed by capital. For example, in the United States, the proportion of agricultural labor force fell more than 78% in more than 100 years while the proportion of the industrial labor force experienced a process from rising to decline, and as maximum reached to about 40%, but in 1990, it only accounted for 26%; the service industry has had a great development since the 1970s, replacing this industry to become the first major industry. In 1990, the employment proportion of the service industry was up to 70.9%, and the proportion of output value accounted for about 70% of GDP.[1] In 1999, the proportion was as high as 77%.[2] It reflects that the sectors which provide "services" for the realization, transfer and distribution of surplus value take an increasingly important economic status in modern capitalism.

---

[1] Chen Ying: *The Evolution of Industrial Structure in Capitalist Countries*; Gao Feng: *The Economic Relations and Operating Characteristics of Modern Capitalism*, pp. 515-520.

[2] Department of Commerce: *Survey of Current Business*, July 2001.

Actual subordination:

Labor's actual subordination to capital is deepened and expanded. As mentioned above, Labor's actual subordination to capital is directly expressed as that capitalists use capitalist mode of production to control workers. The production modes resulted from three scientific-technological revolutions in the history of mankind have provided all kinds of means with their unique characteristics to strengthen labor's actual subordination to capital.

If we say that the machine industry caused by the first technological revolution in the era of Marxism has formed the objective skeleton that capital controls labor, the heavy chemical industry caused by the second scientific-technological revolution in the end of the 19th century has provided more space for the role of this objective skeleton. The rapid rise of departments such as iron and steel, chemical industry, automobiles and aviation, etc. enabled enterprises' scale to rapidly expand and product lines to be widely used. Taking this opportunity, capital once again pushed labor's actual subordination to a new level. The outstanding performance was that in the early 20th century, "Ford system", characterized in controlling and sucking living labor by accelerating of machines, firstly appeared in the United States. The extensive use of such a system made the situation of machines controlling workers reach an extreme point. According to an article published in 1982 in the second issue of *Avant Garde*, a Japanese monthly, the principle for the enterprise managers to arrange the conveyor speed is to not waste 1 second. After visiting this factory, Walesa said with emotion: "This is virtually that the machines use people and it is unacceptable." Because there was no one to greet Britain's Queen Elizabeth when visiting the factory, she said very angrily: "I am greeted with applause in the factories in every country in the world, but only in the Panasonic factory, no one had paid attention to me." How can workers stand up and applaud in an assembly line without a second to spare? The article finally said with emotion: "Capital exposes capitalists' endless pursuit for profit without treating workers as men. But if we think that it is what happened in the 19th century when Marx had lived and a record of the past, it seems a serious mistake. Now it is the 20th century, if Marx came to today's Japan, wherever he would go, he would probably be surprised that the exploitation is much crueler than 100 years ago."

The gains brought by new scientific-technological revolution with information technology as the core for capital are firstly the expanded scope of its activities through the emergence of a series of new emerging industry sectors such as computer, optic fiber, laser, bio-engineering and robot industry and secondly enabling machines to not only have a "musculo-skeletal system" and advanced "nervous system" through the invention of computers and extensive use of machines with a part of the human brain activities transferred from the workers to the machines. The combination of this automatic machine system and more detailed division of labor makes the labor of workers more monotonous, tensional, lacking of initiative and even more under the control of machine system. But in traditional industries, capital is still striving to maintain the traditional means' (such as machine-driven) control over the workers. However, in several knowledge-based industries, it is difficult for capital to insist on control over workers by using the machine-driven method. Therefore, in such industries, strengthening division of labor, making information possessed by workers become a one-sided information and forming a new situation of asymmetric information have become the main means of controlling labor in practice. At the same time, capital also takes employee stock ownership and other incentive measures to mobilize the enthusiasm of scientific and technological workers.[1] It shows that the capital strongly enhances its rule in various fields, especially the industries which represent the new development direction of advanced productive sectors.

---

[1] Even so, the distribution of wealth in capitalist countries remains highly unequal. For example, in the end of the 1990s, in the United States, about 38% of the wealth was still in the hands of the richest 1% families, while 80% families at the bottom only controlled 17% of wealth. The distribution of stock ownership is much more unequal. Calculated according to the market values of the stocks, the 1% stock owners on the top held about half of all stocks (47.7%), while 80% owners at the bottom only held 4.1% of the whole stocks. (Refer to Lawrence Mishel and Jared Bernstein and John Schnitt.

In a wider vision of a global scale, the actual subordination of labor to capital is deepened not only in the scope but also in the extent. After World War II, more than 100 new independent states in fact have all embarked on the road of capitalism. With the progress of science and technology and the globalization of the world economy, more and more population in these countries not only in form but also in actuality is subordinated to the rule of capital. The workers over there have even worse working conditions, bigger intensity and much lower wages than of those in the developed countries. Therefore, they create a large amount of surplus values for the bourgeoisie in their own countries. In addition, because labor productivity in these countries is generally lower than that in developed countries, the developed capitalist countries make use of higher productivity to obtain a large amount of international excess profit, thus preventing a drop in the profit rate to some extent arising from the reduction of direct productive labor. Starting from this point, we can see that it is the expansion of the actual subordination of labor to the capital that capital uses to further maintain its dominance on labor, which is another important feature of capital under the condition of modern capitalism.

2. New Characteristics of the Industrial Relations in the Reproduction Process

As mentioned above, to study the industrial relation of capitalism in the reproduction process mainly investigates the relationship between the bourgeoisie and the working class from the overall macro-economic aspect. To investigate the industrial relation of contemporary capitalism from this perspective needs a broader view and rich information. Due to limited information, this chapter only takes the United States as a representative example to explore this issue by using the research results made by left-wing scholars in the United States.

On the whole, since the 1960s, due to various reasons, the strength of American working class has been weakened, and American working class is in a more disadvantageous position in the struggle with the bourgeoisie.

When analyzing the issues such as why American workers cannot organize a stronger party which is controlled by workers in the period after the American labor unions has experienced a decline, lost their cultural image and political influences since World War II, American left-wing economist David Gordon and others point out that this is because "American working class has been differentiated from the internal in the aspects such as economy, politics and culture,"[1] and thus the struggle power of the working class has weakened. That American working class has encountered an internal differentiation is the consensus of many economists. However, there are different explanations on why the working class has encountered internal differentiation. One view is that this is because the trend of "post-industrialization" effectively blurred the traditional division between workers and capitalists, and this trend made traditional Marxist analysis of the relationship between labor and means of production lose its effectiveness. They believe that the spread of this post-industrialization trend led to the end of the traditional "ideology" and "the rise of elites' ruling". In fact, they believe that with the improvement of science and technology in economic activities and the increasing prominence of the tertiary industry, professional skills and technical ability are improved and even replace the ownership of means of production to become a decisive variable in determining interpersonal relationships so that people no longer treat themselves by the identities of "capitalists" or "workers", but they deem themselves as a part of the group divided by their careers or consumption ability. It is the opinion of the human capital school in the mainstream economics of capitalist countries. They acknowledge the existence of the differentiation of workers, but deny class antagonism and class differences.

　　Contrary to the opinions of mainstream economists, Gordon and others have developed **the theory of the social structure of accumulation** (hereinafter referred to as "SSA theory"), and used it to explain the differentiation among American workers and changes of the balance of strength between labor and capital. In their view, there are indeed differentiations brought by different production practices among American

[1] David M.Gordon, Richard Edwards, Michael Reich: *Segmented Work, Divided Workers.* Cambridge University Press, 1982. p. 8.

workers. Such differentiation is an important reason of sustainable development of capitalism and that an anti-capitalist ideology uniting the working class movement could not be formed. The reason why the workers have different production experiences is the result of the social structure of accumulation in the United States. The so-called social structure of accumulation refers to the special system environment in the process of organizing capitalist accumulation. It offers some important variables that influence and determine capital accumulation, such as a series of systems connected with capitalist reproduction including the monetary and credit system, the pattern of participating in economy, the situation in the labor market and the characteristics of labor process. It is in the combined effect of these variables that the new capitalist accumulation can be carried out and realized.[1]

Gordon and others believe that since the 1920s the evolution of American social accumulation structure has experienced three stages. The first stage, from the 1920s to the 1990s, was the initial proletarian stage. At this stage, the labor market was initially formed, but the labor process did not have substantial changes, and workers still controlled the labor process through their own skills to some extent. Therefore, the workers were affiliated to the capital in form. The second stage was from the 1920s to the beginning of World War II. It was the homogenization stage of the American working class. The capitalist mode of production at this stage had made marked progress, the labor process was increasingly controlled in the hands of the capitalists and their agents, and the labor market became more general and competitive. The workers had begun to be actually subordinated to capital. The third stage was from the 1940s to the 1980s. It was the differentiation stage of the working class. At this stage, due to development of large monopoly enterprises, the American labor market was divided into two markets with major differences, and the labor process of different sectors also had obvious differences. Thus, the working class in the United States

---

[1] David M. Gordon, Richard Edwards, Michael Reich: *Segmented Work, Divided Workers*, pp. 9-13.

was differentiated.

At the third stage, the division of working class was subjected to the important condition of the rise of American large enterprises after the World War II. The economic strength of those huge enterprises made it possible for them to regard the global economy as their "dishes", and the internal company structure formed in enterprises also allowed them to plan investment and production worldwide. Their huge ability and controlling power made them become core enterprises. Such core enterprises were the core part of economy, which controlled key industries, grasped the markets with rapid development and launched innovative technology changes. They enjoyed not only high profit rates but also low risks. Facing the socialized labor force, enterprises could shape the labor management system through negotiations with labor unions. With the development of the capitalist economy, the difference between those core enterprises and peripheral enterprises—a lot of small and medium-sized enterprises became bigger and bigger. The peripheral enterprises engaged in low-profit industries that the core enterprises were reluctant to invest and played an important role for the core enterprises to transfer risks to the periphery and maintain the productive capacity. This division between core enterprises and peripheral enterprises had begun from the 1900s, but the division that really formed the labor market had taken place after World War II. This dual labor market has a significant difference with the labor process associated with it.

First of all, viewing from the perspective of the added incremental value created by the unit production worker, because of having higher capital resources, the core enterprises can carry out continuous technological innovation and investment. Meanwhile because the negotiation strength of labor unions in the core enterprises improve wages and costs and stimulate the enterprises to adopt labor-saving technologies to replace workers, in the core enterprises, the added incremental value created by unit production workers is higher than that of the peripheral companies. Secondly, viewing from the perspective of incomes of workers, because the capital/labor ratio in the core enterprises is high, and the negotiation power of the labor union is stronger, wages of workers in the core enterprises are higher than those of workers in the peripheral enterprises. Thirdly, viewing from the perspective of proportion of productive workers, because the core enterprises need to put more resources for planning, supervision and marketing functions, the proportion of productive workers in the core enterprises is lower than that in peripheral enterprises. Fourthly, viewing from the perspective of workers' dismissal rate, because the core enterprises emphasize promotion ladders and sustained employment, compared to peripheral enterprises, the dismissal rate of the core enterprises is lower than that in the peripheral enterprises, and workers have more job security. In short, the workers in the core enterprises are in a relatively favorable position. And the workers in peripheral enterprises due to low wages, poor benefits, lacking of job stability and also being production workers are in the bottom of the working class in developed capitalist countries. They have weak labor union strength and lack negotiation capability.[1]

The difference of the economic status has caused different political attitudes. The workers from core enterprises and their families perhaps are more concerned about the quality of life, individual autonomy, environment, civil liberties, individual rights and other issues, and they want more freedom from society; or because they can obtain corresponding work security and stable income, they emphasize more on the importance of economic development so that they can ensure the increase of wages. They are also concerned about America's international controlling power and Social Structure of Accumulation (i.e. SSA) that is necessary to endure their work safety. However, the workers of the peripheral or marginal enterprises and their families put more emphasis on the importance of obtaining the support of government services and income so as to make up for the low and unstable income from their labor; the low remunerations obtained from their economic activities have also lowered their enthusiasm to participate in political activities. For example, their degree of participation in voting is low. In this

---

[1] David M. Gordon, Richard Edwards, Michael Reich: *Segmented Work, Divided Workers*, p. 212.

way, through the analysis, Gordon has concluded that since World War II, due to the division of the U.S. labor market, wakening up of the consciousness of the working class had slowed and workers had formed a differentiated political force. Since 1940, the strength of American working class as a whole had been seriously weakened.

Viewing from the perspective of the world, in the beginning of its establishment, capitalism had begun a global expansion. Before the First World War, the important means of this expansion was to include many countries into the scope of their colonies. After World War II, many former colonies broke away from colonial rule and had gained independence. Through growth in the "golden age" for more than 20 years after the second war, developed capitalist countries had basically completed their industrialization. Environmental pollution accompanied by industrialization, increase of labor costs, increase in taxes brought about by the implementation of welfare policies and other reasons forced the bourgeoisie to begin to seek for a favorable foreign investment environment in a larger scale, thus forming the trend of transferring the manufacturing industry to the less developed regions in the 1970s. Japan and "the four Asian tigers" in Southeast Asia, etc. had developed by taking this opportunity. The labor markets in those underdeveloped regions can be said to be the third-level labor markets. The workers in the third-level labor markets also had differentiations as that in the labor markets in the developed capitalist countries. But generally speaking, the unit production added value of workers, wages, benefits and labor security of workers and other aspects in the third-level labor markets were less than the workers in developed capitalist countries, and they were at the bottom of being deprived. Moreover, if directly investing in less developed countries, the goods produced can be sold locally. While reducing transportation costs, it also avoids trade barriers like high custom tariffs. The bourgeoisie in the developed capitalist countries bribed the working class and leaders of labor unions with a great amount of surplus value created by the working class in less developed countries and confused their class consciousness. They also used transferring business to less developed countries to threaten the working class in their own countries, thus making them actively or passively to give up their requirements such as raising wages and improving working conditions to maintain stable employment.

Since the end of the 1970s, a new round of scientific-technological revolution has taken place in the developed capitalist countries first. This round of scientific-technological revolution with innovation of information technology as the main content has a profound influence not only on the production but also on economic relations. Viewing from the perspective of the labor market of the developed capitalist countries, what is mostly affected is the independent basic labor force in the labor market connected with the core enterprises because the swarm of technological innovation, improvement of education level and wide use of micro-electronics and information technology brought by the new scientific-technological revolution have made a part of the independent basic labor force more independent, and meanwhile they have made another part of the labor force become standardized or homogenized. A part of senior managers and senior technical personnel are highly valued by enterprises and have more mobility, higher wages and other benefits, some even can obtain corporate stock, and thus they become the beneficiaries of the new technological revolution. And the careers of ordinary managers, general technical staff, and general professionals, etc. have been standardized and have become a routine work, which can be obtained through vocational training. Accordingly the independence and mobility of this part of workers are greatly reduced, what is accompanied with it is that their wage levels and benefits are at a standstill, even if not lower. Some parts of these workers even fall into the secondary labor market. At the same time, the new scientific-technological revolution has expanded the North-South gap and the third class labor markets in underdeveloped countries are squeezed even more seriously.

III. Historical Trend of the Evolution of Capitalist Industrial Relations

1. Present Situation of Class Relations in Various Capitalist Societies

The new scientific-technological revolution gave rise to changes of the class structure in the capitalist society, and to new changes of class relations in the post-war capitalist countries.

Firstly, the internal class structure of the bourgeoisie has changed. After the second war, ownership and business management rights have separated due to the rapid development of joint stock companies. A large number of high executives such as general managers and brokers, etc. have appeared accompanying with the increasingly dispersed ownership in the company. Not only were they offered large salaries, but also had stocks of companies, received dividends and shared the residual claim. They became a part of the bourgeoisie and played the role of functioning capital. The number of high executives exceeded the average of all hierarchies of the bourgeoisie. For instance, of the 500 largest companies in America in 1976, only 9% were under the leadership of the descendants of the families who used to own the companies. High executives not only had a larger quantity, but also played an important role in the economy and politics of the capitalist society. They received higher education and professional training, had command of the latest scientific and technological knowledge and had rich practical experiences and abilities for making business decisions.

They possessed and controlled crucial means of production and exercised decision-making power and business management rights of the big companies. They exerted great influences upon elections, held senior positions in the governments and influenced the formulation of national policies. Besides, as the development of post-war state monopoly capitalism, production and capital were highly centralized and monopolized, and many large and extra large companies continually sprang up. A new generation of monopoly financial groups emerged and the number of financial oligarchies controlling these financial groups greatly increased. Only in America, the number of individuals with a property of over 10 billion in 1986 exceeded 21. The personal assets of Gates, the president of Microsoft, and Buffett, a portfolio investor were respectively 18 billion USD and 15.3 billion USD in 1996.[1] Most millionaires were "automobile magnates", "oil magnates" and "chemical magnates" in the 1950s and 1960s. However, new millionaires tend to make a fortune in the high-tech industries such as computers and software, etc. and the financial investment industry, etc. after the 1980s and especially the 1990s. Such change in the bourgeoisie reflects changes of the industrial and economic structure driven by the new scientific-technological revolution.

Secondly, the working class structure has also changed. It was primarily represented as the rapid expansion of the working class ranks. After the war, the development of science and technology, and the change of industrial structure as well as social and economic development increased the demand for skilled workers, semi-skilled workers, engineers, technicians and managers. Therefore the working class ranks expanded rapidly. In accordance with the statistics of the International Labor Organization, the number of salaried workers in America increased from 49.3 million in the 1950s to 101 million at the beginning of the 1980s, and that in Japan rose from 18 million to 41 million. The number is still increasing after the 1980s. The working class structure in main capitalist countries tends to have multi-levels as the working class ranks rapidly expands. As mentioned above, this is the result of the differentiation of the labor market in developed capitalist countries. It is mainly represented as: 1) A larger amount of intellectuals were needed as the application and spread of science and technologies in production. For instance, scientific and technical personnel participated in production activities, design, research and development, as well as inspection and adjustments, etc. of products. They took part in the production process

---

[1] *Research on the Major Issues of Contemporary Capitalist Development* (Vol. 1) edited by Li Cong, Jia Huaqiang and Xie Zhiqiang and relevant materials in *Reference News.*

in different ways, either directly or indirectly, and created surplus value for capitalists. More and more intellectuals has become an important part of the working class. The growth rate of employment of scientific and technical personnel in America was 7.9% from 1980 to 1988 and the annual growth rate of employment of all labor forces was merely 1.7% during the same period. 2) As the rapid development of the tertiary industry in developed capitalist countries, the number of employees mainly including low-level intellectuals, such as public servants, accountants and laboratory assistants, etc., has increased sharply. Earning a living by selling their brainwork, they became wage earners and a part of the contemporary working class. 3) Numerous women were employed after the war and increased the working class ranks as well. Based on statistics, the number of employed women at present accounts for approximately 50% of all employed people in main capitalist countries, increasing by more than one time compared with that before the war. In terms of the pursuit of equal economic and political rights, they became an active force in the working class of contemporary capitalist society. 4) After the war, the large-scale mobilization of the working class around the globe has increasingly risen with the rapid development of economic globalization. A large number of laborers from countries or regions which lag in economic development have immigrated to developed capitalist counties. They are mainly engaged in onerous physical work in the construction industry and service industry, etc. and have formed the lowest special group in the working class of contemporary capitalist society.

As the expansion and development of multi-level working class ranks, the overall quality of the working class has improved too. It is prominently represented as increased average time of education received by workers, continual improvement of their labor skills and proficiency levels and other aspects. This is the result of the development of science and technology and the application of scientific and technological achievements in the production process. As the increased application of scientific and technological achievements in the production process, the requirements for the knowledge and skills of laborers are increasingly higher. On the one hand, on their own account, governments and capitalists have increased educational and training expenses, cultivated a great amount of scientific and technical personnel and trained a large number of skilled workers. On the other hand, to maintain employment and gain more income, workers need to constantly improve their labor skills and proficiency levels. This requires more cultural education and frequent participation in vocational training. Based on statistics, the proportion of people who had received secondary education or above among all civil laborers in America has risen from 58.3% in 1948 to 64% in 1970 and 86% in 1989. The proportion of people who had received higher education has increased from 14% in 1948 to 50% in 1999; the period for receiving education has increased from an average of 10.6 years in 1948 to over 14 years in 1999; and the number of American employees receiving on-the-job training has reached 47 million at the beginning of the 1990s, accounting for 41% of all labor forces.[1]

After the war, the scientific-technological revolution has boosted industrial structural adjustments of western developed capitalist countries. It has not only contributed to the thriving tertiary industry and rapid increase of employed people, but also changed traditional labor modes, leading to continual decrease of workers directly engaging in material production. Both the output value and quantity of employment in the tertiary industry (service industry) account for about two thirds of all industries, becoming the largest industry in contemporary developed capitalist countries. Since the service industry directly or indirectly provides services for production, workers in the service industry are directly or indirectly engaged in the social production process, thus engaging in the creation or distribution of surplus value. Same with workers in material production sectors, they do not possess means of production but earn a living by selling their labor force, so they are totally the same in terms of subordination to the capital power. However, since the sectors included in the service industry are more complicated and the enterprises are mainly small and medium-sized enterprises on the verge of capitalist economy, the working class of the service industry has a low level

---

[1] US Census Bureau, *Statistical Abstract of the United States*, 2000, p. 158.

of organization and dispersed forces. This has also affected their collective fighting power.

New Middle Class:

Finally, a new middle class represented by new-type small labor masters and senior white collars was created after the war. This is the outcome of the scientific-technological revolution. They are widespread, numerous and played an increasingly great role in terms of promoting the development of production, tackling economic crisis and absorbing labor forces in employment, etc. Intellectuals of this new middle class can also play an important role in the contemporary capitalist society. They can create new productive forces, raise labor productivity, and create material wealth and spiritual wealth through the scientific-technological revolution, innovations and inventions, and the administrative management and enterprise management, either directly or indirectly. Meanwhile, they play the catalytic, braking and buffering role in the conflicts between the employers and employees since they are a large group in number. They are discontent with the loss of reason and rising crime rate in the capitalist society, as well as the decrease of income and decline in the living standards during the periods of economic crisis. However, they still have several illusions on the capitalist society. They do not wish for convulsive upheavals but only demand for improvements in the capitalist system, which has a great impact on industrial relations.

As what Marx had stated in the past, "its position stays between the bigger capitalists, i.e. the genuine bourgeoisie and the proletariat or industrial workers, which determines its features.... Therefore, this class always vacillates between the two: they wish to enter into ranks of the richer class on the one hand, and are afraid of falling into a position of proletarian or even beggars on the other hand". Marx had named them as the "transition class" based on this features.

The new middle class, as the outcome of post-war capitalist socialization and high development of science and technology, economy, society and culture, had a rapid growth since the 1950s to 1970s. The majority of them, as brainworkers, have received higher education and possess certain professional knowledge, skills, administrative talent and artistic creativities and are the main body of the new middle class. At present, the development momentum of the new middle class has weakened and the polarization momentum significantly strengthens. For instance, American enterprises have dismissed a large number of white collar employees, middle management, engineers and technicians since the 1980s. The middle class who have lost their former jobs can generally find new job opportunities with lower wages and worse welfare. Many people fell into a lower level due to their worsening situation.

Meanwhile, the income of a minority of senior professionals and managers in the middle class has increased sharply. They became "new technical nobles" and leaped to the ranks of the bourgeoisie. Especially after 1995, the income of the bourgeoisie has increased significantly and that of the working class has also increased due to the continual intensive labor market. Only the income of the middle class did not increase and even declined. To maintain the original level of consumption, the middle class had to greatly increase labor time. For instance, the total labor time of typical married couple in the middle class of America was yearly 3,885 hours in 1998, increasing by 247 hours (approximately six-week work time) compared with that in 1989.[1] The social mentality of the middle class was mixed due to their unstable position. On the one hand, their interests are not absolutely consistent with that of the bourgeoisie. On the other hand, they have many conceptual differences with the working class because they have controlled workers' labor to some extent. This mentality makes them a special group for alleviating class contradictions in the capitalist society.

Generally speaking, the respective class status of the bourgeoisie and the working class, the two main aspects of class contradiction and struggle in the post-war capitalist society have not changed. As long as classes with contradictory interests, mutual conflicts and different social status exist, the

---

[1] Lawrence Mishel and Jared Bernstein and Jahn Schnitt. *The State of Working America 2000-2001*, ILK Press, an imprint of Cornell University Press 2001, p. 8.

struggle between classes will not end. Therefore, the opposition, conflicts and struggle between the working class and the bourgeoisie in the post-war capitalist society has not ceased because of the development of the scientific-technological revolution. Not long after the war, large-scale labor movements and labor union movements striving for increase of wages, improvement of living and labor conditions and expansion of political rights have successively occurred in main capitalist countries. To fight against aggressive policies and war policies of imperialism, further improve living conditions and expand political rights, the working class has struggled against the bourgeoisie, and workers' strikes have occurred one after another from the 1950s to 1970s. The number of strikers in developed capitalist countries was 19 million in 1965, 45 million in 1970 and 48 million in 1975. In America, the number of workers' strikes was over 4,800 times in 1950, over 3,300 times in 1960, 5,716 times in 1970 and 3.3 million people had participated strikes. Strikes of the working class have forced the bourgeoisie to make major concessions and carry on social reforms, which have significantly improved working conditions and living conditions of the working class. In the 1980s, due to the transition of the capitalist economy from stagflation to low-rate growth, the bourgeoisie further expanded their power taking advantage of the benefits brought by the new scientific-technological revolution, and the power of the working class was weakened due to the differentiation of the labor market. Consequently, industrial relations of capitalist countries had shown slower quantitative changes on the basis of the older models. This was mainly represented as labor movements remaining at low tide, gradually decreasing conflicts between the employers and employees and a decline in the severity of conflicts between the employers and employees. For instance, there were only 813 strikes in Britain in 1985, and the number of strikes in Italy decreased from 5,174 in 1974 to 1,565 in 1983.

The number of labor conflicts in France also decreased from 4,400 in 1976 to 2,000 in 1985. Strikes and protest demonstrations mainly ended in compromise and failed to meet the original requirements of strikers. The main means of struggle of the working class transferred from strikes and protest demonstrations to direct dialogues and negotiations. Due to the existence of the general middle class, who were discontent with social turmoil caused by strikes and protest demonstrations, the working class mainly had straightforward dialogues and negotiations with capitalists through their representatives in order to alleviate problems. Again, the proportion of workers participating in labor unions decreased and the number of union members decreased, which led to continual weakening influences of the labor unions. Most importantly, the class consciousness of the working class faded and their sense of historical mission to overthrow the capitalist social system weakened. Strikes were only limited to increase of wages, opposition to layoff, opposition to unemployment, improvement of working environment and other aspects.

There are many reasons that contributed to the formation of the present situation of internal industrial relations in capitalist countries. Seen from social environment, the support level of the public to the labor unions decreased from 70% in the middle 1960s to about 60% in the middle 1980s. Till 1998, only about 13% of the public had confidence in labor unions.[1] The first reason was that the public believed that laborers were a cause for a nation's economic problems. For instance, as to the stagflation of developed countries in the 1970s, some people held the view that union members' demand for higher wages was the cause for the upward spiral of commodity prices. America had lacked competitiveness in comparison with some countries from 1979 to the middle 1980s. Some people had attributed the reason as labor forces' lack of competitiveness, not only because of the rigid wage system and their concern about better welfare, but their lack of willingness to cooperate with the management to increase productivity or reduce unnecessary expenses. Secondly, the public and even some union members believed that union leaders no longer stood for workers' interests. Many union leaders had high wages and lived in elite housings while their children studied in quality private schools. The economic gap between

---

[1] Jeffrey E. Cohen: *Politics and Economic Policy in the United States*, second edition, Houghton Mitflin Company, Boston New York, 2000, pp. 132-133.

ordinary workers and union leaders had widened and they even had nothing in common. Last but not least, the public had attained a conservative tendency, the liberal campaigns for deregulation, etc. initiated in the 1970s had won the support of the public. The attitude of the public towards labor union movements has reflected the immaturity and a certain degree of deterioration of labor union movements in developed capitalist countries. The basis for the working class to combat the bourgeoisie was deprived due to the lack of support from the public.

As far as the working class is concerned, the working class ranks had a complicated, multi-level and knowledge-based structure, and it could hardly form unified wills and unified movements. Subject to effects of diversified ideologies, reformism and various non-Marxist ideologies, the party machine and labor unions of the working class could hardly form a scientific guiding ideology for the labor movement. During the transition of the economic structure of developed capitalist countries in the 1970s, the proportion of manufacturing industry which used to be the main component of labor unions had significantly decreased, and the increase in the proportion of service industry had led to the sharp decline of non-agricultural labor forces in labor unions. The structural changes in the economies brought by the new scientific-technological revolution, i.e. the decline of the proportion of traditional blue collars and increase of the proportion of so-called white collars (middle management and technicians), pink collars (general office workers and service personnel), golden collars (senior managers and technicians) has weakened the forces of labor unions. Especially, the conditions of the basic necessities of life of the working class were improved; their social welfare and insurance conditions were continually increased, which has undermined the struggle willpower of the working class. In western economics, the Engel coefficient (proportion of expenditures on food to income) is generally used to measure the change of consumption structures. After World War II, there was a falling tendency of the Engel coefficient in the resident consumption structure of developed capitalist countries, which means that people can satisfy consumption requirements in other aspects at a higher level after satisfying the basic requirements. The improvement of material living conditions has blurred the class consciousness of the working class. Some theories defending capitalism in economics and sociology such as the utility theory of value and the human capital theory, etc. has also misled the working class.

As far as the bourgeoisie is concerned, determined by the development of social productive forces and out of the requirements for competition and protection of interests of the dominating class, on the one hand, the bourgeoisie improved their rule on the working class. For instance, they have increased workers' wages, improved social welfare, improved labor environment, and especially implemented measures of so-called "capitalization of workers" and "democratic management", etc. This alleviated contradictions between the employers and employees to a certain extent. On the other hand, the bourgeoisie strengthened attacks to have control of the working class. They threatened the working class through economic means. For instance, some enterprises terminated existing labor contracts by bankruptcy reorganization, employed non-union members and concluded new labor contracts with lower wages, low welfare and high flexibility. All these were based on their interests under the protection of the bankruptcy law to lower labor costs. This offensive strategy has endowed enterprises with powerful weapons against the labor unions. They were not only able to comprise workers through threats. They have also restricted and opposed workers' struggles through consolidating legislation and administrative measures. For instance, the American government has formed a series of well-conceived measures to suppress labor movements after World War II. The U.S. Congress had passed the "Industrial Relations Act" in June 1946, which stipulated that the disputes between both parties of the labor and capital shall be "mediated" by the FBI. Under the so-called circumstances of jeopardizing national security, the president was entitled to investigate and instruct judicial departments to issue strike prohibitions or relevant injunctions within 80 days; it also stipulated that other units shall not offer sympathy for strikes, it prohibited the labor union from using union funds for political activities and prohibited the Communist Party members from assuming positions in labor unions. The Congress had also formulated the "Labor Management Reporting and Disclosure Act" in 1959, which prescribed that the labor union must report various activities of workers and further strengthened control of the government over labor unions.

Economic globalization also exerted profound influences upon the change of industrial relations as the rapid development of the scientific-technological revolution. In the 19th century, economic globalization had began right after the establishment of the capitalist system, As Marx had commented: "the need of a constantly expanding market for its products chases the bourgeoisie over the entire surface of the globe. It must nestle everywhere, settle everywhere and establish connections everywhere." Economic globalization had a fast development after the 1980s. During the process, multinational corporations became the most crucial driving force. For a long period, multinational corporations were not satisfied with export of their goods to the whole world, but wished that they could carry on production in expected or to-be-developed new markets or places with cheap labor. Meanwhile, investors have transferred enormous capital from one country to another, their capital from various financial derivatives to stocks and from stocks to various financial debentures. The main purpose of multinational corporations regarding the whole world as their market is for one thing, that is "profit!". Multinational corporations have purchased other companies at an unprecedented rate and made trans-border mergers. They kept on looking for the best technicians, the cheapest labor and the quickest suppliers no matter if these people were from Silver Valley, Singapore or other countries or regions. It is a kind of monopoly right without any frontier or any restriction. As Thurow, an American economist said, people do not mean to establish sentimental fixed relations with a certain part of the world in this kind of monopoly. Fundamentally the core of capitalism is to minimize costs and maximize profits.

After capitalist developed capitalist countries are in a developed status for over 100 years, the production cost of wages, welfare, etc. have remained high and affects the profitability of enterprises. So they have turned their attention to cheap labor in developing countries. For instance, German companies preferred to carry on production in countries with lower wages, such as Hungary or Czech since the collapse of the Berlin wall in Germany. Based on the calculation of Siemens' CEO, wages in these countries were 80% to 90% lower than that in Germany. Wages paid by them to engineers in France or Italy were only half of that paid to ordinary engineers in Munich. They were not only concerned about wages. German automobile manufacturers have moved production out of Germany in succession so as to win new customers in America or Latin America. This was also to avoid the risks of fluctuation in US dollar or directly eliminate trade barriers and reduce the effect of protective duties. There were some disputes on how many labor posts need to be transferred out of Germany. The president of Federal German Industrialists had claimed that it should be 300,000 posts within 5 years, whereas the German Federation of Trade Unions had advocated for 75,000 posts. In Europe, such rapid change has roused people's fear. There were fierce struggles centering on production bases and welfare state, competitiveness and additional cost of wages. People have become increasingly aware of consequences of globalization, and there were protests outside the fate of each conference on globalization process no matter in Davos, Europe or Seattle, America.

In developed capitalist countries, the number of unemployed people is about 300 million at present, the largest ever since the great world economic crisis. Meanwhile, there are "poor people with jobs" whose wages are almost the same with that in the Third World countries even if they have jobs. The emerging industrial countries are springing up and making large investments on education. Many highly-skilled and professional technical talents who are more excellent than that in Europe are working in China or India. Although the social welfare network is still preventing Europeans from falling into real recession, the network which has always closely connected with the growing living conditions is paving the way for its disruption. Medical insurance and retirement insurance is slowly going to collapse. The struggle to protect production bases going abroad becomes a competition for social welfare system. Governments of different countries are cutting social welfare benefits. Sweden used to be the country with the highest welfare, but the government has to cut medical insurance premium, abandon the allowance for short-term labor years and stipulates certain qualifications for getting medical allowance. At present, simply oral threat of capitalists can make workers voluntarily reduce wages or welfare level so as to avoid unemployment brought by the move of enterprises. For example, the faith that one must adapt to the changed world market is growing in Germany. In the Wiesmann Company engaging in heating equipment, 3,700 workers have stated that they were willing to adopt the 30-hour working week on the condition of maintaining the original payment, so as to prevent the transfer of the production base to Czech.[1] At the same time, multinational corporations enjoy full development. As mentioned in the expert testimony annually published in America's *Fortune* magazine, the turnover of the 500 largest companies and enterprises in the world had increased by 11% in 1995, and their growth rate was 4 times more than the growth rate of the world economy. In terms of profits, these multinational companies had greater growth; the rate nearly amounted to 15% in 1995 and even reached 62% in the previous year before 1995. It indicates that economic globalization results in the accumulation of social wealth in developed capitalist countries and poverty in developing countries. The class confrontation between the bourgeoisie and the proletariat gradually develops all over the world, mainly represented as the confrontation between the international bourgeoisie and the international proletariat, and contradictions between the monopoly bourgeoisie and the general public of the Third World. These contradictions and confrontations will aggravate as the quickening process of economic globalization.

2. Historical Trend in the Evolution of Capitalist Industrial Relations

After developed capitalist countries have experienced the new scientific-

---

[1] Li Cong, Jia Huaqiang and Xie Zhiqiang et. *Research on the Major Issues of Contemporary Capitalist Development*, Vol. 1, p. 740 (the "30-hour working week" in the original text—notes).

technological revolution after World War II and entered into the information era, the rise of emerging high-tech industries such as the information industry, etc. profoundly changed economic relations among people while contributing to the high development of social productive forces. Some economists have denied the decisive role of the ownership of the means of production; basing their ideas on some new changes in modern economic activities and further deny capitalists' exploitation of wage earners.

American economists Neuberger and Duffy believes that the nature of decision-making right is the most important symbol of an economic system (mechanism). Seen from a historical perspective, the decision-making right has four sources: tradition, customs, enforcement, ownership and information. Marxism regards ownership as the most crucial variable for differentiating between economic classes and determining the nature of a social and economic system. However, this viewpoint is becoming less persuasive within the limit of the increasingly important role of information. Information has become the most important foundation for power under modern conditions.[1] The human capital school has also raised the opinion that the post-industrial wave has effectively impaired the traditional division of capitalists and workers and weakened the Marxist viewpoint that the ownership of the means of production has decisive meanings in class analysis. It has marked the "end of the traditional ideologies" and the "emergence of elite dominance". On the contrary, occupational differences caused by education have been the most persuasive clue or guideline for explaining the differentiation and inequality of different groups in the society.[2] Following the clue, it is inevitable that they have reached to the conclusion that class relations in the capitalist society had already had qualitative change.

It is a significant theoretical and practical issue as to how to evaluate the position of information and the means of production in modern economic activities for the reason that it fundamentally determines the position of information owners and owners of the means of production in the production

[1] Egon Neuberger, William J. Duffy: *Comparative Economic Systems*, pp. 35-36. Beijing: The Commercial Press, 1988.

[2] Bell, Daniel. *The Coming of Post-Industrial*. New York: Basic Books. 1976.

of material means of production and other economic activities as well as their mutual relationships, and determines people's judgments on the nature of the society. I can give several specific answers here.

Firstly, we must admit that information, especially advanced scientific and technological information plays a greater role in modern economic development. By means of modern information processing and communication, etc., information is included in the production process through different factors, such as the main body of production, production equipment, production techniques and production organizations, etc. and is becoming the main factor and variable in economic growth and a crucial factor for an enterprise's survival and development. Competition among nations and enterprises are increasingly represented as the competition for the information with scientific and technological knowledge as the core content and the talents who master the information. It is the competition among these demanders and the competition between the suppliers of this kind of resources, i.e. it is scientific and technological personnel and technical workers and demanders that improve the position of various owners of human resources such as scientific and technological personnel in capitalist countries. This indicates that of all kinds of variables that determine interpersonal economic relations, the role of modern information is strengthened indeed. Fundamentally, it is the requirement for the development of productive forces and the outcome of the struggle between scientific and technological personnel and technical workers.

However, we cannot deny the decisive role of the means of production and ownership of the means of production in economic activities and economic relations based on this. The main reasons are:

1) Under the precondition that the means of production and information respectively belong to different subjects, seen from the fundamental aspect of economic structure, owners of the means of production (or owners of material capital) and owners of information (or owners of human capital) have asymmetrical power. The underlying cause is that the means of production is the premise for the production of material goods under any circumstance,

and labor is not provided with "supernatural creativity". Under the restrictive conditions, owners of the means of production may organize production by themselves and survive without owners of human capital; whereas without the means of production, owners of human capital cannot carry on labor in the real sense and survive, which forces owners of human capital to be hired by owners of the means of production. Even if under knowledge economy conditions of today, there are no pure knowledge products but only knowledge-intensive products. Knowledge labor cannot create economic value without the means of production. Consequently, different relations between men and the means of production are the main reasons for the formation of hired labor system. The basic economic relations of capitalism will not change if the capitalist private ownership of the means of production is not abolished.

2) In capitalist enterprises, owners of the means of production and their agents can use not only power but also some systems to ensure that they can obtain necessary management information, so employees can only receive one-sided information and the situation of information asymmetry between the two come into being. The internal hierarchy in enterprises is such a system: The American left-wing scholar Marglin analyzed this in the essay *What Do Bosses Do? The Origins and Functions of Hierarchy in Capitalist Production*. The investigation of the management system in 48 large and medium-sized manufacturing enterprises in Japan made by Marsh, an American sociologist in 1983 proved once again that the distribution of the decision-making right, thus the distribution of information has a close relationship with the internal hierarchy in enterprises. Marsh had reached a conclusion, "Contrary to the belief of many western observers, systems of participative decision making in Japan have not led to workplace democracy. Although the firms allow workers to present their ideas and suggestions… they deny workers authority to make decisions." It is clear that controlling information by power and system is a crucial mean of the bourgeoisie to safeguard its dominance in capitalist economies. The argument of the human capital theory on the rigid and absolute division of owners of material capital

and owners of human capital is doubtable itself.

Under the knowledge economy conditions, some large or high-tech companies establish their internal information network in enterprises. Based on the relevant information, 64% of 1,000 large companies published on the *Fortune* magazine had established their internal information network in enterprises till 1996. This internal network has strengthened information exchange among employees along with improving labor efficiency, enhanced employees' right of speech and made some enterprise managers realize that "network technologies and their easy access to information are eroding the authority and power of management." It indicates that information network technology has surely provided a convenient technical mean for information exchange and democratic management. It cannot be neglected that the level of use of information means and contents exchanged on the network within enterprises are decided by people. On the use of internal network of enterprises, owners and managers will probably choose the latter and weaken the former, at least meticulously search for a fragile balance between the two. The nature of capitalist economic relations and restrictions of such relations to the use of new technologies are clearly manifested under any circumstance.

3) During the process of the development of capitalism, the labor market was constantly improved and laborers were at a disadvantage in the circulation domain of the economy. The unilateral working capacity and the formation of industrial reserve army (it changes some labor as non-scarce resources) are the outcome of such a dynamic process. Under modern capitalist conditions, the government will also formulate and implement some macro-economic policies aiming to stabilize and promote economic development and increase employment. As the American's left-wing scholar Gordon and others have indicated, its essential goal was to realize the "favorable balance between the environment of labor disciplines (demands for enough unemployment) and the utilization of production capacity (sometimes calls for the expansion of demand).[1]

---

[1] Gordon, David M., Samuel Bowles and Thomas E. Weisskopf. *Beyond the Waste Land: A Democratic Alternative to Economic Decline*. New York: Anchor Press, 1983.

In conclusion, the elevation of the status of high-tech information under new economic conditions may position brainworkers and technical workers at an advantage in some industries and posts. However, since the capitalist private ownership of the means of production does not change fundamentally, the basic economic relations of capitalism, i.e., the capitalist wage labor relations do not change. Different from traditional capitalism, interactivity between capital and knowledge is strengthened within the new framework because of the medium and assistance of information technology. The analysis of Britton Manasco, editor of American *Knowledge Inc. Communication* has pointed out this feature to a certain extent: the formation of global capital market rapidly eliminates the political, legal and economic barriers in the creation of knowledge and its application in production. Meanwhile, knowledge quickens capital movement, so capital especially financial capital becomes the pivotal issue. It is such interaction between capital and knowledge that constitutes the core of new economies.[1] However, when we realize that the nature of industrial relations under capitalist conditions does not change, and movements of the working class are generally at a disadvantage at the current stage, we should also realize that the factors that deny the subordination of labor to capital is also growing as the rapid development of socialized production and the opinion on the subordination of labor to capital is sublated in a sense.

When the capitalist mode of production was transformed to the machine industry stage, Marx had realized that factors that ultimately free labor from capital dominance would gradually appear during the capitalist production process accompanied with the gradually maturing capitalist mode of production. That is: 1) Though the old-type division of work is kept in capitalist enterprise system, the uniform, interchangeable and simple labor capacity caused by machine industry provides technical possibilities for the transition of labor, change of functions and overall flow of workers, for people's free choice of careers and individual development in an all-round

[1] Chen Luzhi: "Knowledge Economy and Functions of Capital", in *Pacific Journal*, 1992.

way. 2) Machines combine natural force and science, greatly improving labor productivity, which cannot only shorten workers' necessary labor time and prolong surplus labor time, but also save labor time, increase free time and offer possibilities for full development of individuals in terms of time. 3) Labor is actually subordinated to production socialization which forms capital, further intensifying its agonistic contradiction with the capitalist ownership. At this time, individual possession of production conditions not only becomes unnecessary but also incompatible with large-scale production. Socialized material productive forces provide material possibilities for the change from the capitalist ownership to the socialist public ownership. 4) The most sound and proper form of machine system is automatic machine system, once production develops into this stage, "labor performance is not included in the production process as before, but is conversely represented in the way men have a relation with the production process itself as supervisors and regulators in the production process." At that time, it is inevitable that workers will get rid of the actual subordination to capital. Seen from Marx's more profound meaning, capitalism is the "last development of the value relation and the production system based on value". Once production develops into the stage of overall automatic machine system, labor time will cease being the measure of wealth, and exchange value will cease being the measure of use value. "From then on, production based upon exchange values will collapse and the immediate process of material production will be stripped of its form and its miserable contradictions."[1] The formal subordination of labor to capital and capitalist relations of production fundamentally is defeated on the basis for its existence and finally will turn to the opposite.

The statements of Marx inspire us that, seen from a dialectic perspective, the factors that confirm the subordination of labor to capital also exactly negate the subordination of labor to capital. Under modern capitalist conditions, higher productive forces formed by the new scientific-revolutionary revolution has increasingly become the factors freeing labor

---

[1] *Karl Marx and Frederick Engels*, Chinese version, Edition 1, Vol. 46 (II), pp. 217-218.

from capital dominance while deepening the subordination of labor to capital.

Firstly, production automation driven by the scientific-technological revolution made some wage earners in developed capitalist countries get rid of onerous physic labor and become the controller of automatic equipment. In the *Capital*, Marx had realized that few "senior workers" such as engineers and mechanists, etc. appeared alongside traditional "factory workers" who worked on a part of the equipment for their whole life. As the extensive application of electronic computers in the industry and the development of automatic and semi-automatic production, the labor structure of developed capitalist countries has dramatically changed. The significance of simple labor and non-skilled labor has gradually declined and that of complex labor and skilled labor has gradually increased. Knowledge laborers are an important part of "general workers", a crucial category raised by Marx. At that time, there were mainly detail laborers engaging in partial labor due to the differentiation within enterprises, and detail laborers with extremely different educational backgrounds have constituted general workers. Consequently, general workers at that time were mainly a micro-category. Marx's category can still be used in the original sense under new economic conditions. However, out of the increasingly intensive social requirements, knowledge labor has gradually developed into a relatively independent part of social division of work and knowledge laborers have become the main body of some industries formed by knowledge labor. At that time, the category could be used in a macro sense, whose meanings were: social division of work gradually resulting in the demand for workers with different educational backgrounds in different industries, making them detail laborers with different knowledge accumulation. They as a whole constitute general workers in a macro-sense and knowledge laborers are laborers with more knowledge accumulation and more brainwork expenditure compared to the whole labor force. For instance, white collars had accounted for 50% and professionals accounted for 15% of all employees in America in 1978.[1]

---

[1] Gao Feng: *Capital Accumulation Theory and Modern Capitalism*, p. 243, Tianjin, Nankai University Press, 1991.

Such circumstance was the result of both technical progress and capital's requirements. Under the conditions of generally shortened working days and increasingly fierce competition among developed capitalist countries, relative surplus value is becoming the driving force for capitalist production. The inherent tendency of capital that "endows production with a scientific nature" has an increasingly prominent expression, which has inexorably led to the increase of senior technicians such as scientists and engineers, etc. who are employed by capital. Besides, owing to the great increase of fixed capital led by the scientific and technological revolution, the functions of live labor for preserving capital are becoming more and more important in these semi-automatic and automatic factories. Those extremely complicated and expensive machines need to be maintained and repaired by live labor, which demand for advanced technologies and knowledge. This has given rise to the increase of senior technicians like machinists, etc. Even though these intellectual laborers are also subject to the control of old-type division of work in capitalist enterprises, they have gained more freedom in the control of the latest labor means, i.e. machines. It indicates that when strengthening the actual subordination of labor to capital, some labors had to be gradually liberated from the actual subordination (or to a certain degree). Besides, there is a mutual-conditional and contradictory tendency between the two trends. Though the part of laborers have got rid of the control of material existence of capital on themselves, they are still subordinated to the requirements for appreciation of capital and were subordinated to capital in form. However, in some high-tech industries, the difficulty of capital's control of labor has increased due to the improvement of knowledge and status of knowledge labor. The requirements for freeing labor from capital dominance are further represented in these industries. The employee stock ownership has shown a rapid development in developed capitalist countries under the context of such indication. Those knowledge labor-intensive high-tech industries were industries with intensive employee stock ownership.

After the decline for several decades, the power of the working class in America had showed indications of recovery in the late 1990s. It was firstly represented as the increase of labor union members in white collar workers. It was probably connected with the above discussed tendency. In the early period, the white collar labor had not participated in labor unions. The reason was that although trained workers did not regard themselves as a part of the management, they thought they were professionals at least. Such feeling had separated them from ordinary workers. Nevertheless, the extensive and profound application of science and technology in production has homogenized or standardized many professional works, such as professions of teachers, policemen, nurses and public servants, etc. Such standardization has lowered their social status, and made them aware of the fact that they were indeed only wage earners. Based on statistics, about one third of all government employees at all levels in America are labor union members nowadays, approximately 2.5 times of employees in private enterprises participating in labor unions.[1]

Labor union struggles have also recovered with the recovery of labor unions. Nearly all important strikes of American workers had failed from the early 1980s to the middle 1990s. Nevertheless, two significant strikes in the summer of 1997 and 1998 have achieved success, demonstrating the relatively bright future for labor unions. In the summer of 1997, the express man of the United Parcel Service Inc. (UPS) had held a strike demanding for work protection and welfare for part-time workers. Workers of UPS have established good personal relationships with their clients on account of their efficient and polite services, which has contributed to the sympathy of the public and a huge wave on supporting strikers. The opinion poll made by the CBS News in the strike peak showed that the proportion of people supporting workers to that supporting the company was 52 to 36. UPS management had signed new contracts in favor of workers under public pressure. The victory of UPS workers' strike has greatly enhanced the confidence of labor unions across the country and resulted in the strike of workers of the General Motors Corporation launched by the labor union of United Auto Workers (UAW)

---

[1] Jeffrey E. Cohen: *Politics and Economic Policy in the United States*, second edition, Houghton Mitflin Company, Boston New York, 2000, pp. 131-132.

in 1988. This strike had also won the support of the public. Investigations showed that the proportion of people supporting the labor union to the company was 42: 31. Again, the management compromised with the labor union supported by the strong public.[1]

Without doubt, victory of two strikes does not mean that American labor unions have restored growth and labor movements have stronger power today. All factors that influence and impair the power of labor unions are still at work. Both strikes had happened in the period when there was a healthy expansion of the American economy and significant growth of enterprises' profits. Under this circumstance, the public had believed that enterprises were capable of providing workers with higher wages and better working conditions. Besides, we can see an important indication that labor unions regained a positive image in the public and the support of the public was a crucial means for labor unions to win the struggle with the management.

Secondly, capital's sublation owing to the movement of the basic capitalist contradiction has loosened the formal subordination of labor to capital to a certain degree. Under modern capitalist conditions, capital's sublation owing to the movement of the basic capitalist contradiction is represented in the evolution of forms of capitalist ownership, the creation of legal person's capital and other aspects on one hand. This is the self-sublation of capital within its limits. This provided a material foundation for full-time managers to play a greater role and for workers to take part in the enterprise management on the surface. On the other hand, contradiction is represented as the positive sublation of capital and the gradual development of workers' cooperative enterprises. Based on statistics, the number of cooperative members around the world has reached about 100 million in 1934. The development of cooperative movements was disrupted during World War II. However, cooperative movements had shown sustainable development after the war; and the number of cooperative members in the world had increased to 120 million in 1953 and further rose to nearly 500 million in 1984. Till

---

[1] Refer to Jeffrey E. Cohen: *Politics and Economic Policy in the United States*, second edition, Houghton Mitflin Company, Boston New York, 2000, p.135.

1995, the total number of cooperative members all over the world has reached 750 million and the number of immediate beneficiaries of them was approximately 3 billion, accounting for over a half of the total population in the world. Various cooperatives have provided job opportunities for 100 million people. This type of enterprises have provided a material foundation for workers to be the owners of production conditions and actually take part in enterprise management, and has enabled the formal subordination of labor to capital be "actively sublated".

After its establishment for nearly 200 years, the capitalist economic system has greatly changed human behavioral motive, way of act and organizational functions. It also has formed a flexible social system, which provides system conditions for the quicker and higher development of productive forces. Information economy appearing earliest in western developed countries was the outcome of that system. While on the one side, realizing the fact that capitalist economic relations can adapt to the development of productive forces within a long period, we should also admit the contradictions between it and the productive forces -contradictions between socialized production and capitalist private ownership. To adapt to the development of productive forces, capitalist economic relations were forced to be adjusted. On the one hand, cooperative economy organized by laborers had a rapid development within capitalism and cooperatives have become economic organizations with certain influences and enjoy widespread recognition by the society. This is the positive sublation of capitalist economic relations. On the other hand, adjustments to economic relations were made within the limits of capitalist systems, and negative sublation is the main aspect of the evolution of capitalist economic relations. Though the nature of capital does not change through negative sublation, its mode of existence has changed from individual capital to monopoly capital, government capital and legal person's capital, and the tendency of socialization of capital is strengthening. To adapt to this, there were also some changes of the management system and distribution system of capitalism. For instance, new ways of distribution such as employee stock ownership has appeared and new-type horizontal management systems such as participation in management have gradually replaced the pyramid hierarchy. These constant marginal adjustments of capitalist economic relations driven by new technologies and new economic conditions has formed some factors of the new society. Workers can probably use and drive these factors under the circumstance of the continual improvement of their quality, unite again in the world, develop labor movements in a larger scale and realize their historical mission by new ways.

Chapter VI

Capitalist Relations of Distribution and Its Historical Evolution

The relations of distribution is an important aspect of capitalist economic relations. After World War II, the relation of distribution in main capitalist countries had significant changes due to profound and complicated internal and external reasons. This was mainly represented as: multiple forms of income of workers, increased income, reinforced role of workers in the distribution of income and gradually improved social welfare system. The basic living conditions of most workers were guaranteed to a certain extent, the social income gap widened and governments interfered into the primary distribution and redistribution process of personal income in an all-around way. Reviewing significant changes in the contemporary capitalist relation of distribution through the basic theories and scientific methods of Marxism is of significant theoretical and practical meanings for us to accurately realize and scientifically grasp the historical process and development trend of capitalism.

I. New Phenomena in the Relations of Distribution

Changes of the relation of distribution in main western capitalist countries after World War II were mainly reflected as many unprecedented new phenomena in workers' income. It is a requisite to explore new changes of contemporary capitalist relation of distribution, see the essence through the phenomena, and systematically and comprehensively understand new changes in terms of workers' income, revenue sources and the mechanism of income distribution, etc.

1. Main Forms of Employees' Income in the Contemporary Capitalism

The forms of income changed with economic and social development, and the forms of income also had continual development and evolution over long-term historical development of capitalist countries. In the development history of capitalism, there are many forms of income. At present, there are many forms of income in capitalist countries, mainly including the following:

Transformation and disruption:

1) wage income. This is the most common income form, referring to the income gained by workers in accordance with the hourly wage standard and working time stipulated in labor contracts. The wage income of workers in modern capitalist enterprises is mainly worked out on hours. In capitalist enterprises, workers' wages are divided in grades, and capitalist enterprises have a set of measures on evaluating the wage standard. There are great differences in the division of wage grade and determination of wage standard in different countries and industries. Generally speaking, the wage standard of workers in different countries and industries are determined based on capabilities, working strength, responsibilities and labor environment, etc. The difference between the wage of the highest level and the lowest level is 30% to 100%. Before the 1950s and 1960s, the piece work system was generally adopted in some industries of some capitalist countries, such as

clothes, shoemaking and cigarette, etc. However, as the improvement of level of mechanism and automation, the piece work system lost its meaning and was generally replaced by other forms of wages.

The salary of managers is also divided into different grades. The monthly pay system is adopted for ordinary managers and the yearly salary system is adopted for senior managers. The grades and standards of salaries are determined by factors such as the length of service, working capacities, positions and responsibilities, etc. There are substantial differences in salaries if grades are different.

The wages of workers and managers account for the largest proportion of all income in contemporary main western capitalist countries. However, seen from the perspective of development and changes, the growth rate of wage income is lower than that of other income (such as bonus, welfare and dividends, etc.). Generally speaking, the proportion of wage income to all income of employees is mainly between 60% and 80%. For instance, the proportion is approximately 70% in America, 60% in Germany, 70% in Sweden and 80% in Britain.

2) Bonus income. Bonus is a kind of income paid to employees when they over-fulfill production tasks, or the income distributed to employees besides wages when enterprises obtain excess profits. During the early period and rising stage of the capitalist development, some enterprises distributed bonuses to workers, but the distribution of bonus income was not common and was not related to enterprises' operating benefits at that time. However, bonus income is relevant to enterprises' operating benefits in contemporary capitalism. If enterprises have good operating benefits, there will be more bonuses; otherwise there will be no or less bonus.

Bonus income is a common income form of employees in contemporary capitalist countries. There are two forms of common bonus income as follows: the first one is the bonus income directly related to employees' amount of labor. Such bonus income, which is based on the employees' individual amount of labor, can be obtained by employees if they finish the work well. The common bonus forms are: Gantt award, which refers to awards granted to people who fulfill or over-fulfill tasks based on the standard time, apart from daily payment of guaranteed wages; Halsey award, which refers to a part of saved time wages gained by employees as awards apart from basic wages, when the actual labor time consumed in production is lower than the norm of working hour, and the other part is owned by enterprises; Roth award, which refers the bonus based on the actual work time and calculated on the basis of the percentage of saved time to the quota standard time; Emerson award, which means that the efficiency index is calculated as the actual work time divided by the standard time, and based on certain efficiency index, wages will be calculated on the basis of the norm of working hour if lower than the standard efficiency index and bonus will not be distributed; and for the part higher than the standard efficiency index, bonus will be distributed on the basis of different ratios and the bonus ratio will be increased as the enhancement of efficiency. The second one is the bonus income indirectly related to the employees' amount of labor. Such form of bonus income does not have a direct relationship with employees' individual amount of labor and labor quality, but is related to the overall operating status of enterprises. Capitalists distribute a part of enterprises' profits to employees as an award based on benefits. For instance, the American automobile industry stipulates that 15% of the industry's profits before tax shall be distributed to employees as bonuses. The amount of bonuses for managers and ordinary workers are significantly different. Bonuses of managers, especially senior managers are much greater than ordinary workers.

Bonus income is a common income form of employees in enterprises of contemporary capitalist countries, which accounts for a considerable proportion in employees' income. It is especially the case in Japan. Based on the statistics of Merton Peck, professor of the Yale University, America, the bonus income accounted for approximately three quarters of the non-wage income of employees in Japan and one quarter of the total amount of their annual income. Bonus has become an important part of workers' income in Japan.

3) Allowance income. It refers to the extra-wage income gained by employees from enterprises, which reflects their positions, skills, specialty of work, and cost-of-living allowances. There is a wide variety and extensive scale of allowance income for employees in capitalist enterprises, such as duty allowance, skill allowance, allowance appropriate to special functions, family allowance, region allowance, house allowance, traffic allowance, allowance for children's education, allowance for work stoppage, allowance for wage adjustment and longevity pay, etc.

4) Employee stock ownership bonus income. It refers to the income form that employees become shareholders of the company after purchasing stocks of the company and obtain bonuses from enterprises on account of stocks in enterprises which adopt employee stock ownership. The bonus income appeared in the early stage of capitalist development and popularized after the 1960s and 1970s. There are two types of employee stock ownership bonuses: one is fundamental employee stock ownership income, enterprises transfer all stock ownership and the ownership of an enterprise to employees, and most of enterprises' profits are distributed to employees. Sometimes employees gain higher income thanks to the possession of the company's stock. The other is employee stock ownership bonus, such as employees' purchase of stocks by wages or purchase of stocks by loans or by savings, etc. America is the source area of employee stock ownership plans. The statistics of the American National Center for Employee Stock Ownership indicate that during the 23 years from 1975 to 1998, the number of enterprises adopting employee stock ownership increased from 1,600 to 11,400, the number of employees with stock ownership increased from 248,000 to 8.5 million, and the total amount of stocks held by employees reached USD500 billion until the end of 1999.

5) Welfare income. Welfare income of employees in capitalist enterprises mainly comes from two aspects: one is the welfare system of enterprises, i.e. welfare provided by enterprises to their employees. The welfare income gained from enterprises in contemporary capitalist countries is very multifarious and common, including a wide variety of contents from

cars, health insurance to free or low-price lunch and public bathhouse for employees, etc. Generally speaking, the enterprise welfare income may be divided into merit welfare income, guarantee welfare income and willingness welfare income. The merit welfare income is the income determined by the significance of employees themselves. It is the award income representing both status and contributions made to the position, mainly including company's cars, awards, bonuses, dividends, stock options and private health insurance, etc. The guarantee welfare income is the welfare income with significant influences upon the long-term interests of individuals, mainly including pension insurance premium and sick-pay insurance income, etc. The willingness welfare income mainly includes holiday wage income, maternity leave wage income, vacation wage income and traffic allowance income, etc. Some insurance are borne by employers whereas some are jointly borne by employers and employees, and most insurance premium are jointly shared by employers and employees. The welfare income refers to the shares borne by employers. Some of the welfare obtained by employees from enterprises are prescribed in national laws and some are stipulated by enterprises themselves. Japan is a country with high enterprise welfare and the employees' welfare accounts for over 60% of their extra-wage income. In Germany, employees' pension insurance accounts for 18.7% of their wages, of which employers and employees respectively pay 9.35%; the average medical insurance accounts for about 12.3% of the average wage of employees, and employers and employees respectively pay 6.15%. Wages are paid within six weeks of employees' sickness, and for the part exceeding the time limit, medical insurance institutions offer sickness subsidies, which account for 80% of wages. The part of these insurance paid by employers is the welfare income obtained by employees from enterprises.

The other is the welfare income from the society, which refers to the welfare provided by the government to all residents. There are many social welfare projects implemented by governments in western countries, their specific contents and regulations are different in various countries and are continually adjusted with changes of economic situation. The welfare income from the society are mainly distributed in cash, and a part (such as medical treatment, education, houses, school lunch, elders and children's nutrition plan, etc.) are distributed in kind. Besides, a kind of indirect income from deduction or exemption of taxes such as some social allowance, scholarships and grants for students, etc. falls into the category of indirect income obtained from social welfare. The direct income and indirect income obtained by residents from social welfare are different because people have different income. High-income earners gain less and low income earners gain more. Generally speaking, the social welfare income accounts for a considerable proportion in residents' income. For instance, the welfare income per capita in Britain had reached 2,000 pounds in 1997.

2. Recent Changes in the Contemporary Capitalist Distribution Relations

Through the aforesaid review of the capitalist relation of distribution, we find out that the capitalist relation of distribution continually changes with the development of capitalism. Compared with capitalism in the early period and rising stage, the contemporary capitalist relation of distribution has distinct features, mainly represented as:

1) For the determination of wages, the former determination of wages by the single party of employers was changed as the determination of wages by the three parties of employers, labor unions and governments. In the early capitalist period, workers' wages were solely determined by employers and workers were powerless in the determination of wages. This is because the working class was weak and dispersed without organization. To extract more surplus value, capitalists always tried every means to force down workers' wages and desperately squeezed out the sweat labor of workers so that some wage systems were named as the "sweating system" in Britain at that time.[1] As the development of social production, the number of workers increasingly grew, the working class gradually developed, expanded and fought against the capitalist class for their own rights and interests. During the struggle

[1] Marx: *Capital*, Edition 1, Vol. 1, p. 606.

process, their organizations—labor unions came into being, which marks that "the collisions between individual workmen and individual bourgeois take more and more the character of collisions between two classes. Thereupon, the workers begin to form combinations (trade unions) against the bourgeois; they group together in order to keep up the rate of wages; they found permanent associations in order to make provision beforehand for these occasional revolts. Here and there, the contest breaks out into riots."[1] After World War II, capitalists were forced to negotiate with workers in labor unions on wages and other issues due to rising labor movements and high-level organization of labor unions. Strong labor unions greatly restricted and balanced the power of capitalists, and many of workers' rights were gained in negotiations with capitalists through labor unions. Meanwhile, governments formulated and improved many laws on industrial relations, which played an important role in resolving conflicts between the employers and employees and regulating their negotiations on wages. Workers' wages such as wage rate, forms of payment of wages, time for payment, wage and welfare increase, wage category and wage structure, etc. were determined through negotiations between labor unions and employers under the recognition and protection of laws. Governments generally did not prescribe workers' wages, but in turn played their role in the determination of wages as to mainly formulate laws relating to wages. The most influential law is minimum wage legislation, social security donation and payment legislation.

2) The social security system plays an increasingly significant role in the redistribution of income. Another important feature of the contemporary capitalist relation of income distribution is the continual improvement of social security system. The modern security system originated from the 1880s. During the period, the struggles of the working class for social security increasingly sprang up due to the worsened world economic crisis. To mitigate social contradictions, the German Empire Parliament passed relevant decrees in succession from 1883 to 1889, ratifying the establishment

---

[1] *Selected Works of Marx and Engels*, Edition 2, Vol. 1, p. 281.

of a series of systems by the nation such as health insurance plans (1883), industrial accidents insurance plans (1984), and retirement insurance plans (1889), etc. It is the first formal social security system in history. After World War II, on account of the formation of a peaceful environment, capitalist countries established the social security system one after another when restoring and developing economy and arranged it as a common system so as to regulate class relations within the society, mitigate social contradictions and realize the steady growth of economy. Table 6-1 indicates the spread of the social security system in different countries of the world after World War II.

Table 6-1 Spread of the Social Security System in Different Countries of the World

item / year	1940	1949	1958	1967	1977	1985
With any kind of guarantee	57	58	80	120	129	142
With old age disability and survivor insurance	33	44	58	92	114	132
With sickness and maternity insurance	24	36	59	65	72	83
With employment injury insurance	57	57	77	117	129	136
With unemployment insurance	21	22	26	34	38	40
With family allowance	7	27	38	62	65	64

Source: *Global Social Security System*, compiled by the U.S. Social Security Administration. Beijing: Huaxia Publishing Co., Ltd., 1989.

As the gradual generalization of social security, it represents the following specific features itself. Firstly, the contents of social security increasingly expanded. After World War II, all main capitalist countries further improved their social security system, improved residents' social welfare and guaranteed the life of low-income earners to a certain extent. The spread of various specific social security systems in different countries of the world since the 1940s, as represented in Table 6-1, indicates such feature to a certain degree. Secondly, the scale of social welfare and guarantee increasingly expanded and the proportion of expenditures to the financial expenditures of all countries was increasing. For instance, the social security expenditure in Japan accounted for 18.8% of Japan's national income in 1998, and the proportion was 18.4% in America, 37.6% in Germany and

46.1% in Sweden. The proportion of expenditure included in the American social security plan to budgets was 28% in 1960 and it rose to 59% in 1994.[1] Thirdly, laws and regulations on social welfare were formulated to further legalize and institutionalize social welfare. Because of the emphasis on legality and institutionalization, the social welfare system in western countries is represented as a legal system constituted by a series of laws and regulations in the legal aspect. For example, the basic laws on social security in Japan are the *Life Protection Activities*, the *Children Welfare Act*, the *Disabled Welfare Act*, the *Act on the Welfare for People in Poor Condition of Body and Mind*, the *Elder Welfare Act*, and the *Act on the Welfare for Mothers, Children and Widows*, etc. In addition, there are 283 specific laws and regulations on social security in Japan. In Germany, there are the *Unemployment Insurance Act*, the *Federation Social Economy Act*, the *Federation Children Subsidy Act*, the *Act on Subsidies for Old Farmers*, the *Labor Promotion Act*, and the *Federation Training Classes*, etc. Other countries also issued a series of social security legislations centering on the establishment of welfare states, such as education act, family allowances act, national insurance act, national medical and health care and national assistance act, etc. These laws and regulations specifically prescribe the items of social security, objects of security, standards, ways for collecting funds, and the methods for implementing management, etc., form definite systems, and make enforcers and objects of security have laws and regulations to abide by. Main western capitalist countries have established sound social welfare and security system through development for several decades.

3) The labor income gap narrows down and the gap between capital and labor income widens. Generally speaking, the difference of individual labor and production efficiency in contemporary capitalist countries is low and gradually reducing. It is mainly represented as the decreasing amount of rich people and poor people and the increasing amount of middle-income earners. Some middle-income earners rely on their labor income and some

[1] Samuelson: *Microeconomics*, the 16th edition, p. 233, Beijing, Huaxia Publishing Co., Ltd., 1999.

rely on capital income, but most of them rely on labor income. At present, the proportion of the income of middle-level families to the total income increased by 10% compared with that after World War II, and reached over 50%; the proportion of the income of upper-level families to the total income decreased by 7.5% compared with that after the war and is approximately 40%. The proportion of the income of the low-level families to the total income increased by 1% compared with that after war and is approximately 5% at present. Therefore, the growth rate of the proportion of the income of middle-level families to the total income of national families is higher than that of upper-level and low-level families, which indicates the tendency that the labor income gap is narrowing down. The gap between capital income and labor income is rapidly widening when the wage income gap narrows down. In fact, it is the amount of fortune and capital that contributes to the increased intensity of income distribution in western society. The pure labor income cannot lead to serious income inequality, concentration of fortune and capital in the minority determines the extremely high intensity of income, and the minority has a large share of social income. Based on the report of American *Business Week*, the annual profit growth rate of the 900 largest multinational corporations in America was 19% in 1999 and the labor cost in America that year only increased by 1.8%. Consequently, workers' income was out of proportion to companies' profits. The disposable weekly wages and disposable income of employees engaging in non-agricultural production in America decreased from 1978 to 1995, and they were still lower than that in the 1970s till 1999 though there was an increase after 1995. Besides, based on the 2000 Development Report of the World Bank, the working time of workers in Germany and Japan had few change in the late period of the 1990s and the beginning period of the 1980s. The value created by workers had a large increase due to the improvement of labor productivity; however, their wages did not increase accordingly. Thus the difference between the value created by workers and labor price greatly increased. Calculated on the basis of per capita, the difference increased from USD 19,237 to USD 46,390 in Germany and from USD 22,150 to USD 60,895 in Japan. The difference between the capital income and labor income in the two countries further widened as well. The circumstances in America, Germany and Japan show that the gap between the rich and the poor widens and enormous wealth is centralizing in the hands of the minority. The polarization tendency is intensifying in contemporary capitalist societies. The rich get richer and the poor get poorer. A large amount of people require relief and there are prominent contradictions between the rich and the poor. From 1973 to 1995, the GDP per capita in America increased by 36% without considering the factor of inflation. However, the actual hourly wage of ordinary employees decreased by 14%. The income gap between the 10% top-level high-income earners and the 10% bottom-level laborers widened from 7.5:1 in 1969 to 11:1 in 1992. The proportion of poor people living below the poverty line was 16.5% is America, 15% in Britain and 10% in Germany.[1]

4) Governments strengthen management and regulation of income distribution. The bourgeoisie generally began to manage and regulate social income distribution by the government after World War II, and contemporary capitalist governments further strengthened such functions. Firstly, different countries actively use legal means to standardize the relation of distribution. Different countries built sound legislation systems to legalize and standardize the relation of distribution, such as the minimum wage act, social security act and occupational protection act, etc. Secondly, governments regulate income distribution by strengthening taxation means. In contemporary capitalist countries, taxes account for a considerable proportion in GNP, approximately between 40% to 50%, and the high amount amounts to 60% (in Sweden). Strong taxation functions provide governments with enough financial resources to guide and regulate economic operation and redistribution of national income. Thirdly, governments directly intervene in the relation of income distribution endangering the objective of governments based on domestic political and economic requirements.

---

[1] Zhu Guohong: "Accurately Understand the Self-Adjustment, Reformation and Improvement in Developed Capitalist Countries", in *Journal of Fudan University (Social Science Edition)*, 2000 (6).

II. Main Reasons for Changes in the Capitalist Relations of Distribution

Enormous changes in the contemporary capitalist relation of distribution happened out of profound and complicated economic and social, internal and external reasons instead of for no reason. The dominant bourgeoisie was forced to continually adjust the relation of distribution due to complicated historical and objective reasons instead of showing compassion and mercy.

1. Influences of Changes in Capitalist Ownership upon the Relation of Distribution

The rapid development of share economy in different contemporary western capitalist countries results in new changes of capital ownership and further influences the relation of distribution.

1) The legal person ownership leads to the change of capitalists' status as the subject of distribution. After World War II, natural person decreases and institutional shareholders rapidly increase because of significant changes in the equity structure of enterprises in western countries. The separation of owners from business managers further socializes the use of the means of production and socializes shareholders as well. Most stocks of companies in western countries concentrated in the hands of a minority of big capitalists before the war. For instance, the Ford family held over 80% stocks of the company in the 1930s. Situations changed after the war. There is a rapid increase of stocks purchased by individual residents and business entities. For example, the Volkswagen AG has 700,000 minority shareholders at present, who hold over 80% stocks of the company. The new development of joint-stock system leads to changes in the distribution of capital income. In the past, the owners of capital were capitalists, who were opposite to laborers as personified capital. However, in modern big capitalist companies, the rising institutional shareholders cut direct relations between natural person as owners of money capital and corporate capital, and weaken their right to control income distribution of the company. The ownership and business

management right within the enterprise are increasingly separated as the extensive development of joint stock companies. Capitalists used to be both owners of capital and operators and managers, whereas owners of capital and operators are separated nowadays. It is the general meeting of shareholders, board of directors and senior managers that operate and manage capital. It is of great significance for mangers to operate capital and managers have increasingly greater power in using capital. They may attach greater importance to the steady and long-term development of enterprises, and pay more attention to the cooperation with employees, thus further lead to a series of changes in the capitalist relation of income distribution.

2) Employee stock ownership promotes socialization of capitalist distribution. Many enterprises promote employee stock ownership plans to strengthen the relationship between employees and enterprises as the development of share economy. Employee stock ownership plans and governments' implementation of preferential tax policies on these plans stimulate employees' enthusiasm in purchasing of stocks in the company, many employees become shareholders of the company and the shareholder team rapidly expands. The number of direct shareholders in America was only 6.5 million in 1952, accounting for 4% of the total population, and it sharply increased to 47 million in 1985, accounting for 25% of the total population. At present, approximately one quarter of American workers have partial fortune of their companies, and such number exceeds the number of employees participating in labor unions. The proportion of employees holding shares in French industrial sectors reached 50% and is even up to 90% in some enterprises. More than 20 million people hold shares in Japan. There are tens of thousands even hundreds of thousands of shareholders in big companies of capitalist countries at present, greatly increasing the decentralization level of capital. Most of the tens of thousands of shareholders are minority shareholders, whose stock quantity only accounts for a small proportion and will not exert decisive influences upon the operation and decision of the company. Nevertheless, such change of capital ownership in contemporary capitalism greatly influences the capitalist

relation of distribution. Because on the one hand, employees possess the right to distribute enterprises' bonuses as they possess a part of enterprises' assets. On the other hand, capital socialization promotes socialization of the relation of distribution, influences and determines a series of changes in the distribution system.

3) The development of state ownership plays an important role in the regulation of income distribution. After the war, developed countries generally develop state-owned or state joint-stock enterprises in the sectors of basic industry, infrastructure, public utility, and emerging risk industries, etc. through nationalization of private enterprises and financial appropriation for new establishment, state share-holding and other channels. Though there was a wave of privatization of state-owned enterprises in western countries in the 1980s and many state-owned enterprises were sold to individuals, the proportion of government capital to the aggregate social capital is between 10% and 15% nowadays. Considerable amount of government capital enable a country to intervene and regulate income distribution with stronger power and enable the smooth implementation of income distribution policies.

2. The Influence of State Intervention in the Changes of Distribution Relations

In the past, contradictions between the employers and employees always led to the opposition between the employers and employees, and strikes continually happened to be a serious social problem. Under stress from workers' strikes and in order to safeguard the long-term interests of the capitalist class, capitalists and countries representing the interests of capitalists adopted many concession and pacification policies towards workers and labor unions after World War II. This was especially evident in the 1960s, which mitigated industrial relations on the surface. In terms of different countries, for the purposes of mitigating class contradictions and maintain social stability and economic development, main capitalist countries, such as America, Britain, France and Sweden, etc. formulated many laws on industrial relations, which specify laborers' rights that can relatively protect workers' interests, and legalize the relations between the employers and employees. In terms of enterprises, developed capitalist countries generally carry on "democratic management" and absorb employees to take part in partial decision-making, supervision, inspection and management of enterprises, mitigate industrial relations and internalize contradictions between the employers and employees through share of interests and other forms. The "joint decision system" in Germany, the "employee representative executive council system" in America and the "worker representative system" in Sweden can be cited as examples. Besides, it is very common for employees to hold shares, and the forms of participation are constantly innovated within capitalist enterprises. The aforesaid circumstances show that the bourgeoisie has limited labor movements within the scale of its permission through macro-economic situation in favor of capital appreciation and various micro institutional arrangements in the contemporary capitalist society. The issue has also been elaborated in Chapter IV.

Changes in industrial relations exert great influences upon the capitalist relation of distribution, which are beneficial to the bourgeoisie. Firstly, "democratic management" enables employees directly to participate in enterprises' decision making. Employees raise their opinions, requirements and suggestions through labor unions when their personal interests are involved and workers have a feeling that their personal interests are seemingly protected. Secondly, employees can gain a part of income from bonuses through stock ownership, which increases income and alleviates their pressure on demanding for increase of wages. Thirdly, the economic situation of increased unemployment rate and declined increase of income caused by the capital's control of labor has not led to big strike upsurges of workers. For instance, the annual unemployment rate in European communities was 2.2% in the 1960s, and the rate increased to 4.3% in the 1970s, reaching 10% in the 1980s and about 9% in the 1990s and 2000. Though the unemployment rate in America, Japan and Canada are lower than that in European countries, it also has an increasing tendency, and the employment rate was respectively 4%, 4.7% and 7.6% in 2000. Employees' income tends to decrease and have slow increase when there is a significant increase of unemployment rate. Except that the income tends to be the same or have slight increase in Japan and Canada, income in America, Britain, France, Italy, Germany, Australia and other countries all decreases. Even though unemployment rate rises and income decreases, they have not caused widespread large-scale resistance and strikes of workers as before. Fourthly, industrial relations determined by governments in the legislation form guarantee employees' interests to a certain extent. America, Britain, France, Sweden, Japan and other countries developed and improved many laws on industrial relations and formed systems, which specify the power of labor unions and group negotiation and group agreement system relatively safeguarding workers' interests. A set of complete laws on industrial relations was formed in America, such as the *Fair Labor Standards Act*, the *Working Time Act*, the *Social Security Act*, the *Equal Pay Act*, and the *Retirement Income Security Act*, etc. There are similar laws in Japan, such as the *Labor Standard Act*, the *Labor Safety and Sanitation Act*, the *Labor Union Act* and the *Industrial Relation Adjustment Act*, etc.

One of the crucial economic features of contemporary capitalist countries is the enormous intervention of the state on economic activities. State intervention exerts great influences upon capitalist economies, especially significantly changes the capitalist relation of income distribution through intervention in income distribution. The influences of state intervention upon distribution are mainly represented as:

Firstly, state intervention leads to the change of subjects of the primary distribution of income. In the past, capitalists actually occupied the decision-making position as subjects and workers were passive objects in the primary distribution of income. After state invention in economy, through the formulation of a series of laws and regulations, such as minimum wage and maximum working hour legislation, etc., it enabled itself to be the important subject of income distribution in the relation of primary distribution, and improved the status of workers' representatives, i.e. labor unions to a certain extent in the primary distribution.

Secondly, the inequality between the rich and the poor was alleviated to a certain extent through regulation of redistribution of national income. Contemporary capitalist countries formulated all kinds of financial and monetary policies in macro-economic regulation, which greatly strengthened the leading role of national financial budgets and currency issue in the redistribution of income. Western developed countries greatly expanded their scale of financial revenue through taxation and other means after the war. The proportion of financial revenue to GNP rapidly increases and is even up to a half in some countries. The reinforcing state financial power provides nations with enough financial resources to formulate a series of social welfare and security systems, thus influencing the contemporary capitalist relation of income distribution.

III. Evolution of Welfare System in Contemporary Capitalist Countries

After World War II, western capitalist countries generally strengthen the government's role in the distribution of income, reform the social welfare system, increase the share of distributed social welfare by increasing taxes, and realize relative "fairness" in the distribution of personal income in contemporary capitalist society through social redistribution as the development of economy.

1. Functions of the State in the Distribution of Income

The functions of capitalist countries in the distribution of income gradually improved after World War II and are mainly represented as the following forms in the contemporary era:

1) Regulate and influence income distribution by taxation means and policies. Taxes include individual income tax, inheritance tax, gift tax and consumption tax, etc., of which individual income tax is the foremost tax form. Taxation greatly regulates distribution in contemporary western society. Firstly, individual income tax is the main source of state revenue.

The proportion of individual income tax to the total tax revenue is above 40% in main western developed capitalist countries and is even up to over 60% in some countries. Individual income tax is the foundation for the implementation of welfare system in contemporary western countries. Most expenditures used by financial departments of different countries for social welfare come from individual income tax. Secondly, regulate the gap in social distribution of income. There are tax threshold and exemptions of individual income tax, which is a kind of protection of the interests of low-income earners. Taxpayers and people raised or borne by them can declare for exemption of the individual income tax in all countries and low-income earners can be exempted from income tax, which relatively increase the income of low-income earners. Individual income tax is generally progressive tax and more taxes are paid for more income. Progressive tax rate can effectively alleviate the concentration of social wealth distribution, increase the proportion of income of middle-income and low-income earners, and narrow down distribution gap. Thirdly, mitigate conflicts between the employers and employees and distribution contradictions. Negotiations between the employers and employees mainly center on the increase of wages. Laborers and capitalists are at a deadlock on whether wages can be increased. Under such circumstances, reduction of tax rate and tax burdens by governments can mitigate contradictions between the employers and employees and increase disposable personal income.

2) Regulate income distribution by donation and jointly assume economic risks. Donation is the tax paid by employers and employees for employees' social insurance. This is to prepare for emergency needs in terms of endowment, medical treatment, employment injury and unemployment, etc. Most of employees' donations are made on the basis of a unified rate of income, so more donations are made for more income and fewer donations are made for less income, and low-income earners are exempted from donations in many countries. The payment of social insurance tax protects the income of low-income earners and reduces the income of high-income earners.

3) Standardize, restrict and regulate distribution of subjects of distribution by laws and systems. Laws play an immeasurable role in the social distribution of contemporary capitalist countries. Negotiations between the employers and employees, wage income, bonus income and social welfare income, etc. are closely linked to laws and systems. Income is distributed under laws and regulations in contemporary capitalist countries. The laws of the state on the distribution of income mainly include minimum wage legislation and various social insurance legislations. Social welfare legislations cover a variety of contents. Its large categories mainly include the endowment insurance act, medical insurance act, employment injury act and unemployment insurance act, etc. and there are multiple and specific laws and regulations under each category.

2. Transition from Welfare State to Welfare Society

During the development of welfare states in the middle 1970s, economic, political and social changes shook the foundation for the original welfare state to a great extent, and the so-called welfare state crisis occurred. Western welfare states all try to find a way to break out of the crisis, which can be generalized as the transition from welfare state to welfare society. The transition from welfare state to welfare society refers to that the social welfare originally assumed by the state is assumed by the society, it is privatized and put on the market so as to alleviate the state's responsibilities and burdens in terms of social welfare. Such changes are unbalanced in different countries and have been merely an endeavor until now.

(1) Reasons for the transition from welfare state to welfare society

Firstly, finance sank into crisis. Welfare states were established on the basis of increasingly growing financial expenditure. During the prior 30 years after the war, there was a great increase in the financial revenue of main western developed countries and governments' financial resources could satisfy incessant expenditures of welfare states because of rapid economic development. However, due to the economic crisis, financial expenditures

which are needed by western developed countries to break out of the crisis
have had a sharp increase since the 1970s, and taxes and financial revenue of
these countries relatively decreased due to the economic crisis. The growth
rate of welfare expenditures nearly exceeded economic growth rate each year
in western developed countries since the 1970s and the growth of financial
revenue is far slower than the growth of financial expenditures. Consequently,
the financial situation of developed countries generally deteriorates and
financial deficits increase. The deterioration of financial situation makes these
welfare states hard to carry on. Huge financial expenditures and financial
crisis inexorably leads to the state's increase of taxes to offset the balance.
Sweden, as the most famous welfare state in the world, is honored as the
model of welfare states. High welfare and high taxes coexist in Sweden.
In the book *Sweden: A Model of Social Welfare Economy*, Zhang Ping and
other people elaborated that how exorbitant financial expenditures of Sweden
lead to a series of economic problems in Sweden. The total tax revenue of
Sweden accounts for over 50% of GDP, and the pressure of rapid increase
of tax revenue directly comes from the rapid increase of public transfer
expenditure. Only through high tax policies can the state ensure its huge
public expenditures. The tax revenue required by the financial departments
of Sweden mainly comes from individual income tax, enterprise income
tax and indirect value-added tax, which leads to the annual increase of tax
rate in Sweden. To ensure public revenue, Swedish people have to assume
enormous taxes for the welfare they enjoy and the taxes per capital account
for approximately 50% to 65% of GNP. Despite all this, the national income
of Sweden cannot catch up the inflation rate of public expenditures, and
financial deficits in budgets appeared in successive years. Many industries
and enterprises in Sweden lapse into serious economic difficulty. To maintain
high employment rate, the government has to offer subsidies to enterprises
and industries in difficulty through financial means, which leads to rapid
deteriorating financial situation and sharply increasing deficits.[1]

---

[1] Zhang Ping, etc.: *Sweden: A Model of Social Welfare Economy*, pp.70-71, Wuhan, Wuhan Press,
     1994.

Secondly, considerable welfare expenditures are not used for those people really in need. The objective of a welfare system is to satisfy basic living requirements of low-income earners and needy people. However, some welfare plans, such as social service items of public education and children subsidies, etc. are provided to all residents, including rich families. For instance, no matter for rich families or poor families in Britain, college students can enjoy grants of 520 pounds per year provided by the government. The state grants same allowance, etc. to children in either rich families or poor families.

(2) Channels for the transition from welfare state to welfare society

There are multiple channels and ways adopted by capitalist countries in the socialization of welfare, which mainly include:

The first one was to replace traditional welfare state with social investments. For instance, the English Blair government tried to change the dependency model welfare of the past. The government declared to invest on human capital, inspiring people to seek new job opportunities, employment and economic independence, criticizing reliance on relief money. And also started to change previous welfare policy to establish public utilities jointly contributed by: government, enterprises and individuals. During the one-year after the new labor welfare plan by the Blair government in April, 1998 to the end of March in 1999, nearly 137,000 people had participated in the project and 44% had found steady jobs, thus greatly reducing the unemployment allowance expenditures of the government.

Secondly, some contribution and management responsibilities on social welfare were transferred to enterprises and social organizations. Capitalist countries had rapidly developed into welfare states after the war and little attention had been paid to the development of enterprise welfare. During the transition from welfare state to welfare society, the governments reduced social functions and emphasized the innovation of enterprise welfare. Financial source of enterprise welfare comes from employers and its aims and goals are totally different from social welfare. Enterprise welfare is formulated and implemented to improve the working efficiency of enterprises and compete for talents on the market, thus fulfilling their overall strategy. Media information applauses that enterprise welfare has notable effects in motivating employees and improving labor productivity. It is expected to eliminate some drawbacks of social welfare. Consequently, contemporary capitalist countries attribute greater importance to enterprise welfare, carry on detailed research and investigations, and design various innovative enterprise welfare plans. Through social legislation and administrative orders, governments impose enterprises to provide all kinds of welfare as much as possible in order to reduce the pressure of excessive government financial expenditures. For instance, the *Economic Growth and Tax Relief Reconciliation Act of 2001* issued by the U.S. Congress had made great amendments to the laws and regulations on enterprises' pension plans, the main amendment was to increase pensions paid by employers. When requiring enterprises to assume more social welfare responsibilities, governments have also encouraged some social organizations—mutual-aid and relief type—to undertake services such as medical treatment and education, etc. Main developed countries are actively encouraging their social community organizations to assume more such social service responsibilities.

The third was to reduce governments' role and transfer some production and supply functions in social service sphere to private organizations. At present, the social services purchased by the American government from profit-making or non-profit organizations each year accounts for one third of the total amount of individual social services. Reliance on private market has expanded in terms of the health insurance sphere in America. The government also puts social service on the market by means of outsourcing, releasing vouchers and providing subsidies, etc. For instance, it contracts out school teaching in some formal public primary and middle schools to profit-making organizations, releases housing, food stamps and some vouchers for higher education, etc. letting beneficiaries to choose or select freely on the market. It also offers wage subsidies or capital subsidies to enterprises, requesting them to employ more disadvantaged workers or develop industries in regions with economic hardship. Britain also tries to contract out those services related with medical treatment, such as cleaning, laundry and catering, etc. to private organizations.[1]

Fourthly, welfare provided by the state was cut and residents were forced to invest for private welfare. The objective was declared as to increase income and reduce government expenditure. At present, in the reform of welfare system in developed countries, most of the measures focus on strengthening qualification inspection, reducing number of beneficiaries, prolonging working years, prolonging the time for waiting for subsidies, increasing service expenses borne by individuals, and imposing income tax for some allowance income, etc.

Through a series of measures on socialization of welfare in capitalist countries, even though states' social welfare expenditures have a continual increase, their growth rate has significantly decreased due to marketization and privatization policies. Of the three key parts of welfare states, i.e. social insurance, social relief and social service, some welfare items have been abandoned and some items have been greatly impaired. Welfare socialization is expanding in various degrees. However, the transition from welfare state to welfare society has just begun, and the reform and adjustments of welfare system in western welfare states have not gained fundamental character yet. The original nature and functions of welfare states have not changed and has only partially changed. Although welfare socialization is growing quicker compared with state welfare, it is not easy to carry on an overall reform in welfare state policy.

3. The Welfare Society Process and Its Effects on the Income Distribution

1) Structural changes in social welfare and social security: The social welfare and social security implemented by developed capitalist countries mainly include three contents: i.e. social insurance, social relief and social

---

[1] Huang Suan, Zhen Bingxi: *Reevaluating Contemporary Capitalist Economy*, pp. 254-255, Beijing: World Affairs Press, 1996.

service. Some scholars generally call social insurance and social relief also as social security; which are the most basic contents of state welfare. The contents of social welfare and social security are composed of certain parts, and each part includes certain detail items. The social welfare and security is a huge system including different levels. For instance, there are over 300 various items related with these issues in USA.

2) Problems in the structure of social welfare and social security: The crisis in welfare states is mainly caused by the structural imbalance of social welfare and social security. The problems in the structure of social welfare and social security mainly emerge as the following: firstly, the structure is too large and diverse. After the development of social welfare and social security in capitalist countries for several decades, the content and scale of welfare and security have become broader, covering security and improvement of different aspects such as labor, unemployment, sickness, reproduction, education, housing and old-age, etc. covering the whole life of all residents. It has a very broad coverage, including all care during child birth, old age, and illness as well as burial arrangements for people. Welfare plans incorporate many issues that could not be managed by the state welfare and security system. Therefore, the proportion of state welfare and security expenses to GDP and governments' financial expenditures has grown and has become difficult to carry on. Secondly, the internal structure is irrational and there has been a serious outflow of welfare and security capital. The irrational aspect of the internal structure of social welfare and security systems in different capitalist countries stifle employee's enthusiasm for work and a large amount of social welfare and security capital deplete.

Changes in the social welfare and social security system have brought important effects on the income distribution. In the reform process of the welfare states, the adjustment and change of social welfare and security system structure has been the main content. They involve many aspects such as the reduction in the social security expenditures of the state, enterprises and individuals, decrease of state financial expenditures and increase of the contributions by the enterprises and individuals. The changes in the two foremost social security systems, i.e., endowment and medical structure can be cited as examples. The pension system includes basic pension and additional pension. Basic pension can be obtained by every person and additional pension is related to working years and employment income in the past. In this reform process some countries have changed the proportion between basic pension and additional pension, prolonged working years for additional pension income and some countries require payment of income tax by receivers of pension or security and welfare. Medical security welfare includes two kinds of medical welfare, one is mainly refers supporting medical health expenses and the other is cash welfare, including payment of wages for sick time, maternity and pregnancy leave, allowance insurance, etc. Almost all countries made adjustments to the medical security structure in the reform of social welfare. For instance, Germany and America increased the part borne by individuals to control rapidly increasing medical expenses. In capitalist countries, social welfare is given by the state accounts for a considerable proportion in personal income. Changes in the social welfare and social security structure have the following impacts on income distribution: Firstly, it leads to the decrease of residents' income. The changes in welfare structure directly or indirectly reduce residents' social welfare. If such changes continue, the actual income of more people will decrease and the amount of people who are in need will probably increase. Secondly, the adjustment of social security and welfare structure is a systematic project. It is not only an economic issue but also a political and cultural issue. The adjustments will break old balance and lead to the overall or partial change of the relation of distribution, such as the determination of income distribution, income forms, income gap, people's living standards, the status and functions of governments in the distribution of income. Thirdly, welfare states were established on the basis of capitalist system. The redistribution form of income in capitalist society with welfare state as the main model will not be threatened in the real sense if there is no fundamental reform of the capitalist economic, political and cultural structure. The adjustments to the social security and welfare structure in will continue to be of partial character and will not fundamentally change its overall structure. The current social security and welfare, as the internal stabilizer will exist for a long period.

IV. Historical Evolution in the Capitalist Distribution Relations

The historical evolution of the relation of distribution in contemporary capitalist countries can be separated into three stages. The first stage starts from the generation of capitalism to World War II, the second stage starts from the end of World War II to the middle 1970s and the third stage starts from the middle 1970s to the present day. In the late period of the first stage, i.e. on the eve of World War II, the contemporary capitalist relation of distribution was an embryo in some aspects. In the second stage, i.e. after World War II, the contemporary capitalist relation of distribution formed and had rapid development. In the third stage, i.e. after the middle 1970s, the relation of distribution was adjusted. The main evolution process is elaborated here.

1. Historical Evolution in the Determination of Wages

During early development of capitalist economy, since the working class ranks were dispersed, and weak in power and organization, their power for fighting against employers had not formed. All kinds of workers' resistance were banned and they did not have the power to resist. Employers could deduct or reduce workers' wages at discretion. This situation began to change after the formation of labor unions. The formation of labor unions dates back to the middle period of the 17th century, but labor unions and employers generally began to negotiate and conclude agreements on income issue from the second half of the 19th century. This can be seen as the beginning of determination of wages by free bargaining between the employers and employees. However, the determination of wages through such wage negotiations was not acknowledged and protected by law. Therefore, legal agreements could not be reached. Until the beginning of the 20th century, especially after World War II, the determination of wages through free bargaining between labor unions and employers was acknowledged and protected by law since in this period, labor movements were more intensive in this period than any other time before and there was a high level of organization of labor unions. Labor unions had the power to contend with capitalist groups, which laid a foundation for labor unions to determine wages. For instance, labor unions in main capitalist countries organized over 4,000 strikes per year, and the proportion of strikes organized by labor unions reached 33% from 1945 to 1948. In the 1950s, American labor unions organized workers' strikes on the increase of wages, etc. and won over the increase of wages comparable with price inflation. In the struggle between labor unions and capitalists, bourgeois governments had acted as mediators, which restricted the short-term interests of the capitalist class to a certain extent through legislation in order to protect their long-term interests, and acknowledged the status and functions of labor unions to a certain extent. For example, the *National Industrial Relations Act* in America had defined the status of labor unions in group negotiations and restricts the power of employers. The recognition by state laws contributed to gradually strengthen the power of labor unions, promoting the development of determination of wages by group negotiations.

Generally speaking, the governments are not directly involved in the process of determination of wages by collective bargaining. The government's role in the determination of wages is mainly to formulate laws on wages, regulate behaviors of the employers and employees in the determination of wages in the form of laws and realize the state's will in the determination of wages. After participation of the government in the determination of wages, collective bargaining is carried out on the basis of the legitimate umbrella of the government. In contemporary era, both labor unions and employers attribute greater importance to protect their interests through laws. The transition from the determination of wages unilaterally by employers to the determination by the three parties: employers, labor unions and the government in contemporary era is a great advance, which mitigates contradictions between the employers and employees in a certain form, and is beneficial to motivating workers and improving labor productivity.

Since the middle and late 1960s, there has been a differentiation within the working class and a declining level of organization of labor unions with the development of science, technology and economy. The proportion of traditional blue collar labor union members gradually decreased after the war with the development of science and technology. Even though the proportion of white collars among labor union members is increasing, its growth rate is low and has not caught up to the decreasing rate of labor union members. For instance, the proportion of labor union members to total number of laborers had a steady increase since World War II and reached 25% to 27% in the 1950s. However, the proportion has decreased to 18% in 1984 and to about 15% in 1993. The proportion of Japanese labor union members to laborers reached 55% at the maximum in 1949, and decreased to 29% in 1985. In Britain, the proportion of members to laborers decreased from 53% to 43% since 1979. In France, the number of labor union members has sharply decreased since 1975, its proportion being only 14% in 1985 and less than 10% in 1990. In Netherlands, the proportion has decreased by 17% from 1975 to 1985. The decrease in the number of labor union members inevitably results in the weakening role of labor unions in the determination of wages. The declining status and functions of labor unions result from their internal reasons as well as the restriction and destruction of labor unions by the capitalist governments in association with capitalist class. In capitalist countries the role of labor unions is increasingly difficult when state legislation becomes more comprehensive and specific. Capitalist countries have formulated many laws on industrial relations. For instance, in Britain, there was the *Trade Union and Labor Relations (Consolidation) Act*, which mainly prescribes the issues on labor unions and their rights, procedures and conditions for industrial relations, organizations for handling labor disputes and their composition, etc. The *Employment Protection (Consolidation) Act* systematically prescribes individual labor rights of employees, including the minimum standards for employment conditions, employment protection right, termination of employment, wrongful dismissal, cutbacks in staff and subsidy expenses, as well as the organizations and procedures for handling disputes on individuals' rights. The *Equal Pay Act*, the *Health and Safety at Work Act*, the *Labor Contract Act*, the *Trade Union Act*, and the *Group Negotiation and Group Agreement System*, etc. were also formulated. Similarly, the *Employment Security Act*, the *Equal Employment Opportunity Act*, the *Employee Dismissal Training Regulations*, the *Work Environment Act*, the *Holiday Regulations*, the *Total Working Hour Regulations*, the *Joint Decision Act*, the *Labor Dispute Lawsuit Regulations*, the *Labor Union Representative Act*, the *Regulations on Employee Representatives of the Board of Directors*, the *Regulations on Deduction of Wages by Employers*, and the *Regulations on Wage Payment after Bankruptcy*, etc. were formulated in Sweden.

2. Evolution of Rewards and Incentives

The reward forms in the determination of wages were mainly based on time wage and piecework wage, and the bonus system was not common before the 20th century. After World War II, work appraisal methods had changed and wage forms multiplied with the development and advance of science and technology, and especially with the improvement of production techniques. Many forms of wages suitable for different industries and different work characteristics apart from time wage and piecework wage gradually developed and improved. After the 1960s, due to the extensive development of automobile technologies, electronic technologies and wage systems, such as job skill wage systems, grading systems, forms of time wage and piecework wage could not satisfy requirements for the development of production, therefore, instead of them wage systems based on ability, work appraisal wage system, etc. had emerged. In the 1970s, the economic growth of capitalist countries had slowed down or stopped, enterprises' profits had greatly decreased and the unemployment rate remained high. To tackle such "stagflation", economists came up with various opinions. American economist Weitzman raised the share economy theory in 1984. He believed that share economy could save capitalism and urged the substitution of share system to wage system. The share system refers to a form of distribution in which income is shared by labor and capital. The difference between the traditional distribution system and the share system lies on the argument that there is no relationship between wages and enterprises' economic benefits in the traditional distribution system. Whereas, in the share system, employees' income will be related to enterprises' benefits, i.e., if the enterprise has higher productivity and high profits, workers will have high income, otherwise they will have low income. The share economy theory was followed by great repercussions in the West once it was raised, and it was even named as the most excellent economic thought after Keynesianism. Share economy theory won the support of governments and acclaim of entrepreneurs. Many enterprises had linked profits with rewards to laborers, and transferred their operational risks to both workers and other employees. At the end of the 1980s and the beginning of 1990s, America, Britain, France and some other countries extensively linked wages with profits. They developed the employee stock ownership to let employees assume enterprises' production and operational risks as well as the responsibilities for long-term development. Consequently, many enterprises were revitalized and many employees retained jobs. For instance, nearly 100 enterprises which were mismanaged have been saved through purchase of stocks by employees, and an average of nearly 1,000 job positions in each factory were maintained in the 1980s.

3. Historical Evolution of Workers' Labor Income

Workers had extremely low wages and no guarantee for life and work before the 20th century. Marx and Engels had elaborately described and analyzed the subhuman, poverty-stricken and miserable situation of the working class in the *Capital*, and the *Situation of British Working Class*, and other works. There was a great increase in the actual income of workers in main capitalist countries from the 1950s to 1960s due to economic prosperity, the struggle of the working class and other reasons. The actual average wage per hour of non-agricultural sectors in USA was 4.87 USD in 1947, 6.79

USD in 1960 and 8.55 USD in 1973. The actual average wage of workers had risen by 37.9% from 1947 to 1973. However, in the 1970s and early 1980s, the actual income growth had slowed down and even decreased due to economic downturn. After the middle 1980s, even though economy growth had recovered, the recovery was weak, and the actual income of workers in different countries had decreased. For instance, the actual wages of workers in the USA had an annual increase of 2.76% from 1951 to 1960, but the growth rate had decreased to 1.07% from 1961 to 1970. The actual wage had an annual decrease of 0.6% from 1971 to 1980 and an annual decrease of 0.4% from 1982 to 1990. The actual income of workers in Britain had an annual increase of 2.68% from 1951 to 1960 and 3.03% from 1961 to 1970. Also the growth has been negative after the 1970s. In Germany, the average growth rate of actual wage was respectively 5.75% and 5.60% in the 1950s and 1960s. It had a significant decrease in the 1970s and the annual growth rate was only 1.55% in the 1980s. The growth rate was only 0.9% in France (1981-1986). There was also a negative growth in Canada with an annual decrease of 1.03% (1982-1990).[1] The income of workers had only a slight increase since the 1990s in capitalist countries. Although there was a significant increase in economic growth for a decade due to the recovery of the American economy in 1991 to 2001, there was a decrease rather than an increase of workers' income.

4. Historical Evolution of the Social Welfare System

With the continual development of society, the welfare system also had continual development and improvement, which can be generally separated into four stages.

The first is the period of establishment of the system. The establishment of the earliest social welfare system dates back to the first *Poor Law* issued by the British Queen Elizabeth I in 1601. Although not being sound, this act was the forerunner of social security. Laisser-faire capitalism had developed

---

[1] Chen Bingcai: *Contemporary Capitalist System of Income Distribution*, p. 222, Fuzhou, Fujian People's Publishing House, 1994.

to the zenith and monopoly organizations were in embryo from the 1870s to the 1880s. During this period, serious economic crisis had occurred in capitalist countries, there was economic depression, serious unemployment problems, surging labor movements and social contradictions were intensified. Social problems including workers' unemployment, employment injury and sickness, etc., were very prominent in Germany. In order to solve these increasingly severe social problems and maintain social stability, Germany successively formulated the *Sickness Insurance Act*, the *Industrial Injury Insurance Act*, and the *Old-age Disability Insurance Act* from 1883 to 1889. The *Sickness Insurance Act* had prescribed that during all kinds of medical expenses occurring during employees' sickness, one third should be borne by employers and two thirds by employees. The *Industrial Injury Insurance Act* had stipulated that employers should pay all medical expenses and living expenses for employees' injury at work. The *Old-Age Disability Insurance Act* had prescribed that employees' living expenses at an old-age should be borne by employers and employees in average due to employees' inability to work at an old age. Consequently, Germany became the first country in the world which enacted formal social security legislation. After Germany, many European countries followed suit and formulated their social welfare and social security regulations at the end of the 19th century and the beginning of the 20th century. For instance, Austria had formulated and implemented the *Industrial Injury Act and Sickness Insurance Act* in 1887 and 1888, Belgium had formulated the *Health Insurance Act* in 1894, Finland the *Industrial Injury Insurance Act* in 1895, Denmark, the *Health Insurance Act* in 1891 and 1892, Sweden the *Endowment Insurance Act* in 1915, and Britain the *Unemployment Insurance Act* in 1911.

The second was the formation period of the social welfare system. World War II brought serious disasters to Europe and people had suffered many hardships. To alleviate the situation, with the entrustment of the British government, Beveridge, who used to be the director of the London School of Economics and Political Science and the director of Labor Exchanges in Britain, drafted the report on *Social Insurance and Allied Services* in

1942, i.e., the famous Beveridge Report. In the report, he had proposed that Britain should establish a social insurance system covering all kinds of different social welfare benefiting all residents. The social welfare and security plan conceived in the Beveridge Report was approved by the British government in principle. On the basis of this report, the British government had passed a series of social security legislations within three years, including the crucial *Education Act* in 1944, the *Family Allowances Act* in 1945, as well as the *Social Insurance Act*, the *National Health Service Act* and the *Industrial Injuries Act* in 1946. The aforesaid acts and other relevant legislations constituted the complete social security system in Britain. The implementation of the social security plan and the establishment of social security system in Britain influenced and drove other capitalist countries to follow suit. Germany, France, Sweden and other countries specifically put forward the social reform plan and formulated many social welfare and security plans after the war.

The third was the establishment of welfare states. Different capitalist countries had rapid economic growth after the war, and due to economic prosperity, gradually supplemented and improved the previous series of social welfare and social security system in the 1950s and 1960s, making the contents of these welfare plans richer, more systematic and broader in coverage. It developed into a "safety net" covering all aspects of the nation from cradle to grave and fundamentally realized welfare states.

The fourth is the adjustment and reform period of welfare states. Economic development had slowed down or even stopped because of economic stagflation, and the material conditions supporting welfare states had disappeared after the 1970s. Meanwhile, many serious problems had occurred in the practices of welfare states, such as financial crisis, irrational structure, emphasis on equity and less attention on efficiency, etc. Under various pressures, capitalist countries began to adjust and reform the welfare and security system in the 1980s. At present, such adjustment and reforms are still in trial; the situation is complex and resistance is at a high level since it involves various aspects of social politics, economy and culture, etc.

5. Historical Evolution of Government Management and Intervention

The management and intervention of capitalist countries on the in income distribution has experienced a process of continual exploration and development, which can be generally divided into three main stages of development. The first stage was before the 20th century. Since the economic principle of liberalism was adopted, governments generally had showed no concern about the distribution of income, and distribution relations had only involved employers and workers. Serious economic crisis which broke out in the western world in 1920s and 1930s, had revealed serious defects of liberal economy. The states had to assume responsibilities for economic management and intervention. During this period, state intervention and management of the distribution of income were not complete and mainly included the minimum wage legislation and collective bargaining legislations, etc. The acts on collective bargaining were primarily formulated in USA: the *Norris-LaGuardia Act*, the *National Industrial Recovery Act*, and the *Social Security Act*, etc. The primarily formulated acts involving minimum wages were the *Davis-Bacon Act*, the *Walsh-Healey Act* and the *Fair Labor Standards Act*. During this period, some people with the vision of the bourgeoisie, such as Roosevelt and Keynes, etc. raised the theory and political advocacy of government intervention in the economy, which was initially adopted in some other countries. For example, a large amount of contents on government intervention and reform of the income distribution system were included in the "New Deal" implemented in America. The American economy gradually got out of the crisis owing to the implementation of New Deal. After World War II, the state intervention theory of Keynes was vigorously promoted and applied, and the functions of the state on the management and intervention of income distribution had rapidly expanded and strengthened. Apart from further improving the laws and regulations formulated before World War II, adjusting the distribution of income, such as the *Minimum Wage Act* and the *Social Security Act*, state had also formulated many new laws and policies, took many measures, forcefully intervened in economy in an all-around way and had managed the distribution of income. The significant changes in the distribution of income in capitalist countries such as welfare state, employee stock ownership, narrowing gap between the rich and the poor and improvement of people's living standards, etc. had occurred and were completed under the forceful guidance and of governments in the period after World War II. The second stage is the 1970s, when serious "stagflation" appeared in the capitalist economy. Production stagnated and commodity prices had soared. Financial deficits had increased in consecutive years and profits of capitalists had severely decreased. Countries adopted new means, i.e. income policies to tackle "stagflation". These income policies refer to freeze wages and price inflations by government regulations. Though income policies had played a role to a certain extent in tackling inflation, they had severe disadvantages and were basically abandoned after the 1980s. During this period, governments changed a policy and vigorously supported share economy and employee joint-stock system to tackle economic recession and economic downturn. For instance, all kinds of taxes exempted or deducted for the employee stock ownership had reached 2.05 billion USD in 1986, which had greatly promoted the development of employee stock ownership and led to the rapid increase of enterprises and employees participating employee stock ownership plans. In the process of capitalist countries' intervention in the distribution of income, the guiding and decisive status of states in the distribution of income had greatly strengthened. For example, the scale of financial revenues in capitalist countries had increasingly expanded after the war, accounting for a rapidly increasing proportion in GNP. The proportion was only 7% to 8% in USA from 1870 to 1910 and had reached to 33.6% in 1985. It was 11% to 14% in Britain from 1825 to 1910, and reached to 43.10% in 1985. The proportion in some countries in Northern Europe, such as Norway and Sweden, etc. has exceeded 50%.[1] The third stage is the period from 1980s, in which states had intervened and managed the distribution of income, and adopted flexible and multiple methods based

---

[1] Han Baojiang: *Salvation of Western World: Transition and Contributions of the Modern Western System of Income Distribution*, pp. 162-163, Jinan, Shandong People's Publishing House, 2000.

on the economic situation at each stage. These countries had generally reconsidered the series of policies formed after the war on intervention in the distribution of income. They believed that while ensuring the leading position of states, they should reconsider the role of market in the distribution of income. They also adjusted the minimum wage acts and carried on the privatization of state-owned economy apart from the reform of social welfare system. Britain had pioneered the privatization movement, it has sold many state-owned companies to individuals since 1979 and two thirds of state-owned enterprises had been privatized in Britain by 1992. The privatization movement initiated by Britain spread to France, Japan, Italy, Spain, Portugal, Belgium, Austria, Australia and other countries.

V. Future Aspects in Distribution Relations

Marxism believes that everything undergoes development and change. Likewise, the capitalist distribution relations had also encountered development and change process.

1. Tendency in the Near Future

At present, the capitalist income distribution relations are adjusted and possibly will remain in the present direction in the next ten to twenty years if there is not a great social reform. Firstly, the functions of collective bargaining in the determination of wages will further narrow down since laws become more specific and broader in applicable scale and narrows down the scale and contents of collective bargaining. Secondly, contradictions between the employers and employees tend to be alleviated. Employers allow workers participate in enterprise management and decision-making, and share interests and risks through share of profits and the joint-stock system. This solves many problems which were demanded by negotiations in the past. However, there will be no large increase in actual income and welfare. With the beginning of 21st century, especially the "9·11" incident, capitalist countries led by America have been heading towards a recession, and economic downturn has become an indisputable fact. Additionally, states' welfare expenditures are too high and many countries are cutting down. Therefore, the actual income and welfare of workers may have a slow increase and or even decrease. Thirdly, the social welfare distribution system will be further reformed, and the international coordination of social welfare may be strengthened. At present the social welfare system of main capitalist countries is difficult to be continued. Different countries have reformed their social welfare and social security system in succession, but the effects are not obvious yet. Reform is an inevitable tendency since governments are not able to bear the heavy burden of social welfare expenditures. Social welfare will be gradually cut down to a certain extent and the proportion of individual responsibility or direct solution of enterprises will further increase. Coordination of these relations demands for prompt solutions by the governments of these countries. The international coordination of social welfare will be strengthened in the future, but the basic model and the core of capitalist social welfare will not have much change even in the face of any reform and will continue to play a role in stabilizing capitalist society and promoting economic development. Fourthly, government intervention in income distribution in form of legislations will be more extensive and specific. Capitalist countries increasingly adopt legislation to intervene in the social relation of distribution after World War II. Practices prove that the legal intervention of governments plays a significant role in adjusting inequality of social distribution to a certain extent, maintaining social stability and promoting economic development. The tendency is expected to continue and legal regulation and intervention will be more extensive in scale and specific in contents. The form of direct intervention in the distribution of income by governments will be more flexible and effective.

2. Tendency in the Long-Term

There are significant changes in the contemporary capitalist distribution relations after World War II. The income of the working class has increased and social contradictions in capitalist countries had tended to alleviate, which enabled capitalism to maintain momentum of development. However, that these significant changes in the capitalist distribution relations did not change the exploitative nature of capitalist economic relations, i.e. capital possessors gain the surplus value without charge, and the exploitation of the working class, as well as polarization between the poor and the rich, the working class and the bourgeoisie remains as before. They could not eliminate contradictions and fundamental opposition between the working class and the bourgeois as well as the basic contradiction of capitalism between socialized production and private possession.

Firstly, the material and cultural living conditions of the working class in post-war developed capitalist countries did improve, and the income and consumption level of the working class had increased based on the great improvement of labor productivity and continual increase of material wealth. This had mitigated conflicts between the employers and employees and unfair distribution. However, for capitalists, not only the profits of capital were realized, but also they had an increase. Consequently, the surplus value rate still increases in favor of capitalists although workers' income have increased. Many data show that the surplus value rate had constantly risen after the war. If we take USA as an example, its surplus value rate was 130% in 1909, 236.7% in 1950, and up to 364.7% in 1987. Of the top 20 biggest companies, the growth rate of profits in 18 companies was from 10%-20% to 40%-60% in 1996. The growth rate of Microsoft was up to 57% whereas the growth rate of workers' wages in these big companies was much lower. This fact implies that most of the value created by workers was usurped by big capitalists. The income of workers increases in the absolute amount. However, the income actually decreases relative to the values created by them. Income increase and improvement of life do not change subordination of wage earners to capital, and such relation is just represented in a more conciliatory form. This verifies the opinion raised by Marx in the *Capital*: it means, in fact, that the length of the golden chain tying the wage earner allows some relaxation. Under the mode of production dominated by the law of surplus value, capitalists purchase labor forces to increase the value of their capital. Therefore, despite any favorable conditions for workers to sell their labor forces, the relation of the subjection of wage labor to capital and exploitation by capital does not change.

Secondly, the welfare system does not fundamentally change polarization in the capitalist society. The social welfare system in developed capitalist countries alleviates the imbalance of social distribution to a certain extent, basically guarantees life of general laborers especially grass roots, and eliminates prevalent poverty only to a certain extent. However, the fundamental principle of the capitalist distribution system is according to one's capital. The social welfare system cannot fundamentally eliminate polarization in the primary distribution of national income. In capitalist countries, wages and social welfare are two main income forms of laborers, wages are paid by employers and social welfare is paid by the government. Social welfare capital is raised from three sources: the first is the insurance paid by laborers, the second is the insurance paid by employers for employees and the third is financial expenditures of the government. Workers' insurance is directly deducted from wages, insurance paid by employers for employees is directly deducted from the necessary labor by capitalists and financial expenditures of the government come from taxes, which is a part of the surplus value created by laborers. Therefore, social welfare obtained by laborers is neither a charity of capitalists nor that of governments of capitalist countries, but a part of the value created by laborers.

Thirdly, employee stock ownership has not only changed the private nature of joint-stock system, but also aggravated capitalist exploitation. The number of residents holding stocks have increased and the so-called tendency of "decentralization of stocks" have appeared in developed capitalist countries after the war. Some have named it as the "democratization of capital" and workers, employees holding stocks became "owners" of company property, i.e. capitalists, and capitalism has become "people's capitalism". When we analyze the nature of the joint-stock system, we cannot see the number of stockholders but we know how many stocks they hold, and who own controlling stocks. In USA, 10% of rich families hold 89.3%

of all stocks and another 1% richer families hold 63% of stocks in the whole nation, whereas 10% of employees engaged in employee stock ownership plans only hold 1% of stocks. In fact, the "decentralization of stocks" is an ingenious form of big capitalists for collecting laborers' funds, with the aim to dominate and pool more capital, reduce investment risk of their personal capital, and increase exploitation of laborers. Even Samuelson, an economist of the bourgeoisie, believed that the changes in workers' income brought by stocks had trivial influences upon their life. It is true. The Enron Corporation, America's energy giant ranking seventh in the top 500 largest companies in the world had gone bankrupt in December 2002, and its 21,000 employees had become the ultimate victims. This was because, based on the regulation of the corporation, the capital deposited in their pension accounts were used as the stocks of the company, and the associated capital provided by the Enron Corporation had been paid in the form of stocks. The stocks of Enron Corporation accounted for 58% of employees' pension funds with a total value exceeding 2.1 billion USD. During the sharp decline of the company's stock price, the company prohibited employees from selling the company's stocks they held. Nevertheless, 29 senior managers of the company sold stocks of 1.73 million shares before the stock price had collapsed and they had obtained huge profits of 1.1 billion USD. The 21,000 employees with greatly depreciated stocks, had severe losses of several billion US dollars.

Chapter VII

Historical Evolution of the Capitalist Economic Operating Mechanism

The macro operating mechanism of contemporary capitalist economy had significant changes, and the basic feature has been the integration of government intervention and market power and the establishment of the regulation system of state monopoly capitalism. Through history, market mechanism has always been the basic mechanism and main force dominating its economic operation in all stages of capitalist development. Nowadays, the question is why there must be the macro-economic regulation of the government under modern capitalist conditions? Why the "invisible hand" must be integrated with the "visible hand" and be assisted or supplemented by the latter? Which kind of power promotes the evolution of the capitalist economic operating mechanism and what is the nature and tendency of its evolution? All these have become unavoidable issues in the capitalist development process.

I. A Historical Review on Capitalist Economic Operating Mechanism

Main contradictions to be solved in the socio-economic development process and their manifestations vary in different stages of the development of capitalist mode of production. The differences in the specific social and economic conditions and main problems confronted in socio-economic development determine the diversification in the social economic operating mechanism in different stages of the capitalist mode of production.

1. Market and Government in the Classical Liberalism Period

I will mainly study practical issues on the relations between the government and the market during the period of capitalist economic development. This is over a period of 240 years from the victory of the English Bourgeoisie Revolution in 1688 to the capitalist world economic crisis in 1929. The reason why I deem the victory of the English Bourgeoisie Revolution in 1688 as the starting point of research is not only because the first bourgeoisie regime was built in human history, but also it implies the transition from feudal economic system to capitalist economic system in human economic history. Besides, from the perspective of world history, the significance of the English Revolution is that it had determined and implemented the principles of liberalism. The reason why we regard 1929 as the end of that historical period is that the serious economic crisis sweeping the whole capitalist world broke out in 1929. It was the explosion of all kinds of contradictions accumulated in the capitalist reproduction process for a long period, both reflecting capital's limitations of self-regulation on the market mechanism and proving the necessity of government intervention in the economy. Governments of main capitalist countries such as Great Britain and America, etc. had strengthened economic regulation and intervention since the 30s, which declared the termination of laissez-faire capitalism era and the beginning of the market economy era with government regulations. During the capitalist historical period for over 240 years, the capitalist economy had experienced state intervention and mercantilism in the early period of capitalism. This was the thriving period of free competition system and the period of the transition from free competition to monopoly.

(1) State intervention in the early period of capitalism

At this stage, market economy ultimately replaced natural economy and the operating mechanism of free competition economy finally replaced the economy dominated by imperial power. It is also the period of the capitalist primitive accumulation stage. With the discovery of America, new world market came into being, commodity exchange had rapidly expanded, and commercial capital had entered the stage of history. Mercantilism also became prevalent in this period, and mercantilists had advocated that countries should realize trade surplus so as to accumulate monetary capital and increase social wealth. Therefore, the aim of state intervention in economy was to control currency movement. The principle of state intervention in the primitive accumulation stage was characterized as the integration of commercial capital and feudal state power. Primary state intervention and commercial capital reflected as mercantilism had a close complementary relationship with unanimous interests. On the one hand, to finance the huge expenditure of central governments, kings and governments needed to combat against feudal lords by allying with the commercial capital, i.e. power of the emerging bourgeoisie. On the other hand, the immature commercial capital appealed to state authority to protect their interests, especially internally to quicken the primitive accumulation process by violence, thus obtained abundant cheap labor forces, developed manipulatory manufacture, and destroyed feudal fetters imposed on socio economic development. Externally, they attacked competitors, grabbed gold and silver, developed navigation, expanded colonies and overseas markets. Owing to this fact, mercantilists had advocated power politics with state intervention. They believed that a strong nation was an important condition for developing the economy and accumulating currency. The conception and reality of primary state economic intervention in mercantilism reflect the deficit of power by emerging capitalist system in the primitive accumulation period, which had demanded state support for economic development.

(2) Rise of industrial capital, the period of laissez-faire

Beginning from the middle 18th century to the 1830s and 1840s. During this period, the First Industrial Revolution had occurred with the invention of steam engine as its symbol. The productive forces had started to generated more than the sum of the previous eras in less than one hundred years. The rapid increase of productive forces brought by the Industrial Revolution had created huge demands for raw materials and strong aspirations for a broad market. At that time, the supply of domestic raw materials fell short of demand, the capacity of domestic market was limited, overseas raw materials could not be imported because of state intervention and overseas markets could not be expanded because of various restrictions. The policies of trade protection became the barrier for the development of foreign trade, and it was imperative to quickly overcome the obstacle of state intervention and transfer to free trade policies. As the factory of the world, Britain had began free trade movements since 1820, including reform of customs tariffs, cancellation of bans against import of silk fabrics, and reduction of raw silk import taxes, etc. Nullification of the "Grain Act" in 1846, which prescribed the imposition of high progressive tax on foreign grain to protect its agriculture was of special significance. The industrial bourgeoisie had believed that the act was a barrier for Britain's industrial development. Besides abolishing the Grain Act, many tariffs on foreign goods were reduced, open door policy was declared, and raw materials required for the industrial production could be imported freely. The free trade policy had replaced the protective tariff policy. With the establishment of free trade system as a breakthrough, the state's role in social and economic life declined in the capitalist history and economic policies was shifted from state intervention to laissez-faire. The transition from state intervention to laissez-faire reflects the policy requirements for the rapid development of productive forces in the economic life of the nations after the Industrial Revolution on the one hand, and the

interests of the rising industrial bourgeoisie on the other hand. Obviously,
the laissez-faire policy was greatly beneficial to the industrial bourgeoisie
who were desperately searching for the raw materials sources and product
markets. Economic theories advocating free competition and free trade were
put forward to adapt to the period. Along the trace of historical development,
the main representatives of these theories were Smith, Say and Marshall,
whose economic thoughts and political advocacies had all emphasized free
competition and laissez-faire. The economic liberalism theory in the early
period of capitalism had acute contradictions with the reality of capitalism in
the 1930s.

(3) Transition from free competition to monopoly and all-around
state intervention

Free competition was transformed into monopoly from the middle of
the 19th century to the beginning of the 20th century. The market mechanism
had played a decisive role in the whole economic operation till the end of
the capitalist world economic crisis in the 1930s. However, many problems
caused by the capitalist economy in this stage revealed that the market
economic system was not a perfect system, and that self-regulation of market
could not realize long-term balanced and steady development of the capitalist
economy. Internal contradictions in the capitalist development process
had mainly emerged as its failure to avoid regular economic fluctuations
and economic crisis. The large-scale industry had just developed from its
childhood. The first economic crisis had occurred in 1825 in Britain just after
the completion of Industrial Revolution. Britain's economy was in prosperity
at the beginning of 1825, however, the situation went into a precipitous
decline, the market stagnated, stock market suffered a drastic decline and
enterprises went bankrupt one after another. In 1825, 1,489 enterprises went
bankrupt, and the number had increased to 3,301 in 1826. There had been
regular economic fluctuations for every 10 years in Britain since the crisis in
1825. Before the middle of the 19th century, the effects of economic crisis
were limited effecting only a single country. Then the capitalist world was
gradually connected to be an interdependent whole with the development of

international differentiation and international trade. The first world economic crisis broke out in 1857 and rapidly spread from USA to Europe on the opposite shore of the Atlantic. In 1857, 5,000 enterprises went bankrupt in America, the whole losses of Britain had amounted 250 to 300 million pounds, and there were 12,030 bankruptcies in France from 1856 to 1858. The depression period lasted for more than five consecutive years. The industrial and agricultural crisis weaved together. The severity of the destruction in industry and agriculture, bankruptcy of enterprises and the number of unemployment of workers in the crisis, as well as the shrinking financial trade, etc. had exceeded previous crises. The crisis had intensified competition among different enterprises, promoted concentration and centralization of production and capital, and had resulted in the extensive development of monopoly organizations. This unprecedented profound world economic crisis marked the transition of capitalism from free competition stage to monopoly stage. This world economic crisis demanded that the governments should act as not only a political force but also the general representative of the economic interests of monopoly bourgeoisie on the historical stage, so it was followed an all-around extensive government intervention. There have been significant changes in the capitalist economic operating mechanism from this period. Since the economic crisis had regularly occurred after the establishment of the capitalist economic system, why had not it break up the worship to the "omnipotent market" in capital economic practice and western mainstream economic theories at that time? Tracing its origin, subjectively, the main task of classical economics at that time was to clear the influence of the residual thoughts of state regulation in the Middle Ages, especially that of mercantilist thoughts and political advocacies, and strengthen laissez-faire thoughts to promote the establishment and development of capitalist market economic system. Therefore, the market system of free competition could only be established through fundamental opposition to state intervention. Objectively, these crises were not as severe as the Great Depression in the 1930s even though they were frequent. New classical economists inevitably adopted the attitude to present a false picture of peace and prosperity in face of the disastrous social background at that time. I believe it was the basic reason for the duration of the free market economic system advocacy for over a century since the Industrial Revolution and the dominant position of the laissez faire economic theory. However, this could not continue after the end of 1920s. The Great Depression shaking all developed countries of market economy in 1929 declared the end of laissez-faire thoughts and the start of all-around state intervention.

2. The Market and the Government in the Keynesian Period

(1) Explosion of the great depression and all-around state intervention

The crisis before the 1930s always had a longer cycle, i.e. once in ten years. They had always occurred in a certain region and there were only a few world crises; they lasted for shorter periods and the losses caused by the crisis were not big enough to arouse suspects on the free market system. However, the crisis from 1929 to 1933 had shaken the whole capitalist world. It was the most serious crisis in the world economic history and had brought the capitalist society to the brink of total destruction. With the collapse of the stock market on the "black Tuesday" on October 29, 1929 as the fuse, the crisis had rapidly spread to all industries. The national industrial production in America had decreased by 55.6% after the crisis and regressed to the industrial production level in 1905. Five thousand and five hundred banks had gone bankrupt, which also had exacerbated agriculture in the crisis and led to its decline to the level in the 19th century. The number of unemployed people was over 12 million in 1932, almost accounting for 24% of labor force of the whole nation. The disastrous crisis starting from USA had rapidly spread to the other shore of the Atlantic and the whole capitalist world. During the crisis, industrial production had decreased by 23.8% in Britain, 40.6% in Germany, 36.2% in France, and 32.9% in Japan. The "Extreme Great Depression" with such a long duration, its large scale and immense destruction was unprecedented in the history of capitalist economies.

The crisis had not only become the turning point in the capitalist economic system, but also the turning point for the development of capitalist economic theories, with the following main characteristics. Firstly, the Great Depression was both the explosion of various contradictions accumulated over time during capitalist reproduction and had exposed the limitations of the self-regulation mechanism in the capitalist market economy. The crisis had originated from the development of the contradiction between socialized mass production and private possession of the means of production. On the one hand, the Second Scientific-Technological Revolution had accelerated the transformation in industrial structure and industrialization and had provided socialized mass production with new features and meanings. The tendency of socialized mass production had become a reality to be faced by monopoly capital. The highly socialized production process demanded more prominent requirements for more rational proportions in social production. However, the fact was that the contradiction between the total supply and total demand which had accumulated during the capitalist production process had become increasingly severe. On the other hand, as private monopoly enterprises had gradually developed into large enterprises, their internal organizational level increasingly contradicted with the anarchy in the whole social production process. Contradictions between the two had become more severe, and the capitalist economy itself had to release its internal contradictions in the form of crisis when the contradictions were accumulated to a certain extent. The occurrence the crisis had strongly demonstrated the limitation of market's self-regulation functions, and the crisis required the state, as the general representative of private monopoly capital, to participate in the capitalist economic operation. Therefore, after the early 1930s, America, Britain and other countries intensified all-around government interventions in their economies, gradually forming the so-called market economic mechanism with government regulation. They also declared the end of the laissez-faire capitalist era and the beginning of the capitalist era with joint roles of government intervention and market regulation. Secondly, the Great Depression announced the failure of the laissez-faire economic theory, and especially broke down the myth of "Say's Law", i.e. "supply creates demand". Symbolized by *The General Theory of Employment, Interest and Money* published by Keynes in 1936, Keynesianism and Post Keynesianism became the theoretical mainstream and replaced the previous mainstream— the neoclassical economic theory- after the big crisis.

The all-around government regulation in developed capitalist countries had began with the "New Deal" policy of U.S President Roosevelt. Roosevelt had immediately set to implement the plans aiming to save USA out of this crisis and revitalizing the economy. The so-called Roosevelt's "New Deal", in brief, was a series of new economic policies and measures allowing government intervention in the economy, was formulated and implemented to revitalize American economy during the six years from 1933 to 1938. Its main contents included the following policies: Firstly, rectification of the financial order and strengthening government intervention in financial activities. The Congress passed the *Emergency Banking Act* on March 9, 1933 to rectify the banking system; it issued the *1933 Banking Act* on June 16, prescribing that the government shall provide insurance for the bank deposits of 5,000 USD or below. Secondly, it issued the *Agricultural Adjustment Act* to strengthen the government's agricultural regulation and control policies. Through this law the government had controlled the production of agricultural products which were facing large price fluctuations. Thirdly, it strengthened state intervention in industry and regulating industry through the *National Industrial Recovery Act*, and tried to establish a legal system of planned production and mitigate contradictions between the employers and employees through adjustments on wage standards. Fourthly, the government invested in public projects and established social welfare system to solve the employment problems.

The "New Deal" had almost covered all aspects of America's social and economic life. The implementation of the New Deal policy implied the state's overall intervention in the whole economic operation. Even though there were disagreements on the evaluation of the "New Deal" policies, the objective fact was that America had gradually walked out of the difficulties caused by the Great Depression in the 1930s during the "New Deal" period. We should acknowledge that on the one hand, the "New Deal" of Roosevelt was a beneficial trial by the capitalist government on economic regulation. The "New Deal" had promoted the development of productive forces through economic intervention in many aspects, such as improving productive forces in some districts, building irrigation and electric projects, water and soil conservancy, and increasing government's subsidies in scientific research and educational undertakings, etc. On the other hand, the "New Deal" had established the form and system of state monopoly capitalism for the first time in American history and it had laid the foundation for the future characteristics of the capitalist system in the USA which still prevails today. Some policies and measures on government intervention in the economy in the "New Deal" period continued and exerted influences on the market economic mechanism; in the 1950s and 1960s in USA and other countries in the West. Additionally, the "New Deal" policies had the most profound influence in the social spheres. Through the "New Deal", the government was involved in the economic process, adjusted industrial relations and implemented the social insurance system. This had all resulted in the redistribution of income to a certain extent and mitigated class contradictions in America to a certain degree. The nature of the "New Deal" was to save and prolong the life of American monopoly capitalism by strengthening state intervention without affecting private ownership during the period when the contradictions of monopoly capitalism had severely intensified and faced the risk of a collapse. The New Deal had transformed the USA from private monopoly capitalism to state monopoly capitalism and promoted the further development of productive forces to a certain extent.

World War II broke out in 1937 when main capitalist countries had not fundamentally eliminated the affects of the Great Depression. Main capitalist governments had strengthened wartime economic controls to meet the requirements during the war-time, and this historical period was named as the period of "war-time controlled economy". Extensive government intervention and regulation had almost involved every aspect of economic life.

The mechanism of state intervention in the economy was established and had become a common operation after the World War II. The main reason for capitalist countries to adopt state intervention in the economy as one of the fundamental mean for regulating economic activities was the outcome of the development of contradictions between capitalist productive forces and capitalist relations of production in the first place. With the emergence and development of new scientific-technological revolution after World War II, huge investments were needed to develop new technologies and to support the establishment of a series of new emerging industrial sectors and industries, and also infrastructure and public projects. Since private capitalists were neither able to nor willing to make such large-scale, long-term and high-risk investments, the state should make direct investments or organize investments. Therefore, main industrial countries generally increased investment share of governments and established a number of state-owned enterprises or joint economic sectors as a mixture of state-ownership and private capital. The improvement of total factory productivity brought by the development of science and technology after the war had generally improved social productive capacities, and the potential or apparent contradictions between supply and demand were more acute. In view of bitter experiences in the great catastrophic crisis before the World War II, and the fact that automatic market regulation could not maintain the basic balance between the total supply and total demand, capitalist governments were to mitigate contradictions by means of government regulations and make up for the deficiencies of the self-regulation mechanism in the markets in the face of fiercer contradictions arising between market supply and demand. Secondly, due to the serious imbalances in economic powers among main developed countries which appeared before and after the war, it was impossible for them to quickly restore their economies and competitiveness to catch up with the USA within a short term under the conditions of the self-regulation of market mechanism. Consequently, during the post-war economic recovery and participation in international economic competitive activities, Japan, the Federal Republic of Germany and other countries had strengthened the government's role to regulate and intervene in the economy, and formed their respective unique market economic models which integrated market regulations with government regulations. Again, as the Keynesian economic theory replaced neo-classical economics and had become the mainstream after the war, the theories and relevant political advocacies of Keynesianism on state intervention in the economy had exerted great influences upon the formulation and implementation of policies in different countries after the war. Keynesianism had even become the main theoretical foundation for the constitution of various economic policies in the developed countries after the war.

The distinctive feature of the post-war capitalist economic operation was that the role of the government's direct intervention in economic life had been increasingly strengthened. The diversity of its means and extensiveness in the scale of intervention in all spheres of reproduction and the sectors involved were unprecedented. The purpose of state monopoly regulation in the economic operation was to maintain the capitalist system, which had alleviated the basic contradiction of capitalism on the one hand, and had accumulated contradictions in a new form on the other hand.

(2) Objectives and means for macro-regulation in economic operations

The basic objective of state monopoly regulation in the main capitalist countries after the war was to realize full employment, stable prices, steady and sustainable economic growth and to reach a basic balance in the international payments. Generally speaking, the contents and means of regulation and intervention in economic activities between the 1950s to the 1960s had mainly included the following: Firstly, they had increased the government's investment share and built state-owned enterprises or mixed ownership enterprises with both state-owned and private capital. The government had protected and supported private enterprises in some sectors and industries, and exerted influences upon whole economic activities through direct or indirect intervention in these enterprises. Secondly, they had strengthened planned guidance for these enterprises. The governments guided and regulated national economic operations through middle-and-long-term national economic plans in association with the relevant fiscal policies, industrial policies and financial policies. Positive results were achieved through planned regulation especially in France, Japan and other countries. Thirdly, the governments had regulated national economies by policies on financial revenue and expenditures, monetary policies and industrial policies. Fourthly, the governments had promoted foreign trade development through formulating and implementing relevant policies on promoting export trade and other activities, and protected their national industries by adopting trade protection policies. Fifthly, the governments had controlled the widening gap between the rich and the poor caused by the market mechanism within certain limits through formulation and implementation of income distribution policies and transfer of payments for the vulnerable groups, they had established and improved the social insurance and social welfare systems, and adjusted social contradictions. Developed capitalist countries had reinforced the state's power to regulate economy through the aforesaid means and promoted the development of productive forces to a large extent.

(3) Several different models of macro-regulation in economic operations

Due to the different historical conditions in terms of politics, economy and culture in different countries, there had occurred unique characteristics in the integration of market regulation mechanism and government regulation means in each country. Thus they had formed different models of macro-regulation in economic operation.

The first was the American and British market economic model. Although the government economic sector had grown after World War II, its proportion was smaller than the other developed capitalist countries. The government's intervention in private sector was weaker than other countries as well, and they had mainly adopted fiscal and monetary policies to intervene in economy. Such model was called as the "free market system model with government regulation". Through mechanism adjustments, USA economy had realized a continual prosperity in the whole 60s, and its annual growth rate had exceeded 4.2%. Britain also had rapid growth with an annual growth rate of 2% to 4% from 1950s to the middle 1970s except a few years.

The second was French market economic model with planned regulation. France had consecutively formulated and implemented nine medium-term plans on national economic development in 40 years from 1947 to 1988. Economic prosperity which had appeared in France after the war in the 1950s and 1960s was deemed as the outcome of the effective combination of plans and the market. The French government had planned the goals of economic development for those plan periods and changed them when necessary and also designed socio-economic development plans. On the basis of the role of market mechanism, France had preferred guiding plans and promoted national economy to operate for the expected goals by coordinating financial policies and monetary policies with industrial policies. Another feature of French model was that although private ownership had always played the dominant role, state-owned economy had accounted for a larger proportion in national economy than other developed capitalist countries. The output of state-owned enterprises accounted for 18% of GDP, the amount of investment accounted for 27.5% of the total national investment, and the export amount had accounted for 25% in 1990. Since state-owned economies had a large proportion especially in basic leading sectors and public sectors, this sector had become the material foundation and support for government regulations. This model had played a significant role in promoting French economic recovery and development.

The third was the social market economic model in the Federal Republic of Germany. Germany's economy needed to a strong recovery after the war, and there were two viewpoints on this issue. One was the "planned economy school" advocating the state's economic control. The other was the "market economy school" represented by Erhard, who had advocated the reestablishment of market economic order through free competition. Finally the market economy school won the elections and gained the opportunity to practice their policies. Advocated by Erhard, the so-called "social market economic model" gradually was formed in the Federal Republic of Germany

in the 1950s and 1960s. Based on the thoughts of its founder Mueller
Armack, this model meant that "social market economy should work on the
basis of market economic laws, but it should be assisted with social security
policies. Its aim was to combine the principle of free market with social
equality. It essentially was an orderly market economy with government
regulation, i.e., the government executed necessary regulation on the basis
of free market competition. The characteristics of government regulation in
the Federal Republic of Germany were that the state's role in stabilizing the
currency was strengthened, and the income distribution and social security
system were established and improved. The measures of joint supervision
on the enterprise operation and sharing enterprise profits by the employees
within enterprises was a typical case. As the result of economic policies
integrating free competition with government intervention, its GNP had
actually increased by four times from 1950 to 1980.

The fourth was the government guided market economic model
practiced in Japan. Main western capitalist countries had generally adopted
the policy of government intervention in economy on the basis of the
market competition mechanism. However, no where, the scale and extent of
government regulation were not as extensive and profound as that in Japan.
The government played the guiding regulatory role in a certain period, certain
scale and certain extent. Consequently, the economic operating mechanism
in post-war Japan was generally named as "East Asian Model". The Japanese
model had distinctive characteristics. Unique enterprise systems, such as
the so-called "rank promotion system", "life-time employment system",
"system of employees sharing enterprise profits", and the "enterprise internal
labor union system", etc. were formed in the micro field. In the macro field,
middle-and-long-term plans and especially the government's industrial
policies played a guiding role besides the implementation of fiscal policies
and monetary policy regulations similar with other countries. In different
stages of development, the government implemented industrial development
plans designed for every stage, determined leading industries, pillar industries
and emerging industries, and offered strong support in various degrees

through fiscal and monetary policies. The success of the Japanese model had determined its rapid economic development. Its actual annual economic growth rate was 9.8% during the 19 years from 1955 to 1973. After World War II, there were other models among various market economic models formed by the integration of government regulation and market regulation besides the above four models, such as the welfare market economic model in Sweden and the model of four little economic dragons in Asia, etc. In a word, developed capitalist countries generally adopted and strengthened the government's intervention in and regulation of economic activities on the basis of market regulation after World War II. Capitalist economy had enjoyed a rapid growth from the early 1950s to the early 1970s, which was called the "golden period" of capitalist economic growth. It was directly related to the partial adjustment of the capitalist relations of production and government intervention to strengthen economic regulation and controls to make up for the defects in the market mechanism. The "stagflation" which occurred in the capitalist world in 1973 marked the end of this historical period and capitalism entered a new period with a new adjustment in economic policies.[1]

The reason for naming the capitalist economy during the historical period from the Great Depression in the early 1930s to the outbreak of new crisis in the middle 1970s as the "Keynesian period" was not only because the Keynesian theory had replaced neo-classical economics as the mainstream economic school in the history of economic thought, but also because the Keynesian economic theory and its political advocacies had exerted significant influences upon economic policies in different capitalist countries.

The laissez-faire thought had suited the requirements for the establishment of capitalist economic systems and the development of market systems which had formed classical economics and neo-classical economics

---

[1] Compiled by Zhu Zhengqi, Lin Shuzhong, etc.: *Development Route of the Federal Republic of Germany—Practices of Social Market Economy*, Edition 1, pp. 35-36, Beijing, China Social Sciences Press, 1988.

to become mainstream in succession during the free competition stage and its transition to monopoly. Then during the popularization of the policy of state intervention in economy, Keynesian economic theory and its political advocacies became the mainstream economic school because it had suited the requirements for capitalist economic operation in such a historical period.

During the post-war capitalist economic prosperity in the 1950s and 1960s, there was an accumulation of contradictions generated in the capitalist reproduction process. Different policies and measures practiced by government's intervention in economies also had created a series of negative effects while exerting positive influences upon the capitalist economies. Economic crisis interweaving with the universal currency crisis and energy crisis finally broke out between 1974 and 1975 and the unprecedented co-existence of depression together with inflation had appeared in the capitalist world. "Stagflation" was considered to be caused by the Keynesian, especially Post-Keynesian policies. Therefore, the Keynesian economic theory was suspected or even denied and its status as mainstream economic thought was shaken. The capitalist economy had entered into a new adjustment period and the neo-liberalism wave thrived in the development of western economic theories.

3. The Market and the Government in the Neo-Liberalism Period

With the oil crisis caused by the increase of oil prices as the fuse, the large-scale world economic crisis, the most influential crisis after World War II broke in 1974, and had led to the re-adjustment of capitalist economic policies. During the crisis from 1974 to 1975, the industrial production index of USA, Japan, the Federation Republic of Germany, France, Britain and Italy had decreased by 15.3%, 20.0%, 12.9%, 13.2%, 4.7% and 13.5% respectively compared with their peak years before the crisis. Total number of unemployment in western industrial countries had exceeded 15 million in 1975. The commodity prices had increased sharply while there was a sharp decline in production and large increase in unemployment. This was the so-called "stagflation" crisis caused by the co-existence of economic stagnation together with inflation.

"Stagflation", the new phenomenon that had never occurred in previous economic crises, had put the policies of government intervention in economy with demand management as the core in a dilemma; they could not tackle inflation and reduce unemployment at the same time.

We especially need to review the phenomenon of "stagflation" to accurately evaluate the theories of Keynesianism. I think, in fact, stagflation was caused by various reasons. Government intervention also had produced negative effects while stimulating economic growth in a positive way. In the heyday of Keynesianism, governments of different countries generally adopted expansionist policies. The increasingly growing government expenditures had led to huge financial deficits and excess issuance of currency which was bound to lead to inflation. Various control and intervention measures of the government on economic activities had stimulated a general macro economic growth in a certain period, but had also restrained the vigorous growth in micro level, i.e., enterprise level. The rises in commodity prices was caused by expansionist policies had increased production costs and inhibited economic development, finally leading to the co-existence of "inflation" together with "stagnation". Therefore, we should review Keynesianism from a dialectical perspective. On the one hand, we should acknowledge that Keynesianism adapted to the requirements for post-war economic adjustments and strengthened government intervention, and promoted economic development. Meanwhile, we should also realize that Keynesianism could not touch the fundamental contradiction of capitalism, but it had only applied palliative remedies. Due to this defect, it could not fundamentally solve the problems in the capitalist economic development, but had only alleviated some problems and had caused some other problems to become prominent. Consequently, Keynesianism could not ensure the long-term, sustainable and steady development of capitalist economy, which was the limitation of this theory.

Firstly, stagflation destabilized the dominant position of Keynesianism and Post-Keynesianism in economic theories and resulted in the rise of neo-liberal economic wave. The theories and political advocacies of some neo-liberal economic schools were adopted by the relevant governments as official economics and gradually replaced Keynesianism. Thatcher who had assumed office in Britain in 1979 and Reagan assuming power in the USA in 1980, provided opportunities for a large-scale experimentation of neo-liberal economic policies. "Thatcherism" and "Reaganism" re-emphasized the market's status, functions and advocated reduction of state intervention in the labor market and financial markets, especially into the public procurement market. Specifically, USA adopted the policy of "robbing the poor and helping the rich" and greatly reduced enterprise tax rates to simulate the economy. The Reagan government had encouraged entrepreneurs to fight against the government's wasteful expenditures, especially high tax policies and propagated that the former taxation policies had severely damaged the entrepreneurship spirit, and had restricted the development of American economy. With Reaganism as the vanguard, monetarists headed by Friedman and supply-side school had denied Keynesianism as an "insignificant thing". They had advocated reduction of taxes, strict controls on currency issuance, reduction of state intervention and had praised privatization. USA was not alone to abandon Keynesianism, in the European continent, Britain practiced a large-scale "privatization" of the state-owned enterprises. In France, Jacques Chirac and Germany's Helmut Schmidt had turned to implement deflationist policies after the failure of expansionist policies with Keynesian features such as the employment expansion and increase of minimum wages, etc. in 1975 and 1978. It should be noted that the collapse of the economic system and political system in the Soviet Union and East Europe in the end of 1980s had provided a rare chance for the expansion of liberal economic theories. The whole 1980s had almost become an era of Reaganism and Thatcherism.

    Influenced by neo-liberal economic theories and relevant political advocacies, main developed capitalist countries have made a series of major economic adjustments from the whole 1980s to present. In sum, the main contents of these policies include the following features: 1) Implementing tight fiscal and monetary policies. In the monetary policies, monetary regulation with adjustments of interest rates as the main instrument in the Keynesian era was replaced by currency supply policies aiming to control the currency amount. For fiscal policies, they greatly cut government expenditures and tightened the budgets. 2) For the macro-goal, they abandoned the economic expansion strategies with the promotion of rapid economic growth and realization of full employment—the main goals in the Keynesian period—and turned to long-term stability strategies emphasizing adjustments and reforms as the focus, and adopted inflation control policy as the emphasis of macro policies. 3) Adjusted share of state-owned economy and promoted surviving state-owned enterprises to market competition. A wave of privatization had emerged in the West inspired by the neo-liberal thoughts. 4) They loosened the government's economic control and intervention, promoted economic liberalism and intensified competitive mechanisms. And some countries practiced tax reduction plans. 5) Loosened the government's regulation on income distribution and social welfare policies, reduced government expenditures and financial deficits by decreasing social security expenditures, etc.

It was the era to criticize Keynesianism in the 1980s, whereas Neo-liberalism had a louder voice in terms of theories and public opinions, and had exerted great influences upon policies of governments in the main capitalist countries. However, no government had indeed abandoned economic intervention and regulations in practice. A simple example was that in the Reagan administration period along with widespread influences of Neo-liberalism, the American government's military expenditure was up to USD 250 billion annually, and public deficits had not decreased accordingly due to reduction of government intervention, but were always maintained at 5% to 6% of the GDP. Besides, government investment had also remained high, which was obviously a manifestation of the government's role. In practice the governments had loosened intervention in some aspects and but instead practiced new interventions at the same time. Then why could

they comprehensively deny the significance of government intervention?
It is mainly because neo-liberal policies were themselves the outcome of
a higher stage in the development of monopoly capitalism. Many giant
monopoly enterprises had formed in the formation of this stage and "perfect
competition" was replaced by monopoly competition. This had objectively
required that the government should implement certain intervention in the
social economy so as to prohibit monopoly, and protect free competition
among enterprises, and coordinate the smooth operation of social economy.
It is obvious that the objective reality faced by capitalism had determined to
continue government interventions.

In sum, main developed capitalist countries have gradually loosened
government intervention in their economies and strengthened regulation
of market competitive mechanisms since the 1980s. However, it did not
mean that they had completely abandoned economic regulation, but only
had decreased the scale of government regulation and the extent of their
influences upon the economy and also changed the pattern of government
regulation in comparison with the Keynesian era. When we carefully review
of the evolutionary history of economic policies, we can find out that the
scale and extent of government intervention were applied dynamically
because the factors and conditions influencing government interventions had
changed. During frequent fluctuations, the scale and extent of government
intervention was expanded and deepened, whereas when social economy
remains relatively stable, government intervention was decreased. As a result,
the scale and extent of government intervention has relatively decreased in
capitalist economic practices since the 1980s.

II. Theoretical Disputes on Capitalist Economic Operating Mechanism

There had always been diametrically opposed voices on the design of
theory and policy models on the capitalist economic operating mechanism.
The argument generally focuses on "government failure" or "market failure".

There were fierce debates on the relationship between the government and the markets among various schools from mercantile school and physiocratic school to classical, neo-classical economic school and Keynesianism, and then to Neo-liberalism and New-Keynesianism. If we classify different economic schools in western modern economics, we can see two basic trends of thought. One is the laissez-faire thought and the other is the trend advocating government interventions. The basic conception of the latter is that the functions of private economic sectors purely relying on market mechanism to regulate economic operation is limited and malfunctions in some fields. Only through government intervention and regulation can they realize the goals of the economic operations. Therefore, they emphasize on the government's role in macro-economic regulation so as to restore, make up and correct the regulations in market mechanism. Mercantilism, Keynesianism and Swedish school, etc. can all be included in the category of government intervention principle. However, their understandings in terms of forms, means and emphasis, etc. of government intervention and regulation are different. On the contrary, modern economic liberalism advocating for laissez-faire holds the view that the market mechanism of private economic operation can be able to ensure balance and stability in economic operations, the governments should only create and maintain required institutional conditions for the free market competition process and control a minority of crucial macro-economic variables influencing the market process. Traditional economic liberalism had totally denied the state's role, whereas new economic liberalism affirms the necessity of limited government intervention and opposes all-around government intervention in economic operations. American monetary school, rational expectation school, public choice school, property rights school, supply-side school and London school all belong to economic liberalism trend.

Theories are reflections of the reality, although they are always unilateral and partial. Differences in modern western economics reflect the contradictions in the operation of modern capitalist economies. To grasp internal contradictions in capitalist economic operations and their development in the historical context is crucial for Marxists. I think we should more profoundly understand the differences among modern bourgeois economics theories and the development trend in the modern capitalist economic operations. Below I will present my ideas on the subject.

1. Economic Liberalism

Economic liberalism in the early stage was the theoretical reflection on the economic operating mechanism of laissez-faire capitalism in bourgeois economies, which intensively reflected as the worship and eulogy of the market. It had eulogized merits of the market economy in terms of harmony and consistence between personal interests and social interests. Both the "invisible hand" proposition of A. Smith and the economic harmony theory of Bastiat were typical.

USA and other European countries had established the "free enterprise system" and gradually formed the modern market system in the free competition period. The Classical economist Smith had raised the idea of regulating economy by free market, i.e., the "invisible hand" at that time. Smith had vigorously advocated free competition. He had believed that a "natural order" existed in economic life, and human intervention in economy would only result in the destruction of that natural order. According to him, economic activities should be controlled by an "invisible hand", and only free competition and laissez-faire were the best policies. His reasons were as follows: firstly, free competition was the most propitious to realize personal interests. He regarded humans as an economic man, who naturally pursues for personal interests. If each person is given enough freedom of movement, individuals could try their best to realize maximum self interests. Secondly, free competition objectively contributes to the increase of social interests. Guided by market laws, and its invisible hand, optimal allocation of resources could be automatically realized. Social interests could be unconsciously realized spontaneously while economic man motivated by self-egoism pursued for personal interests. Thirdly, even though the government may intervene in the resource allocation process by a motive inspired by goodwill or optimization of social interests, the results could only be the opposite. The functions of the government should be limited to certain spheres: the protection of national security, maintenance of public order as well as protection and construction of the infrastructure. In summary, the government should only play the role of a "night watchman" in the market economy. Smith had persuaded many people in the faith of laissez-faire and non-intervention policies, which had occupied a place in peoples' minds for as long as one and a half centuries.

The thought of Smith was not an incidental theory, but was the outcome of the requirements for the establishment and development of market system in the early period of capitalist development. Free competition had suited to the formation of capitalist market economic systems as well as the struggle against feudal economic elements of the era. However, in fact, government had also intervened in economy even in the laissez-faire period; the bourgeois governments had played an important role in the formation of capitalist market system. Meanwhile, the non-mainstream school advocating government intervention had also resisted strongly on just grounds. For instance, Malthus had advocated government intervention in population affairs. The German historical school represented by Liszt hade made an utmost effort to urge government to intervene in economy and implement trade protection policies.

Western economics had developed to the neo-classical stage by the end of 19th century. Industrial Revolution was completed in main capitalist countries and the capitalist economic operating mode had gained a dominant position during this period. Compared with classical economics, neo-classical economics had not needed to struggle with feudal economic elements; it had focused on the methods to improve market economic operations. Neo-classical economics had inherited the laissez-faire thought of Smith and progressed for the perfection of the market mechanisms by introducing the marginal analysis, utility analysis and equilibrium analysis methods. They believed that consumer choices were a "baton" guiding allocation of resources in the market under free competition conditions.

Walras, the representative of Swiss Lausanne School had raised the general equilibrium theory and the British Marshall had amended it as the partial equilibrium theory. "Equilibrium" was an ideal condition in the market operations, and optimum allocation of resources could be realized when the market reached equilibrium. Therefore, neo-classical economists did not advocate government intervention in the market. We cannot say there were no brilliant ideas on the market mechanism in the achievements of neo-classic economists. However, due to their standpoints and goals of research as well as the development of internal contradictions of the capitalist mode of production, they could neither notice or reveal the profound contradictions occurring in the society nor depict shallow contradictions in the social operating mechanism capitalism. However, the latter was the main contribution of various schools advocating for government intervention.

Economic liberalism had begun to revive in the 1960s as neo-liberalism, and in the economic literature they initiated several arguments on the "government failure". There were two practical reasons for the evolution of this economic trend: one is that Keynesian policies promoted by developed capitalist countries had generally resulted in "stagflation" and the reality of high unemployment together with high inflation was contradictory with the government intervention principles of Keynesianism. According to Keynesian views inflation and unemployment rates are mutually replaceable, and the government's macro policies can realize both goals: stabilizing commodity prices and realizing low unemployment rate. Nevertheless, there was a significant difference between reality and theories. Another reason was that in 1960, some socialist countries and many developing countries had reformed their policies in the direction of the market economy. In socialist countries after rapid industrialization in the early construction period, their highly centralized economies generally lacked economic efficiency, and they were seeking for new ways to promote economic development by means of the market.

In comparison with economic liberalism of the early period, Neo-liberalism is a contemporary economic school advocating free competition among enterprises, emphasizing on the market mechanism as the basic regulatory mechanism in the economic operations, and limited government intervention. As mentioned before, even neo-liberalism has various sub-schools but they all believe one thing in common, i.e., the market mechanism in modern economy has limitations and failures in the markets indeed exist. However, this is not caused by the market mechanism itself, but due to excessive government intervention. Excessive government intervention causes market mechanism fail to operate freely, and the merits or functions of the market mechanism can not play their roles in a normal way. They further believe that the only way for eliminating market failure is to re-establish the role of market mechanism and reduce government intervention accordingly. Neo-liberalism had also raised the concept of "government failure" corresponding to "market failure" based on the argument that government intervention may inevitably have drawbacks. They believe that government officials are also economic men, same like ordinary people. They also have the nature of pursuing private interests and neglecting public interests. The governments led by these officials are not more holy and wiser than other organizations. Therefore, government intervention unavoidably may have many drawbacks, mainly in the following aspects: Firstly, since government intervention is also man-made and subject to political objectives rather than economic goals, such interventions and regulations are not always reasonable. It could be very dangerous to regulate economy depending on the morality and virtue of officials. Secondly, government intervention and regulation are prone to lead to excessive centralization of power, and further to monopoly and autocratic behaviors, which may impair the normal operation of economic system and civil peoples' material and spiritual welfare or interests. Additionally, the means of government's regulation are limited and various means and tools are mutually restrictive and offset one another. Last but not least, the influences of the governments on economic activities contain less rational or morality than that of market. Since government's actions are executed by officials seeking personal gains and authority, these actions not only lack the competition concept but also lack cost and profit notions, thus they are also prone to safeguard the narrow interests of the government departments rather than social interests. Therefore, they are inefficient and even invalid. Since the failures are rooted in the government intervention itself, it is unrealistic to employ government with a task to correct the market failure. Nevertheless, we should underline one point. Due to the characteristics of monopoly capitalism, neo-liberalism cannot completely deny the necessity of government intervention, and holds the view that government intervention should be controlled within the irreplaceable limit of market mechanism, and the purpose of government intervention should be to ensure the smooth operation of market mechanisms.

In sum, the neo-liberal economic thought gradually had occupied a dominant position in the development of economics and became the new doctrine of theories in developed capitalist countries as well as the standard for measuring the success of economic policies in the developing countries since the end of 1970s. Many developing countries—including former Soviet Union and East European countries—have followed the theories of the neo-liberal economic wave. They have carried policies such as liberalization of trade and investment, financial liberalization and privatization, but they could not achieve rapid economic growth as they have assumed. The impacts of Asian financial storm and problems in the international monetary and financial system itself have impelled many economists to reconsider the neo-liberal economic wave. Many people started to blame and criticize the extreme aspects in this model. Firstly, they have criticized that neo-liberal economic wave was too keen on privatization. Its approach was based on the incidental facts ignoring the fundamental problems, confuses means and purposes and finally loses direction. Either trade liberalization or economic privatization can only be means to an end. The result would be irrational if we only pay attention to privatization and liberalization rather than nurturing a competitive market. Therefore, the criticizers suggest that the privatization myth should be abandoned. In fact, privatization cannot be the objective but only a way for promoting market competition at best. Secondly, neo-liberal economic wave had inappropriately emphasized open economies, trade liberalization and financial liberalization, and led some developing countries into serious troubles. Thirdly, the neo-liberal economic wave had rejected government intervention in economy and that could exert negative effects on the economic efficiency. While admitting and recognizing the existence of government failure, some people have also realized the limitations of the market. They have suggested that markets have failures especially under those circumstances of inadequate information and during their immature stage of development. Under such circumstances, government intervention can offer a Pareto improvement effect, i.e., government intervention can make some people better-off without making others suffer. Through reconsideration of neo-liberal economic wave and its long-standing mistaken ideas, public can push better economic development strategies on a more solid foundation and avoid more mistakes.

2. Government Intervention Principle

During the history of capitalist development, the government intervention principle had existed since the primitive accumulation period of capitalism, which was mainly represented by the theories and political advocacies of mercantilists at this stage. Mercantilism was the general integration of economic thoughts of the commercial capital's pursuit of gold/ silver currency and the policy system emphasizing government intervention in Europe from the 15th to the 17th century. Government intervention at this stage can be summarized as the original state intervention principle, i.e. the state intervention principle at the primitive accumulation stage by the alliance of commercial capital with the feudal state power. Its progressive aspect lies in that feudal monarchy had become the "crutch" in promoting and supporting the growth of the capitalist mode of production which eventually buried itself. Mercantilism at the early stage had advocated both the restriction and impairment of private economic scale and direct regulation through nationalization or state monopoly. States should not only intervene the economy by administrative means and legislation, but also spare no hesitation to seize gold and silver through political, diplomatic or even military means. French Colbertism and Germany Cameralism which appeared in the late mercantilism stage, made such original state intervention principle reach a peak, and equipped it with the features of feudal autocracy and state monopoly. Such original state intervention principle had gradually weakened with the development of mercantilism. Eventually its leading position was finally replaced by economic liberalism.

It should be pointed out that though mercantilists had strongly advocated popularization of intervention policies by state power politics and government organizations, they did not simply welcome the behaviors of placing state authority and will of the monarchy above private economic behaviors in handling some economic issues except foreign trade spheres. We should also indicate that monopoly commercial capitalists who differentiated from small and medium commercial capitalists were the main beneficiaries of state intervention policies, whereas small and medium commercialists did not have monopoly rights. They were not the beneficiaries of state intervention policies and some of them were naturally against the state intervention principle.

The internal contradictions of capitalism featured by free competition had gradually become visible after its steady development for a period. The Great Depression in 1929 had announced the failure of traditional laissez-faire economic theory. The crisis was not only a significant turning point in the development of capitalist economies, but also a crucial turning point in the development of western economic theories. Suffering severe attacks, economic liberalism had left the stage. On the one hand, though the former economic liberalists still continued to believe in liberalism, they could not advocate "laissez-faire" as before; they had to acknowledge that state intervention to a certain degree was a necessary condition for market economic operation and began to show up in the face of neo-liberalists. On the other hand, most economists had turned to the government intervention principle, analyzed market drawbacks in an all-around way and explored the necessity of government intervention—naturally—with the precondition of safeguarding the basic capitalist operating mechanism. Their main arguments include the following aspects which mainly focus on "market failure":

1) Existence of monopoly. Arguments of neo-classical economists were based on the perfect competitive market. However, perfect competition requires a large amount of buyers and sellers on the market, sufficient market information, full free flow of resources, and homogeneous products, etc. But most competitions on the real markets are imperfect competition or monopoly competition. Monopoly infringes the functions of the market, due to the inappropriate distribution of resources for different purposes caused by monopoly; monopolists are no longer the receivers of market price but the manipulators of price. Monopolists restrict the flow of resources in monopolistic sectors of the economy; thus due to their choices flow of resources are less than the optimal amount; production amounts are also restricted to reach monopolistic prices, etc. Thus allocation of resources distances from the equilibrium point. Therefore, government intervention is required.

2) Existence of externalization. Externalization refers to the favorable or detrimental effects on a manufacturer's economic activities by the economic activities of other manufacturers or consumers. However, this manufacturer will not gain relevant rewards and assume relevant responsibilities. Since the subject of market does not consider externalization when making decisions, seen from the perspective of social interests, if the market system operates freely, negative effects of externalization will be too high and positive effects will not be maximum, which leads to obvious problems in the allocation of resources.

3) Existence of public commodities (goods). Public goods refer to those commodities or services produced by government investments since private individuals are unwilling to or unable to invest for that production. They are featured as non-competitive and non-exclusive consumption. Since the internal economic benefits of public products (providers can gain benefits) are far less than the external economic benefits (total social benefits), there will inevitably be a lack of supply for these goods if they are provided through the market. Then free economics cannot suit for public goods.

4) Markets cannot focus on both efficiency and fairness at the same

time. There is an unequal distribution of income and wealth in the market economic system. Smith had already realized such drawback of market economy in the period of laissez-faire capitalism. He had once pointed out: "Wherever there is big property there is a great inequality. For one very rich man there must be at least five hundred poor, and the affluence of the few supposes the indigence of the many." The main reason for income inequality are based on differences in property, differences in individuals' abilities, differences in education and opportunities as well as differences in age and health conditions, etc. And polarization had become more and more obvious with the transformation from free competition to monopoly capitalism. Such social problems could not be solved by the market itself, but through government policies and measures.

Keynesian school was the most influential school in government intervention theories. Keynes had criticized employment theories of neo-classical economists, criticized Say's Law of "supply creates demand" theory, integrated economic theories with monetary theories, replaced universal analysis with specific analysis, validated in theory that there should be economic crises and unemployment in the capitalist society. He had strongly criticized laissez-faire in economic policies and raised a set of concrete policies and measures for avoiding economic crises and eliminating unemployment through state intervention in economy, which was named as "Keynesian revolution" in the history of economic thoughts. Keynesian revolution is a fundamental turning point for the theories of government intervention in an economy to replace laissez-faire trend, and is the historical outcome related with the rapid development of state monopoly capitalism. Keynesianism had thrived for a period after the war and occupied a dominant position in economics. The overriding reason was that Keynesianism, the new economic theory had well suited to the formation and development of monopolistic state capitalism, adapted to the requirements of a series of measures for the state intervention in the reproduction process and had adapted to the requirements for the monopoly bourgeoisie's pursuit for maximum profits during the period after its occurrence. By attacking Say's

Law, Keynes had abandoned the argument of the traditional economics that the capitalist market economy can automatically regulate and realize full employment. He had acknowledged the existence of crises and unemployment in capitalism. These reflected some facts in the monopoly capitalist economy in a more realistic way compared to traditional economics of laissez-faire. Another important reason was that the Keynesian school had indeed supported profit concerns of the monopoly bourgeoisie, by maintaining the stability in the capitalist economy and promoting its development. It laid more emphasis on quantitative analysis and research on economic management, economic benefits and economic policies and reflected some general development trends in the modernized mass production by exploring those specific economic aspects. However, the ultimate mistake of Keynes' government intervention economic theory was that it had undermined the basic contradiction of capitalism, i.e. the contradiction between socialization of production and private capitalist possession of the means of production, and only focused on the forms of some phenomena rather than content. It was impossible for Keynes to find out the root of the problem in the capitalist mode of production and reveal the main drive of the capitalist society. Keynes could not reach a scientific analysis, since he had studied economic crisis without considering the capitalist production relations and had explained the cause for the crises and unemployment by the effective demand theory, even though he had acknowledged that there was overproduction and scant demand in the capitalist society. Even though his theoretical practice had contributed to the prosperity of the capitalist world for nearly 20 years after World War II, it could not fundamentally solve the problems of the capitalist economic crises and unemployment, etc., and finally led to a series of phenomena as "stagflation", etc. in the 1970s that could not be solved by Keynesianism either.

3. Integrating Economic Liberalism and Government Intervention Principle

The crucial issue on the capitalist economic operating mechanism at

the end of the 20th century was still whether to return to Smith or Keynes.
Specifically, more popular is the economic liberal theory which originates
from Smith's laissez-faire in this period, which was later developed by
Hayek and enriched by Friedman's monetarism. The other alternative is the
government intervention theory of Keynesianism. The two opposite views
can be found in almost each crucial turning stage of economic cycle in the
whole 20th century especially after the Great Depression in 1929-1933.
The confrontation between these theories also exists nowadays and was
also debated during the Asian financial crisis towards the end of the 20th
century. As the supporter of foreign exchange control in the emerging market
economies, the views of Krugmann, professor of the Massachusetts Institute
of Technology are obviously a modern reflection of Keynesian views. On
the contrary, Sax, professor of the Harvard University believes that it's better
to devaluate a currency rather than maintain exchange rates by tight budget
policies and high interest rates, which obviously is the latest manifestation of
Smith's views.

Between Krugman and Sax, there is another voice from Stiglitz, the
representative of New Keynesianism, and Samuelson, the representative
of neo-classical synthesis and the winner of the Nobel economic prize.
New Keynesians have absorbed some views of Neo-liberalism insisting
on the basic theories of Keynesianism, their new synthesis emphasizes
proper government intervention to solve market failure on the basis of
Keynesianism, and explicitly advocates the pattern of "mixed economy".
Such moves of economic schools effectively reflect mutual interaction
between the two main opposite trends debating on the capitalist economic
operating mechanism. They approach each other and absorb some elements
from its opposite to suit the new conditions.

New Keynesianism:

New Keynesianism has inherited basic theories of Keynes and opposes
to the advocacies of Neo-classics which argue on the inefficacy of macro-
economic policies and abandonment of state intervention in economy. The

"coordination failures" theory of New Keynesianism provides theoretical foundation for the efficacy of macroeconomic policies and merits of the active state intervention. However, in terms of guiding ideas, New Keynesianism puts more emphasis on the role of market mechanisms compared with the traditional Keynesianism. It advocates "moderate" state intervention rather than excessive frequent interventions. It also advocates the government's "macro regulation" and disapproves "micro regulations" on the economy. This is the typical achievement made by new Keynesians which admits the effective role of market in an interaction with neo-liberal economics. However, on the other hand, the "coordination failures" theory has also revealed that even price is completely flexible, and all economic participants are reasonable economic men, the market mechanism cannot successfully coordinate overall economic activities in the society; since in the social economy generally multiple equilibriums with different efficiencies appear. The existence of multiple equilibriums constitutes the basis or possibility to transform the economy from an equilibrium with lower efficiency to an equilibrium with higher efficiency by employing government intervention. The "coordination failures" theory also reveals that due to the existence of multiple equilibriums, economic participants can choose actual equilibriums according to their social consciousness or expectations. The reason why social economy can reach a state of equilibrium with lower efficiency is that each participant in the economy has lower predictions and expectations, and there is no incentive factor that can change their behavior. New Keynesian economics believes that under such circumstances, not only the government can influence the actual output through total demand management policies as advocated by traditional Keynesianism, but also it offers a new "scope for demand management policies", i.e., by considering the influence of faith or expectation of the economic participants; government's economic policies can increase the actual output. The government's macro-economic policies can be effective and compatible with rational behaviors of micro-economic participants if they can influence people's choice on multiple equilibriums and coordinate people's expectation for a higher-level equilibrium. In sum, compared with traditional Keynesianism, New Keynesianism is more progressive in terms of theories on the capitalist economic operating mechanism and suits better to the reality of capitalist economics. However, New Keynesianism also has some major defects, for instance, their propositions on the ways of mobilizing external variables to overcome non-equilibrium and avoid stagflation, etc. are incomplete. Some judgments lack solid internal logics and empirical evidence; and there is a lack of internal relations among its different theories. Therefore, we can say that New Keynesianism has cured some deficiencies in the traditional Keynesianism theory to a certain extent, but it could not free mainstream economics from the predicament of a crisis.

The neo-classical synthesis:

The neo-classical synthesis has combined neo-classical micro economic theories with Keynesian macro-economic theories and advocates the "mixed economy": co-existence of private economic activities and governmental economic activities side by side, i.e. on the basis of the capitalist private ownership of the means of production. The allocation of resources for different kinds of purposes should be determined freely by individual activities through price mechanism on the one hand, and on the other hand, the government should intervene to stimulate total output through fiscal and financial policies by regulating income distribution through progressive taxes and welfare support. Therefore, the neo-classical synthesis has put forward the policy of "micro economic regulations" to realize steady economic growth and ideal full employment, which is also the difference between the neoclassical synthesis and the new Keynesians. As far as the theories on capitalist economic operating mechanism are concerned, they believe that the government and the market were mutually complementary rather than mutually replaceable. This neither means that the optimum result can be guaranteed by the market itself, nor that the government is required to assume all responsibilities of the market because of market failure risk when the government is involved. Under some circumstances, the government can be deemed as the force for creating markets and promoting the creation of the markets. In some fields, such as education, government and private departments, undertakings can be jointly assumed as cooperating partners. In some other fields, such as the financial sector, the government should be deemed as the provider of regulations and systems necessary for normal market operations. The government should also assume a special task apart from playing the role in the above aspects, i.e., create the institutional infrastructure so that the market can play its effective role. To ensure effective market operations, there should be a clearly established ownership system and a sound property system, effective competition, effective anti-trust laws, people should have confidence in the market and fluent contract institutions and practices.

In conclusion, on the one hand the mixed economic theories manifest the fact that modern capitalist economies are fundamentally based on and guided by the market economic mechanisms or market power and secondly assisted by the government's macro-economic controls. However, on the other hand they advocate the mutual relationships between the market and the government, acknowledge their respective roles but not in fixed patterns; instead relative and mutually ebbing and fluent relations. This approach is the dividing line and interaction line between them and the Samuelson's "mixed economy" theory. Samuelson had believed that the government should assist or supplement the market mechanisms. The government should not do things that can be done by private individuals, it should do things that have not been done. Secondly, for Samuelson the foremost issue of social economics is to determine the proper line between the market and the government. Samuelson had believed that the monopoly, externality and social inequality lead to market failures, and the government should with the "visible hand" intervene to avoid those defects. For Samuelson, the government should undertake three main economic functions in the modern market economy. First one is to increase efficiency by promoting competition; secondly, to redistribute income to promote equality by means of tax and government expenditures; thirdly, to promote growth, reduce unemployment and prevent inflation by fiscal and monetary policies. These fields are deemed as the

boundaries in the integration of the market and the government. Through his
views, we can see the development trend in the mainstream economics and
people's value orientation on the debate about the market and government
relations. We believe that in that heated debate, the mixed economy argument
of the neo-classical synthesis better accords with the practical realities of the
current capitalist market economy. However, the theories of the neo-classical
synthesis were bound to be incomplete since this school also treats the market
economic operating mechanism on the basis of safeguarding the capitalist
economic system.

As we observe the evolution of modern capitalist economics—especially
the trend of New Keynesianism and the neo-classical synthesis—the
tendency of mutual integration between government intervention principle
and economic liberalism is more and more prominent. Economic liberalism
gradually makes a reasonable transition from complete laissez-faire to
the acknowledgement of government's partial intervention. Government
intervention principle gradually acknowledges the efficiency of the market
economy and pays attention to integrate government intervention with market
regulation. I guess such a trend will also be active in the future development
of the theories on the capitalist economic operating mechanism.

4. Models and Criterion on Integration of Market and Government Functions

In fact, today hardly any serious economist completely denies
the functions of the market or the government in the socio-economic
development. Most of their analysis on the market failure or government
failure focuses on the argumentation and descriptions of the priority of
government regulation or market regulation, i.e., the selection of the
appropriate model how to integrate the market and government functions.
Nevertheless, the relevant debates cannot grasp the key and fundamentals
of the issue, due to their world views and methodologies. There must be a
criterion for selection and what is the criterion for that selection under the
conditions of the capitalist economic operating mechanism? It needs to be

deeply analyzed by the theories of Marxist economics, and it is the necessary precondition for realizing the historical and current debates among schools.

It is the basic principle of Marxist social economics that the relations of production should adapt to the development of productive forces. Modes for the integration of government functions and market functions fall into the category of institutions-regulations- or theoretically put; relations of production. The basic criterion for a reasonable mode to integrate the government and market functions should be that it can enable the totality of the integrated governmental and market functions adapt to the requirements for the development of productive forces and realize appropriate allocation of the sources. In brief, that totality should be both be flexible in the micro sense, include effective motivating mechanisms and enable good macro co-ordination, so as to combine the advantages of market regulation with that of government regulation. We should accurately analyze specific factors influencing the relations between the government and the market so as to achieve this goal. It is necessary to realize that the government and the market are not two independent economic organizations, but two relatively independent components in an integrated social economic structure. Their generation, development and mutual relationship depends on the overall situation of the socio-economic structure and under the effect of mutual interaction of all kinds of factors constituting the whole socio-economic structure. There are many factors influencing the relationship between the government and the market, such as the natural and social environment of a nation, constitutional system, level of economic development, the government's economic policies and historical and cultural traditions, etc., which can be summarized in the following aspects as a whole. I suggest them as the selection criteria for designing the functions of the market and the government.

Level of productive forces: The functions and integration form of the government and the market, as the category of market mechanism or institution, are fundamentally are inter-related to the development of productive forces. Here I consider the market as a category including market mechanisms or institutions; according to general accepted definition institution is a series of regulations or norms which influences human activities. Superficially, a market economy is a mode of resource allocation in the first place, and price signals dominate the process of economic operations. However, price is based on value, which reflects the interest exchange relations between independent producers, while the extensive development of the exchange relations is the result of social division of labor and the width and depth of the division of labor determines the width and depth of exchange activities. Therefore, the development level of a market is fundamentally determined by social division of labor and productive forces driven by it. In history natural economy which needed a primitive division of labor had come into being on the basis of original natural productive forces, and small commodity production economy could only occur and function on the basis of the handicraft—guild like—industry, whereas commodity economy relations could only be generalized and universalized on the basis of socialized mass production, requiring the market mechanism as the foundation for the allocation of resources. The nature, position and functions of the government are fundamentally decided by the development level of productive forces as well. Socialized mass production had broken the fetters of natural economy on producers, and had contributed to extensive economic relations among people and had promoted extensive political participation. Meanwhile, with the continual deepening of the contradiction between socialization of production and private capital ownership and the difficulties of capital appreciation led by this contradiction, the government's planned economic regulation became the necessary condition for the normal operation of socialized production and inevitable requirement to create the conditions for capital appreciation. The free market economy was replaced by the market economy with regulations. It is the fundamental reason for the fact that "western market economic countries also attach importance to the role of planning. The models on the integration of government and market functions would be reasonable and effective only by adapting to the requirements for the development of productive forces and their further development needs.

Ownership relation or property system: The determinant role of productive forces on the relations of production and the model on the integration of government and market functions are generally realized through the property system. Property system or ownership is the foundation for social economic and political relations, which determines the basic interest relations and interest structure of a society. Therefore, the nature of property relations is the most crucial factor for deciding the combining mode of government and market functions. Market exchanges are essentially exchanges of property rights by nature and the nature of property relations directly determines the nature of market exchange. Likewise, based on Marxism, the class dominant in economy is also dominant in politics, so the nature of property system decides the class nature of the government. Government intervention in economy is the requirement for the fundamental economic interests of the capitalist class, and state ownership is the foundation for its macro adjustment and control. In capitalist market economies, the basic function of the governments is to protect private property rights with due consideration to fairness and a spontaneous market order is a normal manifestation of private ownership. Only when the spontaneous market order is destroyed by troubles, or social polarization is too severe such that it hurts the capitalist market order, the state has to make market intervention. Therefore we can say that rationalization of property relations is the foundation for the rationalization of government and market relations.

Social ideologies and cultural conditions: Ideology is the ideological system of the dominant class, which significantly influences a state's choice of economic mechanism. Not only the formation of traditional socialist planned economy in the Soviet Union and China and many other countries was the outcome of special historical environment, but also it had great relations with traditional and original socialist theory and ideology. The classical viewpoint that socialism is a planned economy and capitalism is a market economy had greatly influenced the process of institutional change in the socialist countries. Culture, as an informal rule, accumulated in the

long-term acculturation of one generation after another and reflects the
lifestyle of a nation and a nationality. Different cultural backgrounds have
great influences on the behavior they react to institutional changes. Seen
from a historical perspective, Hellenism featured by freedom, personality and
rationality, the Roman Law centering on ownership contract relations, and
protestant ethic with rational tendencies all constitute the cultural origin of
contemporary capitalist market economy. Compared with Confucianism and
Daoism in China, Hinduism and Buddhism in India and Moslem in Arabia,
western cultural traditions were more convenient for the development of
capitalism and market economy in history and have greatly promoted the
generation and development of capitalist system. I should suggest more
attention to the profound internal relation between culture and economic
development and institutional change. Different market economic models
and marketization ways in various countries reflect the differences in
national and ethnic cultural traditions to a large extent. The circumstances
are also different in capitalist countries. While USA and Britain are forts for
liberalism, authoritarianism prevails in Germany and Japan, Nordic people
have a spirit of mutual assistance and the cultural tradition of East Asia is
familial. Different market economic models have formed because of different
cultural traditions, for instance, the free market economy in Britain and USA,
the social market economic model in Germany, the government oriented
market economic model in Japan and welfare states in North Europe were
all produced in the long history of institutional changes and have profound
influences upon the market economy and the relationship between the
government and the market.

In sum, the relationship between the government and the market are
historical, specific instead of being abstract. Since the development level of
productive forces in different periods varies, the nature of property system as
well as historical and cultural traditions are different in different countries, thus
the models of market economy and the relationship between the government
and the market cannot be the same. Therefore, when studying the capitalist
economic operating models, i.e. the model on the integration of government

and market functions, we have to proceed from the historical background of a nation in a certain period, give full consideration to all kinds of economics, political and cultural factors, combine the general requirements of the market economy with specific national conditions and specific historical conditions and systematically combine effective government regulation with effective market regulation aiming at the promotion of development of productive forces to the most extent as the fundamental criterion.

The differences between two different theoretical models on the capitalist economic operating mechanism are mainly represented as either affirming or denying the respective status and role of regulation by the free market competition mechanism and government intervention and regulation, and their judgment on the degree of integration between the two. The main issue debated is the regulation and control of capitalist economic operation. The common foundation for the two different theoretical models is to ensure that private ownership and private economic decision rights play the dominant role and protect private property from being infringed, thus they do not involve in form of ownership, the decisive issue in economic mechanisms. In other words, they do not touch the system itself under the precondition of capitalist private ownership, which decides that no such theoretical model can fundamentally solve the contradictions in the capitalist economic operation.

III. Nature and Tendency of Contemporary Capitalist Economic Operating Mechanism

Through the above analysis, we have formulated our research results on the historical evolution process of the capitalist economic operating mechanism from the dual aspects of theory and practice. We also have given detailed picture on the basic features of the contemporary capitalist economic operating mechanism. On this basis, I will further explore the nature and development trends in the evolution of the contemporary capitalist economic operating mechanism.

1. Essence of the Evolution of the Capitalist Economic Operating Mechanism

The evolution and changes in the capitalist economic operating mechanism is inevitable, which can be explained from two aspects:

Firstly, the internal contraction of capital is the direct reason for the evolution of the capitalist economic operating mechanism. On the one hand, capital exists on the basis of capitalist private ownership, and possesses distinctive features of private capital. On the other hand, capital exists on the condition of socialization of production, capital can exist, develop and increase in value, only if it can continually obtain subjective and objective conditions for production and continually promote its products in the society. Therefore, capital has also distinctive properties of social capital. Any capital is the unity of opposites of that dual nature as: private capital and social capital. Only by continual transformation from private capital to social capital can the capital reserve itself and increase in value. In the period of laissez-faire capitalism, the internal contradiction of capital did not have an external form of development; the general social nature of the single private capital which existed in the form of family capital did not have the external independent form of existence, and the social capital nature of private capital was revealed only after it assumed commodity form—rudiments of capital market—thus single private capital was recognized by the society, i.e., after its independency on the surface and independent form of existence were sublated. Under such new circumstances, the private capital form of the capital could satisfy its requirements for capital movement. The necessary role expected from the state was to be the guard of private capital, and its main function was to protect sufficient competition among private capital(s). Therefore, the capitalist economic operating mechanism had mainly existed in the model of free market, the government's role was relatively weak and its scope of intervention had focused on relatively minor spheres; those affected by market failures. However, there were profound changes in the technological base and the industrial structure of social production after the Second Scientific-Technological Revolution; not only a series of new emerging industrial sectors were created, but also traditional industrial sectors have undergone re-construction process. The degree of mutually relative, mutually independent and mutually conditional socialization among different links of the production process and different production processes were further strengthened. The social nature of capital should be further strengthened with the further development of socialization of production.

The social nature of capital was a necessary requirement in the market and different links of the social reproduction process, which inevitably led to capital's constant form changes with new social forms; for the realization of private capital ownership. Without a change in its fundamental nature as private ownership of capital, the forms of the realization of private capital ownership was transformed from private ownership to joint-social ownership forms, i.e., legal person's capital, the form of state-owned capital and then to the form of international capital. In the course of time, the social nature of capital had become more prominent and capital could only move smoother in that way. Once capital was transformed to legal, state-ownership and international forms, the state was inevitably required to act as the general representative of monopoly capital, in the capitalist economic operating mechanism. Therefore, for the above reasons, an evolution in the capitalist economic operating mechanism is an inevitable requirement for the self movement and appreciation of capital.

Secondly, the basic contradiction of capitalism is the fundamental reason for the changes in the capitalist economic operating mechanism. Directly to say, the evolution of the capitalist economic operating mechanism is the result of the contradictory movement of the dual nature in capital. However, since capital's inner contradiction is the reflection of the basic contradiction of capitalism in the capital itself, then we can say that it is fundamentally the inevitable outcome of the movement of the basic contradiction of capitalism. We can thus explain the relation between changes in the operating mechanism and basic contradiction of capitalism. Constant socialization in the capitalist production pushes capitalists to use capital as social capital as much as possible within the scope of private ownership, in other words, it requires that the social nature of capital be revealed in a more prominent way. This requirement as socialization of capital is realized throughout the evolution of the capitalist economic operating mechanism, such as: legal person's capital, state-owned capital and international capital. Such new forms—carriers or undertakers—with relatively independent and distinct contents finally comes into being, therefore enterprises—with different forms—operate side by side are connected and linked in a more stable way, which mitigates the basic contradiction of capitalism to a certain extent.

In the following we will make a detailed analysis in the changes of the capitalist economic operating mechanism in different stages determined by the basic contraction. The basic contradiction of capitalism determines the inevitable occurrence of economic crises based on relative overproduction, which forcefully balances total supply and total demand and makes economic crises cyclical. Cyclical economic crises constantly intensify the competition and the competition promotes the continual development of productive forces and continual progress in the socialization of production process. On the basis of continual increases in the level of productive forces and the level of socialization of production, the social attributes of capital helps for the concentration process thus stock capital form as the proper form of capital's concentration and centralization records a rapid development. Monopolistic enterprises had come into being on the basis of constant concentration of production and capital. Laisser-faire capitalism had developed into monopoly capitalism during the end of the 19th century to the beginning of the 20th century. During the stage of monopoly capitalism, the basic contradiction of capitalism has deepened and become acute, which led to the Great Depression shocking the whole capitalist world between 1929 and 1933. The Great Depression had announced the failure of theories and policies since Smith, which had idealized market mechanism, the "invisible hand", believing that social economy could be adjusted with pure reliance on the spontaneous role of market power. Great Depression had also raised objective requirements for adjusting capitalist production relations, reforming the capitalist economic operating mechanism and curing the deficiencies of pure market mechanism in both theory and practice. The formation of Keynesianism as well as the formation and development of state monopoly capitalism were the specific manifestations of such objective requirements. The New Deal policies of Roosevelt was a new practice of state monopoly capitalism. After World War II, production became more socialized with the big progress in science and technology and further deepened social division of labor. Higher socialization and modernized mass production brought in a series of new problems for solution. For instance, modernized mass production has a larger scale and demands much larger sum of capital. The development of science, technology and modernized mass production demand rapid improvement of educational training in all fields. Environment protection and ecological balance need to be maintained, economic and financial globalization demand for coordination and division of labor among different countries, etc. Private monopoly capitalists were neither able to nor willing to solve these problems; which all exceeded the capacities of the private monopoly capital and required the state as a direct investor and as a "general capitalists" come forward or required its cooperation with private monopoly capital. After World War II, a new pattern of an economic operating model based mainly on market regulation and which was assisted by government's macro intervention and regulation had generally formed in developed capitalist countries under the circumstances of the development of state monopoly capitalism.

From the above analysis we realize that the capitalist economic operating mechanism adapts to the requirements of capital movement and appreciation, and its fundamental motive is the continual evolution of the basic contradiction of capitalism caused by the socialization of production. Production socialization is the tendency of capitalist economic development, and the constant accumulation and leaps in the basic contradiction requires that the form of capitalist appropriation of the means of production should continually adjust and adapt to this tendency of the socialization of production. Regulation and control of the capitalist market by the government as the general representative of private property right and capitalists had mitigated contradictions to a certain extent and promoted the progress of the productive forces in the capitalist society. However, its basic contradiction is insurmountable and the form and extent of contradictions are developing with the constant progress of production socialization tendency, which objectively determines that the capitalist economic operating mechanism dynamically changes.

2. Recent Changes in the Capitalist Economic Operating Mechanism

The overall feature of contemporary capitalist economic operating mechanism is characterized by an increasingly obvious trend: integration of government intervention and market mechanisms. This is a kind of progress in the theory and practice on the relations between the market and the government in the capitalist development process. In the past, although people once misunderstood and had incomplete ideas on the relations between the market and the government, we cannot deny that these approaches were the reflections on the then evolution of the capitalist economic mechanism itself. Observing the historical process of the evolution of the capitalist economic operating mechanism, we can clearly see that the objective law of the evolution in the capitalist economic operating mechanism as: the tendency of the constant integration of market mechanism and government intervention determined by the basic contradiction.

Although the rise of Neo-liberalism has resulted in the impairment of economic intervention by governments in developed capitalist countries since 1970s, no force can fundamentally alter the main trend of capitalism. We also observe some new features in capitalist economic operation, especially related to government intervention, specifically represented as:

Firstly, the aim of intervention has changed from stimulating total demand to stimulating total supply. The view that the supply-side school is a return to the Say's Law is biased. Say's Law is against government economic intervention in any form and nature. However, today's supply-side school does not utterly reject state intervention, and their suggestions stimulating supply by tax reduction is itself a kind of state intervention.

Secondly, changes in the structure of budget expenditures: although governments of different countries advocate reductions in financial expenditures and financial deficits, they actually maintain huge budgets but only adjust structures, they cut welfare expenditures, increase expenditures on the development of science and technology to adapt to the requirements for enhancing state's international competitiveness.

Thirdly, the privatization of enterprises: they do not fundamentally undermine state ownership, as the foundation for state monopoly capitalism. On the one hand, the amount of privatization is limited; on the other hand, the state-owned part and government interventions still account for a considerable proportion in today's capitalist economy. Additionally, state monopoly capital investments focus on some high-tech industries, which is also a kind of structural adjustment.

Fourthly, even though governments have reduced intervention in some economic fields domestically in different degrees, they have further strengthened and greatly developed regulation on the international economy.

The new characteristics in the capitalist economic operating mechanism seem as the structural adjustments in the state's operating mechanisms by new policies. Governments reduce intervention in some economic fields and strengthen intervention in some other economic fields at the same time, impair the application of some intervention methods, and initiate some other intervention methods at the same time. The monetary approach is against Keynesianism since it believes that monetary policies are more important than fiscal policies but it opposes abandoning fiscal policies. The supply-side school is against Keynesianism since it believes that supply management is more crucial but opposes abandoning demand management. American economic policy in the 1980s called as "Reaganomics" was the state intervention system with the integration of the supply-side school and the monetary approach. Therefore, I think there is no essential change on economic intervention and regulation in developed capitalist countries. In sum, major adjustments in macro-economic policies do not totally deny state intervention, but to adjust the methods, scale and degree of intervention to adapt to objective requirements for the further development of modern

economy. This is an objective requirement determined by the development
the basic contradiction of capitalism.

3. Tendencies on Capitalist Economic Operating Mechanism

Recent economic recession had started in America and spread to the
whole world, and pushed people to question neo-liberal economic policies
in the last few years of the 20th century. The highly praised regulatory role
of market mechanism has declined and even lost its effect in some fields
along with the quickening process of economic globalization and economic
liberalism. Thus inherent contradictions and various drawbacks of market
economic system were further exposed. Russia and East European countries
have encountered many difficulties during their transition to the market
economy. Severe financial and monetary crisis has occurred in succession
in Latin America, Asia and Russia, and the establishment of a larger market
within EU could not meet the expectations. More fundamentally, those
countries practicing structural changes in economy were confronted with
some new problems, such as continual structural unemployment accompanied
by traditional unemployment as in the Keynesian era, social security
expenditures, costs of scientific and technological research and social costs in
trade globalization and international competition have massively increased.
The outcome of financial liberalization practiced in developing countries was
to shoot fire against oneself, and all these problems demand for breaking the
old decision-making frame. When we observe economic theories, the micro-
economic foundation in the former macro-economic theories has already
changed greatly, which makes scholars to re-reconsider the significant role of
government in economic life and try to reform or seek new patterns for state
regulation. Such tendency is quite popular in capitalist developed countries.

Rising criticism on market fundamentalism:

People have good reasons to criticize the "supreme market liberalism"
ideology, in the new century. In the first half of the 20th century, people were
at a loss as when they were faced with the "Great Depression" between 1929
and 1933. Then capitalist market economy had a continual steady growth for

about 20 years with Keynesian theories. Nevertheless, due to the inherent contradiction in the capitalist economy and the drawbacks of Keynesian theories and policies, economy had almost stagnated in the 1970s. Together with the gradual dissolution of the planned economy, people had also worshipped market liberalism again and pushed to spread it to different places of the world with the mindset of the Savior. Promoted by the global voice of "marketization and liberalization", Southeast and East Asian economies with high saving rates attempted to further release foreign exchange controls, quicken open their capital markets and weakened government intervention. But these policies turned out to be immerse in uncontrollable abyss due by the strike of international speculation. At the beginning international capital speculators invested massively in these countries and later took drastic measures to withdraw money and solicited a crisis. In the efforts to overcome the Southeast Asian financial crisis, USA and IMF not only failed to react in time and pull these countries out of crisis but also caused its spread from Asia to economically developed countries like Russia, Western Europe, USA, etc. by adopting their conventional "extreme free market rules". USA stock market was also the victim of naïve worship of market liberalization. In the first half of 1988, famous economists in USA still acclaimed the everlasting prosperous "American new economy", disquietedly repeated the viewpoint in the 1920s, and insisted on laissez-faire for the markets.[1] They believed

---

[1] Based on an opinion poll made at the end of 1997, on the relations between the state and the market, most people had agreed that there should be a balance between the state and the market rather than prefer one party. The number of people approving such view accounted for 92% in America, 90% in Germany, 77% in Italy, 76% in Britain, 67% in Spain and 63% in France. Accordingly, there were also changes in views of the public on issues related the capitalist system, profit and globalization, etc. Due to different social history in different countries, the proportion of people for and against "globalization" in America was at that time higher than that in France. Based on such an opinion poll, for the pursuit of profits, the proportion of supporters to dissenters was 93%:5% in USA, 83%:8% in Italy, 79%:20% in Britain, 69%:30% in Germany and 61%:36% in France. For the views on economic globalization, the proportion of supporters to dissenters was 56%:38% in USA, 51%:40% in Italy, 51%:45% in Britain, 48%:51% in Germany and 26%:68% in France. For the views on capitalism, the proportion of supporters to dissenters was 64%:31% in USA, 43%:52% in Italy, 36%:59% in Britain, 48%:50% in Germany, 31%:68% in France and 36%:44% in Spain. Source: French L'Expansion, p. 101, December 4 to 17, 1997.

that deregulation, globalization, low inflation rate and technical progress should support increases in stock prices. Due to such a wrong estimate, the stock market was overvalued like a soap bubble and the Wall Street stock market recorded a sharp decline. In fact, such high risks not only exist in the securities and other financial markets, but in the whole economic operating process. Even Kutner, the American neo-liberal economist has acknowledged that USA is not a solitary island in the world nowadays. The disasters in Asia, Russia and Latin America were also caused by exported American ideologies to some extent, which was bound to affect America and Europe in return. In all these events, the most dangerous thing was economic collapse in Russia, which made people recollect the fact that the West had failed to help Germany's disastrous economy after World War I, thus leading to the reign of Hitler and World War II. The practice in the 1990s has proved that blind market liberalization in Russia supported with the intentions of Europe and America could only result in "laissez-faire mafiatic capitalism".

The erred and lopsided approach of neo-liberal economists in terms of the relations between the state and the market lie in that they only emphasize that the market can motivate individuals, and or are unwilling to realize the fact that if the government does not adopt some regulation and intervention policies in economic development and intervene in social economic life by means of regulation, support, restriction or other measures, there would be no economic development and social stability. Their ideologies of liberalism and historicism make them fail to realize the significance of the government's regulation of and intervention in social economic life. They can at most admit the limited role of the government from the aspect of guaranteeing free play of the market's role. Neo-liberalists believe that the market and the state are only the tools for allocating scarce resources. They hold the view that the market is established on the basis of contractual exchange and subject to the price system, aiming to achieve maximum allocation of resources in exchanges among economic men. On the contrary, the government should improve administrative organizations and allocate resources in a batch according to plans. However, the government is a complicated political organization with multiple functions, including political, economic, social, military and others. We cannot simply regard the government as a system for the allocation of resources. Similarly, the market also has multiple forms and mechanisms instead of being uniform. Consequently, we cannot say that the government and the market are two different regulatory mechanisms in general terms. Undoubtedly, we also cannot say that only market regulation or government regulation is effective any time and in any place. The efficiency and quality of economic activities practiced by these two different institutions are dependent on the national and international economic and social conditions, and a nation's development level of productive forces at that time. At present, although the guidelines of liberal parties or the conservative parties in different European countries do not include "invisible hand" and "laissez-faire" programmatically, they still firmly believe in the fundamental role of self-regulation of individuals or groups, and are suspicious in the efficacy of government regulation and intervention. Facts have proved that market economy is more efficient because it offers freedom and democracy, encouragement and competition. The trouble is market economy also has insurmountable defects in itself. Yet, market liberalists have not voiced more valuable opinions than that. However, the error of market liberalization could be observed in the Southeast Asian, East Asian and Russia financial crisis since the Baht depreciation on July 2, 1997, and the upheaval in USA's capital market in the fall of 1998.

Among critics on neo-liberal economic policies and theories, some new theories advocating "internal growth" has appeared, voiced by "neoclassical synthesis" school, "new institutional economics" and "regulation school", etc. Even though the neoclassical synthesis do not approve Keynesian pattern of state intervention, they acknowledge the role of macro-economic policies and industrial policies in improving economic growth rate. They criticize side effects of traditional economic policies, but do not deny macro-economic policies. They advocate new contents in macro-economic policies, emphasize the significance of economic information and economic participants' extensive information needs, and believe that macro-economic policies should not only be the decision of public authorities, but also a series of gaming roles between the state and private sectors with a contractual nature and reputation and reliability of policies playing an important role. They believe that the state should not make decisions independently but need to cooperate with other partners. The state should establish a cooperative rather than hierarchical coordination system, and promote a set of regional and nation-wide coordination mechanisms. They emphasize that economic growth is not only dependent on the progress of scientific technologies, but also has direct relations with the ownership system and closely related with the innovation of socio-economic system. They acknowledge that the enterprise system and market system are relatively effective institutional bodies since they can reduce transaction costs. However, they also stress that a state's fiscal policies and industrial policies also have significant roles in improving economic growth rate. They reject traditional Keynesian theories especially for its expansionist aspect. Meanwhile, they insist that government regulation still has great meaning. Some of them have raised the fact that the old economic and social mechanisms cannot meet the requirements of the era and are obsolete. They advocate that the role of state regulation should be given full play while fully improving the role of market regulations; which have similarity with "mixed economy" thought raised by Samuelson.

The extreme difficult circumstances faced by the world people nowadays require each country to change traditional social conception and economic logics. At present, governments' strategic calculations or optimization of selfish state interests are quite strong in many countries. But on the other side, there has appeared great differences on the functions and roles of the government and traditional views are questioned and challenged under the impact of economic globalization, regionalization and scientific-technological revolution. The reason lies in that economic globalization progresses rapidly and multinational corporations have formed a strong international network. The government have transferred some rights to regional international economic organizations and domestic local administrations. Many people believe that the role of the government has necessarily weakened and the form of government regulation should be adjusted to that requirement. However, after the Asian financial crisis, some people have raised strong suspicions on commented that the new vitality injected into market economy by the so-called "globalization" was temporary and the nation state's regulatory role should be strengthened. In recent years, the capitalist model itself is also questioned, and the debate between "two capitalisms" (capitalism of "Anglo-Saxon model" and capitalism of "Rhein model") has re-staged. There are big changes in both theoretical circles and public opinion on the understanding of the relations between the state and the government. Some people also raise several new views such as "European social model", "social Fordism" and "wage earners' republicanism", again.

In sum, these recent changes in the economic operating mechanism of capitalist countries (or in the debate on the relations between the state and the market) hint the future trend in the capitalist economic operating mechanism. In a word, as Samuelson has mentioned, the economic operating mechanism of capitalist countries tends to be the integration of market mechanism and government intervention. There is neither pure market nor pure government in the current economic operating mechanism of capitalist countries. Different countries practice a choice suitable for their circumstances focusing on optimum relations between the market and the government. They design their policies to meet the actual development requirements of their productive forces and attach due attention to their unique socio-cultural traditions. However, they share one thing in common, that is, not emphasizing one and abandoning the other as before. They pragmatically intend to combine "two hands" for economic development. As Mirabeau, the French revolutionist said, "If a nation is too tough, it will weigh us down; if it is too weak, we will be dragged down as well." Recently the famous French sociologist Michelle Guille has made a public statement as "modern states are modest states" which suggests decrease of state intervention, but the former French president Chirac had replied him with a comment as: "In this era a modest state should be an ambitious state as well." The current debate is not whether the state and the market should co-exist in economic operation, but how the two will co-exist and the degree to which their integration should be extended, i.e. the border lines of integration of the state and the market.

4. Using the Two Hands

The debate on the relations between the "market" and the "government" is actually an old issue, and there are multiple views and schools in the international academy and political spheres. Sometimes market liberalism was at an advantage and sometimes the government intervention principle has become the theoretical mainstream. The two theories were employed alternatively in different periods. Generally, the governments in a period can always accept useful theories in actual practice. In the history, we can observe alternatively and cyclic changes between "failure" and "validity" of economic liberalism and government intervention principle. In the first half of the 20th century two world wars and a disastrous global recession had occurred. Inspired by the thoughts of Ricardo, and others, Keynesians had raised the government intervention thought that was deemed as the cure for market economic crisis not long after the "great recession". Meanwhile, the successful practice of Roosevelt's "New Deal" showed people that government intervention can be effective. Even people have returned back to "economic liberal theory" after two oil crises in 1970s (See Fig. 7-1); people may well remember that the "government intervention principle" was used for about 30 years in capitalist countries. Due to the financial storm uncontrolled by the free market occurring at the turn of the century; more and more countries and regions had to strengthen government intervention and started measures to regulate capital movements. Without doubt, the governments no longer emphasize unilateral government interventions, but instead a government intervention mode based on dual integration.

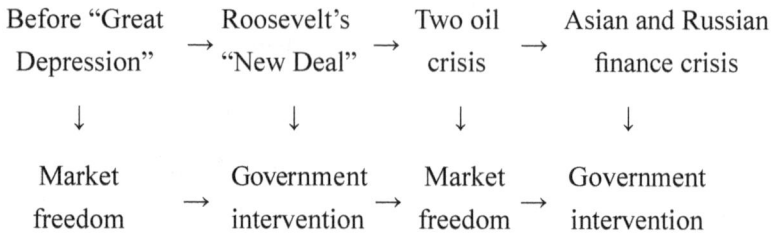

Before "Great Depression"	→	Roosevelt's "New Deal"	→	Two oil crisis	→	Asian and Russian finance crisis
↓		↓		↓		↓
Market freedom	→	Government intervention	→	Market freedom	→	Government intervention

Fig. 7-1

5. Focusing on the Main Contradiction

We have considered the evolution process of the theories on the relations between the market and the government, and reviewed the historical changes in the relations between the market mechanism and government intervention. I would like to offer a brief review as follows:

The status of self-regulatory market mechanism and government regulatory mechanism in different historical stages and their integration patterns is fundamentally determined by the development of that contradiction between productive forces and relations of production. During the period of the establishment of the capitalist economic system, the main goal was to bury the remains of feudal system, especially economic intervention and controls by monarchic noble forces remaining from the Middle Ages, and establish the market economic system meeting the requirements for the development of capitalist economy, which determines the dominant role of laissez-faire ideas. After the establishment of capitalist economic system and its market economic system, the self-regulatory market mechanism had played an active driving role in the development of capitalism at the free competition stage. Moreover, the contradiction between capitalist production relations and socialized mass production had not fully exposed in the rising period of capitalist economic development. Self-regulation of the market became the main economic operating mechanism since it had basically suited with the level of productive forces at that time. The defects and problems were gradually exposed as the contradiction between socialized mass production and capitalist production relations became acute and pushed the government to participate in economic regulation. Strengthening the government's economic intervention and regulation mechanisms on the main basis of market regulation had mitigated the contradiction between productive forces and relations of production and promoted capitalist economic development for a certain historical period. However, the defects of government intervention theories and policies themselves led to prominent drawbacks in socio-economic development. Thus capitalism entered into another adjustment period to improve the integration of market and government. Therefore, the evolution of the whole capitalist economic operating mechanism can be generally divided into three stages: The first stage is that when the market regulatory mechanism was established, while it gave full play to that role and in practice, the defects of market mechanism were gradually exposed; the second stage is that when the government regulatory mechanism was established, while it gave full play to that role and in practice, the defects of government intervention in economic gradually were gradually exposed; the third stage is an adjustment stage when market regulation and government regulation jointly play their respective roles. Historical review shows that, yet an optimal pattern for the integration of market regulation and government regulation is not found or established in capitalist countries. A general and stable economic mechanism that can both overcome the defects of market mechanism and defects of government intervention, able to give full play the market role and government regulation role, and realize systematic integration and complementation of the market and government regulatory mechanisms has not been formed.

Realistically observing the economic operating mechanisms in capitalist countries, the government and the market respectively play an important role in terms of promoting economic development and maintaining social reproduction. The two parties have different functions but both are indispensable. State regulation and market regulation are two totally different regulatory mechanisms, they are a unity of oppositeness and mutually complementary. Today, it is crucial to employ the respective irreplaceable roles of the state and the market and practice that for a considerable long period in the future and carefully avoid their side effects and possible negative effects at the same time. The state should formulate accurate economic and social policies, and the market should continually establish a sound competition mechanism, the relations between the state and the government should be constantly adjusted to maintain balance between the state and the market and constantly achieving new balances.

Different unique models of integration had gradually formed in the capitalist world after World War II. These unique models were determined by the particular historical conditions of these nations, and were formed through the interaction of several elements as: their special foundation as productive forces, special economic, political, cultural and other complicated factors. All models reflect special requirements for economic development in different countries under different levels of productive forces and different economic, political and cultural background. Therefore, each model has its special reason for existence, special operating mechanism, special circumstances, specific application scope and its historical limitations. Naturally, an effective model integrating the market and the government can only be efficient under specific environmental conditions in specific stages of history and within specific scope. There can be no abstract model apart from specific historical conditions and national conditions. People may choose and learn from current models rather than simply transplant or blindly apply them.

Meanwhile, I should clearly mention that the historical evolution in the capitalist economic operating mechanism is fundamentally determined by the inherent law of capitalism. Generally expressing; the basic economic law in the whole development of human society is that social relations of production should adapt to the requirements for the development of productive forces. In the capitalist stage this economic law is specifically reflected as the law: constant socialized development of capital relations should adapt to the requirements for the development process of socialization in production. Seen from the facts, it is purely a political preference of administrators of a nation's government to choose a type of socio-economic operating mechanism. However, an effective social operating mechanism should adapt to the development of the basic contradiction of capitalism and all effective institutional innovations are bound to reflect objective requirements of the law of socio-economic development. The trend of socialization in production and socialization in capital's forms not only raises the objective requirement for government intervention in economy, but also constitutes its real economic basis. Therefore, the integration of market regulation and government intervention is not a temporary or occasional historical phenomenon, but the inevitable outcome of the development of the basic contradiction of capitalism, and the inevitable result of the above economic law active in capitalism. Undoubtedly, the economic operating mechanism in the capitalist society cannot fundamentally eliminate the basic contradiction of capitalism no matter how it is adjusted; thus twists and turns and deep turmoils are inevitable in the capitalist development process. Nevertheless, we can realize that the historical evolution process of capitalist economic operating mechanism is a process of self-denial of private capital relations and has progressive meaning for the development of social economic operating mechanism. Therefore in the future the contradiction between the market mechanism and state intervention and their integration will be represented in a new, more extensive and profound way. In the course of time, the space for the self-regulation of the basic contradiction of capitalism will be smaller, and the economic operating mechanism adapting to the requirements of the new society will reveal itself in a more prominent way in the womb of the old.

Chapter VIII

Globalization and Capitalist International Economic Relations

The most crucial feature of the contemporary world economy is economic globalization in which all countries in the world participate or are involved in the wave of economic globalization. There are extensive debates on economic globalization. Some people actively advocate that globalization is a bright way for human society to gain wealth. However, some people have strong opposition, believing that globalization is a trap, immersing general laborers in poverty and oppression. Such opposition and differences in attitude are bound to result in different strategies of different countries in coping with globalization. Then what is economic globalization, when did it appear and what are the underlying reasons for its formation and development? Does economic globalization mean development in a capitalist way and what influences will economic globalization exert upon the world economy, what are its impacts on nation states and which kind of opportunities and challenges will it bring to the general developed countries? It is of significant theoretical and practical meaning to get a clear view of these issues, so as to scientifically understand contemporary capitalist international economic relations and realize the historical process of capitalist development from one aspect.

I. Economic Globalization Process

1. Development Stages of World Economy

The first and foremost thing to understand about economic globalization is the process and stages of world economic development. Since capital is born to have a worldly nature, and the expansion of capitalist economic relations is represented as the development of commodity economic relations, the formation and development of capital relations are the starting point and contents of a true world economic history.[1] It is represented as the formation and development of commodity economic relations in the international scale.

We can divide world economic development into three historical stages based on the above understanding. The first stage was from the 16th century to the 1860s when the world economy centering on the capitalist economy came into being on the basis of the Great Geographical Discoveries at the end of the 15th century and the beginning of the 16th century and the colonial rule of backward eastern countries afterwards. Its main form was internationalization in the movement of trade capital, i.e., international trade development. At that time, such international trade was mainly represented as colonialist countries' plunder of natural resources and human resources from colonies and semi-colonies. With the establishment of modern industry in

---

[1] Marx and Engels once pointed on capital competition, "It has produced the world history for the first time, insofar as it made all civilized nations and every individual member of them dependent for the satisfaction of their wants on the whole world, thus destroying the former natural exclusiveness of separate nations." (*Selected Works of Marx and Engels*, Edition 2, Vol. 1, pp. 114.)

European capitalist countries and the expansion of production capacities, the demand for either labor forces and raw materials or the commodity market was greatly strengthened. The development of commercial industry, sailing industry and land transportation had promoted industrial development and caused the scale of capital's search for raw materials and market to expand. European colonialists began to plunder human and natural resources in Asia, Africa and Latin America starting from the end of the 15th century. The principal mode of plunder by colonialists was a trading company. The East India Company established by British colonialists in 1600 was the largest and most influential organization, which did not only monopolized freight trade to South Asia and China, but also plundered China's labor forces even dumped opium to strive after exorbitant profits. The result of such monopoly was that capitalist economic central areas gained the opportunity for specialized production by means of the division of labor and division on international trade. The industrialization process had gradually continued on such basis. However, the cost was that colonial countries were severely deprived of political and economic sovereignty.

The second stage had started from the end of the 19th century to World War II, which was based on the Second Scientific-Technological Revolution and transition of main capitalist countries to monopoly capitalism and their further expansion and plunder in colonies, and its main form was internationalization of industrial capital. The Second Scientific-Technological Revolution had given rise to the upgrade of industrial structure in capitalist countries and promoted the rapid development of industrial production. Enterprises' scale was increasingly larger and capital production was more and more centralized in a minority of large enterprises. Highly centralized production and capital provided conditions for the formation of a monopoly. Monopoly organizations established in different sectors in succession and had developed to the rule of financial capital integrating industrial monopoly capital and bank monopoly capital. The capitalist's pursuit of profits could not be satisfied within one state because of the falling tendency of the average rate of profit, and the wish of capitalists for external expansion so as to seek higher monopoly profits had become more fervent. Monopoly capital had spread to all parts of the world by capital export. Capitalists had directly engaged in commodity production and carried on activities to extract surplus labor. Monopoly capital then incorporated the national economy of colonial dependent countries to its exploitative system and made them the vassal nations of the capitalist world economic system. For the colonial dependent countries importing a large amount of capital, inflow of foreign capital had promoted the development of capitalist industry and commerce and quickened the dissolution of natural economy. Meanwhile, foreign capitalists have plundered a large amount of their national wealth from colonial dependent countries. The effect of capitalist countries to the colonially dependent countries had integrated them to the world market and made them the place for manufacturing raw materials for industrialized countries as well as their investment place and market for commodity export. Capital export and commodity export was integrated and the links between production and consumption among different countries have become closer. However, the unreasonable division of labor among central areas and peripheral zones of the capitalist economy has increasingly deepened and the gap between the rich and the poor.

The third stage was from World War II to today, when the Third Scientific-Technological Revolution and the new world economic system was gradually formed, featured by highly internationalized commercial capital, industrial capital and financial capital. The Third Scientific-Technological Revolution has greatly reformed human life, especially the application of electronic computers and the development of communications have enabled people to span space with a larger scale, with a quicker speed and at a cheaper cost. The important feature of such globalization was that it was driven by a motive in the economic system. More and more economic activities have expanded beyond national borders targeting at the global market, and the dependency of different economic subjects to the market have strengthened even more. Economic elements in international relations have increased and the world economic globalization process has greatly quickened especially after the Cold War. From the completion of the Uruguay Round Negotiation of the General Agreement on Tariffs and Trade to the establishment of WTO, different countries have adjusted policies to integrate with the world economy to the most extent. The WTO has become more authoritative and effective in mediating economic disputes among different countries, and created more favorable conditions for the improvement and stability of world trade environment and world trade development. In this stage, the world trade volume has continually increased, capital flow among nations has grown higher and more frequent, and some developing countries have shown rapid development. Nevertheless, we cannot deny that developed capitalist countries still play a dominant role in the world economy.

2. Process of Economic Globalization and Evaluation Criteria

Although we cannot understand economic globalization process outside the history of world economic development, we cannot equal world economy with economic globalization. I believe that economic globalization is only a new stage of world economic development and the economic globalization process has truly began in when different countries participate in the commodity based economic activities in an all-around way and become a part of those relations. In other words, we should deem the status and attitude of nation states, the subject of economic activities in the world as well as the extent of commodity economic development in the world as the direct symbol of economic globalization. Firstly, all nation states should be the subject and focus of research in understanding the evolution of the development of world economic relations. If we neglect the changes in economic relations of different subjects of the world economy and their status, we will lose the standard for scientifically judging the economic globalization process. Reviewing from the subjects of economic globalization and based on the relations and status of different subjects, we may arrive at the following conclusion: in the first two stages of world economic development, general colonial and semi-colonial countries and regions entered world market under the threat of a minority of developed capitalist countries; they were totally passive, and their political status and economic power had determined that they could not possibly have economic exchange with developed capitalist countries on the basis of commodity economic relations in the true sense. On the contrary, these backward countries and regions have always appeared as exporting countries of natural resources and human resources as well as importing countries of commodity and capital. They were totally involved in the world economy in a passive way, thus forming international economic relations with the basic feature of developed capitalist countries exploiting and plundering backward countries and regions. Whereas today the subjects, i.e. countries and regions in different places around the world under economic globalization conditions actively and consciously participate in the world economy. Different subjects actively and mutually influence each other and there is an interactive relationship instead of unilateral behaviors that some subjects actively control some other subjects and the latter are passive. Secondly, seen from the perspective of the development degree of world commodity economy, the first two stages of world economic development respectively was centered on the internationalization of commodity capital and industrial capital, and the fields, scale and influences of such internationalization were limited. Whereas in the third stage not only did commercial capital and industrial capital move out of national borders, but also they had rapid development (represented as rapid expansion of international trade and international investment after World War II), and the internalization level of financial capital movement has obviously increased and represented a highly internationalized tendency. We can say that the internalization tendency penetrates in different aspects of the world economy in the third stage of world economic development and the economic globalization process is truly initiated.

In sum, we cannot equal economic globalization with world economy, and there are both differences in their development levels and qualitative differences. The economic globalization process began only when most subjects of the world economy have participated in the world economy in an all-around way.

At present, some people deem the factors of market and system, etc. required in economic globalization as the criteria for judgment and thus they offer three different methods of evaluation. The first viewpoint is that economic globalization had originated from the beginning of the 16th century, i.e., the first stage of world economic development and its process was promoted by western capitalist countries. The globalization of the world economy at present has went through three stages, or to say, such viewpoint is that the process of world economic development is the process of the development of economic globalization, which totally mixes economic globalization with the world economy. The second view is that the process of economic globalization had originated from the 1860s to 1870s. As the formation of the world market explored by industrial capital from the 1860s to 1870s, there were a series of profound reforms in international economic relations: the system of international division of labor had taken shape initially, international economic and trade relations had increasingly strengthened, the international financial system was gradually improved, production internationalization had risen to a higher level and economic globalization had started. The third view is that globalization occurred at the end of 1980s and the beginning of 1990s in a strict sense, which was mainly based on the definition of the International Monetary Fund (IMF) on globalization in 1997, i.e., the increase of scale and form of multinational commodities, service trade as well as international capital flow and widespread technologies had increased the mutual independency of economies in different parts of the world.

Even though the three viewpoints are reasonable in certain degrees, they have not realized issues from the perspective of different relations among subjects participating in world economy and their changes of status. In other words, they attach importance to the quantitative change instead of qualitative change in the development process. In fact, economic globalization process has began only when the majority of countries and regions consciously took part in world economy. The process began after World War II, and such tendency has become more obvious and the development process has quickened especially since the 1990s because of changes in different conditions of world economy.

3. Main Manifestations of the Development of Economic Globalization

What I will further study is that to what degree economic globalization develops under the new world economic situation and its specific representations.

In the world today, the primary content of economic globalization is internationalization of capital movement, of which no part can be independently carried on within one country without international economic relations. For instance, in the purchase stage of capital, people are increasingly dependent on the international capital market. They purchase labor forces through international scale, regard global laborers as their hiring object and realize allocation of global material resources for production. In the production stage of capital, an increasing number of large companies demand worldwide production layout, cooperation based on the division of work and commodity production so as to directly internationalize the production process. Finally, in the sales stage of capital, enterprises need to sell products, realize international surplus value and gain huge profits in the international market. We can see from this that the coexistence and successive movement of money capital, production capital and commodity capital in the world constitutes capital internationalization and form economic globalization. Therefore, we need to elaborate from the above three aspects when introducing the manifestations of economic globalization.

The main form of internationalization of production capital movement is the rapid increase of foreign direct investment. The capital internationalization tendency has strengthened year by year in recent years, specifically represented as the increase of investment abroad. Only 17 countries had attracted foreign capital of over USD 10 billion in the world, and 10 countries had made foreign investment of over USD 10 billion in 1985, whereas the number has respectively reached to 51 and 33 at the end of 2000. During this period, the number of developing countries among main participants of IMF has increased as well, and the number of developing countries among main countries attracting foreign investment rose from 7 in 1985 to 24 in 2000. Also the number of developing countries among main countries making foreign investment has risen from zero to 12. Some emerging industrialized countries and regions (such as Hong Kong and Singapore) also became the home country and host country of multinational corporations. The share of developing countries in foreign direct investment rose from 5% in the 1980s to 9% in 2000.[1] Multinational corporations are the carrier of internationalization of production capital. They are both the supplier and the regulator of foreign direct capital. Based on the statistics of UNCTAD, the number of global multinational corporations has increased from more than 10,000 in the 1980s to 44,500 in 1996 and the number of their foreign subsidies and branch offices rose from over 100,000 to over 276,000.[2] The number of multinational corporations rose to 63,000, and the number of their foreign subsidies and branch offices were more than 700,000 in 1999. The total number of multinational corporations decreased to about 60,000 in 2000 through a large amount of multinational merger and acquisition, but the number of their foreign subsidies and branch offices rose to over 820,000.[3] It is the continual expansion of the scale of multinational corporations and their mutual M&A and reconstruction that promote the development of internationalization of production capital.

Internationalization of money capital movement refers to the expansion of movement of capital existing in the form of money from one nation to the world. It mainly refers to the movement of capital always in the form of money, we should exclude the exchange in the form of money in international commodity exchange and exchange in the form of money in foreign exchange transactions. After the 1970s, developed capitalist countries represented by America, Britain have implemented neo-liberal

[1] IMF: *International Investment Report*, 2001.
[2] UNCTAD: *World Investment Report*, 1997.
[3] UNCTAD: *World Investment Report*, 2000.

policies in succession, widened financial control, thus expanding the areas of activities and rule space of financial capital to most parts of the world. The globalization of money capital is also the most prominent manifestation of economic globalization. Some large banks and organizations named as institutional investors such as insurance companies and endowment funds, etc. dominate financial globalization. In the last five years of the 20th century, the merger wave of large commercial banks has developed to a huge scale. The Chemical Bank ranked the fourth in America announced to amalgamate the Chase Manhattan Bank ranked the 6th in August 1995, the acquisition cost was high up to USD 10 billion and the total assets after acquisition was USD 299 billion. The American Fleet Bank announced to annex the Bank of Boston in March 1999, and the new bank after amalgamation named as Fleet Boston Bank became the eighth largest bank in America with an asset of nearly USD 174 billion. The Citibank amalgamated the Travelers Group on April 6, 2000, named as the Citibank Group. Involving acquisition cost of up to USD 82 billion, a market value of USD 166 billion and an asset of nearly USD 700 billion, such acquisition not only became the largest financial merger in the world until now, but also made the Citibank Group the largest financial service company in the world (calculated based on market value) and the largest enterprise in the world (calculated based on assets). Financial globalization led to the unprecedented development of debt economy and national debts had sharply increased. The external liabilities of America was USD 446 billion in 1998 and its banks borrowed USD 126 billion from outside in the same year. Some high-debt countries also had huge inflow of money, for instance, Thailand contracted a foreign loan of 247 billion Baht, and Indonesia contracted a foreign loan of 450 billion Rupees in 1998.[1]

The scale of international trade further expands. International trade is in fact the internationalization of commodity/trade capital movement. As an important feature of the capitalist mode of production, it had occurred in the early capitalist period. However, as widespread globalization of today, it is reciprocal and mutual independent with globalization of production capital

---

[1] *International Financial Statistics Yearbook*, 2002.

movement and money capital movement, being a crucial representation of today's economic globalization. Table 8-1 and Table 8-2 introduce changes in international trade scale since the end of 1990s, which directly reflects changes in the internationalization of global production and extent of international economic exchange.

Table 8-1   Changes in Import Turnover of World Trade

Unit: USD 1 Billion

	1997	1998	1999	2000	2001
Total	5624.7	5545.6	5776.8	6528.6	6302.5
Developed Countries	3632.0	3727.6	3929.3	4335.0	4138.5
Developing Countries	1992.61	1817.97	1847.46	2193.56	2164.01
Growth Rate (%)	3.37	-1.41	4.17	13.01	-3.46
Developed Countries	2.21	2.63	5.14	10.32	-4.53
Developing Countries	5.53	-8.76	1.62	18.73	-1.35

Source: IMF: *International Financial Statistics*, 2002, 3.

Table 8-2   Changes in Export Turnover of World Trade

Unit: USD 1 Billion

	1997	1998	1999	2000	2001
Total	5530.0	5436.0	5635.8	6340.5	6114.8
Developed Countries	3643.1	3664.2	3741.2	3993.0	3862.5
Developing Countries	1886.95	1771.86	1894.01	2347.27	2252.88
Growth Rate (%)	3.49	-1.70	3.68	12.5	-3.56
Developed Countries	2.21	0.58	2.1	6.73	-3.27
Developing Countries	6.05	-6.10	6.89	23.93	-4.02

Source: IMF: *International Financial Statistics*, 2002, 3.

From the table above we can see that the value of import and export in the world continually increases; the trade volume of developing countries have a more rapid increase compared with developed countries, which shows that the market of developing countries is gradually included in the world commodity sales network, and becomes an inseparable part of the world market. However, the import growth rate of developing countries is higher than its export growth rate. Besides, the main role of developing countries is still being the commodity export destination of developed countries and commodities produced by them still have low international competitiveness in international trade.

In sum, the extent of capital internationalization nowadays continually deepens, and the international capital movement is more and more frequent. Without doubt, developed countries still hold an advantage during the process. But statistics show that generally developing countries are actively participating and have an increasingly important position in the capital internationalization movement at a higher growth rate than that of developed countries.

Economic globalization is the inevitable tendency of capitalist development and an objective historical stage. The most crucial thing for different countries is not to debate whether there is economic globalization, but to find the effective way for them to develop and be strong in the process of economic globalization.

II. Main Reasons for the Formation of Economic Globalization

Economic globalization does not come out of nothing, and there is an internal cause for its generation and development. Only through the analysis of these reasons can we fully explain the fact that economic globalization is the result of and a necessary step of capitalist development. It contributes to our sufficient understanding of its historical inevitability.

1. Fundamental Reason for the Development of Economic Globalization

The level of productive forces determines the scale/degree of market division and a reasonable market division promotes the development of productive forces. Young's Theorem summarizes such view as the determination of the division of labor by the division of labor and the transmission mechanism is that market scale depends on purchasing power, i.e. actual income, while income depends on productivity; productive forces rely on the division of labor, which relies on market scale. Each expansion of the division of labor in history is based on the development of productive forces. Marx had once said, "Modern industry has established the world market, for which the discovery of America paved the way. This market has given an immense development to commerce, to navigation, to communication by land. This development has, in its turn, reacted on the extension of industry; and in proportion as industry, commerce, navigation, railways extended, in the same proportion the bourgeoisie developed."[1] The new technological revolution rising in the middle of the 20th century had technologies of micro-electronics and electronic computers, etc. as the main symbol, science and technologies highly mediate and the time span of scientific-technological achievements turning to productive forces is shortening (since according to Marx science should be applied to production to become a productive force) thus leading to the unprecedented increase of social productive forces. The higher degree of complexity of production process and expansion of production scale give prominence to the reliance of production to modern sciences. Therefore, the rate of communication of knowledge has a decisive role on the development of productive forces. The greatest achievement of the application of electronic computers is the Internet, which leads to an unprecedented revolution in the communication field, and the spread of information has been very rapid and cheap. On the one hand, knowledge has no national boundary, and on the other hand, it can flow worldwide at the highest rate and lowest cost. Then the division of labor based on knowledge must be developed worldwide and the globalization of the division of labor promotes production globalization in turn.

2. Economic Globalization as the Intrinsic Demand of Capital's Nature

Capital itself has a world nature, and capital is the unity of opposites as private and sociality. Though it is owned by individuals, it includes social economic relations and stands as a social force. "Capital is a collective

---

[1] *Selected Works of Marx and Engels*, Edition 2, Vol. 1, p. 273.

product, and only by the united action of many members, nay, in the last resort, only by the united action of all members of society, can it be set in motion. Capital is therefore not only personal; it is a social power."[1] "Society" here is global instead of being restricted to one nation. The direct reason for economic globalization is capital's pursuit of profits. Marx had believed that globalization of capital movement is the intrinsic demand of the capitalist mode of production. Marx had argued, "It is only foreign trade, the development of the market to a world market, which cause money to develop into world money and abstract labor into social labor.... Capitalist production rests on the value or the transformation of the labor embodied in the product into social labor. But this is only [possible] on the basis of foreign trade and of the world market. This is at once the pre-condition and the result of capitalist production."[2] Lenin had also believed that capitalism cannot survive and develop itself without drawing all countries in the world into the economic globalization system and it is the historical "mission" of capitalism to promote economic globalization. He had pointed out, "What is important is that capitalism cannot exist and develop without constantly expanding the sphere of its domination, without colonizing new countries and drawing old non-capitalist countries into the whirlpool of world economy."[3] Ricardo had once indicated that capitalist economic growth may have a stagnate trend subject to the influence of "income decreasing principle". As the continual growth of population, the demand for grain is increasing, and it is inevitable to expand from superior land to inferior land when reclaiming land. Because land is limited and contributing labor forces are increasingly concentrated, the contribution margin of grain production constantly decreases and there is a tendency of decreasing land returns. At the same time, profit rate decreases as the increase of nominal wages and rentals. When the profit rate constantly decreases, the motive for capital accumulation declines and economic

[1] *Karl Marx and Frederick Engels*. Chinese version, Edition 1, Vol. 4, p. 481, Beijing, People's Publishing House, 1958.

[2] *Karl Marx and Frederick Engels*. Chinese version, Edition 1, Vol. 26 III, p. 278, Beijing, People's publishing House, 1975.

[3] *Selected Works of Lenin*, Vol. 1, p. 232, Beijing, People's Publishing House, 1995.

growth would be inhibited. However, even though Marxist economics is greatly different from western economics on the issues of the definition and role of capital, etc., it also has a theory of the "falling tendency of the rate of profit" corresponding to the "income decreasing principle". Such theory argues that constant increase of organic composition of capital, i.e., the relative proportion of actual living labor input to total capital tends to decrease, and the surplus value created by living labor also has a relatively constant decrease compared with the value of total capital used in the capital accumulation process. Then there is a tendency of decrease of profit rate, represented as the lower growth rate of total surplus value than that of total capital.

There was a falling tendency of the rate of profit in western developed countries in real economy. The nature of capital is to pursue huge profits, so when there was a falling tendency of the rate of profit in a given country, it was inevitable for capital to break through the limitation of national boundaries and seek higher profit rates in the world. When the scale of production was restricted by the scale of domestic market in the first place, commodity/trade capital firstly went beyond national boundaries and has entered the world market, then there was a tendency of the globalization of production capital and money capital. Economic globalization began and developed in the capital's pursuit of profits. As Thomas Jefferson said, merchants have no country. The mere spot they stand on does not constitute so strong an attachment as that from which they draw their gains. Lenin had also pointed out, "As long as capitalism remains what it is, surplus capital will be utilized not for the purpose of raising the standard of living of the masses in a given country, for this would mean a decline in profits for the capitalists, but for the purpose of increasing profits by exporting capital abroad to the backward countries. In these backward countries profits are usually higher."[1]

---

[1] *The Collected Works of Lenin*, Chinese version, Edition 2, Vol. 22, p. 233, Beijing, People's Publishing House, 1958.

3. Information Industry Revolution and the Economic Globalization

The Information Industry Revolution, especially the establishment of Internet quickens the speed of transfer of information, reduces costs, and becomes the new motive for world economic development. The Information Industry Revolution has profound influences upon the development of social industrial structure. The information industry is named as the "fourth industry". The revolution also pointed a way of industrial development, i.e., high dependency on scientific technologies in future industrial development. One of the important factors for constant high economic growth in America for nearly eight years was the promotion by the information industry. The development of information industry also makes impossible long-term monopoly of a given technology. The network is flooded with a large amount of information and a new technological invention can be made public in an instant. Michelle Wofsi said, "Online services turn a home computer screen from nothing to libraries, notice board, mailbox and municipal conference."[1] Therefore, no one can possess monopoly advantage for a long time because of a given technology, which promotes the development of new technologies on the one hand and strengthens specialization on the other hand. Strengthened specialization also stands for strengthened socialization and globalization. Because of this, we can see an American made Intel motherboard, a Sony Japanese CD-ROM and a Chinese made case all in the same computer.

E-commerce came into being with the integration of information technology and economics. It is a brand new commercial model which connects customers, sellers, suppliers and employees by unprecedented network, freeing business contacts from limitations of space and time, and promoting the development of global commercial contacts. Moreover, the form of E-commerce has huge space for development in the future. Different countries are actively promoting E-commerce in recent years. America issued the *Framework for Global Electronic Commerce* on July 1, 1997 and the US

[1] Nicholas Baran: *Inside the Information Superhighway Revolution*, Edition 1, p. 38, Haikou, Hannan Press, 1998.

Department of Commerce issued the *Emerging Digital Economy*, the first report of the government on the influences of information technologies upon economics in April, 1998. It passed the Internet Tax Freedom Act on May 14, 1998. Meanwhile, developing countries were unwilling to be lag behind. Based on the report of Singapore *Lianhe Zaobao* on September 23, 1998, the Singapore Economic Development Board established the goal of making Singapore a global E-commerce center, and the goal of "reaching electronic trade volume of SGD 4 billion in Singapore in 2003". We can imagine that when the information superhighway system in different countries is linked together, time and space will no longer restrict economic transactions and economic and commercial relations around the world will be closer, which will greatly promote the development of economic globalization.

4. State Monopoly Capitalism and the Economic Globalization

State monopoly capitalism had come into being when the bourgeoisie countries integrated with private monopoly capital. Capitalist states integrate with private monopoly capital and take part in social reproduction on the one hand and regulate economic operation on the other hand. When capital moves both within one nation and in the world, the bourgeoisie states, as the general representative of monopoly capitalists, are bound to expand their economic regulation to the world arena. The main contents of state monopoly capitalism in actively promoting policies on foreign economic expansion are: 1) Encourage foreign direct investment. Western developed states provide various subsidies and favorable conditions to multinational corporations for foreign investment, such as providing investment guarantee and insurance, and offer taxation preferences, etc. 2) Promote international trade. Western developed countries vigorously promote sale of products to developing countries through tariff or non-tariff means. 3) Promote capital internationalization through the international monetary financial system. During the process, western monopoly capitalist countries exert influences upon developing countries by means of their advantages in the international monetary financial system, which promotes capital globalization in an objective way and provides important institutional conditions for the development of economic globalization. In addition, state monopoly capitalism also promotes the development of globalization in terms of the system. Developed capitalist states not only exert economic influences upon other countries as the development of foreign economy but also spread to economic intervention and cultural infiltration. The market economic system was broadly established worldwide as greatly promoted by developed capitalist states. The reasons include both the independent choice of general developing countries in exploring a way for its development and influences even more pressure of developed states. Developing countries are forced to accept some additional conditions when receiving international assistance and "quickening the establishment of the market economic mechanism" is the most common condition. In terms of the forms, the market economic mechanism is beneficial to the free flow of resources and strengthening international economic transactions. However, developed capitalist countries gain the most benefits. In this sense, the market economic mechanism is an important institutional condition for the foreign economic expansion of capitalist countries.

In conclusion, the development of productive forces is the fundamental reason for economic globalization, the development of science and technology provides technical conditions for economic globalization, and the development of the capitalist system itself provides a direct motive in the process of the formation and development of world economy. The development of economic globalization becomes inevitable when all these factors are provided at the same time.

III. Influences of Economic Globalization on World Economy

We have arrived at a conclusion from the above analysis that economic globalization in an irreversible trend. What will such trend bring to us? The overall evaluation of economic globalization will be the basis for different countries to accurately understand this issue and choose rational strategies. When economic globalization was just exposed to and discussed by people in the early 1990s, most people held an optimistic view towards the influences of economic globalization on the world economy. Especially some scholars vigorously advocated that globalization would create for us a world with rich individuals and sufficient employment. Influenced by them, some scholars of our nation were also very passionate about economic globalization, but most of them only realized the positive role of economic globalization. At the same time, there was an entirely different view expressing a pessimistic attitude. These pessimists believed that economic globalization was more like a trap, leading to imbalance and loss of control of market forces, causing unemployment and crisis, and pushing the world economy to the abyss of crisis. Not only scholars in developing countries but also people in some western developed countries have held such a view. The anti-globalization wave which has appeared from time to time in western countries in recent years is a reflection of such view. In fact, everything is a unity of opposites, and it is unilateral to simply regard economic globalization as "heaven" or "trap". The reason why economic globalization became an irreversible tendency lies in that it adapts to capitalist production and promotes economic development. Meanwhile, economic globalization also has some impacts. We will make a comprehensive analysis from the two aspects as the research on economic globalization deepens.

1. Positive Influences of Economic Globalization on World Economic Development

(1) Economic globalization promotes improvement of productive forces

The foundation for the capitalist mode of production is socialized mass production while the division of labor is an important feature of socialized mass production. Therefore, capitalism always strives for broader market space and expands its scope of division of labor during its development process. The European big powers had plundered gold, silver and other precious metals all over the world in the capitalist primitive accumulation stage. They centralized these resources in their hands by trade or wars, and rapidly went on the path of capitalist development. In the development period of capitalist industrialization, capital gained extortionate profits and rapidly expanded through unequal exchange with economically backward countries and predatory exploitation of natural resources in these countries. The global expansion of capital has lasted up until today and its increasingly strong economic globalization tendency facilitates the capitalist international division of labor worldwide. Information Technology Revolution is the important driving force for economic globalization. Popularity of computers in different fields and the establishment of information network worldwide have brought the human society to the information age. Informatization accelerates internationalization of the market economy and gradually incorporates different countries in the world to the system of international division of labor, while the development of the division of labor further promotes the improvement of labor productivity. Fig. 8-1 shows the development of actual GDP in the world from 1970 to 2000, indicating that the global actual GDP had a low increasing tendency from 1970 to 2000 and such tendency was maintained till 2005.

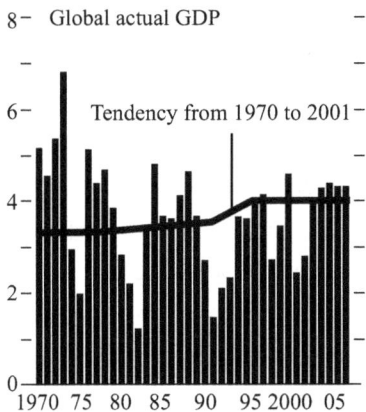

Fig. 8-1 Map of Actual GDP Tendency in the World

Source: IMF: *World Economic Outlook*, 2002.

At present, the system of international division of labor centering on developed countries has been established with developed capitalist countries staying on the top of the pyramid. Such structure of international division of labor is highly beneficial to developed countries. Table 8-3 shows improvement of American labor productivity.

Table 8-3 Changes in American Labor Productivity since 1960   (1992=100)

Output per Hour	1960	1970	1980	1990	1991	1993	1994	1995	1996	1997	1998	1999	2000
Commerce	48.8	67	80.4	95.2	96.3	100.5	101.9	102.6	105.4	107.8	110.8	113.8	116.9
Non-agriculture	51.9	68.9	82	95.3	96.4	100.5	101.8	102.8	105.4	107.5	110.4	113.2	116.2
Non-financial Business	55.4	70.4	81.1	95.4	97.7	100.7	103.1	104.2	107.5	108.4	112.3	116.2	119.9
Manufacturing	41.8	54.2	70.1	92.8	95	101.9	105	109	112.8	117.1	124.3	129.6	146.3

Source: *Monthly Labor Review*, 2002.

(2) Economic globalization gives rise to profound changes of international relations

Different countries are more mutually interdependent, and collision between multi-polarization and unilateralism increasingly intensifying. Economic globalization brings in closer political and economic relations among different countries, truly links the world as a whole, and mutual interdependence among different countries further strengthens. At present, global awareness has been enhanced unprecedentedly, and many hot spot issues concerned by people, such as environment, resources, technological innovation and sustainable development, etc. are based on globalization. The hot spot issues above cannot be solved without joint coordination and efforts of different countries in the world especially major countries; no country can develop independently out of the world economy. In case there is economic crisis in some countries and regions, not only developing countries will suffer a great deal, but also developed countries cannot keep themselves out of the crisis. Out of the interests of their nations, those developed countries sometimes support developing countries and offer some assistance so as to fundamentally nurture market for themselves and stabilize source of their revenues. For instance, when the Asian financial crisis and Latin American financial crisis broke out, some developed countries and international organizations offered economic assistance to developing countries immersed in the crisis to help them overcome difficulties and recover economically. Therefore, global economy demands for global cooperation. All members of the international society are bound to jointly safeguard the stable development of world economy following the spirit of sharing responsibilities and risks. Without doubt, the above economic crisis was fundamentally the outcome of the impact of multinational corporations and financial magnates in these developed capitalist countries and economic liberalization carried out by the governments in these countries, and the assistance provided by them were not unconditional. All these show that there are profound and complicated economic relations behind the further strengthening interdependence among different countries. The nature of such relation is determined by those who dominates or controls the interdependent relationship under globalization conditions.

There are obvious debates between the trend of multi-polarization and unilateralism in world economy and politics on this issue. After the collapse of the former Soviet Union and East Europe, the former bipolar structure had ended. Then what is the future structure of world economy and politics? Most countries in the world demand for active promotion of world multi-polarization process to protect their own rights and interests and maintain long-term stable development of the world economy. However, a minority of countries led by America vigorously promotes unilateral politics to safeguard their hegemony, and attempts to further strengthen hegemonic dominance with America as the core in the world. The military invasion of a minority of countries led by America to Iraq since March 20, 2003 was a crucial strategic step for realizing such goal. It further proves that the formation of a new structure will be a long and complicated process. Under the circumstances of economic globalization, it demands long-term and arduous struggles and efforts of people in the world to build a new economic and political order beneficial to the general development and interests of different countries in the world and maintain lasting peace in the world.

(3) Under the precondition of general benefits and common prosperity of different countries, globalization may improve the income level of people in different countries and improve labor employment

If the world economic and political structure develops along the way favoring people of developing countries on account of joint efforts of people in different countries around the world, then related with general benefits, common prosperity and economic growth in different countries, economic globalization may bring the world economy to a new stage of stable development, improve employment and increase people's incomes. Economic globalization realizes flow of elements around the globe and achieves optimal allocation of resources. The development of economic globalization promotes the growth of international trade. It is predicted based on statistics that the volume of export in the world will have an annual increase of 7% in the next 10 years and developed countries will surely be the ultimate beneficiary. It is estimated that the growth rate of export of goods into America will reach 21.7% in 2005, and the rate will be 19.4% in the European Union, 18.3% in Japan and 16.6% in Canada. Increase of export will directly increase employment within the exporter nation. Developing countries will also gain benefits during this process, such as attracting foreign capital, increasing employment, optimizing industrial structure and enhancing international competitiveness, etc. Oskar Lafontaine, the former chairman of the Left Party and former German finance minister once had commented about the globalization wave, "do not fear economic globalization". He believed that globalization can bring people with richness and employment. Kim Dae Jung, president of the Republic of Korea was also an active supporter of economic globalization. Based on his views, "The boundaries in the world would disappear in a few years. The world has become a market connecting national economy in different countries as a whole. Each nation must produce and provide the best and the most economical goods and services to the whole world.... In my view, freedom, human rights, justice, peace and efficiency are the common values that should be accepted and pursued based on the principle of globalism."[1]

2. Negative Effects of Economic Globalization to World Economic Development

(1) The gap between the rich and the poor widens and world economic development is more imbalanced.

From the statement above we realize that it requires conditions to realize positive functions of economic globalization, of which an important condition is to actively promote world multi-polarization politically, promote harmonious co-existence of various forces and maintain stability of the international society. However, the reality nowadays is that no fundamental change has been made in the old, unfair and irrational international political and economic order, uncertainties impeding peace and development are on the rise, the elements of traditional and non-traditional threats to security are intertwined, and hegemony and power politics have new manifestations. Therefore, developed capitalist countries always occupy the favorable status and gain more benefits in the process of economic globalization, which intensifies polarization between the rich and the poor in the world. Some scholars had once pointed that: "In fact, the current financial system and its liberalization only benefit those countries enjoying privileges and dominating the world economy. However, the price is paid by developing countries, especially the poorest countries among them."[2] The income gap between the 20% richest people and the 20% poorest people in the world widened from 30:1 to 61:1 over the past 30 years. The five countries with the highest GDP per capita in 1995 were Luxembourg, Switzerland, Japan, Norway and Demark with a GDP per capital of 36,524 USD. The five countries with the lowest GDP per capita were Mozambique, Ethiopia, Zaire, Tanzania and Burundi, with the GDP per capita of merely USD 116, which is 315 times lower than the highest one.[3] Secondly, polarization between the rich and the

[1] Kim Dae Jung: "It Will Be the World of Global Economy in the Future", recorded in the Hong Kong *Standard*, 1998-11-19.

[2] Gerald Boxberger. *The 10 Globalization Lies*, p. 143, Beijing, Xinhua Press, 2000.

[3] World Bank: *World Development Indicators 1997*.

poor is very severe within different countries. Taking America for example, the gap between the top 20% average income of American families and the lowest 20% widened from 7.3 times in 1966 to 10 times in 1995.[1] Seen from another perspective, the average income of the poorest 1/5 Americans decreased by about 5% while the average income of the richest 1/5 Americans rose by about 9% from 1977 to 1990. During these years, the average income of the poorest 1/5 American families declined by approximately 7% while the average income of the richest 1/5 American families rose by about 15%. The income of the poorest 1/5 Americans accounted for 3.75% of the total national income in 1990, while the top-level 5% Americans had 26% of the total national income.[2] Globalization also leads to the change of employment structure. The speed of information transmission quickens and transmission cost rapidly decreases as the establishment and constant improvement of Internet, which shortens the cycle for a renewal of technologies. Companies in different countries invest a large amount of human and material resources on scientific and research activities to ensure that their technical skills will not fall behind and even occupy a leading position. In addition to the localization of R&D activities of multinational corporations as mentioned before, the demand for scientific and technological personnel in the whole world increases, the number of professional technicians and their income increases. On the other hand, high-value enterprises brought by the knowledge economy, such as consulting firms, advertising companies, and investment consultancy corporations, etc. are thriving. These enterprises require talents with rich knowledge. Generally speaking, professionals who had received higher education increase and these people generally have higher income. For ordinary laborers engaging in ordinary works, since globalization results in more convenient flow of resources and capitalists can always find the cheapest labor forces, the competition for work posts are more severe and the wage income of these people relatively decreases.

---

[1] *Forbes*, April 21, 1997. Quoted from Robert Reich: *The Work of Nations: Preparing Ourselves for 21st Century Capitalism*, Shanghai, Shanghai Translation Publishing House, 1998.

[2] Robert Reich: *The Work of Nations: Preparing Ourselves for 21st Century Capitalism*, p. 200.

(2) Economic globalization leads to more turbulent world economy.

The prominent representation of economic globalization is international flow of capital. Transnational flow of capital must rely on the international capital market and multinational banks. International capital flows across countries through the integrated financial market, forming the trend of financial globalization. Some problems confronted in the process of financial globalization cannot be fundamentally solved and becomes the potential danger to the world economy. The Asian financial crisis in 1998 and the Russian and Latin American financial crisis afterwards sounded the alarm and made scholars realize the severe force and destructive power of the financial crisis under the context of economic globalization. Firstly, over-speculation activities in the global financial market are the direct reason for the financial crisis. The slump of world stock market in October 1987 and speculation in the foreign exchange market in September 1992 had almost resulted in the collapse of the exchange rate mechanism of the European monetary system. In the 1980s and the early 1990s, the bankruptcy wave of financial institutions had hit the highest record since World War II and affected many developed countries such as America, Germany, Switzerland, Norway, etc. The Japanese government even considered implementing the plan of "rescuing banks". Since the middle 1990s, Mexican financial crisis, bankruptcy of Britain Barings Bank, etc. shook the whole international financial field once again. Secondly, international hot money which is hard to be managed is always the immediate cause for the crisis, and the Asian financial crisis can be taken as an example. Based on the estimate of IMF, the amount of international hot money reached 7,200 billion and 1,200 billion capital flows around the globe every day. International hot money has become a strong economic force, which directly influences economic security and stability. Developing countries are looking forward to control it. However, people in western countries advocate freedom in holding, using and benefiting from money, and the unrestricted flow of capital is protected by laws. It is unlikely for developed countries to cooperate with developing countries to control international hot money, whereas developing countries can hardly block hot money when opening-up; especially when opening their capital markets. Thirdly, many developing countries have heavy foreign debt burdens due to financial internationalization, and once such foreign debts are not controlled well, they will have a great impact on different countries even the world economy. The liability ratio (the ratio of balance of foreign debts to GNP that year) in China, which always emphasizes on the risks of foreign debts, is also increasing in recent years. It had increased from 5.2% in 1985 to the maximal 17.1% in 1994, and decreased afterwards to 15.2% in 1998, while the foreign debt ratio (proportion of the balance of debts in the previous year to the trade and non-trade income of foreign currency that year) was 56% in 1985, 96.5% at the maximum in 1993, and reached 70.4% in 1998.[1] From Fig. 8-2 we can see that the ratio of foreign debts to GDP also increased from 1996 to 2000 compared with that during the two periods of 1980 to 1990 and 1991 to 1995. Once such a debt crisis explodes, its impact on the world economy would be beyond our imagination. People still have a lingering fear about the international debt crisis which broke out in 1982. There was a national political and economic turmoil in Argentina in May 2002 because of its inability to repay debts.

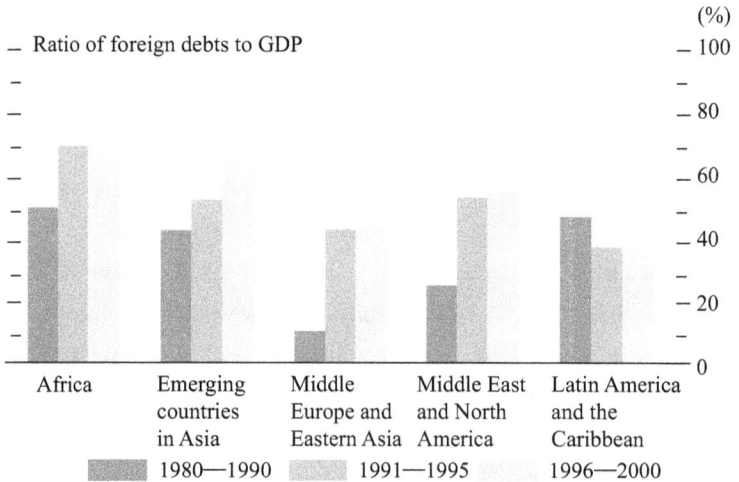

Fig. 8-2 Ratio of Foreign Debts to GDP in Main Districts in the World

Source: IMF: *The World Economic Outlook*, 2002.

[1] *China Statistical Yearbook*, 1999.

In recent years, there is a popular saying that economic globalization is a "double-edged sword". Then what is "double-edged" sword? Just as the name implies, "double-edged sword" can not only sweep the obstacles on the way, carve out a way for advance and beat opponents, but may hurt people. Therefore, the most crucial thing is to know how to use it. Arguing that globalization as a "double-edged sword" is more than simply listing the impetus and unfavorable conditions of globalization, and simply indicating opportunities and challenges. Wu Jinglian, a famous economist once commented on China's entry to WTO, "If we handle well multiple problems after the entry to WTO, it would be an opportunity; if we do not take proper countermeasures, it would be a challenge." It is also the same with the issue "economic globalization is a double-edged sword". Most countries in the world have participated in the process of economic globalization nowadays, and each country wishes to gain more benefits in the process. Those countries which make accurate economic policies are likely to use global resources instead of their country's resources and other advantages brought by economic globalization to develop their economy and economic globalization may be their "ladder" to success. If a government fails to adjust way of approach in time and adapt to the changes brought by the trend of economic globalization, it may be passive in the globalization wave and become a dependent country of other countries, then it is bound to fall into the "trap" of economic globalization.

IV. Nature of Economic Globalization

1. Position of Developed Capitalist Countries in Economic Globalization

Reality shows that developed capitalist countries have occupied an advantageous position in economic globalization. They not only have strong economic, scientific and technological powers, but also launch international economic organizations and are designing main international economic treaties. They command the dominant vote rights in international economic and trade organizations and international economic rules and enjoy a series of preferential treatment in international economy, therefore they benefit the most from globalization and general developing countries are at a disadvantage as a whole. As the dominance of developed countries, economic globalization further differentiates the status and level of different countries and regions in global development. Developing countries are confronted with many new challenges, their development tends to be more difficult, and the gap between the rich and the poor, between the North and the South further widens. It is not only against the healthy development of world economy, but also against the peace and stability of regions and the world; what needed is economic globalization with equality, mutual-benefits, double win and co-existence among different countries in the world. Firstly, we must acknowledge that developed countries occupy the dominant position and affect development orientation of economic globalization to a large extent during the economic globalization process at the present stage. From the changes brought by economic globalization in terms of the society, science and technology, and institution, etc., we can see that:

1) Economic globalization has formed the system of international division of labor in the world and realized global allocation of production elements. At present, the system of international division of labor centering on a minority of developed countries and based on general developing countries has gradually formed in the globalization process. Some scholars have described the system as a pyramid type structure (as shown in Fig. 8-3). Twenty-four developed countries are situated at the top of the pyramid, emerging industrialized countries and India are at the second level, China, Thailand, Indonesia, Malaysia are all at the third level, former socialist countries in Eastern Europe are at the forth level, the industrialized level of rich OPEC is only level five since it mainly relies on resources, while some countries in Africa and Latin America are at the lowest two levels. Even though information, capital, technology and other resources can flow freely in the world, the requirements of developed capitalist countries for resources

are satisfied in priority in such system of division of labor. The gap between developed countries and developing countries will become more and more widened in such a trend and general developing countries will be more and more dependent on a minority of developed countries. They gain meager rewards simply by offering processing and raw materials with low technical level to developed countries and become their supplier countries of resources and marketing places of products.[1] Therefore, economic globalization is the fact that the bourgeoisie "creates a world for itself with its own image"[2]. Though developing countries actively participate in competition in the world nowadays, it cannot fundamentally but partially change such nature under the circumstance of the significant advantage and dominant position of western capitalist countries led by America in economy. A minority of developed capitalist countries dominate the globalization process of world economy. As the global expansion of economy, the bourgeoisie is trying to export the capitalist system and its ideologies to the whole world; economic liberalism, political hegemony and cultural imperialism are on a rampage.

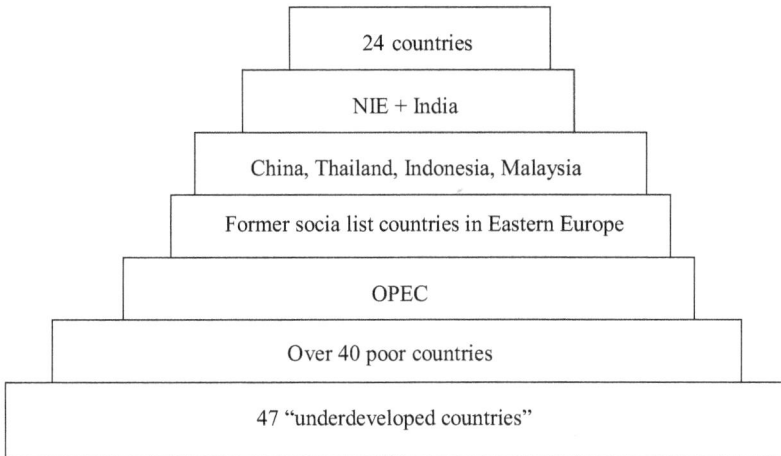

Fig. 8-3   System of International Division of Labor

[1] Richard J. Barnet, John Cavanagh: *Imperial Corporations and the New World Order*, Edition 1, p. 275, Haikou, Hainan Press, 1999.
[2] *Selected Works of Marx and Engels*, Edition 2, Vol. 1, p. 276.

2) International organizations are playing an increasingly important role in international relations. Main international organizations at present are the United Nations, World Trade Organization, International Monetary Fund and World Bank, etc. These international organizations have certain influences upon the sovereignty in terms of politics and economy, etc. of their member states. Western developed countries have occupied the dominant position, and both the formulation of principles and tenets of these international organizations, and the decision and implementation of some international affairs embody their wills. Without doubt, developing countries also made some achievements in safeguarding their interests through cooperative efforts. However, their forces are comparatively still weak, the guiding orientation of the World Bank's credit policies is mainly to emphasize the role of market orientation and primacy of private sector, and the mission of developing assistance is to guide and support developing countries to implement economic structural adjustment orientated by the market economic mechanism and political reforms, and help developing countries build a market economic mechanism beneficial for development. Under the guidance of those principles, a group of developing countries have established the market economic mechanism. However, the World Bank always spreads its economic policies through its credit policies, and some countries especially developing countries have to accept these attached conditions if they want to get loans, which is actually forceful implementation of liberal economy advocated by developed countries. After the explosion of the East Asian financial crisis in 1997, international economic organizations led by IMF and the World Bank had offered huge capital support to East Asian countries with very strict conditions, and forced recipient countries to implement financial liberalization and make economic reforms. For instance, Malaysia was forced to submit the schedule for implementing market economy in its nation to the World Bank and IMF when receiving subsidies.

Economic globalization is a historical process during which the open economy continually breaks national and cultural boundaries. In fact, developed countries are ahead of other countries in economic development because they enjoy more open-type economic interests at an earlier time. On the contrary, underdeveloped countries fail to get rid of poverty and backwardness owing to self-enclosure. For instance, China's national economy has deeply imbedded in globalization after opening up for over 20 years, the ratio of dependence on foreign trade in China was only 9.8% in 1978 and it reached to 33.8% in 1998. China can not develop its economy without the world. Economic globalization also needs China's participation. Increasingly opening economy in different countries of the world is breaking long-standing national or cultural boundaries in the social production and consumption process, and historically transforming the economic life of human society. Economic globalization provides broader markets and more opportunities for developing countries to introduce advanced scientific technologies and learn management experiences. Developed countries are more willing to offer help to developing countries in this aspect than any previous time since developed countries can gain broader markets only if backward countries develop their economy. Meanwhile, the assistance provided can bring benefits to developed countries. Economic development or recession of any region can exert either positive or negative influences upon the whole world. At present, a slight move of the world economy may affect the overall situation, and no country can show utter neglect for other's trouble so long as one is safe oneself. Some preferential policies of WTO on developing countries and the assistance provided by western countries after the Asian financial crisis, etc. are all proper examples.

Different countries actually communicate on the basis of their economic powers in economic globalization. Countries of different natures can win political and economic status only by developing themselves after participating in the international economic system. Developing countries are able to protect and further develop themselves, and break the dominant role of capitalist developed countries in economic globalization nowadays only by actively participating in the international economy and obtain the right of speech on the international stage by their economic development.

2. The Nature of Economic Globalization Is Capital's Internationalization

Based on the analysis above, we believe that the nature of economic globalization is capital's globalization. Capital appreciation is the basic activity and fundamental objective of market economy, reflecting the basic property, feature and law of the movement and development of market economy. The capital appreciation relation is the nature of market economy, and it is the nature of capital's pursuit of appreciation that leads to the internationalization of capital. In the development history of capitalism, capital has several stages of free competition capital, private monopoly capital and state monopoly capital, and economic globalization at present reflects the stage of state monopoly capital. The objective of globalization is to realize capital freedom, and the objective of any investment in any form is to realize maximum profits. Economic globalization reflects the West's requirements for plundering capitalist development, and its nature is that large monopoly capitalists attempt to gradually control world economy on account of their economic power. Marx had commented on that, in the *A Contribution to the Critique of Political Economy* that "capital must ... strive to tear down every spatial barrier to intercourse, i.e., to exchange, and conquer the whole earth for its market".

The internal contradiction of capitalism also develops along with economic globalization. As Robert Kyloh had commented in the *Governance of Globalization: ILO's Contribution*, industrialized and emerging industrialized countries have significant structural changes in the globalization process, such as continual slowing down economic and employment growth, rapid technical innovation, reform in social welfare system brought by population structural changes, obvious expansion of service sector and informal sectors, explosive development of non-traditional employment methods such as part-time jobs, odd jobs, and SOHO, etc., increased women labor ratio, increased significance of migrant workers, and strengthened flexibility of labor market, etc. The integrated role of these changes has negative effects upon the force of labor unions and interests of the working class. John Bildillo, professor of the Université d'Evry-Val d'Essonne held the view that the class struggle mentioned by Marx in his work still exists in western enterprises nowadays for the reason that class and class contradictions have not vanished in the capitalist society. Nevertheless, capital power is at an advantage and has the initiative in class struggle nowadays, while the working class is in passive defense, and the means of the working class for safeguarding its interests and scope of activities are restricted. Class struggle is more complex. Union and conflicts among different groups can be sometimes deemed as the reflection of the class struggle between the capital and labor, and sometimes as disparities and conflicts among interests of different industrial groups that are practically unrelated to industrial relations. Liquidity of both monetary capital and human resources greatly intensifies in the process of economic globalization. Different enterprises all seek cheaper labor forces, leading to more fierce competition among labor forces and forcing workers to receive lower welfare. The great strike of Hong Kong Aircraft Engineering Company (HAECO) Limited is a typical example. HAECO used to monopolize the aircraft maintenance engineering market in Hong Kong and workers had enjoyed higher payments. After the new airport was opened in July 1997, Hong Kong government introduced in competition to improve service quality and HAECO had cut employees' wages and welfare on a large scale to strengthen competitiveness. The company cut down welfare again under the circumstance of gaining profits of HKD 60 million in October, 1999, finally leading to the strike of workers. However, the company was not in a panic since it had transferred a large number of workers from Xiamen to cover the jobs of strikers. Even though the strike ended honorably, the labor union had to acknowledge that the strike did not gain any material achievement for workers. We can see that economic globalization has further deepened the class contradictions. Even though the power of the working class is impaired at present, fiercer struggles are nurtured as well.

V. Economic Globalization and Nation States

1. Challenges of Economic Globalization to Nation States

The rapid development of economic globalization has brought unprecedented challenges to nation states. Under the context, the focus of debate includes the impacts on the sovereignty of nation states, changes of government functions and the role of states. Firstly, I will make an analysis on challenges to the sovereignty of nation states.

(1) Impacts of international organizations

In the era of economic globalization, economic relations among different countries are increasingly closer and relevant international rules and international organizations are needed to ensure the normal operation of international trade and international investment. Nowadays, main international organizations have influences upon the sovereignty in terms of politics, economy, etc. on their member states. I will only discuss their economic influences here. Firstly, when the international law and local law contravenes, the international law shall prevail. Taken the first case of WTO in resolving disputes as an example, U.S. Congress passed the amendments to the *Clean Air Act CCAA* in 1990, requiring the Environmental Protection Administration (EPA) of the federal government to amend the gasoline technical standards for the purposes of reducing hazardous gas emission from engines and reducing pollution. However, some regulations of US EPA in the specific implementation process violated the principle of GATT, i.e., signatory countries cannot place foreign products similar with national products at a disadvantage according to the laws, regulations and technical requirements. Then Venezuela and Brazil respectively lodged a claim to the Dispute Settlement Body (DSB) of WTO in January and April, 1995. DSB offered a final report on January 17, 1996, awarding that America lost the lawsuit and suggesting America change its national legal regulations and make it consistent with the requirements of GATT. From this case we can see that the power of nation states in regulating an economy by legal means is restricted to a certain extent. Nation states transfer a part of their economic power so as to ensure their relevant legal regulations are consistent with principles of international organizations. Secondly, some policies of international organizations have a guiding role towards nation states and developing countries are more influenced. Take the World Bank as an example, the World Bank promotes its idea of economic development by adjusting credit policies to promote economic and social development of developing countries. From the 1980s to nowadays, the World Bank regards the guiding goal of its credit policies as to emphasize market orientation and functions of private sectors, and it aims to develop assistance so as to guide and support developing countries implement economic structural adjustments oriented by the market economic mechanism and political reform and also to help developing countries establish a market economic mechanism favorable to development. Some developing countries established the market economic mechanism under the guidance of these principles. However, since the World Bank always promotes its economic policies through its credit policies, some countries especially developing countries have to accept these additional conditions if they wish to obtain loans, thus transferring part of their economic sovereignty. A financial crisis broke out in East Asia in 1997, international economic organizations led by IMF and the World Bank had offered huge capital support to East Asian countries with very strict conditions, and forced recipient countries to implement financial liberalization and make economic reforms. For instance, the Republic of Korea received a subsidy fund of 55 billion, of which 10 billion came from the World Bank, but it had also accepted a series of harsh terms, including decreasing the economic growth rate from 6% in 1998 to 3%, keeping price inflation rate below 5%, reducing deficits in revenue and expenditure of economic items to 1% of GDP or below, immediately rectifying financial institutions and implementing deflationary policies, changing the mutual guarantee system among enterprises of large-scale enterprise groups, permitting foreign banks and security institutions establish subsidiary companies in the Republic of

Korea, allowing the increase of limit of each Korean stock held by foreigners from 25% to 56%, and approving opening Korea's capital market in advance. Public opinions in the Republic of Korea had regarded this as "national humiliation" and "forfeit of economic sovereignty" and believed that the Kim Yong-sam government was placing Korean economy under the "trusteeship" of foreign forces.[1] Both tax reduction and relevant negotiations of GATT and economic adjustments forcefully made by countries with financial crisis for assistance can be seen as the transfer of national economic sovereignty in a certain degree.

(2) Challenges from multinational corporations

Multinational corporations are independent economic entities, whose goal of activity is to maximize profits. While nation states have to consider issues in many aspects such as their political and economic sovereignty, utilization of resources and labor employment etc. Therefore, interest conflicts between multinational corporations and states are unavoidable. On the one hand, multinational corporations may deviate from the goal of their home countries. Since large-scale multinational corporations are generally the main forces for the national economy of different countries, the government of home countries always need to take into consideration of interests of their large-scale multinational corporations when making political and economic policies and even make concessions sometimes. For instance, America has a series of anti-monopoly laws aiming to ensure market competition in a certain degree and prevent excessive monopoly. However, the government always makes concessions to multinational corporations in specific cases. The Daimler-Benz AG, Germany claimed to amalgamate with the Chrysler Corporation in America on May 7, 1999, and announced to establish the Daimler-Chrysler Motor Corporation. The merger was carried out in the form of mutual exchange of stocks, shareholders of Daimler-Benz AG held 57% shares of the new company, while shareholders of Chrysler Corporation held 43%. Both the Benz Corporation and the Chrysler Corporation are the "giants"

---

[1] Liu Cheng: "Influences of Credit Policies of the World Bank on the Economy of Developing Countries", in *International Economic Cooperation*, 1999 (3).

in the world automobile industry. The Benz Company is the largest industrial group in Germany with 300,000 employees, while the Chrysler Corporation is the third largest car manufacturer in America with 128,000 employees. The market capital involved in the merger of the two companies was up to 92 billion and the market capital of the Daimler-Chrysler Motor Corporation after merger had ranked the second in the world, its sales ranked the third and sales volume ranked the fifth in the world. However, such merger was not resisted by the American and German governments. Why the anti-monopoly law was not applicable? Under the context of globalization, decision-makers of the automobile industry realized that they must expand the space for survival and enhance their competitiveness from nowadays if they wish to gain a firm foothold within the industry and gain further development in the next century, and the best way for achieving such goal is union of enterprises. The state also made concessions to multinational corporations to ensure their local enterprises' competitiveness in the international market. On the other hand, although citizens in capitalist countries have the election rights, influences of votes of ordinary citizens upon politics of such nation are far less than that of large companies' donation to candidates. In other words, large companies, especially multinational companies can eliminate various obstacles to a certain degree and ensure they can gain maximum economic profits by donating money to candidates of different parties in their home countries. These multinational corporations and rich people constitute the "lobby", directly influence decision-makers by donations, and embody their will in national policies. For instance, America's state power was dominated by the Democratic Party and the Republican Party in turn for a long period. However, in fact, people become more aware of the fact that policies of the two parties have no significant differences any more since the late 1980s. Both the Democratic Party and the Republican Party become the pro-business Party. Many suggest that actually America has a single-party system dominated by the "Democratic Party". A corporate PAC director once described the elections as: "There was a genuine movement, the closest thing I've ever seen on the part of business in this country, almost a phenomenon that occurred in that year and a half or two years of that particular election. It was a genuine virtual fervor. Let's go out there and we can do it, we can change the system. The Chamber of Commerce and NAM (National Association of Manufacturers) and everybody (rich) beat the drum."[1]

The national economic sovereignty of host countries especially those among developing countries are more challenged by multinational corporations generally represented as the following aspects. Firstly, foreign private capital inflow increases the home currency rate of host countries, increases the price of their products in the international market and reduces their competitiveness. The independency of monetary policies can hardly be maintained with the free flow of capital. The famous Mundell-Fleming Model has discussed this issue, indicating that a nation will face significant collisions between an independent monetary policy and a fixed exchange rate under the condition of free capital flow. A nation can at best realize two aspects among the three: totally free capital movement, independent monetary policy and steady exchange rate. Therefore, free capital movement becomes a basis feature in the process of economic globalization. A nation needs to transfer monetary sovereignty to multinational private capital in a certain degree or gain independence in the monetary sovereignty by the frequent fluctuation of exchange rate so as to maintain a steady exchange rate. Secondly, short-term speculative capital can easily lead to a financial crisis in the country receiving the capital as seen by the explosion of the Southeast Asian financial crisis. The development in the Southeast Asian district had been called as a "miracle" for a long term and these countries and regions were publicly known as the most vibrant investment hot spots with the quickest growth and strongest foreign exchange reserve strength. Nevertheless, the economic development of Southeast Asian districts had relied on international capital inflow to a large extent, and it was the international capital inflow that imbedded the hidden trouble of the financial crisis. Southeast Asian countries all had experienced the period of rapid economic growth, however, both

---

[1] Quoted from Dan Clawson, Alan Neustadtl and Mark Meller, *Dollars and Votes: How Business Campaign Contribution Subvert Democracy*, Temple University Press.

their increase of investment and credit expansion of domestic banks had greatly relied on foreign capital. For instance, the domestic savings ratio in Thailand was 34.5% in 1996, the investment ratio was up to 43.5%, and the total amount of foreign loans was up to 90.8 billion USD, accounting for 50.3% of GDP, far more than the internationally recognized 20% warning line.[1] Such undue dependence on international capital results in the fact that once international capital ceases to inflow or practices massive outflow, domestic investment and economic growth will severely be affected. The fuse of this financial crisis was the impact of international hot money. After the crisis, there was a sharp decline in the stock market and foreign exchange market and multinational corporations withdrew their investment from different Southeast Asian countries one after another. The large-scale outflow of such international capital undoubtedly exacerbated difficulties. Meanwhile, economic recovery of Southeast Asian countries relies on the re-flow of international capital. "If the government wants to repay debts, attract investment, create job opportunities and satisfy people's expectation on the standard of living, the government must accept multinational corporations and even curry favor with them."[2] In the middle 1990s, some developed countries actively advocated establishment of a global multilateral structure to replace the existing 1,600 bilateral treaties at present, and drafted the *Multilateral Agreement on Investment* (MAI). The aim of such agreement is to provide a comprehensive international investment structure, protect investors, institutionalize economic liberalization and settle disputes, of which the important content is to request host countries of multinational corporations not to legislate or formulate regulations to discriminate foreign capital. If some behaviors of the government in a given country are realized as jeopardizing the interest of foreign capital, the government shall assume legal liabilities. Such regulations are bound to impose a threat to the national sovereignty of weaker countries. Even though the MAI was not reached a final agreement due to the boycott of many countries, such agreement

[1] *The Yearbook of World Economy*, 1998.

[2] George Lodge: *Managing Globalization in the Age of Interdependence*, Edition 1, p. 13, Shanghai, Shanghai Translation Publishing House, 1998.

basically reflects the impact of multinational corporations to the national sovereignty in the age of globalization.

2. National Sovereignty and State Functions in Economic Globalization

People have different opinions on the role of states in view of challenges to the national sovereignty in economic globalization. Some people believe that economic globalization is the grave-digger of states and a single nation state will lose its sovereignty and material contents. Globalization will gradually erode core power collectively represented as tax imposition by the sovereignty, maintaining public order, formulating diplomatic policies and safeguarding military security, etc. by establishing a world society and transcending boundaries of nation states. The welfare state and sovereignty awareness will be fundamentally weakened. The final result of globalization will be that nation state will gradually lose power and the state can no longer assume historical roles of social coordination. It descends to be a spectator, like a "court clerk, who just records decisions made in other places and has no power to make any decision". "Globalization destroys sovereignty of states, links world domain, abuses established political community, challenges social contract and prematurely erodes the 'useless' concept of national security ... thence, sovereignty is no longer an indisputable basic value like before, and the infiltration of external ideas is surely changing the connotation of sovereignty, although in a slow way."[1] This view is apparently extreme. There are certain limitations in exercising national sovereignty under the situation of globalization. Due to intensified capital flow, globalization destroys the autonomy of national macro-economic policies. Countries are not able to counter-balance the foreign exchange market and their controlling power on interest rates declines. The nation's legality in national welfare is infringed as well. Because state's taxing power is strengthened, the welfare expenditure of states is close to the utmost limit though it is increasing. Besides, nations' selection of ways for development, planning of overall

---

[1] Quoted from Alain Benoit: "Facing Globalization", in *Telos*, 1996, summer edition.

development strategies, etc. are all impaired because of the development of world market economy. The British plutonomist Susan Strange had once pointed out, "The impersonal forces of world markets, integrated over the postwar period more by private enterprise in finance, industry and trade than by the cooperative decisions of governments are now more powerful than the states.... In many key fields in which the state dominated the market, nowadays the market dominates the state."[1] The statement that globalization makes the state decline or even die out has become the basis of some people in advocating so-called statement of "human rights above sovereignty".

It is diametrically opposed that some people believe that economic globalization will lead to both transcendence of sovereignty and consolidation of national sovereignty. Economic globalization divides collective space under the management of capitalist economy and nation state's space under the management of political society, which demands both giving priority to global economic management and protecting core contents of the national sovereignty from being infringed. The national sovereignty can be transferred in a tangible way and corroded in an intangible way, and it can be redistributed and adjusted through the two forms of upper transfer and lower transfer. "Depression theory" exaggerates the previous power of states and their consistent reaction to globalization. Both strong countries and weak countries have certain adaptive capacity. Besides, the depth and width of globalization are not that great and home countries are still very crucial for multinational corporations. The role of nation states strengthens rather than weakens and it promotes advance rather than obstruct development in the globalization process. Nations are not the victims but the facilitators of globalization. Opening market is the direct outcome of government behaviors in some countries. For instance, economic officials and industrial circles have close relations in Japan and its economic policies are realized upon consultation of both parties, therefore its "internationalization" strategy goes smoothly. To help enterprises adjust themselves and adapt to external environment in a more effective way, the Japanese government applies

---

[1] Susan Strange: *The Retreat of the State*, Cambridge, 1996, p. 4.

"foreign development assistance", which not only guarantees the export of Japanese products, but also asks officials to stay abroad to contribute to the spread of Japanese model.

As we analyzed above, economic globalization exerts influences upon the sovereignty of nation states. Nevertheless, it is better to say economic globalization changes the role of states than simply say that economic globalization strengthens or weakens the national sovereignty or makes it die out.

(1) National economic security

The relative limitation of world resources and "anarchy" of the international society definitely result in conflicts during the cooperation of different countries. Different countries attempt to strengthen the dependency of other nations for themselves through strengthening their power so as to reduce cost to the utmost. Clinton had commented on that: "We will deem our nation's economic security as the main goal of our foreign policies."

(2) Actively create conditions and strengthen opening up

Opening up will be still the mainstream of international economy in the future based on the trend. The government of different nations shall create conditions for their enterprises to participate in international economic cooperation and competition and develop their national economy in competition and cooperation. Opening capital markets is the direct outcome of government behaviors, and many countries are trying to directly promote rather than restrict the internationalization of companies in trade, investment and production.

(3) Strengthen logistics service

Galbraith believes that modern economic life has transcended national boundaries and formed complicated and global cooperation on the one hand; and the state's social responsibilities in terms of employment, education and hygiene, etc. are increasingly larger on the other hand. For instance, many European countries especially Sweden and Germany always make great efforts to alleviate the influences of changes in external environment on the labor market and minimize the impact of globalization to their nations by implementing a large number of national technical training and labor employment programs.

Are human rights above sovereignty? The argument of "human rights above sovereignty" seems to be a wave in some developed countries. Based on the argument of depression or impairment of nations, people holding such view believe that an open society should be most requisite and the nation is only an old tool, which must be adjusted in coordination with social requirements. The nation should transfer partial political and economic sovereignty since people's interests are above national interests and the power of people's pursuit of economic interests and a happy life are more important than a nation's safeguarding self-interests. Soros had commented on that: "The society shall mobilize and demand that national behaviors abide by some principles, which are the principles of opening the society."[1]

It seems that these people portray a very beautiful picture. In fact, such argument of "human rights above sovereignty" is only another version of "limited sovereignty theory" that has been advocated for many years, as well as an excuse for the few countries that intervene in internal affairs of other countries. Regulations of the international law to replace national rules as they have advocated said in fact based on the standards of capitalist countries. Under current situation, inequality also exists in the UN, an international organization aiming to maintain world order based on the principle of equality among different member states. A minority of developed capitalist countries manipulate the UN to a certain degree. As long as the gap between economic powers of different countries cannot be narrowed or eliminated, the political status of different countries cannot be equal and the world order and international regulations cannot be truly balanced. Major countries in the capitalist world outrageously put the theory of so-called "humanistic intervention" into practice on account of their economic and military advantages. The NATO led by America had forced Yugoslavia to

---

[1] Soros: *The Crisis of Global Capitalism*, p. 260, Harbin, Heilongjiang People's Publishing House, 1998.

accept its principles and methods on handling the minority nationality issues of Kosovo and bombed Yugoslavia savagely for a length of two months in 1999. Then had advocated such illegal behavior on the Kosovo issue in the "new strategic ideas" passed on the summit meeting celebrating NATO's 50-year anniversary, and acclaimed that "NATO built on the common values of democracy, human rights and the rule of law will strive for the realization of the order of justice and long lasting peace in Europe, therefore, the union needs to not only ensure the defense of its member countries but also make contributions to the peace and stability"[1]. As Deng Xiaoping indicated, aiming at the attempt of western world on propaganda in raising turmoil and peaceful evolution, "People who value human rights should not forget the rights of the state. When they talk about human dignity, they should not forget national dignity. In particular, if the developing countries of the Third World, like China, have no national self-respect and do not cherish their independence, they will not enjoy that independence for long." "Actually, national sovereignty is far more important than human rights." He specifically emphasized that in opening-up, "the first priority should always be given to national sovereignty and security"[2]. General people of developing countries can protect their human rights only by safeguarding national sovereignty. Having a clear understanding of this point is of great significance for different developing countries when participating in economic globalization and formulate reasonable strategic plans.

VI. Economic Globalization and Developing Countries

1. Dual Influences of Economic Globalization on Developing Countries

Economic globalization is a driving force for quickening world

[1] *NATO Handbook 2001*, Chapter 2, www.nato.int.

[2] *Selected Works of Deng Xiaoping*, Edition 1, Vol. 3, P331, p. 347, Beijing, People's Publishing House, 1993.

competition and the development of productive forces worldwide. However, as analyzed before, economic globalization is at least led by developed countries at present. Therefore, the prevalent view is that developed countries are the greatest beneficiary in the economic globalization process and there are some debates on the influences of globalization on developing countries. We can say that developing countries assume more costs in the current economic globalization. However, it does not mean that developing countries are destined to be marginalized and deprived of the possibility of developing economy and finally catching up with developed countries. Opening-up policy may make economic policies of the government in developing countries subordinate to the impacts of developing countries to a certain degree, but it is not bound to be fundamentally controlled. Since these countries are sovereign countries, they can build a firewall and protect themselves through implementing a series of policies. The precondition for such "firewall" is to regard the positive and negative effects of economic globalization on developing countries in an objective way.

Positive influences of economic globalization on developing countries are: a considerable portion of developing countries had cut economic relations with developed countries, implement the closed-door policy and had a slow economic development for a long term. In comparison, a minority of developing countries and regions represented by Mexico and four little economic dragons in Asia have actively participated in economic globalization and achieved success in economic development. Many experiences show that there is a positive relationship between opening-up and economic growth.

The reasons are: 1) economic globalization promotes accumulation of favorable elements for developing countries. And they can have more advantages to attract and use foreign capital. Trade liberalization can promote investment since it provides opportunities to enter larger markets, permits obtaining larger returns based on scale-economy and can import capital goods that cannot be obtained before or obtain cheaper capital goods. It is undoubtedly beneficial to solve the shortage of capital in developing countries. 2) Economic globalization enables developing countries further optimize and adjust their industrial structure. Through opening up, developing countries may learn new technologies and knowledge, which are included in trade commodities, machinery relevant to opening economy and foreign direct investment. They can take this chance, vigorously quicken the development of high-tech industries, and especially transfer advanced labor-intensive industries of developed countries to their countries on the basis of the requirements of domestic and international market. At present, it is surely a shortcut for optimization and adjustment of industrial structure in developing countries. 3) Economic globalization provides more job opportunities for developing countries to improve employment. Developing countries possess a large amount of labor resources and have lower wages, so they are very attractive to developed countries. Many large-scale multinational corporations transfer their production base to developing countries and provide a large amount of local job opportunities. 4) Economic globalization enhances competitiveness of developing countries. As the expansion of foreign trade and continual introduction of foreign capital, the national industry of developing countries would be connected with international regulations in a closer way and they would understand the requirements of the international market and international regulations in greater depth. In addition to new technologies learned and application of foreign management experiences, it is inevitable that they can strengthen the competitiveness of their products in the international market. This paves the foundation for developing countries to enter the international market and participate in the formulation of international regulations on the basis of favorable positions. The report with on the theme of *Globalization: Opportunities and Challenges* published by IMF in 1997 had indicated that one of the main lessons in the past decades is that multiple pressures of globalization made people aware of the advantages and costs of good or bad policies. Generally, countries which comply with the globalization wave and make efforts to reform and open markets and pursue macro-economic policies with discipline probably step on the way similar with developed countries such as those successful Asian emerging industrial economies. These countries following the wave may gain benefits from trading, obtain share of the global market and continually receive benefits from larger private capital inflow. In comparison, countries which did not adopt these policies may face the difficulties of gradually decreasing world trade share, gradual impoverishment of private capital inflow and being relatively lagged behind. The Mexican and Asian financial crisis was relevant to economic globalization to a certain degree, but they went on the track of rapid economic development again after the short crisis. Therefore, we cannot deny that economic globalization offers a lasting economic development for these countries and regions. More importantly, economic globalization provides developing countries with opportunities to give full play to their advantages as late-comers and catch up with developed countries. Economic globalization is conducive for developing countries to attract foreign capital and make up for the shortage of domestic funds for construction, quicken technical transfer and adjustment of industrial structure, introduce advanced technologies and equipment and realize spanning technical development, give full play to their comparative advantages, make full use of rich labor resources and human resources and develop foreign trade. Therefore, although economic globalization is dominated by developed countries today, we cannot accordingly hold the view that developing countries can only be passive and accomplish nothing in the economic globalization. Practice has proved that the general backwardness of developing countries cannot be completely attributable to economic globalization, and globalization can promote economic development of developing countries if these countries can avoid their disadvantages in policies.

Without doubt, developing countries assume mostly higher costs and are more negatively affected in economic globalization. Because of the impact of economic globalization on government functions, some governments of developing countries which are not good at managing national economy further lose their functions on economic management, and make them more dependent on developed countries. Firstly, developed countries monopolize high and new technologies and further take the lead in medicine, electronics, global natural resources and other aspects. In the current system of world division of labor, global natural resources are used to satisfy the requirements of a minority of people, and oil in the Middle East is "no longer oil of Arabian countries, but oil of the West". Secondly, developed countries still control global capital. International capital flow mainly comes from large-scale multinational corporations and multinational financial institutions, and they control global capital to a certain degree. The famous center-peripheral theory of Wallerstein, believes that Marx has pointed out the capitalist system is international: "The proper task of bourgeois society is the creation of the world market, at least in outline, and of the production based on that market."[1] The social and historical nature of capitalist international division of labor on that basis is that it adapts to capitalist production and is beneficial to the development of capitalist production in strong capitalist countries. The capitalist economy in primitive colonies and dependent countries serves for capital of strong capitalist countries in central areas and is subject to its control. In the specific international division of labor, it is represented as a large group of newest emerging industries, such as atomic energy industry, computer telecommunication industry and biochemistry industry, etc. had appeared in central areas with the Third Scientific-Technological Revolution. These industrial sectors with great knowledge contents have great vigor and driving force for the economy. The previous labor-intensive industries and spare parts production or its several production processes relying on new emerging industries are transferred to peripheral developing countries. Besides, peripheral countries also provide agricultural products and mineral products to countries in central areas. Especially in Latin American countries, one or few kinds of agricultural and animal husbandry products or mineral products generally account for over 70% of their total volume of export, of which oil in Mexico and Venezuela respectively account for 95% and 70%. Developing

[1] *Karl Marx and Frederick Engels*, Chinese version, Edition 1, Vol. 29, p. 348, Beijing, People's publishing House, 1972.

countries are at obvious disadvantage in the international competition of industrial products with higher capital technical contents. In China, the automobile industry developing for many years fails to counter-balance with that of western developed countries, and developing countries and regions still have limited export of automobiles. For instance, the three largest car exporting places of China in 1997 were Hong Kong, China, 2,677, Korea, 2,310, Saudi Arabia, 1,277.[1] Although developing countries have established their industrial system goals and composition of industry based on their conditions and interests, they are always excluded by dominant multinational corporations and are not able to change the current entire allocation system in the capitalist international division of labor. Finally, developing countries are more dependent on developed countries in the financial markets. There are mainly two ways for developed countries to export capital to developing countries, one is multinational banks, and the other is export of state loaned capital. Thus developing countries are severely dependent on the exchange rate with USD, Pound, Euro and other currencies. Developing countries assume extremely large risks in the changes of exchange rate in developed countries, and these countries will be severely impacted in case of a debt crisis. The debt crisis in 1982 was a typical example. The International Bank Group had accumulated a large amount of hot money from 1975 to 1980 and was eager to find the way out, then it exported loaned capital at an extremely low interest rate, and many developing countries chose a way of growth with dept, of which Brazil, Mexico and Venezuela had the most remarkable economic growth. Developed countries have began to attract hot money and tighten monetary policies after 1980, leading to soaring lending rate, that is, 6.11% in 1981, 6.91% in 1982 and 6.71% in 1983. Latin American countries have paid more interests of 49 billion from 1979 to 1982 due to increase of American interest rate. The interest of foreign debts paid by Brazil accounted for up to 57% of its foreign exchange earnings obtained by the export of commodities and labor services in 1982, and the proportion was 54.6% in Argentina. In order to repay huge foreign debts, Latin American countries had

[1] *China Foreign Economic Relations and Trade Yearbook, 1998/1999.*

to greatly increase exports of primary products, which even led to shortage of domestic materials and rises in price. Meanwhile, developed countries tried to keep down price of primary products and increase price of the means of production and immediate products were exported to developing countries. Production in Latin American regions had decreased in an all-around way under the attack of both sides. Mexico firstly declared that it was unable to repay due interests of loans in August, 1982, and then Brazil, Argentina and Peru had declared their inability to repay due interest one after another, Latin American countries were stuck in the mire of debt crisis. From the whole process of this event we can see that developed countries were dominant and were beneficiaries at all times, whereas developing countries were passive and have assumed risks. It had also sounded the alarm for all developing countries. Iglesias, secretary of the Economic Commission for Latin America and Caribbean had commented on this issue: "Explore development model relying on their own power independent of foreign countries and debts." There is no doubt that it is impossible for them to develop totally relying on their own power in globalization nowadays and nations should be interdependent with each other, nevertheless, it is absolutely necessary to maintain certain independence and security. This has been a consensus of many scholars in developing countries.

2. Developing Countries and the Challenges of Economic Globalization

We must admit that developed countries are main beneficiaries and developing countries assume more costs in economic globalization at the present stage. Developing countries can only advance and leap by seeking opportunities in economic globalization under the current international economic order. Analyzing the main forces in current world economy, we may find out that America still holds a safe lead in world economy. The American economy has two advantages in comparison with other countries, one is the advantage of knowledge innovation and technical innovation and the other is the advantage of rapid transformation rate of science and technology to (production) productive forces through fiscal and financial system and policies. The two advantages ensure America's growth at a higher productivity rate than that of other countries in the foreseeable future. The principles of America for formulating international economic policies are: firstly, America must lead the formulation of multilateral regulations and multilateral organizations; secondly, America's authority in leading international economic issues mainly relies on the power of American economy; thirdly, the foremost goal of American trade policies is to further open foreign markets rather than protect domestic market; fourthly, implementation of policies on economic integration in new emerging countries including China accords with America's interest, since it contributes to the prospects of these countries' economic reform and political liberation; fifthly, for USA national economic interests are not a secondary issue, national security shall include the concern of economics and geopolitics. We can see that America is still the No.1 economic power in the world today, and only the European Union can content against it. EU has also entered the new knowledge-based economic era. There is a gap between new economy in Euro area and American new economy, the scale of new economy in Euro area only equals to a half or two thirds of America and the gap is rapidly narrowing. The economic power of EU not only stems from the development of science and technology, the formation of European Monetary Union as well as the expansion of EU will also strengthen its economic status. The Euro accounts for 40% circulation of the world bond market after it was issued. As time passes by, Euro may impose a challenge on the dominant financial position of America. Even though the Japanese economy has been weak in recent years, it is still the most important economic power in the Asian region. After the bubble economy shattered in the 1990s, the Japanese economy has been in depression for a very long period. During the period, the Japanese government made reforms and adjustments of many social economic systems, especially concentrated efforts to improve trade imbalance and reformed the financial market. If Japan can walk out of recession and achieve reforms, it would still be an indispensable part of world economy based on the foundation of its economic power. The third important force comes from developing countries. Although developing countries nowadays are still incomparable with developed countries in power comparison at present, they have a rapid development speed. In economic globalization nowadays, developing countries actively participate in north-south dialogue on the one hand, and on the other hand strengthen South-South cooperation and seek greater development. Table 8-4 reflects the net capital inflow to emerging market economies. We can see from this that the net private capital inflow to these countries reached a peak in 1996, sharply declined because of the Asian financial crisis, had an increase in recent years and it is expected that such increase will go on.

Table 8-4   Net Capital Inflow of Emerging Market Economic Countries

Unit: A Hundred Million USD

Net Private Capital Inflow	1994	1995	1996	1997	1998	1999	2000	2001	2002	2003
Net Private Capital Inflow	150.9	212	234.2	111.9	65.4	69.4	7.7	31.3	58.0	76.8
Net Official Capital Inflow	3.5	26.9	-1.5	64.9	60.5	13.7	5.7	37.2	32.7	15.2

Source: IMF: *World Economic Outlook*, 2002.

In face of such a situation, developing countries should actively take measures, formulate countermeasures to safeguard their interests against negative effects of economic globalization, and seek opportunities to develop and catch up. Firstly, developing countries should not lag behind contently for the developed countries' monopoly of technologies and resources, and have a proper place in high and new technological field. A country should be equipped with comparative advantages if it wants to develop in international trade, and increasing technical contents of products is the fundamental way for obtaining comparative advantages. On the one hand, they may give priority to the selection of projects with high technical contents when attracting foreign direct investment and learn advanced technologies by means of its technical diffusion effects. On the other hand, they should go on the way of independent development, establish talent training strategies, fully realize the fact that the world competition is in fact the competition on talents. They should elevate the development and protection of talents to an important strategic position and reduce talent drain as much as possible. Secondly, targeting at risks encountered by national economic security under the context of economic globalization, developing countries should actively safeguard national economic security while opening-up gradually or moderately. Firstly, should improve the state's ability for managing economy. The government must play a larger role in the construction of macro-economic management mechanism as well as the formulation and implementation of macro policies, further straighten out functions of macro management authorities of the government and improve the government's abilities to comprehensively coordinate various macro-economic policies and economic levers. It is more difficult to coordinate policies especially under the circumstances of further opening the market. Therefore, fiscal policies, monetary policies, income distribution policies and foreign trade policies, etc. should be integrated, and economic levers such as interest rate, exchange rate, price, taxation, etc. should be used well to ensure the healthy operation of national economy. Secondly, strengthen supervision of the financial market, establish a system to comprehensively guard against and risks, strengthen abilities to resist and guard against foreign risks, and safeguard national industrial and economic security. These measures have been a consensus after the Asian financial crisis and Latin American financial crisis. In fact, protection of national economy in the present stage as we mentioned above is to conditions to establish a sound internal structure and mechanism suitable for the development of globalization and prevent lag of internal development in comparison to external environment, which is also a way of active participation in globalization. Thirdly, seize opportunities and greatly develop new-technological industries. The latest technological revolution, i.e., information technological revolution has created a new emerging industrial sector, information industry, which is both an opportunity and challenge for many developing countries. Because different from other sectors, it does not have high requirements for capital and equipment but mainly relies on people's knowledge accumulation. Developed countries and developing countries stand on the same starting line in this industry.

Industrial regulations are not sound and competition is the fiercest in the initial stage of the industry, those who seize opportunities and open up a new prospect would probably be dominant in future industries.

Referring to the Third World under the context of globalization, the famous Egyptian economist Samir Amin had once pointed out, "I am only against capitalist globalization instead of globalization in general terms. We may imagine globalization in another kind of society and in another form … maybe after one to two hundred years, we will have socialist globalization."[1] We live today in the capitalism-based era, so in the short term globalization is led by capitalism, and it is a trap in which developed countries reap all the benefits and developing countries bear all the costs. However, in the long term, only if they actively participate in the wave of globalization and make efforts to seek opportunities for development can they have power to combat against developed countries some day and create conditions for institutional reforms worldwide. Then it is possible that economic globalization will truly belong to the people all over the world.

---

[1] Wang Yizhou: "The Third World under the Context of Globalization—Interview with Samir Amin", in *World Economy and Politics*, 2001 (2).

Chapter IX

Historical Status of the Capitalist Mode of Production

S ame as previous social modes of production, the capitalist mode of production is bound to have a historical process of formation, development and extinction. Such a historical evolution process of the mode of production in human society is determined by the law that the means of production must adapt to the requirements for the development of productive forces. It is an objective natural historical process independent of people's will. In the historical process of the development of human society, each social mode of production has its historical progressiveness and historical limitations; it finishes its special historical mission and has its special historical status, and so is for the capitalist mode of production. This chapter will mainly elaborate the historical progressiveness, historical limitation and historical inheritance nature of the capitalist mode of production as the summary of the book.

I. Historical Progressiveness of the Capitalist Mode of Production

The historical progressive nature of capitalist relations of production is relative to its nature in comparison with the previous social relations of production as well as its historical mission. Marx had revealed the exploitative nature of capitalist relations of production on the one hand and fully affirmed its historical progressive nature on the other hand.

1. Capitalist Economic Relations and the Socialized Production

In fact, serfdom no longer existed in Britain in end of the 14th century, and most farmers had become free dirt farmers in the 15th century. Farmers had their lands and could freely carry on agricultural production on common land. Cottage industry also had sufficient development in the countryside. Guild handicrafts also had great development in cities along the Mediterranean, handicraftsman were directly connected to their labor conditions. The private ownership of laborers to their means of production was the foundation for small production.

Small producers' mode of production:

Small producers' mode of production was the requirement for developing social production and free personality of laborers themselves. Small producers had displayed huge enthusiasm for production under the condition of private ownership based on their own labor and this had greatly promoted the improvement of labor productive forces. Small producers' mode of production was a proper form for the development of individual productive forces, and had later created necessary conditions for individual productive forces to develop into social productive forces. Nevertheless, no matter which level did productive forces had attained by small producers, they were characterized as individual productive forces and had never existed as an integrated social force. Division of labor could only naturally occur within small circles of families. Therefore, it was not a kind of socialized productive force. The physical work and brainwork of small producers were totally and directly linked together, they used production technologies handed down from generation to generation and in case of an invention, it was embodied and fixed on labor tools and passed to forward generations without change. Spiritual productive forces were insignificant in comparison with material productive forces in such mode of production, in a more accurate saying, spiritual productive forces had not represented an independent force, and scientific technologies had not gained proper conditions for development. Production experiences of individual labor and craftsmanship handed down from generation to generation had constituted the technical foundation for the mode of manual labor, which was conservative in nature. Small private ownership by direct producers were the social relation of production in conformity with such individual productive forces. Marx had pointed out, "This mode of production pre-supposes parceling of the soil and scattering of the other means of production. As it excludes the concentration of these means of production, so also it excludes co-operation, division of labor within each separate process of production, the control over, and the productive application of the forces of Nature by society, and the free development of the social productive powers. It is compatible only with a system of production, and a society, moving within narrow and more or less primitive bounds.... At a certain stage of development, it brings forth the material agencies for its own dissolution."[1] In other words, although such small private ownership of dispersive direct producers was a proper form for developing individual productivity of laborers, it was incompatible with social productive forces, and such mode of production was bound to decline with the development of productive forces and development of social division of labor as well as gradual transformation of individual productive forces to social productive forces. Then later; the private ownership based on the integration of each independent labor and his labor condition was eliminated by the capitalist private ownership. The capitalist private ownership was the inevitable outcome of development of social productive forces and social division of

---

[1] *Karl Marx and Frederick Engels*, Chinese version, Edition 1, Vol. 23, p. 830.

labor, and the outcome of polarization of small producers. The capitalist mode of production did not stem from direct transfer from slaves and serfs to wage earners, but had required the deprivation of direct producers, i.e., the dissolution of private ownership based on individual producers.

The capitalist private ownership was based on the deprivation of small private ownership of direct producers. Its precondition was the accumulation of currency and wealth in the first place and to accumulate social means of production and labor forces, organize socialized production process pattern and successfully transform individual productive forces to social productive forces. Under the social mode of production integrating capital and wage labor, the capitalist private ownership had adapted to the objective requirements for all-around flow of production elements needed in commodity production based on spontaneous division of labor and could effectively organize the socialized process of commodity production. The capitalist private ownership also contains an internal motive and mechanism for self development. Based on the broad world market, capitalist production faces huge social demands and it can make allocation of the means of production worldwide on the basis of production conditions created by the world market. Meanwhile, the development of capitalist production constantly creates new markets for itself. Therefore, it is not commerce that restrains huge production but the amount of functional capital and the development level of labor productive forces. It is an internal demand of capitalist movement to further develop other kind of capitalist private ownership forms. To expand capital's ability for appreciation, capitalists must constantly accumulate capital, turn surplus value into capital, develop various forms of capital accumulation, explore capital markets, combine private capital and transform them into social capital, and constantly dominate more production elements. To improve capital's efficiency in appreciation, they need to transform all individual productive forces into social productive forces, create various organizational forms of social labor and make management innovations in the social labor process. It must develop spiritual productive forces when developing material productive forces at the same time so as to support the technical basis of production required for its development. It integrates development of science and technology into material production process and creates huge social productive forces. We can see that capitalist private ownership can obtain material means leading to its rapid expansion, and has immense internal motive and realization mechanism for its development. It is both the reason for the development of capitalist private ownership and an important manifestation of its historical progressiveness.

2. Internal Trend of Capital as to Social Productive Forces

The direct objective and decisive motive of capitalists in organizing social commodity production is to gain surplus value. "Production of surplus value is the absolute law of this mode of production."[1] It must firstly produce goods and the exchange value to achieve this objective, and developing production and improving labor productive forces are the foundation for production of surplus value. Therefore, the relation between production of surplus value and labor productive forces is that between the objective and means for production. Capitalists must develop those means for achieving the objective if they want to realize the objective. Some capitalists always try every means possible to improve production techniques and labor productive forces to gain excess surplus value, so as to make the individual value of commodities lower than their social values. The pursuit of excess surplus value is the direct motive of some capitalists for improving production technologies and social labor forces. The internal incentive of capital in pursuit of excess surplus value and external pressure formed by market competition lead to general improvement of social production technologies and labor productive forces. Marx had pointed out, "Production which has; as its incentive value and surplus-value implies, as we have shown in the course of our analyses, the perpetually effective tendency to reduce the labor necessary for the production of a commodity, in other words, to reduce its value, below the prevailing social average. The effort to reduce the cost price to its minimum becomes the strongest lever for the raising of the social

---

[1] *Karl Marx and Frederick Engels*, Chinese version, Edition 1, Vol. 23, p. 679.

productivity of labor, which, however, appears under these conditions as a continual increase of the productive power of capital."[1] Frequent reforms in the material mode of production and constant improvement of labor productive forces is an inevitable process accompanied with the production of surplus value. Capital needs to regulate all forces through social integration and social exchange while regulating all forces of science and nature, so as to improve labor productive forces and increase production of surplus value.

The capitalist production process with the goal of surplus value is a process of infinite appreciation of capital value. Such internal nature of capital movement is an important social condition for infinite development of social productive forces. Marx had commented on this issue: "It is one of the civilizing aspects of capital that it enforces this surplus-labor in a manner and under conditions which are more advantageous to the development of the productive forces, social relations, and the creation of the elements for a new and higher form than under the preceding forms of slavery, serfdom, etc."[2] Capital possesses productive forces and is able to squeeze out of workers' surplus labor in the form of wage labor and surplus value. Such a special method for possessing surplus labor has given rise to internal requirements for capital's continual and systematic development of social productive forces. In the previous relations of production of slavery and feudalism, labor was illiberal "forced labor", and owners of the means of production had appropriated producers' surplus labor in the form of use values or specific labor, aiming to enjoy wealth rather than accumulate value. Such form of exploitation itself decides the natural boundary of greed for surplus labor. This natural boundary reflects the parochialism of the form of exploitation, and they cannot be the lasting motive for the development of social productive forces. Marx had written: "It is, however, clear that in any given economic formation of society, where not the exchange-value but the use-value of the product predominates, surplus-labor will be limited by a given set of wants which may be greater or less, and that here no boundless thirst

---

[1] *Karl Marx and Frederick Engels*, Chinese version, Edition 1, Vol. 25, p. 996.
[2] *Karl Marx and Frederick Engels*, Chinese version, Edition 1, Vol. 25, pp. 925-926.

for surplus-labor arises from the nature of the production itself."[1]

Surely we do not deny the extreme extravagance of slave holders and feudal lords, and neglect that the nature of their mode of production itself had not generated requirements for boundless greed for surplus labor. They had rather attached importance to the consumption of wealth rather than improvement of productive forces for accumulation. It had been those dominant relations and not the capital that was opposite to direct forced labor, therefore only such dominant relations were reproduced on the basis of direct forced labor in previous economic systems. As far as this relation is concerned, in the past, wealth itself only had a hedonistic meaning instead of its meaning as wealth, so a general industry could not be created by those previous economic relations. Since capital uses the free laborer to accumulate wealth, capital pursuits the general form of wealth and general social power, the contradiction between infinite quality and limited quantity of surplus value, capital's boundless desire to make wealth and the only condition that can realize such desire is to constantly drive the development of labor productive forces. Hence, capital was productive and was an important relation for developing social productive forces. In this sense, the mission of capital is to develop productive forces.

3. Capitalist Mode of Production and the New Society

With the development of capital accumulation process, capitalist relations have fundamentally reformed social production, created huge social productive forces and increasingly improved its level of socialization. Socialized productive forces created by capital have promoted increasingly socialization of capitalist relations and this has produced a strong motive for self- sublation in capitalist relations. Meanwhile, it provides necessary material conditions for the formation of a new society. The reason for the inevitable formation of a new social form is its social nature which enables its adapting to the development of social productive forces. The formation of a new social form demands certain social material foundations or a series

[1] *Karl Marx and Frederick Engels*, Chinese version, Edition 1, Vol. 23, p. 263.

of conditions for its material survival and development, which are the natural outcome of long-term and miserable historical development. It is a long-term miserable process because on the one hand, the level of people's practical abilities for dominating nature is the outcome of human's long-term arduous efforts in the paradoxical movement of man and nature, and more importantly, on the other hand, only by experiencing and overcoming reversed relations between man and materials. When relations between men and men are represented as relations among materials, and materials dominate human, on the other side a strong material foundation can be created to realize a fundamental rupture between human society and private ownership as well as private ownership mentality. In history, such reversed relation includes to forcefully create wealth by sacrificing interests of the majority of the people. However, it is the necessary step for creating infinite social labor productive forces, and only infinite social productive forces can constitute the material foundation for a freely associated human society. To create infinite social productive forces, the capitalist historical stage is a necessary period and is also a long-term miserable process. It was very hard to imagine that capitalist relations could create such social labor productive forces in such a short period. As Engels had indicated in his later years, "History has proved us, and all who thought like us, wrong. It has made it clear that the state of economic development on the Continent at that time was not, by a long way, ripe for the removal of capitalist production; it has proved this by the economic revolution which, since 1848, has seized the whole of the Continent, has really caused big industry for the first time to take root in France, Austria, Hungary, Poland and, recently, in Russia, while it has made Germany positively an industrial country of the first rank—all on a capitalist basis, which in the year 1848, therefore, still had great capacity for expansion."[1] Engel's argument reflects his strict scientific attitude. He had insisted on the historical materialism principle in studying the capitalist mode of production based on the most solid historical facts. Even though Marx

---

[1] *Karl Marx and Frederick Engels*, Chinese version, Edition 1, Vol. 22, pp. 597-598, Beijing, People's publishing House, 1965.

and Engels had judged and explained the historical process of class struggle in France in a historical materialist view based on economic conditions, their methods for understanding issues and basic points also apply to the judgment and explanation of the whole development process of the capitalist mode of production. We shall, on the basis of the most solid historical facts, explain the development situation and development trend of modern capitalist economy using their methods. "Development of the productive forces of social labor is the historical task and justification of capital. This is just the way in which it unconsciously creates the material requirements of a higher mode of production."[1] The existing history of the capitalist mode of production has undoubtedly created a strong material base and predicted the infinite power imbedded in the labor of human society. It has made a huge step towards the "infinite social labor productive forces", and determined by the historical mission of capital, it is bound to give play to its full potential to create necessary material conditions for the formation of a new society as the continual development of the capitalist mode of production.

Besides, capital provides necessary forms of organization for the formation of a new society:

On the one hand, production organizations created by capitalism provide usable forms of organization for the new society to organize socialized mass production. Modern industry should be construed as a kind of organization and system in the first place. Capitalists established the modern enterprise system on the basis of factory system to organize modern industrial production. There are many features in the formation and development of huge modern enterprise organizations: 1) Such enterprise organizations have a labor system with thorough division of labor and scientific management established in strict accordance with natural scientific laws as required in the socialized labor process; 2) These enterprises can organize production for the huge social demands of the world market based on the world market and can realize allocation of resources using production conditions created in the world market, greatly save resources and transaction costs and have

[1] *Karl Marx and Frederick Engels*, Chinese version, Edition 1, Vol. 25, pp. 288-289.

a very high productivity; 3) These enterprises have generally established their scientific and research centers, integrated development of scientific technologies with production and have become organizations that can rapidly transform scientific technologies to real productive forces. In sum, production and circulation of these enterprises are actually organized by an "expert team" for operation, and these experts on engineering technologies and management raise requirements for distribution of profits to owners of assets. The "human capital" theory in the bourgeoisie economics is in fact a theoretical reflection of such requirement reflecting the rise of experts group. Capitalist enterprise organizations have dual natures, i.e., they are not only the form of organization of socialized production, but also a production system in which capitalists squeeze out of surplus value. However, if a new society sublates its capital property, they can be reconstructed in a proper form for organizing socialized mass production.

Secondly, capital creates a system of social division of labor in socialized mass production and form of organization compatible with social regulation. Capital occupies all sectors and industries of social production driven by the law of surplus value and law of competition and thus forms a system of social division of labor. The system of division of labor in social production is subordinated to the production of surplus value since it is established on the basis of private ownership, and it is bound to be spontaneous and blind. Without doubt, such system of division of labor process is also dominated by the natural scientific laws and market laws. Although it is reasonable to a certain extent by realizing a balance in imbalance, such a balancing operation costs a high price and it is generally realized by forceful destruction of productive forces in economic crisis times. The production system based on co-operation in social division of labor objectively demands proportional and balanced development of all production sectors in the economy and a balance between supply and demand. However, this objective law of development of socialized mass production is an external alienated power for some capitalist sectors and groups, and it is inevitable to establish social regulatory and supervisory organizations in the development of socialized production. These regulatory mechanisms were formed through banking systems as well as national macro-economic management and regulatory organizations were established for conscious interventions to the economy. The banks in the capitalist society, act as a computing center, information center, supervisory center and regulatory center of social economy. Commercial banks carry on these functions through credit activities. However, their basis of insufficient market information, profit pursuit of banks themselves and competition among banks, etc. all influence defects in those functions. The functions were significantly improved after the central banks consciously assumed the role as regulating center of social economy. In order to regulate social economic life in a more effective way so as to overcome economic stagnation and crisis, capitalist states also play the regulatory role of "functional fiancé", intervening in and regulating social economic life by the taxation systems. Meanwhile, the capitalist state has also established special committees composed of various experts or other organizations, and makes a large amount of predictive study on social economic operations and offers all kinds of regulatory and operational plans. This kind of planning activity is practiced in big banks and large enterprises, too. Even though the establishment and development of these forms of regulatory organizations cannot fundamentally eliminate the inherent contradictions of capitalist economy, they indeed play an important role in mitigating contradictions, and significantly avoid regular turbulences and crises of the capitalist economy. These forms of organizations provide a direct organizational foundation for the new society to organize and regulate social production and will have a more complete development in the new society.

Finally, capital accumulation itself includes capital's self-sublation. Such form of self-sublation is a form of transition to the new society. 1) Capital's self-sublation is an internal trend of capital accumulation. With the development of social productive forces, in history the technical foundation for the large-scale machine industry had rapidly increased the socialization level of the production process, production conditions were increasingly socialized, and the minimum productive forces to be possessed by a single capitalist had increased accordingly. At this time, capital accumulation in which relying on the cumulating of surplus value of single capitalist could not adapt to the requirements for the development of social productive forces, and the concentration of capital was bound to develop. The initial primitive stock capital system established by old merchant capital was bound to be introduced to the concentration process of industrial capital. It was a quite more moderate mean of concentration in comparison with today's mergers & acquisitions, but it could rapidly integrate formed and forming capital since it had protected the private property right of the former owner of individual capitalist, and would not run up against the resistance in forceful annexation. Relying on a giant bank credit system, it could rapidly concentrate formed and forming capital, gathering social dispersed funds and offer them for the disposition of industrial capitalists. Once the stock capital system was integrated with accumulation of industrial capital, the scale of industrial enterprises had rapidly expanded and industrial departments that failed to develop had rapidly risen. The formation and development of industrial stock companies, as an enterprise system, was crucial for them to more extensively organize the labor process of social cooperation and re-construct dispersed traditional production process employing scientific production process. Therefore, I believe that stock capital was an inevitable outcome of capital concentration in the process of capital accumulation and a proper form of capital socialization driven by the socialization of production. Stock capital was a form of social capital opposite to private capital and the external form of the contradictory relation between the personality and sociality inherent in capital's nature. Joint stock capital had transformed the individual power of capitalists to social power, turned private power of capital to social power, and changed capital from private enterprises to social enterprises. Consequently, a social form of capital was realized in its self-sublation process. 2) Joint stock companies is a transitional form for the transformation of capital to the property of direct producers in the future society, as well as the transitional form for the change from capital's functions of reproduction, to social functions. Within the stock companies for the first time the ownership and functions of capital was separated and capital owners were separated from capital's operation. Although capital owners still maintain the power of dominating capital's operation, it is its agents rather than owners themselves that actually organize capital operation. No matter whether agents actually have capital, they are only appointed agents of owners in nature. Labor process was completely separated from the ownership of the means of production and the ownership of surplus labor; and capitalists do not need to organize labor process by themselves. The extreme development of capitalist production is the transition point required for the transfer of capital to producers' "individual" property. On the other hand, it is also the transition point for the transformation of its functions in the reproduction process, which is still integrated with capital ownership till today, to the pure functions of freely associated producers and for social functions in the future society. These are the forms of development in the capital's movement, and the required forms for the transition to a new society. Meanwhile, the credit and banking system also disconnect capital ownership with capital's functions. Likewise, it sublates the private nature of capital since it includes capital's self-sublation in a sense. 3) Joint stock companies are the negative sublation of capital while cooperative factories/enterprises are the positive sublation of capital. Workers' cooperative factories were established on the old forms of capitalist factory system and credit system, and were the first niche opened in the old form within the boundaries of the old form. The antagonist relation between capital and labor has been sublated here and workers, as a union, have become their own capitalists. The antagonistic nature in labor supervision/control has disappeared because managers are paid by workers and they are no longer antagonistic to workers. "The capitalist stock companies, as much as the co-operative factories, should be considered as transitional forms from the capitalist mode of production to the associated one, with the only distinction that the antagonism is resolved negatively in the one and positively in the latter."[1]

---

[1] *Karl Marx and Frederick Engels*, Chinese version, Edition 1, Vol. 25, p. 498.

II. Internal Contradictions and Historical Limitations of Capitalist Mode of Production

Marxist economic theories reveal the internal contradictions of the capitalist mode of production, and clarify the historical law of generation, development and extinction of the capitalist mode of production on this basis. The historical limitation of the capitalist mode of production originates from its inherent internal contradiction. The theory of Marx on the paradoxical movement of the capitalist mode of production is a theoretical system with rich contents. Below, I will give a brief analysis on the basic contradiction of the capitalist mode of production and its direct relevant contents.

1. Basic Contradictions of the Capitalist Mode of Production

The contradiction between production socialization and capitalist private possession of the means of production is the basic contradiction of the capitalist mode of production. It had further development, attained new contents and new natures when simple commodity economy had developed into capitalist commodity economy. Capital gathers socialized productive forces in the first phase, since workers' cooperative labor process is the starting point and basic initial form of capitalist production, and such material mode of production has a social nature, in other words, the capitalist private ownership and socialized productive forces it contains constitute the basis for the capitalist mode of production. Many Marxists seldom mention this point; it seems to them: as if the nature of productive forces will not change when the technical foundation/conditions for production does not change. In fact, change of labor mode (different forms of organization of labor process) can also result as: transformation of individual productive forces to social productive forces. In fact, the interaction between material production mode and form of capital—the basis for capitalist production— had greatly promoted the development of productive forces and pushed increases in capital accumulation. Therefore, we believe that the basis for the capitalist mode of production includes the contradiction between production socialization and capitalist private ownership.

Contradiction is not confrontation, and confrontation is only the intensified form of the antagonistic nature of contradiction. The basic contradiction in the early period of capitalism was such a relation including mutual promotion and adaptation. Such contradiction was the motive for the development of productive forces and capital accumulation. If capital wants to transcend small production, it must develop into socialized productive forces, if it wants to effectively utilize socialized productive forces, it needs to constantly increase accumulation. Such contradiction not only determines the fact that the amount of capital needed by capitalist enterprises must be more than the amount of the means of production dominated by small producers, but also determines that capital can be accumulated endlessly, due to the new existing conditions of production technologies, capital improves laborer's productive abilities (forces) relying on scale advantages and better maintenance of the means of production (instruments) and also saves labor time through the co-operative labor process.

Its internal contradiction has changed in two aspects during the development of the capitalist mode of production: on the one hand, with the completion of Industrial Revolution, the technical foundation for large-scale machine industry was established and social productive forces were developed into socialized mass production in a real sense as far as its technical nature was concerned. The scale of enterprises had become increasingly larger with socialized mass production based on higher work division and co-operative work of a large amount of workers. Production conditions were increasingly socialized, and the whole social production forms a socialized systematical pattern; the market expands, and the formation and development of domestic and international uniform markets combines production, exchange and consumption in a larger scale and all material modes of production in the social reproduction process are all socialized. On the other hand, production socialization requires socialization of social relations of production, and the first result is the socialization of relations of capital ownership. Accumulation of individual capital(s) and could no longer satisfy rapidly developing productive forces since insufficient pure dependence reliance on the capitalization of surplus value. Therefore, the basic contradiction of the capitalist mode of production manifests itself and result in capital's concentration and socialization in the relations of capital ownership. Capital concentration itself has dual functions. One function is it unites private capital(s) and transforms them to social capital. The socialized nature of capital adapts to the requirements for the development of productive forces, creates a new form of paradoxical movement, also later effectively promotes the development of social productive forces. The second function is that it adjusts property rights within the boundaries of the capitalist private ownership, which is in nature beneficial to the form of big capital's dominance on small and medium capital, thus becoming a favorable factor for strengthening the capitalist private ownership. Therefore, capital concentration promotes the development of productive forces on the one hand, and strengthens the capitalist private ownership on the other hand, thus strengthens the contradictory nature of the basic contradiction of the capitalist mode of production. The nature of socialized mass production demands the following: distribution of means of production and allocation of production resources should be in accordance with the internal proportion of the development of social productive forces, however, the capitalist private ownership disassociates the internal relations in the social production, which is represented as a blind competitive relationship.

The nature of capitalist private ownership is opposite to the objective requirements for the development of social productive forces, and such opposition is bound to be represented as external antagonistic economic crisis. The contradiction between the development of production socialization and capitalist private possession of the means of production, as the basic contradiction of the capitalist mode of production, is the contradiction between the dual basic characteristics of this mode of production: The relation between the material foundation for capitalist production and its social form, and it is the direct representation of the contradiction between productive forces and relations of production under capitalist conditions.

This contradiction is the cause of other economic contradictions. The basic contradiction of the capitalist mode of production is both the fundamental motive for the development of social productive forces and reform of economic relations and also the fundamental reason for the final dissolution of the capitalist mode of production.

2. The Contradiction of Private Power and Social Power within Capital

On the basis of the main contradiction of capitalism, the ownership relation of private capital is bound to have a dual nature. As a special social ownership relation, capital is a unity of private power and social powers. The private power of capital is represented as the actual power of capitalists, the owner of capital possesses and is able to dominate and use capital. The private power of capital depends on the amount of single private capital fund. Such private power of capital in economic relations is represented as the sacred and inviolable right of capitalists on their private capital in will relations and legal right relations, i.e., private property right. Such power and right relation constitutes the relatively stable content of capital relations and determines the nature of capital's exploitative relations, and the exploitative relation between capital and wage labor is formed on this basis.

Capital, as a kind of social integration force, is also manifested as a kind of social power. In particular, different single private capital(s) have formed social power relation of capital with their integration to realize exploitative relations. Such social power relation encounters constant changes in capital relations and it is reflected with the constant transformation in the forms of capital, i.e., the changes in its internal pattern of integration, with the development of social productive forces it possesses. The social nature of private capital roots in the social nature of its material content, in which it possesses. Capital as a transitional form of social labor and a special form of social existence of socialized productive forces has sociality and is embodied as a kind of social power. The relation between private power and social power of capital is only the manifestation of the relation between the form and its content (of) ownership, as well as a representation of the basic contradiction of the capitalist mode of production in terms of the nature of capital itself. The contradiction between the private power and social power of capital inevitably evolves with the development of the capitalist mode of production and constitutes capital's basic contradiction. In history production conditions increasingly transform to social production conditions, organization of the labor process and productive forces increasingly socialize with the scientific developments and continuous improvement of production technologies. Single private capital becomes unable to independently possess or control such higher socialized productive forces. Capital must unite to organize production, transform private capital to social capital and transform private power of capital to social power. Nevertheless, this transformation process embodies and reflects the self-denial character in the relations of capitalist private ownership. As the continuous improvement of social level of productive forces and constant increase of capital accumulation, the sociality of capital power constantly strengthens in terms of qualitative and quantitative aspects, thus the social power possessed by capital develops into a kind of power differentiated from private power and becomes a kind of social power that cannot be totally dominated by private capital. Marx had commented on this issue: "The contradiction between the general social power into which capital develops, on the one hand, and the private power of the individual capitalists over these social conditions of production, on the other, becomes ever more irreconcilable, and yet contains the solution of the problem, because it implies at the same time the transformation of the conditions of production into general, common, social, conditions. This transformation stems from the development of the productive forces under capitalist production, and from the ways and means by which this development takes place."[1] Therefore, we can say that the contradiction between the private power and social power of capital is both; first, the direct reason for pushing the relation of private ownership of capital to higher socialized forms and second, fundamentally leading to the dissolution of

---

[1] *Karl Marx and Frederick Engels*, Chinese version, Edition 1, Vol. 25, p. 294.

private power relations of capital.

3. Contradiction between the Objectives and Means of Capitalist Production

The production and appropriation of surplus value constitute the essence of the fundamental economic law of capitalism. K. Marx had pointed out that "production of surplus value is the absolute law" of the capitalist mode of production.[1]

Such production for value and surplus value includes a constant functioning trend, that is, reduce individual labor time for producing commodities below the social necessary labor time. Efforts made to reduce the cost price of producing commodities to the minimum become the most effective lever for improving labor's social productive forces. Since improving social labor's productive forces is the necessary method for capital appreciation, the capitalist mode of production contains the internal motive and mechanism for improving social labor forces and the also the trend of continuous development of productive forces. However, continuous development of social productive forces, as the means for realizing appreciation of capital's value in the capitalist society is contradictory to the goal itself. Because the general improvement of social labor forces is bound to reduce the value of products and regularly give rise to capital depreciation. On the other hand, the development of social productive forces is accompanied with the improvement of organic composition of capital, and leads to the decrease of the average profit rate of social capital. The contradiction between the objective and means of capital production is that capitalist production tries to maintain or infinitely increase the value of capital by infinitely developing productive forces. Nevertheless, this method itself contains regular deflation of the capital's value as well as the falling tendency of average rate of profit.

Within capitalist production; the contradiction between expansion of production and appreciation of capital's value becomes a kind of restriction

[1] K. Marx and F. Engels: *Soch.*, 5th ed., Vol. 23, p. 632.

for the development of capitalist production. The objective of capital production is to pursue appreciation of its self value, however, the expansion of production will cease when its leads to the deflation of capital value and encounter decreases in the profit rate. Stagnation of production is more prominently represented in regular economic crises. Capitalist production always attempts to exceed such limit and try every means possible to prevent decreases in the profit rate. Nevertheless, the effects of methods for avoiding decrease of profit rate are temporary, no matter by increasing level of exploitation or saving from constant capital part. These methods for preventing decrease of profit rate are generally based upon expanding production and raising labor productivity and its long-term effects will inevitably become the factors for a rise in the organic composition of capital and decrease of profit rate. Therefore, such contradiction firmly indicates that "capital is not, as the economists believe, the absolute form for the development of the forces of production—not the absolute form for that, nor the form of wealth which absolutely coincides with the development of the forces of production."[1]

4. Contradiction between Capitalist Production and Its Realization

The objective of capitalist production and accumulation is to gain maximum surplus value. This means; capital not only squeezes out the surplus value created by workers in the direct production process but also realizes capital value and surplus value included in commodity through the exchange process. Capital movement process is a unity of production process and exchange process, i.e., unity of production and realization of surplus value. Nevertheless, the process of the unity of the two is relatively independent and separated processes, and their respective conditions of movement are totally different. The process of production of surplus value, as the process of the integration of capital and wage labor, is determined by capital amount, labor amount, exploitative level of capital and current level

[1] *Karl Marx and Frederick Engels*, Chinese version, Edition 1, Vol. 46 (I), p. 399.

of productive forces in the society. The production of surplus value expands with the increase of capital accumulation. On the other hand, the process of the realization of surplus value is determined by the objective proportion of different sectors in social production and that between production and consumption, as well as the current level of consumption in the society. On the one hand, social production is an anarchical blind competition on the basis of private ownership of capitalist means of production, and it is inevitable trend that the proportions among different sectors of production will be imbalanced. This contradiction in the production process is surly manifested as imbalanced supply and demand in the exchange process and leads to difficulty in the realization of surplus value. On the other hand, social consumptive power is neither dependent on absolute productive forces, nor absolute consumptive power, but is dependent on the payable purchasing power in the society. Nevertheless, such purchasing power is restricted within a relative smaller scope due to the capitalist exploitative relation, the purchasing power of laborers lag behind the growth of social productive forces, and the consumption of a minority of exploiters will always be restricted by their desire for accumulation. The capitalist antagonistic relation of distribution is bound to lead to the contradiction in the production and realization of surplus value, difficulties of realization of surplus value will regularly appear and economic crises of overproduction will occur.

III. Historical Transition and Development Trend of the Capitalist Mode of Production

1. Law of the Development and Evolution within the Capitalist Mode of Production

If we connect Marx's arguments on the law that social relations of production must adapt to the requirements for the development of productive forces in the analysis of the historical nature of the formation, development and extinction of the capitalist mode of production, we may arrive at the following theoretical conclusions:

1) Social relations of production are definite (certain) forms of realization of social productive forces. Their relations between two are those between the form and content of social production. The relation between capitalist production relations and the definite social productive forces contained in it; is only that between the specific/definite historical form of production and its material foundation. Such material form and social form of production constitute the dual basic character of the capitalist mode of production, reflecting the most basic and essential relation and contradiction within the capitalist mode of production.

2) Social relations of production adapt to a certain level/phase of development of material productive forces and its formation is an outcome of the constant development of productive forces in the human society, a historical bestow and the inevitable outcome of a series of reforms in the social relations of production. Capitalist production relations have their historical inevitability, and it is only a special historical stage in the development of modes of production in the human society.

3) Any form of social production undertakes a historical mission to develop social productive forces and reform the relations of production. The capitalist mode of production cannot exist if it does not constantly reform production technologies, form of labor and social economic relations, because it has its historical mission and historical reasonableness to develop social productive forces and reform social relations of production. The different stages of development of capitalist relations of production in the historical process of its development can only be explained by the development level and requirement for development of social productive forces. Capital relations are bound to be reformed accordingly with the development of productive forces, and the capitalist mode of production constantly develops in the paradoxical movement of interaction and mutual promotion of capitalist relations of production and productive forces.

4) Each significant advance in social material production will give rise to **major adjustments** in production relations, and a certain social

relation of production is fundamentally reformed through partial qualitative changes through these adjustments. The capitalist mode of production experiences a process from quantitative change to qualitative change, from partial qualitative change to a final fundamental reform. Therefore, the only standard for judging the dissolution of capitalist relations of production is whether it allows for the development of productive forces, or whether it can promote the continual development of productive forces within the scope of its fundamental nature through reform when it is in contradiction with productive—forces.

5) Any social formation—also capitalist society—will never die out before its contains play their full roles, and new higher relations of production will never appear before their material conditions mature in the womb of the old society. Conditions for the extinction of capitalist relations of production and conditions for the formation of a new society are internally integrated, which is determined by the continuity of the historical development of human society. When social productive forces push capitalist relations enter into its late stage, that is, when material conditions and type of organization for the formation of a new society gradually mature thus a large amount of socialist factors gradually come into being at the same time. The capitalist mode of production creates conditions for its self-denial in the process of its development, represented as a gradually expiring historical process. In other words, destruction of capital itself is a natural historical process. Such historical process is inevitably full of fierce class struggles and class contradictions no matter which form of a transformation pattern it follows.

Marx had summarized his analysis of the basic contradiction of social mode of production, i.e., it is the law of development of modes of production in the human society that social relations of production must adapt to the requirements for the development of productive forces. It is the basic law of development of productive forces in the human society. The alteration of different modes of production in the human society and occurrence of development stages in a specific mode of production are dominated by this law. If we make deeper research based on this theory of Marx and we can find out that the basic law of development of the mode of productions in the human society can be subdivided as the following three aspects:

Firstly, there is a law that social modes of production with different characteristics progresses from low-level forms to high-level forms in the long historical process of development in the human society. This is the law of transition of social system through a high-level form's negation of the low-level form. It is an inevitable historical process of progressive journey of social productive forces and progressive innovation and evolution of social relations of production with different characteristics.

Secondly, there is a law that the social mode of production in a specific stage of development in the human society has gradual qualitative evolution in its development process. It is the historical inevitability of its self-denial in its self development and improvement and it is the law of self development of a social mode of production. This law dominates the development process of the social mode of production from quantitative change to qualitative changes, from partial qualitative changes to a complete qualitative change.

Thirdly, the law of transition between different social modes of production is that elements for the formation of a higher-level social formation mature in the late period of an older lower-level social formation and pushes the evolution of human society manifest itself as an inseparable social development process. The next stage both negates and inherits the former stage and it is the inevitability of social production and constant historical development. The three laws are different but consistent and their integration constitutes the basic law of development of mode of production in the human society. I suggest to differentiate them as above to overcome simple and unilateral understanding on the issue. Some people neglect the second law and directly link the starting point and end point of the capitalist mode of production. It seems that the capitalist mode of production is in antagonistic confrontation in its whole process and thus the development and historical mission of capitalism is neglected. In fact, this seemingly "revolutionary" view cannot answer the basic historical theoretical question why and how capitalism is progresses and approaches forward to its opposite, and they simply abandon scientific Marxist theories. Some people neglect the third law. They separate internal relations of different social modes of production and "design" different historical stages in development of the human society. They neglect the law of historical inheritance and theoretically stuck scientific socialism in the mire of utopian socialism. Marx's and Engels' researches on the capitalist mode of production always follows the basic view of historical materialism, i.e., approaching to social development as a natural historical process as well as a systematic development process. The movement of the capitalist mode of production, as a natural historical process, is an inevitable historical stage in the development of human society, and assumes certain historical missions of developing social productive forces. Therefore, it is bound to contain a dual nature: historical reasonableness and historical transition. On the other hand, the capitalist mode of production is a constantly changing social entity and constantly reforms itself. The constant development of social productive forces and corresponding frequent reforms in social relations of production are the prominent features of such mode of production, differentiating from other previous modes of production.

The capitalist mode of production could not come into being without the development of social productive forces, growth of surplus value in a certain degree and development of commodity economy. Capitalist production relations imbue productive forces with capital and make them capitalist productive forces, after this process socialized mass production and high material civilization are created. Capitalist production relations are not fixed and unchangeable social forms of production. They change with the development of productive forces. Today's capitalism is greatly different from its previous stages of development. The changes occur in a paradoxical movement: mutual adaptation and contradiction; to and with the development of productive forces. "Its production moves in contradictions which are constantly overcome but just as constantly posited."[1] Modern capitalism is experiencing a profound historical reform. If it can make more

---

[1] *Karl Marx and Frederick Engels*, Chinese version, Edition 1, Vol. 46 (II), p. 393.

splendid achievements in the 21st century compared with the 20th century, it will inevitably drive socialization of productive forces to a new stage, then capitalist production relations will further socialize, which will prepare more mature material conditions and forms of organization for the formation of a new society.

2. Capital's Socialization and the Evolution of the Capitalist Mode of Production

Capital is the subject of the movement of the capitalist mode of production. The law that social relations of production adapt to the requirements for the development of productive forces is represented as the inevitable trend of the development of capital's socialization in conformity of the development of socialization of productive forces within the capitalist mode of production. The relation between production socialization and capital socialization is a real special form of existence of the relation of unity of opposites between social productive forces and social relations of production. Production socialization is the material content of capital socialization and capital socialization is the social form of realization of production socialization. Based on the basic principles of historical materialism elaborated by Marx, we may arrive at the following conclusions: 1) The development of capital's socialization is a natural historical process. Capital relations must adapt to the requirements for the development of productive forces, so production socialization is the fundamental reason and driving force for capital's socialization; whereas capital's socialization is only an inevitable reflection of production socialization and a proper social form for the realization of production socialization. Therefore, capital's socialization is an objective and inevitable evolution process of capital relations. Social capital, as an opposite of private capital, is the inevitable result of this process and the form of development of internal contradictions of capital. 2) The development level of capital's socialization is increasing, and constant development of production socialization demands constant development of capital's socialization. The two mutually promote and grow in the same direction. Social capital, as the outcome of the reform of capital relations, is bound to have multiple forms of development in the reform of capital relations, and the connection and differences of these forms are represented as socialization of capital relations. The development of social capital itself is represented as the improvements in the levels of capital socialization regarding its nature and evolution of different historical forms of capital in phenomenon (external appearance). 3) The development of capital's socialization is an uncompleted reform process. The development of capital's socialization will not end as long as capital relations have room for reform and social productive forces have considerable vitality within the scope of capitalist relations. In fact, capital's socialization will gain larger space for development and gain newer forms along with production socialization through further self adjustments of capital relations. 4) The development of capital's socialization will ultimately transform as a historical transition process. The development of capital socialization is a self-sublation or alienation of capital with private property within the scope of the capitalist mode of production, and apparently this process contains self-denial of capital relations and partial changes in capital's nature. This self-sublation process can be completely consistent with several future stages of capital relations. It is the general development law for everything in the world, including socio-economic forms to seek self development in a self-denial pattern. However, when this sublation process finally reaches its limits, those regarding capital's nature, then capital's socialization will completely lack space for further development. Social capital will develop into a form of transition to the new society in its self development, and it is possible that it will be the time for the transformation from social capital to "public capital". The development of capital's socialization is necessitated with that nature of historical transition (its historical finiteness), and it will enter the transitional stage to develop to new higher relations of production, and such process will be completely dependent on the level of maturity of social capital itself. 5) Socialization of capital is the law of the development and evolution of the capitalist mode of production. It embodies the development trend of the inherent contradiction of the capitalist mode of production, regulates the whole process of development and reform of capital relations, and dominates the evolution process of all aspects of capital relations. This law is the specific form of realization of the basic law of development of modes of production in the human society in the capitalist mode of production. After the establishment of the capitalist mode of production, it practices a development and evolution driven by the law of development of capital's socialization. Dominated by this law, the historical evolution in capital's forms constantly regulates the inherent contradiction of capitalist economy and promotes the continual development of social productive forces and capital relations. Meanwhile, on the other side the result of this law is constantly enriching the material foundation and historical elements required for the formation of a new society.

All internal contradictions in the capitalist mode of production prominently demonstrate historical limitations and historical finiteness of this mode of production. It is bound to be replaced by a new higher mode of production with the development of these contradictions. Marx had commented on this issue: "The capitalist mode of appropriation, the result of the capitalist mode of production, produces capitalist private property. This is the first negation of individual private property, as founded on the labor of the proprietors. But capitalist production begets, with the inexorability of a law of Nature, its own negation. It is the negation of negation. This does not re-establish private property for the producer, but gives him individual property based on the acquisition of the capitalist era: i.e., on co-operation and the possession in common of the land and of the means of production."[1] Marx had further explained on this subject: "That it itself begets its own negation with the inexorability which governs the metamorphoses of nature; that it has itself created the elements of a new economic order, by giving the greatest impulse at once to the productive forces of social labor and to the integral development of every individual producer; that capitalist property, resting as it actually does already on a form of collective production, cannot

[1] *Karl Marx and Frederick Engels*, Chinese version, Edition 1, Vol. 23, p. 832.

do other than transform itself into social property."[1] In sum, it is objectively inevitable for socialism to replace capitalism. At present, this objective inevitableness is represented in various forms raised in this book in the developed capitalist countries.

---

[1] *Selected Correspondence* of *Karl Marx and Frederick Engels*, p. 346, Beijing, People's Publishing House, 1962.

Main References

1. *Karl Marx and Frederick Engels*. Volumes 23, 24, 25. Beijing: People's Publishing House, 1972, 1974

2. *Karl Marx and Frederick Engels*. Volumes 22, 26, 29, 46, 47, 49. Beijing: People's Publishing House, 1965, 1972, 1972, 1979, 1979, 1982

3. *Selected Works of Marx and Engels*. Volumes 1, 2, 3, 4. Beijing: People's Publishing House, 1995

4. *Selected Works of Deng Xiaoping*. Volumes 1, 2. Beijing: People's Publishing House, 1994

5. *Selected Works of Deng Xiaoping*. Volume 3. Beijing: People's Publishing House, 1993

6. Jiang Zemin. *Comment on "Three Represents"*. Beijing: Central Party Literature Press, 2001

7. *Jiang Zemin's Comment on Socialism with Chinese Characteristics (an Extraction of Special Topics)*. Beijing: Central Party Literature Press, 2002

8. Ernest Mandel. *Power and Money: A Marxist Theory of Bureaucracy* (Chinese version). Beijing: Central Compilation & Translation Press, 2001

9. Thomas K. McCraw. *Modern Capitalism* (Chinese version). Nanjing: Jiangsu People's Publishing House, 1999

10. Meadows. *Limits to Growth* (Chinese version). Beijing: The Commercial Press, 1984

11. Gao Feng ed. *Economic Relations and Operating Features of Modern Capitalism*. Tianjin: Nankai University Press, 2000

12. Chen Ying. "Some Controversies about Post-Industrial Economic Structure". *Nankai Economic Studies*. 2001 (3)

13. Maddison. *Monitoring the World Economy, 1820-1992* (Chinese version). Beijing: Reform Press, 1997

14. Marc Linder. *The Anti-Samuelson* (Chinese version). Shanghai: Shanghai: SDX Joint Publishing Company, 1992

15. Berle and Means. *The Modern Corporation and Private Property* (Chinese

version). Taipei: Bank of Taiwan, 1981

16. Lin Huici, Zhang Tongyu and Li Yuanheng ed. *Theories and Practice of Modern Capitalist Economy*. Tianjin: Tianjin People Press, 1999

17. Zhang Tongyu. *Social Capital Theory—Research on Socialized Development of Industrial Capital*. Jinan: Shandong People's Publishing House, 1999

18. Sun Zhizhong ed. *Japanese Monopoly Capital*. Beijing: People's Publishing House, 1985

19. Paul Sweezy. *Monopoly Capital* (Chinese version). Beijing: The Commercial Press, 1977

20. Gorbachev, Brant, etc. *The Future of Socialism* (Chinese version). Beijing: Central Compilation & Translation Press, 1994

21. Gao Feng, Ding Weimin, etc. *Study on the Ownership of Developed Capitalism*. Beijing: Tsinghua University Press, 1996

22. Gong Weiping. *On Category of Ownership*. Xi'an: Shaanxi People's Publishing House, 1994

23. Zhang Yu, etc. ed. *Advanced Political Economics – Latest Development of Marxist Economics*. Beijing: Economic Science Press, 2002

24. Hiroshi Okumura. *The Future of Shareholding System* (Chinese version). Beijing: China Planning Press, 1996

25. Hiroshi Okumura. *Corporate Capitalism* (Chinese version). Shanghai: SDX Joint Publishing Company, 1990

26. Li Cong, Jia Huaqiang and Xie Zhiqiang ed. *Research on the Major Issues of Contemporary Capitalist Development*. Volume 1. Beijing: Central Party Literature Press, 2000

27. Gao Feng: *Capital Accumulation Theory and Modern Capitalism*. Tianjin: Nankai University Press, 1991

28. Ding Weimin: *Analysis of the System of Western Cooperatives*. Beijing: Economics and Management Press, 1998

29. Egon Neuberger, William J. Duffy: *Comparative Economic Systems* (Chinese version). Beijing. The Commercial Press, 1988

30. Ma Jianxing, Gao Feng, etc. *Introduction to Monopoly Capital—Marxist*

Theory of Imperialism: *History and Contemporary*. Jinan: Shandong People's Publishing House, 1993

31. Tao Dayong ed. *Modern Capitalist Economics*. Nanking: Jiangsu People's Publishing House, 1996

32. Huang Suan, Zhen Bingxi: *Reevaluating Contemporary Capitalist Economy*. Beijing: World Affairs Press, 1996

33. Han Baojiang: *Salvation of Western World: Transition and Contributions of the Modern Western System of Income Distribution*. Jinan: Shandong People's Publishing House, 2000

34. Chen Bingcai: *Contemporary Capitalist System of Income Distribution*. Fuzhou: Fujian People's Publishing House, 1994

35. Zhang Ping, etc.: *Sweden: A Model of Social Welfare Economy*. Wuhan, Wuhan Press, 1994

36. Buchanan. *Liberty, Market and State*. Beijing: Beijing Economics College Press, 1988

37. K. Cashbot. *Debates on Macro Economic Policies*. Beijing: China Economy Publishing House, 1988

38. Tang Zaixin, etc. *Macro-Control: Theoretical Foundation and Political Analysis*. Guangzhou: Guangdong Economy Publishing House, 2001

39. Wu Yifeng, etc. *Market Economy and Government Intervention*. Beijing: The Commercial Press, 1998

40. Chen Dongqi. *New Government Intervention Theory*. Beijing: Capital University of Economics & Business Press, 2000

41. George Lodge. *Managing Globalization in the Age of Interdependence*. Shanghai: Shanghai Translation Publishing House, 1998

42. Robert Reich. *The Work of Nations*. Shanghai, Shanghai Translation Publishing House, 1998

43. Soros. *The Crisis of Global Capitalism*. Harbin: Heilongjiang People's Publishing House, 1998

44. Peter Drucker. *The Post-Capitalist Society*. Shanghai: Shanghai Translation Publishing House, 1998

45. Gerald. Boxberger, Harald Klimenta. *The 10 Globalization Lies*. Beijing:

Xinhua Press, 2000

46. François Chesnais. *The Globalization of Capital*. Beijing: Central Compilation & Translation Press, 2001

47. François Chesnais. *Financial Globalization*. Beijing: Central Compilation & Translation Press, 2001

48. Alan Rugman. *The End of Globalization*. Shanghai: SDX Joint Publishing Company, 2001

49. Robert Gilpin. *The Challenge of Global Capitalism*. Shanghai: Shanghai People's Publishing House, 2001

50. World Bank. *China's Participation: Integration with Global Economy*. Beijing: China Financial & Economic Publishing House, 1998

51. Nicholas Baran. *Inside the Information Superhighway Revolution*. Haikou: Hainan Press, 1998

52. Samuelson: *Microeconomics*. Beijing: Huaxia Publishing Co., Ltd., 1999

53. Du Chuanzhong. "Reasons and Trend of Rise in Industrial Concentration of Western Countries since the 1990s". *World Economy*, 2002 (5)

54. Zhu Yunwei. "The New Trends of Global M/A & Its Enlightenment in 2001". *World Economy Study*, 2002 (3)

55. Zhong Guohong: "Accurately Understand the Self-Adjustment, Reformation and Improvement in Developed Capitalist Countries". *Journal of Fudan University (Social Science Edition)*, 2000 (6)

56. Ding Weimin. "Historical Process of Capitalist Development: Research Centering on New Economy". *Contemporary Economic Research*, 2001 (9)

57. "Several Circumstances of Contemporary Capital Socialization" edited and translated by Zhou Tong, *Foreign Theoretical Trends*, 2002 (3)

58. He Zili. "Economic Globalization and Modern Capitalism". *Journal of Nankai University (Philosophy and Social Science Edition)*, 2002 (2)

59. Liu Changli. "Rapid Development of Foreign Direct Investment and Multinational M&A". *World Economy & Politics*, 2002 (1)

60. Jiang Ruiping. "Corporate Monopoly Capitalism—An Analysis of Japanese Model". *Social Science in China*, 1998 (5)

61. Gong Weiping. "Comment on the Basic Structure of the Category of Ownership". *Study & Exploration*, 1995 (5)

62. Gong Weiping. "Three Forms of Historical Evolution of Ownership". *Journal of Jinan University (Philosophy and Social Science Edition)*, 1995 (3)

63. Wu Yifeng. "How to Differentiate Public Ownership of Productive Means and Private Ownership of Productive Means". *Copy Material of Renmin University of China—Socialist Economic Theory and Practice*, 2001 (8)

64. Hua Min. "Development Momentum, Institutional Innovation of Capitalism and Its Crisis". *Journal of Fudan University (Social Science Edition)*, 2000 (6)

65. Tang Renwu. "Comment on Polarization Brought by Globalization and Its Countermeasures". *World Economy and Politics*, 2002 (1)

66. Zhang Tongyu. "On the Historical Development of Capitalist Ownership Relations". *Nankai Economic Studies*, 2001 (2)

67. Guo Jinlin. "Strategic Change of American Institutional Shareholders and Their Corporate Governance Principles". *World Economy*, 2002 (4)

68. Gao Zilong. "97 New Progress on the Research of New Changes in Contemporary Capitalism". *Teaching and Research*, 1998 (3)

69. Sun Shichun. "Comment on Post-war Japanese Corporation Capital Ownership". *Japanese Study*, 1999 (4)

70. Yang Mengzi. "Brief Comment on the Social Contradiction and Inevitable Extinction of Modern Capitalism". *Socialism Studies*, 1994 (4)

71. Xiao Liang. "Ten Issues to Be Explored and Reconsidered in Current Ownership Theories". *Tianjin Social Sciences*, 1997 (5)

72. He Weida. "New Changes in the Development of Stock Companies in Western Countries". *World Economy*, 1999 (3)

73. Zhi Xiaohe. "Discussions on the Nature of Shareholding System". *Economic Science*, 2000 (6)

74. Zhou Dunren. "The Gradual Alienation of Capital's Ownership". *Copy Material of Renmin University of China—Socialist Economic Theory and Practice*, 2001 (8)

75. Lin Qingsong, etc. "Enterprise System of Workers' Ownership". *Economic Perspectives*, 1987 (6)

76. Zhu Guohong. "On Self-Adjustment, Reformation and Improvement of Developed Capitalist Countries". *Journal of Fudan University (Social Science Edition)*, 2000 (6)

77. Liu Cheng, Gao Yan. "Influences of Credit Policies of World Bank on the Economy of Developing Countries". *International Economic Cooperation*, 1999 (3)

78. Wang Yizhou. "National Economy, Politics and Security in the Globalization Era". *World Economy*, 1998 (8)

79. Francois Chesnais. "History and Current Situation of Financial Globalization". *Xinhua Digest*, 2000 (1)

80. Mark Cook and Nigel M. Healey, *Growth and Structural Change*, Macmillan, 1995.

81. Edward N. Wolff, *Growth, Accumulation, and Unproductive Activity*, Cambridge University Press, 1987.

82. Harold G. Vatter and John F. Walker ed., *History of the U.S. Economy since World War II*, M.E. Sharpe, 1995.

83. Kenneth E. Bolding, *The Structure of a Modern Economy*, Macmillan, 1993.

84. William J. Baumol and Kenneth McLennan, *Productivity Growth and U.S. Competitiveness*, Oxford University Press, 1985.

85. John Cornwall, *Modern Capitalism*, Martin Robertson, 1979.

86. Bell, Daniel, *The Coming of Postindustrial* [M], New York: Basic Books, 1976.

87. Marsh. R. M., "What Do Bosses Do? The Origins and Functions of Hierarchy in Capitalist Production" [J]. *The Review of Radical Political Economics*, 1974, 6.

88. Marsh. R. M., "The Difference Between Participation and Power in Japanese Factories" [J]. *Industrial and Labor Relations*, 1992, January.

89. David M. Gordon, Richard Edwards, Michael Reich: *Segmented Work, Divided Workers*. Cambridge University Press, 1982.

90. Jeffrey E. Cohen: *Politics and Economic Policy in the United States*, second edition, Houghton Mitflin Company, Boston New York, 2000.

91. US Census Bureau, *Statistical Abstract of the United States*, 2000, p. 158.

92. Lawrence Mishel and Jared Bernstein and Jahn Schnitt, *The Sate of Working America* 2000-2001, ILK Press, an imprint of Cornell University Press, 2001.

93. Department of Commerce, *Survey of Current Business*, July 2001.

94. Bishop, Libby and David I. Levine, "Computer-Mediated Communication as Employee Voice: A Case Study" [J]. *Industrial and Labor Relations*, 1999, 52.

95. Gordon, David M. and Samuel Bowles. and Thomas E. Weisskopf, *Beyond the Waste Land: A Democratic Alternative to Economic Decline* [M]. New York: Anchor Press, 1983.

96. Robert Pollin, "The 'Army of Labor' and the 'Natural Rate of Unemployment': Can Marx, Kalecki, Friedman and Well Street All Be Wrong?"[J]. *Review of Radical Political Economics*, 1998, 30 (3): 1-13.

97. Bruce, Greenwald, and Joseph Stiglitz, "New and Old Keynesians", *Journal of Economic Perspectives*, 7, 1993.

98. Dornbusch, Rudiger and Stanley Fischer, *Macroeconomics*, McGraw-Hill, New York, 1990.

99. Blinder, Alan S., *Macroeconomics under Debate*, University of Michigan Press, New York, 1989.

100. Barro, Robert J., "Rational Expectations and Macroeconomics in 1984", *The American Economic Review*, 74, 1984.

101. Houndmills, Basingstoke, Hampshire: *Globalization and Nation State*, Macmillan Press; New York, St Martils Press, 1998.

102. Berch Berberoglu, *The Internationalization of Capital*, New York: Praeger, 1987.

103. A. S. Bhalla, *Globalization, Growth and Marginalization*, Ottawa: International Development Research Centre; Houndmills, Basingstoke, Hampshire: Macmillan Press; New York: St, Martins Press, 1998.

104. Bruno Amoroso, *On Globalization Capitalism in the 21st Century*,

Houndmills: Basingstoke Hampshire Press, 1998.

105. Yoginder· K·Alagh, *Coping with Global Economic, Technological and Environmental Transformations: Towards a Research Agenda*, downloaded from www.globalization.org.

106. Neustadtl and Mark Meller, *Dollars and Votes, How Business Campaign Contribution Subvert Democracy*, Temple University Press.

Printed in P.R.C. by order of Canut-Berlin.